TAKING SIDES

Clashing Views in

Urban Studies

Selected, Edited, and with Introductions by

Myron A. Levine
Wright State University

Mc
Graw
Hill

Connect
Learn
Succeed™

TAKING SIDES: CLASHING VIEWS IN URBAN STUDIES

Published by McGraw-Hill, a business unit of The McGraw-Hill Companies, Inc., 1221 Avenue of the Americas, New York, NY 10020. Copyright © 2013 by The McGraw-Hill Companies, Inc. All rights reserved. Printed in the United States of America. No part of this publication may be reproduced or distributed in any form or by any means, or stored in a database or retrieval system, without the prior written consent of The McGraw-Hill Companies, Inc., including, but not limited to, in any network or other electronic storage or transmission, or broadcast for distance learning.

Some ancillaries, including electronic and print components, may not be available to customers outside the United States.

Taking Sides® is a registered trademark of the McGraw-Hill Companies, Inc.
Taking Sides is published by the **Contemporary Learning Series** group within the McGraw-Hill Higher Education division.

1 2 3 4 5 6 7 8 9 0 DOC/DOC 1 0 9 8 7 6 5 4 3 2

MHID: 0-07-805043-X
ISBN: 978-0-07-805043-5
ISSN: 2164-9944 (Print)
ISSN: 2164-9952 (Online)

Managing Editor: *Larry Loeppke*
Senior Developmental Editor: *Jill Meloy*
Permissions Supervisor: *Lenny Behnke*
Senior Marketing Communications Specialist: *Mary Klein*
Lead Project Manager: *Jane Mohr*
Design Coordinator: *Brenda A. Rolwes*
Cover Graphics: *Rick D. Noel*
Buyer: *Nicole Baumgartner*
Media Project Manager: *Sridevi Palani*

Compositor: MPS Limited, a Macmillan Company
Cover Images: Group of People on Subway: © Getty Images RF; Kids Talking with Police Officer and Young Hispanic Children: © The McGraw-Hill Companies, Inc.

www.mhhe.com

Editors/Academic Advisory Board

Members of the Academic Advisory Board are instrumental in the final selection of articles for each edition of TAKING SIDES. Their review of articles for content, level, and appropriateness provides critical direction to the editors and staff. We think that you will find their careful consideration well reflected in this volume.

TAKING SIDES: Clashing Views in URBAN STUDIES

EDITOR

Myron A. Levine
Wright State University

ACADEMIC ADVISORY BOARD MEMBERS

Editors/Academic Advisory Board continued

Preface

Urban affairs deals with important issues and policy questions. It is at the local level—at the regional, city, and even at the street level—that government decisions concerning law enforcement, schooling, housing, transportation, land use, and the environment, have the greatest impact on people's lives.

Major urban problems, however, are not easily solved. Some of the most serious urban problems—like poverty, crime, and students dropping out from school—are seen as "wicked" as they yield no easy, workable, and just answers. Simply put, we do not know how to solve these intricate social problems.

Attempts to solve urban problems also entail serious tradeoffs. Simply put, we can improve some aspects of urban society only by worsening problems elsewhere. The gentrification or renaissance of inner-city neighborhoods may help a city economically, but only by displacing poorer residents from their homes to accommodate the new development. Deporting illegal immigrants to their home countries may reduce the service costs that immigration imposes on cities and states; but the exclusion of immigrants will also deny cities the labor, talents, and entrepreneurial talents of the new arrivals. The expulsion of immigrants also means that newcomers will not be able to repopulate inner-city neighborhoods, breathing new life into areas suffering severe decline and abandonment. Increased "school choice" may enable some students to find a new school more responsive to their needs; but such a policy may also shrink the resources provided to a city's regular schools, diminishing the quality of education provided to students who are not reached by choice programs.

As the above examples underscore, urban policy questions often entail quite difficult tradeoffs. A policy that works well and helps to solve problems from one perspective may be a "loser" when judged from another perspective. No policy is perfect and can do all things well. This is why urban policies are the subject of contentious debate. A policy that helps to achieve certain goals will be opposed by citizens committed to competing values.

Taking Sides: Clashing Views in Urban Studies does not give students *the* answer to any issue. It does not tell the student just what is the best policy solution. Instead, *Taking Sides* provides important background information on an issue and then presents the reader with conflicting points of view that are well-argued. Students are encouraged to "open their minds" to competing perspectives on an issue and to search for additional information (especially by referring to the list of sources and websites that accompany each issue in the book). The student will then evaluate the information gathered to formulate and defend his or her own position.

Taking Sides draws on a variety of sources: books, newspaper articles, academic journal articles, testimony before Congress and the state legislatures, reports issued by "think tanks," and advocacy pieces written by policy intellectuals and issue activists. As editor, I sought the inclusion of insightful articles that could engage students. I did not include more statically based analyses that would enmesh the reader in a sea of data, bogging down the student in the intricacies of methodological discussions and arcane debates of the proper operationalization of variables and the relative merits of alternative data collection instruments and measurement techniques. *Taking Sides* is meant to be a readable book, not a statistical tome. Data-based studies, the application of advanced statistical techniques, and the debate over proper methodology *are* indeed quite relevant to the discussion of urban policy, and such studies help to inform the advanced student in the field. But such a statistics-based discussion lies beyond the realm of the present volume.

Each chapter in *Taking Sides* is structured around a pair of articles that reveal a clash of perspectives on important urban problems. However, no single article or pair of articles can cover all important facets of a debate. Also, some of the articles were written for an audience that already has a fair familiarity with the topic that is being debated and may use terminology and refer to concepts that are not readily understood by nonspecialist citizens. As a result, *Taking Sides* provides an *Issue Summary* that introduces each set of paired YES–NO articles. The reader will find these introductions quite useful, as they will help the reader understand the contending points of view that follow. Each *Issue Summary* also contains important points of view and information that are not revealed—or are reviewed way too quickly—in the featured articles. A list of *Learning Outcomes* further helps the reader to focus on just what he or she should "take away" from the issue debate.

In each chapter, an *Exploring the Issue* section follows the featured articles. Questions for *Critical Thinking and Reflection* seek to have the reader probe and evaluate the contending points of view and decide just which have more merit than others. Most importantly, just what does the informed reader believe is the "right" answer? The *Critical Thinking and Reflection* sections force the reader to take a position on an issue and to organize information to defend that position and rebut critics.

Is There Common Ground? is a section written specifically to encourage creative critical thinking. Too often, debate-style presentation of an issue encourages students to think in terms of polar extremes. Critical thinking, of course, entails more than that. A student may discover that there is always another position: something in the middle. *Is There Common Ground?* leads students to ask if there are possible middle-ground solutions that can meet the needs of many—if not quite all—of the parties in a debate. This section embraces a community-building approach to leadership that rejects the more simplistic conceptualization of politics only as combat, with each side fighting for its point of view while giving little concern to the perspectives voiced by opponents. In place of oppositional combat, the *Common Ground* sections seek to uncover the possibilities for collaborative action, for finding "win-win" and principled solutions even amid seeming dissensus. Can students discover creative solutions and compromises that give each side something useful, something with which each side can live?

Each chapter concludes with a list of *Additional Resources* that the student can use to find more in-depth information on an issue. A list of some of the more important scholarly writings in the field accompanies each set of articles. A fairly long list of *Internet References* steers the engaged student and activist to some of the more important and useful websites. When used properly, the Web can be a valuable asset that allows students to quickly aggregate intelligent arguments and quality information from a variety of perspectives—although the critical user must be aware of the possible biases and incompleteness of any single article gathered from the Web. The Internet researcher must be especially aware of the biases contained in the information presented by the more "interested" or partisan advocacy websites.

Adopters of *Taking Sides: Clashing Views in Urban Studies* may find it of interest to visit www.mhhe.com/cls for materials that will be helpful in using the volume in the classroom. The www.mhhe.com/cls site includes a number of tips on *Using Taking Sides in the Classroom*. The site also has a listing of the Table of Contents for other volumes in the *Taking Sides* series, should an instructor be interested in using a *Taking Sides* volume in some other subject areas. The *Taking Sides* series covers a far-ranging set of subjects.

My thanks go to Jack Dustin, the Chair of the Urban Affairs and Geography department at Wright State University for his continued support of this writing project and for his commitment to teaching and public service. I owe Larry Loeppke at McGraw-Hill Higher Education my gratitude for his belief in the promise of this book. Jill Meloy and Debra Henricks at MHHE were amazingly helpful in steering this volume to completion. I thank them for their gentle advice and patience.

Most of all, my thanks and love go to Nancy for her extensive support, wisdom, sacrifice, and love that have sustained me over the years in my teaching and writing.

Contents in Brief

Contents

UNIT 1   URBAN GROWTH AND CHANGE: RECENT TRENDS   1

Issue 1.   Does the New Immigration Burden Cities?   3

YES: **U.S. Congressional Budget Office**, "The Impact of Unauthorized Immigrants on the Budgets of State and Local Governments" (2007)   *7*

NO: **Julia Vitullo-Martin**, "Mayor Bloomberg: Right on Neighborhoods, Right on Immigration" (*The Manhattan Institute's Center for Rethinking Development*, January 2008)   *14*

The U.S. Congressional Budget Office was created to provide Congress with expert nonpartisan analysis of issues that have major budgetary impacts. In the section of the report *The Impact of Unauthorized Immigrants on the Budgets of State and Local Governments* presented here, CBO explores the service burdens that states and localities bear as a result of unauthorized or illegal immigrants. Julia Vitullo-Martin, a scholar at the conservative Manhattan Institute, argues that America's cities have a strong immigration tradition and that immigrants contribute to the national economy and to the making of strong cities. She applauds New York Mayor Michael Bloomberg for recognizing the critical importance of immigration to the vitality of cities and for endorsing a policy that seeks to welcome immigrants, a sharp contrast to the more punitive approach demanded by politicians in other immigration gateway cities.

Issue 2.   Does Neighborhood Gentrification Benefit the Inner-City Poor?   20

YES: **Lance Freeman**, "There Goes the 'Hood: Views of Gentrification from the Ground Up" (Temple University Press, 2006)   *24*

NO: **Kathe Newman and Elvin K. Wyly**, "The Right to Stay Put, Revisited: Gentrification and Resistance to Displacement in New York City," *Urban Studies* (vol. 43, no.1, 2006)   *32*

Lance Freeman, associate professor of urban planning at Columbia University, argues that most studies that have pointed to the ills of gentrification suffer from an important methodological flaw. Such studies often fail to ask the residents of poor neighborhoods how they perceive the changes that are taking place in their neighborhoods. Freeman, who is African American, worries about gentrification-related displacement. Still, he finds that the low-income African American residents in two gentrifying sections of New York City see benefits in the upgrading of their neighborhoods. Urban studies professor Kathe Newman (Rutgers) and urban geographer Elvin Wyly (British Columbia) dispute Freeman's contention that gentrification brings substantial benefits to the inner-city poor. Newman and Wyly argue that such studies understate the extent of gentrification-related displacement and the ills that such displacement inflicts on the lives of poor people. They fear that studies that overstate the benefits of gentrification will be used by developers to gain approval for new development projects that will lead to still further displacement of the poor.

Dick Carpenter is a research director and John Ross is a research associate at the Colorado-based Institute for Justice, a conservative political organization committed to protecting the rights of individuals against governmental encroachment. The Institute for Justice provided the lead lawyers in the *Kelo* lawsuit that sought to limit the use of eminent domain authority for economic development purposes. Carpenter and Ross believe that government abuses its eminent domain powers when it takes property from one owner and then transfers it to another owner who desires to build a new development project. They argue that government takings and urban renewal projects too often victimize working-class homeowners and the poor, with local governments acting on behalf of powerful corporations interested in reaping a profit from new development. Bart Peterson, then-mayor of Indianapolis, testified on behalf of the National League of Cities. He argues that public law recognizes the authority of governmental authorities to take property for public purposes, including for economic development purposes, is a long-recognized aspect of public law, with the government obligated to pay an owner just compensation for the property seized. He further argues that severe restrictions on local economic development authority would impair the ability of cities to promote new economic development and job creation, reversing a city's long-term economic decline.

Mark Rosentraub, Bickner endowed chair and professor at the University of Michigan's Center for Sports Management, argues that cities can invest wisely in sports facilities, using new stadiums as part of a strategic plan to leverage new private investment in a declining downtown district. Rosentraub points to how planners in San Diego used the construction of a new ballpark as part of a larger project that transformed the surrounding neighborhood. Economics Professors Dennis Coates and Brad Humphreys summarize the findings of a large number of studies that all point to the same conclusion: that public subsidies for sports facilities seldom add to a region's overall wealth and in some cases may even retard economic growth. Consultant studies typically understate the costs and overpredict the benefits that a city will receive from a stadium project. They further observe how the investment in sports facilities can divert public resources from more productive uses.

Lori Healey, former Chicago Commissioner for Planning and Development and later chief of staff to Mayor Richard M. Daley, and John F. McCormick, financial manager in city's Department of Finance helped arrange many of the initial tax increment financing (TIF) projects in Chicago. These authors argue that the TIF program has been an enormous success, attracting billions of dollars in new investment to Chicago and promoting the rejuvenation of distressed sections of the city. Dan McGraw, a freelance writer living in Texas, worries that TIFs have become little more than a standard "handout" given to big and profitable businesses when such assistance is not justified. TIFs diminish the revenues available for public services, increasing the tax burden placed on homeowners and small businesses in a city.

William Bratton was Commissioner of Police in New York City under Mayor Rudolph Giuliani before he moved on to Los Angeles to serve as Chief of Police. James Q. Wilson (emeritus professor UCLA, Ronald Reagan Professor of Public Policy at Pepperdine University, and past president of the American Political Science Association) and George L. Kelling (professor of criminal justice at Rutgers University) are the academic theorists who are generally credited with publicizing the theory of broken-windows policing. These three experts talk about the importance of order maintenance and why they believe that police must respond to smaller crimes and incidents of disorderly conduct in order begin a process that will also reduce major and violent crimes. Bernard Harcourt, law professor at the University of Chicago, argues that the advocates overstate the achievements of order maintenance policing. He shows that the reduction in major crimes occurred across the nation and not just in New York and in other cities where police departments adopted a broken-windows approach to order maintenance. Harcourt further argues that the new emphasis on order maintenance poses a threat to individualism and civil rights. Minority communities will bear the costs of a more aggressive policing approach that criminalizes nonthreatening behavior.

Issue 7.   Are School Vouchers Overrated as a Strategy for Reforming Public Education?   141

Sol Stern's "School Choice Isn't Enough" produced a considerable stir of controversy, especially in conservative political circles. Stern, a long-time advocate of school vouchers, explains why he has reassessed his position. The evidence, according to Stern, shows that school vouchers seldom lead to significant improvements in student test scores or the restructuring of public school systems. Stern argues that greater emphasis should be given to reforming and strengthening a city's public schools, rather than continuing to place so much emphasis on fighting for vouchers. Professor Jay P. Greene, professor of education policy and author of *Why America Needs School Choice,* heatedly disputes Stern's reading of the evidence. According to Greene, voucher programs produce limited but still significant educational gains. The parents of voucher children also express their great satisfaction with the schools they have chosen. Robert Enlow, president and CEO of the Friedman Foundation for Educational Choice, argues for the need to reduce state regulations that continue to insulate public school systems from the competitive pressures that a voucher system was intended to create.

Issue 8.   Do Charter Schools Improve Education?   163

Stéphane Lavertu is a member of the faculty at the John Glenn School of Public Affairs at The Ohio State University. John Witte, nationally renowned education policy analyst, is professor of political science at the University of Wisconsin and former evaluator of the Milwaukee Parental Choice Program. Lavertu and Witte assess the performance of Milwaukee charter schools, observing both their achievements and their disappointments in the all-important area of student educational gains. Gary Miron, an expert in policy evaluation and professor in the College of Education at Western Michigan University, testified before Congress, noting the many flaws in charter school performance. He observes mediocre student performance, lax accountability standards, and the dominance of concerns for business-like efficiency in schools run by educational management corporations.

Susan J. Popkin is senior fellow at the Urban Institute and lead researcher on the *HOPE VI Panel Study* that looked at the fate of families displaced by the demolition of aging public housing projects. She reports that HOPE VI families moved to safer neighborhoods with lower concentrations of poverty and greater economic opportunity. Sheila Crowley is president of the National Low Income Housing Coalition, sharply criticizes the extensive demolition and displacement that were part of the HOPE VI effort. She questions just who are the real beneficiaries of the HOPE VI program.

Margery Austin Turner and Susan Popkin, housing researchers for the Urban Institute, review the many benefits of housing vouchers. They argue that evidence shows that vouchers add to the life chances of poor people, increasing the job prospects and educational opportunities available to low-income families. Christopher Swope edits the website *Stateline* and previously served as the managing editor of *Governing* magazine, a publication devoted to the analysis of state and local policy issues. Swope argues that the housing vouchers have wound up creating new concentrations of the poor in vulnerable neighborhoods, speeding the decline of fragile but otherwise stabile working-class communities.

Peter J. Wallison, former general counsel at the United States Department of Treasury holds the Arthur B. Burns Chair in Financial Market Studies at the American Enterprise Institute (AEI). A political conservative, he is critical of governmental intrusion in the free market. Wallison argues that the CRA helped to undermine the industry's normal standards for home loans, leading mortgage institutions to make loans to persons who were not good credit risks. Philip Ashton, associate professor of Urban Planning and Policy at the University of Illinois-Chicago, argues that it is unfair to blame the CRA for a home foreclosure crisis that occurred three decades after the act's passage. Ashton observes that the lending industry has been critical of the CRA since its very beginning and has used the recent mortgage crisis as a pretense to launch yet one more attack on the CRA. The greatest abuses did not occur in CRA-covered loans but in loans made by institutions that were exempted from CRA requirements. Ashton argues that it was deregulation, not regulation, that contributed to the home foreclosure crisis.

A public interest group with a formidable record of lobbying for clean air, the Environmental Defense Fund (EDF) is a strong advocate of congestion zones. Case studies of London, Singapore, and cities in Norway demonstrate how a toll system can reduce traffic congestion and enhance the livability and economic attractiveness of the center city. The Keep NYC Congestion Tax Free Coalition is an alliance of businesses, labor organizations, and ideological groups that organized to oppose to Mayor Michael Bloomberg's effort to have New York City adopt a London-style congestion zone. The Coalition emphasizes the potential harmful impact that a congestion zone would have on the city economy as well as the burden that a congestion zone would impose lower-income and working-class citizens.

U.S. Public Interest Research Group (PIRG) advocates stronger governmental action in such policy issues as environmental protection. PIRG looks at the high-speed rail systems of other countries and argues that the United States can similarly build a high-speed rail that can reduce pollution while promoting both national economic growth and local urban revitalization. Robert Poole is a policy analyst who, over the years, has questioned a number of the more orthodox big-spending solutions to urban problems. Poole questions whether high-speed rail in the United States is capable of attracting a great number of riders. He argues against investing so heavily in a transportation system that ultimately will accomplish so little.

James M. McElfish, Jr., senior attorney and director of the Sustainable Use of Land Program at the Environmental Law Institute, reviews the numerous environmental, health, social, and economic problems that result from sprawled development. Robert Bruegmann is professor of art history at the University of Illinois at Chicago where he also holds appointments in the School of Architecture and the Program in Urban Planning and Policy. In this excerpt from his controversial book *Sprawl: A Compact History*, Bruegmann argues that critics often exaggerate the problems that result from sprawl. He views sprawl as progress and the inevitable result of the free choice of citizens who see considerable advantages in residing in lower density settlements located at some distance from congested urban centers.

Randal O'Toole, a Cato Institute senior fellow, argues that environmentalists overstate the achievements of Smart Growth policies. O'Toole points to a number of problems that he sees resulting from Smart Growth efforts in

Portland, especially increased traffic congestion and the escalation of housing prices. Michael Lewyn teaches a seminar on sprawl and the law at the Florida Coastal School of Law in Jacksonville. Lewyn contends that Portland's growth management system has succeeded in protecting recreational spaces and agricultural acreage and in reducing automobile reliance. Lewyn also counters the assertion that the UGB is responsible for home price inflation.

Issue 16. Are Environmentalists Too Often the Unwitting Allies of Suburban Exclusionists? 350

The late Bernard Frieden, the director of the MIT/Harvard Joint Center for Urban Studies at MIT, argues that unnecessarily strict land-use regulations serve to drive up the price of housing, impairing the ability of the working class, the poor, racial minorities, and young married couples to find quality, affordable housing. Frieden contends that affluent suburban communities have used the rhetoric of environmental protection as a cover for exclusionary land-use and housing policies. W. David Conn, professor of city and regional planning at California Polytechnic State University, San Luis Obispo, responds that Frieden understates the harm that growth projects can impose on fragile natural areas. Conn worries that developers will use Frieden's claims to leverage approval of environmentally unwise growth projects.

Issue 17. Does New Urbanism Represent a Viable Strategy That Can Transform Suburban Communities? 367

Robert Steuteville and Philip Langdon, the coauthors of *New Urbanism: Best Practices Guide,* argue that New Urbanism is a reaction-sprawled development. The New Urbanism builds compact mixed-use developments that, in a number of ways, resemble the small towns that dominated the U.S. landscape before the rise of the automobile. Steuteville and Langdon show how New Urban design emphasizes environmental sustainability while also seeking to reinvigorate the sense of "community" critical to neighborhood life. Myron A. Levine, professor of Urban Affairs at Wright State University and the author of the present volume, argues that the New Urbanism, despite its laudable goals and many achievements, does not really pose a challenge that is capable of reshaping the American landscape. Most Americans are quite content to live in large detached homes in automobile-reliant suburbs. As a result, developers will continue to build, and the vast majority of Americans will continue to buy, homes in conventional suburbs rather than in New Urban communities.

UNIT 5 DEBATING THE FUTURE DIRECTION OF URBAN POLICY 387

YES: **Elisabeth Rosenthal,** from "Across Europe, Irking Drivers Is Urban Policy," *New York Times* (June 26, 2011) *393*

NO: **Joel Kotkin,** from "The War Against Suburbia," *The American: The Journal of the American Enterprise Institute* (January 2010) *396*

Elisabeth Rosenthal, reporter for *The New York Times,* reviews the various means by which European countries discourage automobile use and encourage walking, bicycling, and public transit. Joel Kotkin, presidential fellow in Urban Futures at Chapman University and author of *The City: A Global History,* argues that Americans prefer automobile-orientated lives and the freedoms and privacy of large single-family homes as contrasted the smaller housing units and greater population densities of Europe.

Topic Guide

Courses focused on contemporary urban issues can be organized in a variety of ways. The issues debated in this book relate to a number of subject areas. The following list categorizes each of the book's chapters (that is, the issues discussed) under a variety of alternative subject headings. On the Internet References pages, a number of websites have been gathered specifically for this book. They are arranged to reflect the issues of this *Taking Sides* reader. You can link to these sites by going to www.mhhe.com/cls.

Housing

9. Should Federal Programs Seek to Deconcentrate Inner-City Poverty?
10. Should Section 8 Housing Vouchers Continue to Serve as the Backbone of the Federal Government's Assisted Housing Efforts?
11. Did the Government's Regulation of Lending Institutions Under the Community Reinvestment Act Lead to the Mortgage Foreclosure Crisis?

Immigration

1. Does the New Immigration Burden Cities?

National and State Urban Policy

3. Should State Governments Impose Strong Limitations on the Ability of Cities to Use Eminent Domain Powers for Economic Development Purposes?
9. Should Federal Programs Seek to Deconcentrate Inner-City Poverty?
10. Should Section 8 Housing Vouchers Continue to Serve as the Backbone of the Federal Government's Assisted Housing Efforts?
11. Did the Government's Regulation of Lending Institutions Under the Community Reinvestment Act Lead to the Mortgage Foreclosure Crisis?
13. Should the United States Invest in High-Speed Intercity Rail?
18. Should Urban Policy in the United States Be Guided by the Model of the European City?

Neighborhood and Community Development

1. Does the New Immigration Burden Cities?
6. Does Broken-Windows Policing Reduce Crime?
9. Should Federal Programs Seek to Deconcentrate Inner-City Poverty?
10. Should Section 8 Housing Vouchers Continue to Serve as the Backbone of the Federal Government's Assisted Housing Efforts?

Power in North American Cities

4. Are Public Subsidies for Sports Stadiums a Good Investment by Cities?
5. Should Cities Rely on Tax Increment Financing (TIF) as a Primary Tool in Their Efforts to Promote Local Economic Development?

Public Choice Theory

7. Are School Vouchers Overrated as a Strategy for Reforming Public Education?
8. Do Charter Schools Improve Education?
14. Is Urban Sprawl a Sufficiently Important Problem to Merit Government Corrective Action?

Race and Ethnicity

1. Does the New Immigration Burden Cities?
2. Does Neighborhood Gentrification Benefit the Inner-City Poor?
6. Does Broken-Windows Policing Reduce Crime?
9. Should Federal Programs Seek to Deconcentrate Inner-City Poverty?
10. Should Section 8 Housing Vouchers Continue to Serve as the Backbone of the Federal Government's Assisted Housing Efforts?
11. Did the Government's Regulation of Lending Institutions Under the Community Reinvestment Act Lead to the Mortgage Foreclosure Crisis?

Schools and Education

7. Are School Vouchers Overrated as a Strategy for Reforming Public Education?
8. Do Charter Schools Improve Education?

Suburbs: Sprawl, Smart Growth, and Exclusion

14. Is Urban Sprawl a Sufficiently Important Problem to Merit Government Corrective Action?
15. Do Portland-Style Smart Growth Policies Raise Housing Prices and Hurt Urban Livability?
16. Are Environmentalists Too Often the Unwitting Allies of Suburban Exclusionists?
17. Does New Urbanism Represent a Viable Strategy That Can Transform Suburban Communities?

Tax Policy

4. Are Public Subsidies for Sports Stadiums a Good Investment by Cities?
5. Should Cities Rely on Tax Increment Financing (TIF) as a Primary Tool in Their Efforts to Promote Local Economic Development?

(Continued)

Introduction

The Persistence of Urban Problems

Is the urban crisis over? The last few decades have seen significant improvements in the urban condition. Big cities have enjoyed a downtown revival that was all but unimaginable in the 1970s. Numerous inner-city neighborhoods, once seemingly caught in a spiral of decline, too, have "come back" as the sites of new residential activity and investment. Cities have been able to maintain their vitality even during a period of national economic recession. Although the slow-growth national economy of the early 2000s meant new fiscal problems for cities, cities as a whole did not teeter on the edge of bankruptcy, as New York and Cleveland did in the 1970s.

Reason for optimism can also be found in the falling crime rates in inner-city neighborhoods, apparent over the last two decades. Community-based organizations have sustained poorer neighborhoods through a variety of bottom-up activities, including neighborhood watch programs, community cleanup days, and the operation of after-school tutoring programs. Community development corporations have entered into partnerships with banks, investment institutions, and government agencies, piecing together the financing necessary for the construction and rehabilitation of tens of thousands of units of quality affordable housing.

Racial discrimination also no longer poses the same barrier to residential mobility that it did in the past. Today, racial minorities make up approximately 35 percent of the suburban population, a figure that is roughly the same as their overall share of the national population (2010 census figures, as reported by The Brookings Institution). The all-white suburb, a common feature of the American landscape in the mid-twentieth century, has virtually disappeared. Racial progress is also apparent in the work place, as affirmative action programs have helped to increase the access of racial minorities to managerial positions from which they were previously excluded.

Yet, the urban crisis is not over. Despite the important gains cited above, all is not well with America's cities and suburbs. Severe urban problems persist. Even a partial listing of urban ills points to the depth and broad scope of a continuing urban crisis:

- Deindustrialization has meant the loss of jobs in the city, with low-skilled workers, especially in areas of concentrated poverty, virtually shut out of a transformed American economy.
- The crisis in public education continues, as measured by intolerable student dropout rates and poor performance on standardized exams. In the nation's 50 largest cities, only 53 percent of first-year high school students go on to graduate, as compared to a 71 percent graduation rate in the suburbs. In Cleveland, only one-third of entering high school students go on to graduate; in Indianapolis, the graduation rate was even worse, only 30 percent (see *Cities in Crisis 2009: Closing the*

Graduation Gap, a report of America's Promise Alliance, available at www
.americaspromise.org/Resources/Partner-Resources/c/Cities-In-Crisis-2009
.aspx). A substantial racial gap in reading and mathematical test scores
also remains (and on some tests even appears to be widening), with the
scores of African American children lagging considerably behind those
of whites and Asians.

- The resegegration of school classrooms reveals the United States is no
  longer making progress on the road to school integration. The racial
  integration of the public schools has actually diminished as localities
  have abandoned earlier efforts that the courts once required to end
  segregation. As the Civil Right Project (http://civilrightsproject.ucla.edu)
  reports, the result is a resegregation of schools that limits the opportunities of both racial minorities and whites: Three-fourths of African-
  American and Latino students attend predominantly minority schools.
  White students in the public schools have less and less contact with
  students from other racial or ethnic backgrounds.
- Despite the noteworthy reduction of violence in inner-city communities in recent years, cities continue to suffer higher rates of violent
  crime than do suburbs. Though the gap has narrowed, cities are still
  perceived as more dangerous than suburbs (see the 2011 Brookings
  report *City and Suburban Crime Trends in Metropolitan America,* available at www.brookings.edu/papers/2011/0526_metropolitan_crime_kneebone_
  raphael.aspx).
- Cities and older suburbs lack the resources to effectively battle the
  problems they face. Over the years, central cities and the nation's "first
  suburbs" have lost both population and tax base to growing communities on the edge of the metropolis.
- The continuing shrinkage of municipal tax bases has forced municipalities to institute wave after wave of spending and service cutbacks.
  Cities and counties have reduced social and mental health services,
  pared back parks activities and recreational programs, delayed much-
  needed infrastructure repairs, eliminated training and other support
  activities, and dismissed public workers, sometimes even taking the
  politically difficult step of laying off police and fire personnel.
- Cities and declining older suburbs face the seemingly impossible
  burden of having to cope with a huge stock of abandoned housing
  and vacant property. A 2008 survey by the United States Conference
  of Mayors reports the existence of more than 79,000 vacant properties in just 42 cites. Baltimore had 16,400 vacant properties, Buffalo
  10,000, and Las Vegas 8,000. These cities face staggering responsibilities, not only in struggling to find the monies to maintain the properties and public safety, but also in attempting to figure out some
  way to fill vacant dwelling units and return idle properties to productive use.

Vacant properties have long-term causes and are not simply the product
of a housing finance system that went "bust' in the early 2000s. Simply put,
many cities are shrinking in terms of demographic numbers and no longer
have need for the same stock of housing that once sheltered a much larger
population.

Vacant properties accelerate the decline of already fragile neighborhoods. Even just one or two vacant properties can lead to severe problems for properties located nearby. Vacant structures often become the sites of drug dealing and other illegal activities. Unscrupulous builders may even strip a building of its copper pipes, plumbing fixtures, bricks, and anything else of value, leaving an ugly scar in the middle of a poor neighborhood. In the worst cases, abandoned homes become the target of arson. "Good" families with the means to do so will leave areas plagued by abandoned housing. Their move away is quite understandable; nonetheless, their exodus leads to the area's further decline.

- Poverty is no longer exclusively a central city problem but a condition of suburban life as well. As The Brookings Institution reported, between 2000 and 2008 the number of poor people living in suburbia rose by 25 percent. One-third of the nation's poverty population can be found in the suburbs. The total number of poor people who reside in the suburbs is actually a bit larger than the number found in central cities (www.brookings.edu/papers/2010/0120_poverty_kneebone.aspx).
- Immigration places new burdens on both cities and suburbs. Port-of-entry cities (also called "gateway cities") are particularly affected. Over 60 percent of Miami's population is foreign born. In Los Angeles 41 percent, New York 37 percent, and San Francisco 35 percent of the local population come from outside the nation's borders (2007 figures). Contemporary immigration, however, no longer affects only traditional port-of-entry communities. The nation's suburbs and cities in America's heartland are also absorbing new arrivals from other countries. Large numbers of arrivals from Mexico, Central America, and East and South Asia have skipped traditional port-of-entry centers and have moved directly to the suburbs, where they are welcomed by extended family and friends. "Little Saigon" is found in Westminster, California, south of Los Angeles. Hicksville, on New York's Long Island, is popularly referred to as "Little India." As Richard Jones recounts in *Immigrants Outside Megalopolis* (2008), large concentrations of residents from other countries can also be found in such heartland cities as Denver, Nashville, Oklahoma City, and St. Paul.
- Municipalities suffer from a weakened bargaining position when working with business. In a global age, municipal officials know that a major corporation often has a choice of a number of suitable sites across the country and around the world for new office headquarters or expanded production facilities. Local officials feel that they have little choice but to raise their own offering of business incentives in order to meet or surpass the package of incentives offered by competitor cities. As a result, municipal budgets are skewed in favor of the infrastructure investment and other actions demanded by businesses. Other policy areas—including the provision of housing and social and health services—are given less priority.
- Intercity, interregional, and global competition also weaken the municipal tax base. In a desperate search for local job creation, cities offer sizable tax breaks and other concessions, including expensive public investment in upgraded public infrastructure, as part of their efforts to lure new development and to keep existing businesses from relocating

elsewhere. Taxpayer-subsidized sports stadiums and convention centers are justified on the basis of their promised contribution to the local economy. It is a matter of debate, however, just how much a city and its citizens receive as a return on such investments. Economists argue that much of the favorable tax treatment given to new business projects actually has little impact, as the city winds up providing subsidies for favorable investment decisions that in many cases would have taken place even with the provision of much less generous taxpayer support. Such concessions reduce the revenues that a city derives from a project, a loss of revenues that municipal authorities could have used to support public education and other vital services.

- Although suburbia is more racially and ethnically diverse than ever, African Americans (and Latinos, to a somewhat lesser degree) have gained entrance to a different suburbia than that enjoyed by whites. African Americans and Latinos are disproportionately found in declining older suburban communities located adjacent to the central city. Such inner-ring communities tend to share many of the same problems of central-city communities.
- Sprawled development threatens the loss of wildlife habits, wetlands, and agricultural acreage while bringing with it associated problems of water and air pollution. The Sierra Club, the nation's oldest conservation organization, estimates that each year the United States loses over two million acres of farm land, parks, and open space (www.sierraclub.org/sprawl/overview).
- Traffic congestion is getting worse and costly. According to 2005 estimates of the Texas Traffic Institute, traffic delays lead to losses in productivity and increases in fuel consumption that cost the United Sates economy $65 billion a year!
- The energy-intensive nature of suburban growth raises questions as to the long-term sustainability of the "spread" or sprawled metropolis.

Writing in 2003 in the *National Civic Review*, Peter Dreier described "America's Urban Crisis a Decade After the Los Angeles Riots." Dreier observed the persistence of concentrated poverty, a widening of the income gap between the rich and poor, rising home foreclosures, an "intense spatial segregation" of populations reinforced by local zoning laws (p. 52), the declining conditions of older suburbs, shrinking municipal revenues, suburban sprawl fueled by federal subsidies and tax breaks, and a "fend-for-yourself-federalism" (p. 50) where reduced levels of intergovernmental assistance diminish the ability of cities and suburbs to tackle urban ills. Unfortunately, Dreier's description of the urban crisis is just as accurate today as it was a decade ago. Little has changed for the better since Dreier's article appeared.

The New Normal

Economists use the phrase "The New Normal" to refer to the fundamental changes that they expect to see in American business in forthcoming years, even during periods of economic growth. The economic woes of the early twenty-first century were not simply the result of a downturn in the business cycle. Instead, they indicate more fundamental long-term problems caused by the restructuring of the national and local economies. Advances in technology and communications coupled with globalization, have eroded the economic position of the United States and its cities. Even the end to the economic recession will not bring a return to the prosperity similar to that of economic rebounds of decades past. Fundamental economic restructuring will continue to cause dislocations and heighten social problems. The new information-based economy will place a premium on advanced education and the command of sophisticated technological skills, skills that the inner-city and suburban poor largely lack.

A new economic upswing is not likely to bring a repeat of the high growth rates that the United States enjoyed during the boom years of previous decades. Instead, even during future "good" years, cities will likely face relatively slow growth rates, depressed housing markets, low investment returns, and the loss of economic activity to overseas competitors. Confronted by the need to take actions to attract and retain businesses that can choose to locate elsewhere, municipalities will continue to give their top priority to economic development activities, with lesser commitments made to battling other pressing community problems. Congress also is highly unlikely to restore the severe cuts that were made in urban assistance programs. The antitax sentiment of voters will continue to constrain action at both the national and local levels. Urban problems will continue to persist even amid the return to better times.

As Detroit and numerous aging once-industrial communities have already discovered, the urban crisis is permanent, the result of a long-term economic transformation that has seen the disappearance of manufacturing and the relocation of economic activity and jobs to the suburban areas, to the Sunbelt, and overseas. Corporate chief executive officers who shut down aging and more costly facilities during the nation's economic slowdown will not reopen them during an economic upswing. Instead, many CEOs will continue to "rationalize" production, shifting a firm's activities to its more modern and productive facilities.

Public Policy Analysis: Evaluating Alternative Urban Problem-Solving Tools

The rest of this chapter reviews various tools or approaches that government can use to help solve public policy problems. For many students, the discussion that follows may seem a bit detached and technical. The reader who is more interested in the debate over urban issues and is less interested in a more systematic discussion of alternative policy tools can simply skip the rest of this introductory essay and proceed directly to the individual issue chapters where the "clash" of competing issue positions is presented.

The rest of this chapter is written for the student who is interested in acquiring greater familiarity with the alternative approaches or "tools" that are available to government in a great many policy areas. As the readings in this book reveal, there is no perfect policy tool. Rather, each tool in the policy tool box has its particular advantages and shortcomings. Advocates for effective policy change need to identify the policy tool that is most appropriate to the task at hand.

The more traditional or orthodox policy approaches include government service provision, taxation, transfer payments, and regulation:

- **Direct government provision of service.** Municipalities can seek to solve a problem by providing a service itself, by having a public agency perform an action. Direct service provision includes: firefighting by a municipal fire department, road construction by a public agency, mass transit system operated by a municipal or regional authority, a city's public schools, county provision of health services to the poor, and the provision of public housing for low-income residents by a governmental authority.
- **Taxation and government-imposed fees.** Government can set high taxes or special fees in an effort to deter undesired actions. High excise taxes can be used as part of the public health effort to curb smoking and the consumption of alcohol. High vehicle registration fees, fuel taxes, and parking charges can be part of a strategy to reduce automobile use. Taxation and fees, of course, also have the added advantage of increasing the revenues that government can use in its attempts to solve problems.
- **Transfer payments to individuals.** Oftentimes, government gives people money. Public assistance to low-income people is often characterized as "welfare." But transfer payments also include unemployment compensation, Social Security and veteran's benefits, and even taxpayer-funded college scholarships.
- **Regulation.** Regulation entails a law or an agency-imposed rule that requires certain actions by private actors or bans or limits certain specified activities by private actors. Federal health care reformers, for instance, have sought regulations that would force employers to offer health care coverage to workers. In housing and employment, federal regulations prohibit discrimination on the basis of race and ethnic origin. Environmental regulations seek to curb pollution. The regulations imposed by the Community Reinvestment Act not only ban "redlining" (the refusal to extend loans to properties located in poorer sections of a city) but also require housing finance institutions to take positive steps to meet the credit needs of home buyers in poor and minority communities located in an institution's depository area.
- **Mandates.** A mandate entails a binding order issued by one body of government that forces another to provide a service or follow a specific course of action. Federal "civil rights for the handicapped" laws, for instance, require local authorities to retrofit public transit systems to ensure equal accessibility by disabled riders. Judicial mandates have protected the civil liberties of patients residing in long-term mental health institutions, preventing states and localities from continuing to confine individuals who pose no obvious threat of harm to themselves or to others. Deinstitutionalization, unfortunately, has been a factor that has contributed to the rise of the homeless population in numerous communities.

There also exist a number of more flexible, less government-centered alternative approaches for solving public problems. The full list of alternative policy tools is fairly large, and the student interested in the field would be wise to consult a public policy textbook. The more important alternative policy approaches include:

- **Privatization.** It is not always necessary for a government agency to deliver an important service. Instead, governments can "contract out" service provision, entering into a contractual arrangement by which government compensates a private firm or nonprofit organization for delivering a specified service. Privatization arrangements are increasingly commonplace. Many small and medium-sized cities hire private trash haulers rather than have a municipal sanitation agency pick up the garbage. Numerous communities have contracted private information technology firms to update municipal data-keeping and computerization systems rather than have such specialized tasks done in-house by government workers. Similarly, governments can contract to have nonprofit agencies run drug rehabilitation and after-school recreational programs. The elderly may be more willing to accept services provided by members of their immediate community than by more anonymous governmental agencies. The award of contracts can also create a competitive environment among potential service providers, who submit sealed bids in an effort to win a municipal service contract. Such competition should serve to keep bid prices low, enabling the city money. When the concept is used more broadly, privatization goes beyond contracting and refers to a range of government efforts to borrow managerial practices, such as benchmarking and statistically based performance measurements, that have proven popular in the private sector.
- **Vouchers.** Some reformers seek to create a market for services that will end the "monopoly" conditions that exist when citizens have no alternative other than to rely on a government agency for a service that may be poorly provided. Housing and school vouchers—also called certificates—represent an effort to break the government's monopoly hold by giving the recipient the ability to choose the rental unit or school they prefer. Choice should generate market pressures that lead public agencies—in this case housing authorities and the public schools—to "shape up" and improve their performance from fear of seeing clients take their voucher-supported funding elsewhere.
- **Deregulation**. Deregulation is the reversal of regulation. Antigovernment critics argue for the need to relax overly rigid governmental rules in order to encourage more innovative and entrepreneurial activity. Deregulation, for instance, can allow new private car services to operate in a city, extending service to neighborhoods that were not adequately served by government-regulated medallion taxicabs. Free-market advocates argue for relaxation of rules where cities attempt to constrain increases in the rent that a landlord can charge; deregulating rents should make investment in rental housing more attractive and expand the supply of rental units in tight housing market. Of course, deregulation can be quite controversial, as the purposes served by

governmental regulation may be jettisoned by a return to an unregulated market. As we shall see, deregulation of the mortgage lending field did succeed in increasing the number of firms working in the field, offering home seekers a variety of creative borrowing instruments that enabled more borrowers to gain access to the capital needed to buy a home. Yet, the narrowing of governmental regulation and oversight also led to an increase in deceptive lending practices and the issuance of loans that could not be repaid, factors that contributed to the wave of home loan defaults that plagued the nation's cities and suburbs.

- **Intergovernmental grants.** A grant-in-aid refers to the assistance that one level of government provides to help another level of government provide an important service. Federal grants-in-aid provide states and localities with financial assistance for a very wide spectrum of program activities, including crime prevention; the protection of women against domestic violence; training programs and compensation for local activities in support of homeland security; the acquisition and "clean up" of contaminated brownfield properties; community development programs; regional planning efforts and the coordination of transit activities; and increasing the capacity of local sewage processing systems. Typically, the assistance awarded is accompanied by numerous regulations, as the grantor seeks to ensure that the grant recipient is following though on program expectations. Recipient governments, however, complain about the loss of flexibility and the costly administrative and paperwork burdens that result from detailed program rules.

- **Grants to businesses and nonprofit corporations.** Governments also award grants to private firms and nonprofit corporations. A government grant may support job training efforts designed to increase the employability of low-income people. Other grants support the provision of day care activities by nonprofit organizations. Federal grants also support the various activities of community development corporations, including their efforts to expand health clinics and the availability of affordable housing. The U.S. Department of Justice, as authorized by the Violence Against Women Act, offers grants to community groups that seek to deter domestic violence and aid the victims of sexual assault.

- **Tax deductions, credits, and abatements.** Just as a government can reduce regulations in an attempt to spur new activity, a government can also lower (or "abate") taxes in an effort to encourage new investment. Tax deductions and credits are somewhat different tools that share the same overriding principle: each lowers a person's or corporation's annual tax obligation for having taken actions that the government deems desirable. The federal government has offered tax incentives to encourage home weatherization and the installment of more energy-efficient appliances. The federal tax code's generous treatment of home mortgages provides a sizeable subsidy for home buying; home owners can deduct from their taxable income the interest they pay each year on their home mortgages, reducing the tax obligation they owe the federal government. The Low Income Housing Tax Credit (LIHTC), by contrast, is a much different tax incentive program that seeks to encourage private investment in low-income housing; investors gain

important tax advantages when they invest in the affordable housing activities of community development corporations.
- **Loans and loan guarantees.** As most college students know, government loans can help facilitate a desired action, such as a student's enrollment at a university. Other government loans assist small business start-ups, encouraging entrepreneurial activity and job creation. State governments offer loans to smaller communities for the improvement of schools and other public facilities. For the government that extends the loan, a lending program is much cheaper than a similar program of government grants; the government that issues the loan is normally repaid, sharply reducing its overall cost of promoting a desired activity.

A loan guarantee program operates a bit differently. The government does not itself advance a loan; instead, the government promotes private lending by assuring creditors substantial repayment in cases where a borrower defaults and fails to make the required payments. Loan guarantees essentially remove much of the risk from private lending. The home loan guarantee programs of the Federal Housing Administration have been enormously successful in encouraging banks and mortgage finance institutions to extend home loans to working- and middle-class people who, in the program's absence, would not otherwise been able to borrow the money necessary for the purchase of a home. Loan guarantees can be very cost effective; if borrowers repay creditors and the government does not have to cover an extensive number of defaults, loan guarantees cost the government very little.

- **Informal partnerships**. Municipal leaders work in partnership with private institutions in order to arrange joint action. Informal meetings held outside the normal processes of government can coordinate strategy and joint public–private undertakings. Many regional partnerships seek to coordinate public and private investment, job training, transportation, and economic development initiatives, in effect formulating a plan that can attract major new employers to a region. Public–private partnerships can also be aimed at smaller goals, such as the initiation of a mentoring program where public school students are led to think more seriously about their futures as they follow local professionals as they perform their daily jobs.

As the reader can readily see, there exists a wide variety of tools or policy approaches that government can use when attempting to tackle a specific urban, social, or economic problem. The list of policy tools presented above is far from exhaustive.

The alternative policy tools, however, are not equally effective in their abilities to solve each and every problem. Each policy tool embodies a unique set of tradeoffs. Businesses may see deregulation and public–private partnerships as providing much-needed flexibility. But deregulation can also entail diminished governmental oversight and lost public accountability, as private firms and nonprofit organizations gain greater freedom to act and use public grant funds as they wish. Regulations that prohibit the conversion of rental properties to condominiums may seek to restrain a landlord's ability to oust tenants, but in doing so may intrude on private property rights and impair a city's economic development by diminishing its ability to attract major corporations and their upscale work forces. Tax abatements entail another set of tradeoffs: reduced taxes can help stimulate new investment but may also represent a sacrifice of revenues that a city could have used to fund schools and local social service and public health programs.

The readings in this book—and the recommended supplementary sources and websites—debate the relative desirability of alternative policy tools for fighting salient urban problems. Just what are the policy choices that are available when confronting specific urban policy challenges? To highlight just a few:

- **Immigration** (Issue 1): Opponents of illegal immigration urge strong direct government action—more vigorous action by federal officials to protect the nation's border, even the construction of a fence along the border with Mexico. Complementary approaches rely on grants to law enforcement agencies and programs that seek to coordinate the joint action of various law enforcement and immigration-related agencies. A regulatory approach entails the levying of substantial fines on firms that continue to hire undocumented workers. Some cities, however, have taken a quite different approach, providing protection and other governmental services to newcomers and assisting the activities of ethnic- and community-based organizations. These cities hope that such assistance will accelerate the integration of newcomers into American life, encouraging their employment and entrepreneurial activities while helping to bring new life to inner-city neighborhoods that, in the absence of immigration, would face continued steep decline and abandonment.
- **Gentrification and Displacement** (Issue 2): Gentrification (the rediscovery of inner-city areas by younger professionals) has contributed to cities' economic growth. However, new investment by upscale tenants and home buyers can lead to displacement of the poor who find that they no longer have the means to live in a suddenly "hot" neighborhood with soaring property values. Antidisplacement advocates argue for legislation to regulate rents and to prevent landlords from ousting tenants and converting rental units to condominiums. An alternative approach relies on government tax incentives and grants to help fund public–private partnerships and the activities of community development corporations as they seek to build and rehabilitate affordable housing units in neighborhoods facing the pressures of change.
- **Eminent Domain** (Issue 3): In recent years, new state restrictions imposed on the local exercise of eminent domain powers have led cities to search for alternative approaches to economic development. Rather than "take" land, localities in recent years have given greater emphasis to individual purchase agreements, with free-market negotiations determining the price that the government will pay to acquire land parcels critical to a development project. Some cities have even begun to turn away from major development projects that are

dependent on the exercise of government's eminent domain authority. These municipalities emphasize investment in infrastructure improvements and the award of grants to community-based organizations to assist smaller scale and "locally owned" jobs development efforts.

- **Local Economic Development** (Issues 4 and 5): Local governments rely on a variety of tools in their efforts to attract new commercial development and to attract and retain major league sports franchises. Cities and counties pay for street upgrading and other infrastructural improvements demanded by business. Cities and counties have also paid for the construction of new sports facilities. Cities across the country offer property tax abatements— the promise of reduced taxes—to businesses that make investments that raise property values. Alternative development strategies entail loans to important businesses as well as the formation of joint public–private efforts to provide the skills training and quality workers demanded by major corporations. But just who pays for the subsidies provided business? State and national grants and provision of services by a county or regional authority can help spread the burden of financing a project more widely, rather than having the residents of a single community pay for a project that brings benefits to an entire region.

- **Law Enforcement and Policing** (Issue 6): Community policing and broken-windows policing see law enforcement and order maintenance as joint actions where the police must work in partnership with community groups and businesses to effect the changes that will bring about a reduction in crime.

- **Public Schools and Education** (Issues 7 and 8): School choice advocates seek to break the monopolistic tendencies that exist in government-run school systems. Vouchers, tax credits, and the contracting of school operations to private educational management organizations are all privatization strategies that seek to borrow private-sector managerial and marketing practices while adding a healthy dose of flexibility and competition to the provision of public education. Critics, however, worry about the inequities that they believe will result from marketization. Some reformers argue for the limited deregulation approach of charter schools represents an appropriate balance, providing for new flexibility and opportunities for innovations while maintaining public control and a concern for equity. More market-oriented reformers, however, argue that charter schools do not go far enough to shake up the performance of public education. For the defenders of public schools, privatization is a move in the wrong direction; they would rather see greater investment in the public schools rather than reform initiatives that wind up draining resources away from public school classrooms.

- **Housing Programs and Community Development** (Issues 9–11): Government once built public housing projects as the backbone of its efforts to provide a decent living environment for low-income people. The past decades, however, have seen a fundamental shift in the nation's housing strategies, with the direct production of public housing ceding way to an alternative strategy that relies on the issuance of housing vouchers to help poor families find an appropriate dwelling unit in the stock of rental housing that already exists. Federal HOPE VI grants helped local authorities to tear down some of the worst-off public housing and build replacement housing. Deregulation made the demolition-and-reconstruction project possible, with a repeal of a one-for-one replacement requirement that previously made it financially unviable for local housing authorities to tear down structures that were largely uninhabitable. The award of housing choice vouchers has empowered poor families to move to better—or at least less dangerous—neighborhoods.

In terms of home ownership and rehabilitation, the regulations of the Community Reinvestment Act (CRA) virtually forced banks and other depository institutions to undertake new initiatives to extend their lending services to inner-city neighborhoods that they had previously ignored. Business-oriented conservatives, however, contend that the United States has paid a steep price for such efforts, as the CRA and similar regulatory programs placed banks under pressure to approve loans they otherwise would have never considered. Liberals argue quite the contrary, that it was deregulation—the narrowing of the scope of existing regulations—that permitted the rise of new mortgage financing businesses that seduced and "ripped off" home owners with deceptive marketing practices and the issuance of loans that home owners could not repay.

- **Transportation** (Issues 12 and 13): Government can ease traffic congestion by building new roads. Alternatively, government can use a system of fees assisted by new technology—automated and flexible road-pricing systems and congestion zones—to reduce the flow of traffic at peak travel times and in highly busy downtown areas. Government grants and contracts have also supported investment in High-Speed Rail (HSR) technology and construction.
- **Suburban Growth, Sprawl, and Sustainability** (Issues 14–18): Environmentalists and Smart Growth advocates argue for strong government regulations backed up by patterns of government infrastructure investment to promote infill development rather than continued urban sprawl. In cases where restrictive local land-use regulations serve to drive new development to the outer edges of the metropolis, environmentalist argue for deregulation—a relaxation of local zoning codes—to allow for more dense patterns of development and a greater diversity of activities in existing suburbs. Deregulation can also reduce the costs of new home construction by thousands of dollars, eliminating regulations that require unnecessarily expensive building materials and practices, including local zoning regulations that require the construction of houses on large lots of land. Practitioners of the school of "New Urbanism" urge voluntary efforts by builders to construct more walkable communities with site design plans that emphasize more dense development, the preservation of open space, and the provision of mass transit. Government planning grants, housing subsidies, and "smart code" deregulation are all tools that can assist the construction of New Urban communities. Critics, however, argue that most Americans will reject the introduction of the sort of strong urban policies found in Europe: high vehicle registration fees and taxes on

gasoline, a reduction in the number of parking spaces, the exclusion of private cars from central pedestrian zones, greater taxpayer investment in public transit and bicycling lanes, and the development of compact communities with relatively small houses built on small plots of land.

This book describes the debate over some of the more critical issues facing urban American. It seeks to provoke thoughtful assessment of the alternative policies. The reader is asked to wade into the debate, to assess the competing claims and evidence, and to decide for himself or herself just what approach—or what combination of policy tools—offers the greatest promise for improving life in urban America.

Urban Growth and Change: Recent Trends

U.S. cities and suburbs are undergoing a never-ending process of change, with emerging patterns of growth and decline serving to alter the shape of the urban landscape. In recent years, newspapers and magazines have focused considerable attention on globalization and gentrification, the newest "wrinkles" in urban development.

Cities in early America were vastly different than the giant metropolises of today. Early settlements were concentrated around harbors, rivers, and waterways, key means of transportation essential to commerce and growth in the preindustrial United States. Later on, other cities were built focused on rail lines. Urban growth, however, was severely constrained by the primitive nature of transportation; a city could expand only as far as a person could reasonably travel on foot.

Cities, however, continued to grow as centers of administration, commerce, and industry, attracting arrivals from the countryside and immigrants from overseas searching for jobs and opportunity. In the twentieth century, the mechanization of agriculture in the South led to the Great Migration, with dislocated African American tenant farmers and poor whites moving to cities, especially to cities in the North, in search of prosperity.

Each new advance in transportation—the horse-drawn jitney, the electric streetcar, and commuter rail systems—allowed the urban population to spread further and further outward. For a long time, cities were able to annex areas of population growth, incorporating the growing rim areas into the expanded borders of the city. Eventually, though, suburbanites spurned annexation, preferring to maintain local autonomy rather than face being swallowed up by the central city with its immigrant population and its corrupt political party "machine."

The automobile, of course, radically altered the shape of the metropolis, allowing new settlements further and further away from the old central city. Suburban residences were eventually followed by warehousing, distribution, retail, and office developments, all of which began the shift from the central city to suburbia. Intersections of major highways became the site of shopping centers and office development, economic hubs that allowed the metropolis to sprawl even further out.

Airports, too, served as the hub of industrial, warehousing, and shipping activities, with nearby suburban sites offering more accessible locations than congested cities with their narrow streets, antiquated warehouses, and undersized loading docks. Air travel also opened the Sunbelt to new development. Computerization and other advances in communications further served to free businesses from dependence on their old central-city sites; business could now move to the suburbs and the Sunbelt (the growing Southwest and West). The regional shift in population and jobs, coupled with the continuing pressures of suburbanization, led to the decline of older industrial cities and even many inner-ring suburbs.

By the latter half of the twentieth century, globalization had become an increasingly prominent factor in shaping urban development. Globalization denotes the increased vulnerability of a city to forces from outside its borders. Cities now found themselves competing not just with cities across the nation but also with cities around the world in the search for attractive new businesses. Industrial cities suffered job losses as corporations shifted production not just to the suburbs and to the Sunbelt but also to lower-cost sites overseas. New York saw the virtual disappearance of its old manufacturing base but eventually was able to recover, reemerging as a global command-and-control center of finance and corporate headquarters. A large number of industrial centers, however, were not able to make a similar transition, with the result that cities such as Cleveland and Detroit suffered unabated steep decline, including depopulation and extensive property abandonment.

Heightened immigration, too, is a part of globalization, with a "new" immigration coming to the United States from Mexico and the rest of Latin America, Asia, and Africa. Advanced communications serves to advertise the American dream to people in countries around the world. Advances in transportation decreased the difficulty of reaching America's shores.

Cities and states have the burden of meeting the costs of schooling and other service provision that result from extensive immigration. Such increased service demands diminish the availability of resources for other municipal activities. Some cities, however, have begun to take a more positive view of immigration, seeing an economic advantage in attracting immigrant entrepreneurs who have an interest in small-business development and who have access to financing and markets in their native countries. The arrival of new immigrant populations also helps to fill distressed inner-city neighborhoods, thereby preventing the extensive property abandonment, arson, and crime that plague a neighborhood that is marred by boarded-up homes.

Recent demographic patterns also reveal an important exception to the long-term narrative of suburban growth and central city decline. By the latter part of the twentieth century, cities were beginning to experience gentrification, as once-poor inner-city communities were "rediscovered" by younger and more professional home seekers who desired residences close to the corporate job base of downtown and close to a city's nightlife and cultural districts. For cities, gentrification was an affirmation of an urban rebirth. Upscale technologically competent workers were valuable assets that made cities attractive to technology-oriented and creative firms. Critics, however, focused on displacement pressures, as poorer residents were effectively ousted from their neighborhoods to make way for more upscale residential and commercial development.

- Does the New Immigration Burden Cities?

- Does Neighborhood Gentrification Benefit the Inner-City Poor?

ISSUE 1

Does the New Immigration Burden Cities?

YES: U.S. Congressional Budget Office, "The Impact of Unauthorized Immigrants on the Budgets of State and Local Governments" (2007)

NO: Julia Vitullo-Martin, "Mayor Bloomberg: Right on Neighbor-hoods, Right on Immigration" (*The Manhattan Institute's Center for Rethinking Development*, January 2008)

Learning Outcomes

After reading this issue, you should be able to:

- Show the various ways by which the "new immigration" differs from the old waves of immigration to United States cities in the 1800s and early 1900s.
- Differentiate between legal immigrants and undocumented or illegal immigrants.
- Explain how advances in technology have changed just what it means to be an immigrant; describe how the identity and allegiance of the new immigrants differ from that of the older waves of immigrants.
- Identify the costs that the new immigration imposes on cities.
- Identify the benefits that the new immigration brings to cities and to core urban neighborhoods.

ISSUE SUMMARY

YES: The U.S. Congressional Budget Office was created to provide Congress with expert nonpartisan analysis of issues that have major budgetary impacts. In the section of the report *The Impact of Unauthorized Immigrants on the Budgets of State and Local Governments* presented here, CBO explores the service burdens that states and localities bear as a result of unauthorized or illegal immigrants.

NO: Julia Vitullo-Martin, a scholar at the conservative Manhattan Institute, argues that America's cities have a strong immigration tradition and that immigrants contribute to the national economy and to the making of strong cities. She applauds New York Mayor Michael Bloomberg for recognizing the critical importance of immigration to the vitality of cities and for endorsing a policy that seeks to welcome immigrants, a sharp contrast to the more punitive approach demanded by politicians in other immigration gateway cities.

Some of the most heated debate in the United States in recent years concerns immigration. California voters in 1994 adopted Proposition 187, denying schooling and other state-funded services, even emergency medical care, to undocumented immigrants. The measure also mandated local authorities to report persons suspected of having entered the county illegally. But the federal courts effectively barred enforcement of the measure as the 14th Amendment of the U.S. Constitution guarantees all "persons" the "equal protection of the laws." The 14th Amendment's use of the word "persons" means that even noncitizens enjoy certain constitutional protections.

Living along the border with Mexico, Arizonans objected that they were bearing the costs of a failed federal policy. The State of Arizona took matters into its own hands with a 2010 measure requiring immigrants to carry their documentation papers. Critics objected that the law was unconstitutional as it would lead to the stops of law-abiding citizens on the basis of their ethnic appearance. Critics further charged that the law was an improper invasion by the state to regulate immigration, a responsibility explicitly given to the national government and not to the states under the U.S. Constitution.

Alabama in 2011 enacted the harshest state immigration statute, making it a crime for an undocumented person to work or rent housing in the state. The measure threatened to revoke the license of businesses that employed undocumented workers. Landlords faced penalties for renting to persons who lacked proper papers. The Alabama law mandated that the police ask for a person's papers at routine traffic stops and also investigate persons they suspect of having entered the country illegally. Public school officials were similarly required to check the immigration status of students. The Supreme Court promised to rule on the law's constitutionality in 2012.

In Arizona, Alabama, and elsewhere, state and local leaders have often helped fuel the backlash against undocumented immigration. But a number of big-city mayors have taken a much different view. They see continued immigration as essential to the health of the local economies. They also recognize that immigration provides the life blood of inner-city neighborhoods facing the scourge of property abandonment.

The character of immigration has changed markedly over the years. Today's *new immigration* is quite different from the waves of immigration that came to the United States from Europe in the 1800s and early 1900s. The new immigration comes primarily from Mexico (about half of the new arrivals to the United State in recent years have came from Mexico), Latin America, the Caribbean, East Asia (notably China and Korea), South Asia (India and Pakistan), and even Africa. The new immigration is also the result of important changes in U.S. immigration policy that removed the old system of per-country quotas that favored immigration from Europe and sharply restricted the number of new arrivals from Latin America and Asia. United States foreign policy commitments have also led to an influx of refugees from Korea, Vietnam, Cambodia, Laos, and Cuba.

A century or so ago, immigrants from Europe settled in big cities. Today the situation is quite different. Although large concentrations of immigrants continue to settle in *port-of-entry* or immigration *gateway cities,* the new immigration is increasingly a part of the fabric of suburban life. In recent years, a large number of immigrants have been able to "skip" the central city, and, with the help of family and friends who are already living there, settle in the suburbs (Singer et al., 2008). Westminster, a suburb south of Los Angeles in Orange County, is popularly referred to as "Little Saigon." Outside New York City, Hicksville, a Long Island community with a large population from South Asia, has similar become known as "Little India."

The new immigration has also filtered into the American heartland. Atlanta, Las Vegas, Salt Lake City, Minneapolis-St. Paul, Wausau and LaCrosse (Wisconsin), and Raleigh-Durham (North Carolina) are only a few of the heartland cities to have large immigrant concentrations (Jones, 2008; Massey, 2008; Singer et al., 2008).

Advances in transportation and communication technology have also changed the immigration experience. When for the earlier waves of immigrants from Europe, the transition was they essentially cut their ties with the "old world" to begin life anew in the United States. Today, however, jet travel and relatively affordable airfare enables a new-style back-and-forth immigration. Many new immigrants send parts of their paychecks to family members back home and return with frequent visits to family back home. Cheap phone cards, the Internet, Skype, and ethnic-based cable and satellite television programming also make it relatively easy for new arrivals in the United States to maintain their native language, customs, and ties to their former homelands. As a result, new immigrants are essentially *transnational citizens* who preserve strong attachments to their native lands.

Much of the criticisms focus on the service costs imposed on existing Americans who must often pay for the schooling, health, social services, and law enforcement costs associated with unauthorized immigration. Americans further fear that the arrival of new immigrants will diminish the job prospects and the bargaining position of Americans who are working at the margins of the economy.

A focus solely on the costs of immigration overlooks the benefits that immigrants bring to both the national economy and to cities facing decline. Leaders of the agricultural industry point to their need to hire undocumented immigrants to work the fields. If the flow of illegal immigration were shut off, agricultural interests argue that the United States would have to adopt a new "guest worker" program, giving immigrants temporary permits be in the country so that the crops do not rot in the field. In cities like Los Angeles, a largely low-wage, female-dominated immigrant work force has led to revival of a manufacturing jobs sector that decades earlier had seemingly deserted the city for good.

Not all immigration fits the stereotype of impoverished Mexican immigrants paying "coyotes" to smuggle them across the border. The new immigration also entails the arrival of educated and high-skilled populations that help the United States to compete in a global economy. In information technology, the United States reaps benefits from a "brain gain" as opposed to the "brain drain" the nation suffers when talented workers are denied entry and wind up working for competitors overseas (West, 2011; also see Herman & Smith, 2010).

Immigrant entrepreneurs arriving from China, Korea, Cuba, and other countries open retail stores and factories, often in overlooked areas of U.S. cities (Kotkin, 2000; Kloosterman, & Rath, 2003). The investments made by immigrant entrepreneurs have served to rejuvenate Los Angeles' textile manufacturing and fashion industries. Cuban entrepreneurs similarly placed a large role in Miami's revival. Ethnic entrepreneurs were able to draw on the financial capital of ethnic networks and take advantage of trade connections that they maintained with businesses in their former countries.

Immigrant-driven activity has been a key to the recovery of distressed neighborhoods in cities as diverse as New York, Los Angeles, St. Louis, Dallas, and Washington, DC. In *shrinking cities* that have suffered steep population loss, immigrants help to fill housing, preventing property abandonments and thereby providing a key to community vitality and safety.

In Chicago, where more than 485 people died in the "killer" heat wave of the summer of 1995, the deaths were not evenly distributed in poor neighborhoods. In poor African-American areas of the city, residents died behind locked doors and bolted-shut windows, afraid to venture out among the area's many vacant lots or even to open their door to aid workers. In contrast, in South Lawndale, an area of Mexican immigration known as "Little Village," there were few heat-related deaths. Fueled by immigration, Little Village had little property abandonment. The area benefitted from the presence of a large number of churches where members visited the elderly to make sure that they were all right. The elderly were also less afraid to venture into the streets, seeking the relief provided by the area's many air-conditioned stores and restaurants, especially those located along the neighborhood's vibrant 22nd Street central shopping artery (Klinenberg, 2002).

By the early 2000s, a number of major U.S. cities had begun to look to immigrants more as a resource than as a threat. Philadelphia sought to recruit immigrants to fill neighborhoods marred by a large number of abandoned properties. In Detroit, a Chamber of Commerce–backed New Economy Initiative looked to immigration as a means of reversing the city's long-term decline by filling depopulated neighborhoods and of nurturing new international investment partnerships.

The YES and NO selections presented in this issue underscore the competing perspectives on the immigration debate, especially of whether illegal immigration is an economic help or hindrance to cities. In the YES selection, the Congressional Budget Office (CBO) compares the taxes and revenues generated by illegal immigrants to the costs of services that state and local governments must provide. The CBO observes that the revenues generally do not cover the full costs of additional state and local service provision. CBO based its conclusions on its review of 29 published studies on the subject.

Julia Vitullo-Martin takes a quite different perspective, noting how the contribution of immigrants throughout its history has helped make New York City a national and global financial engine. She applauds the efforts of Mayor Michael Bloomberg, who like the mayors of a number of other big cities, has initiated efforts to attract immigrants in order to tap their entrepreneurial talents and overseas connections. Immigration also helps to fill once-abandoned neighborhoods.

YES ⬅ U.S. Congressional Budget Office

The Impact of Unauthorized Immigrants on the Budgets of State and Local Governments

Introduction

Over the past two decades, most efforts to estimate the fiscal impact of immigration in the United States have concluded that, in aggregate and over the long term, tax revenues of all types generated by immigrants—both legal and unauthorized—exceed the cost of the services they use.[1] Generally, such estimates include revenues and spending at the federal, state, and local levels. However, many estimates also show that the cost of providing public services to unauthorized immigrants at the state and local levels exceeds what that population pays in state and local taxes. It is important to note, though, that currently available estimates have significant limitations; therefore, using them to determine an aggregate effect across all states would be difficult and prone to considerable error.

The impact of unauthorized immigrants on the federal budget differs from that population's effect on state and local budgets primarily because of the types of services provided at each level of government and the rules governing those programs. For instance, most unauthorized immigrants are prohibited from receiving many of the benefits that the federal government provides through Social Security and such need-based programs as Food Stamps, Medicaid (other than emergency services), and Temporary Assistance for Needy Families. At the same time, the federal government requires that state and local governments provide certain services to individuals, regardless of their immigration status or ability to pay, in order for those states or localities to participate in some of its assistance programs. Various court decisions also restrict the authority of state and local governments to avoid or constrain the cost of providing services to unauthorized immigrants who reside in their jurisdictions. In general, state and local governments bear much of the cost of providing certain public services—especially services related to education, health care, and law enforcement—to individuals residing in their

From *The Impact of Unauthorized Immigrants on the Budgets of State and Local Governments,* Congressional Budget Office, (2007).

jurisdictions. Such programs constitute a major portion of those governments' annual expenditures, but spending by state and local governments on services specifically provided to unauthorized immigrants makes up a small percentage of those governments' total spending.

Another factor that affects state and local spending is the extent to which the unauthorized population uses certain public services. For example, because unauthorized immigrants are less likely to have health insurance, they are more likely to rely on emergency facilities or public hospitals for treatment of nonemergency illnesses and other health-related problems. In 2000 and 2001, researchers from the RAND Corporation and the University of California surveyed immigrants in Los Angeles County and found that 65 percent of those respondents who identified themselves as unauthorized had no health insurance in the two years preceding the survey. In a separate study, the Pew Hispanic Center estimated that in 2004, more than 50 percent of those children who were themselves unauthorized immigrants and almost 60 percent of adult unauthorized immigrants were uninsured. Moreover, 25 percent of those children who, by virtue of their birth, were U.S. citizens—but whose parents were unauthorized immigrants—also lacked health insurance. In terms of public education, unauthorized immigrants who are minors increase the overall number of students attending public schools, and they may also require more educational services than do native-born children because of a lack of proficiency in English. Analyses from several states indicate that the costs of educating students who did not speak English fluently were 20 percent to 40 percent higher than the costs incurred for native-born students.

In addition to differences in the types of services that federal, state, and local governments provide and the extent to which the unauthorized population participates in those programs, the income that unauthorized immigrants earn and the taxes they pay also contribute to their net impact on state and local budgets. Unauthorized immigrants typically earn less than do native-born citizens and other immigrant groups and, partly as a result, they also pay a smaller portion of their income in taxes.

One study conducted by analysts at the Urban Institute found that in 1998, unauthorized immigrants in New York State paid an average of 15 percent of their income in federal, state, and local taxes; other immigrant groups paid between 21 percent and 31 percent. The average household income for unauthorized families is significantly less than that of both legal immigrants and native-born citizens; therefore, that income is taxed at a lower rate than the income of other groups. The Pew Hispanic Center estimates that in 2004, the average annual income for unauthorized families was $27,400, compared with $47,800 for legal immigrant families and $47,700 for native-born families.

A related effect is that lower-paying jobs also result in unauthorized immigrants' having less disposable income to spend on purchases subject to sales or use taxes. State and local governments typically rely more heavily on revenues from those and other sources (such as property taxes) than revenues generated by taxes on income.

The Budgetary Effects of Unauthorized Immigrants

In preparing its analysis, the Congressional Budget Office (CBO) reviewed 29 reports published over the past 15 years that attempted to evaluate the impact of unauthorized immigrants on the budgets of state and local governments. . . . CBO did not assess the data underlying those estimates or the validity of the models used to prepare them. The estimates—whether from formal studies, analyses of data on particular topics, or less-formal inquiry—show considerable consensus regarding the overall impact of unauthorized immigrants on state and local budgets. However, the scope and analytical methods of the studies vary, and the reports do not provide detailed or consistent enough data to allow for a reliable assessment of the aggregate national effect of unauthorized immigrants on state and local budgets. . . . After reviewing the estimates, CBO drew the following conclusions:

- **State and local governments incur costs for providing services to unauthorized immigrants and have limited options for avoiding or minimizing those costs.** All of the estimates that CBO reviewed, regardless of the jurisdiction examined or programs considered, reached this conclusion. Rules governing many federal programs, as well as decisions handed down by various courts, limit the authority of state and local governments to avoid or constrain the costs of providing services to unauthorized immigrants. For example, both state and federal courts have ruled that states may not refuse to provide free public education to a student on the basis of his or her immigration status. Furthermore, many states have their own statutory or constitutional requirements concerning the provision of certain services to needy residents.
- **The amount that state and local governments spend on services for unauthorized immigrants represents a small percentage of the total amount spent by those governments to provide such services to residents in their jurisdictions.** The estimates that CBO reviewed measured costs associated with providing services to unauthorized immigrants that ranged from a few million dollars in states with small unauthorized populations to tens of billions of dollars in California (currently the state with the largest population of unauthorized immigrants). Costs were concentrated in programs that make up a large percentage of total state spending—specifically, those associated with education, health care, and law enforcement. In most of the estimates that CBO examined, however, spending for unauthorized immigrants accounted for less than 5 percent of total state and local spending for those services. Spending for unauthorized immigrants in certain jurisdictions in California was higher but still represented less than 10 percent of total spending for those services.
- **The tax revenues that unauthorized immigrants generate for state and local governments do not offset the total cost of services provided to those immigrants.** Most of the estimates found that even though unauthorized immigrants pay taxes and other fees to state and local jurisdictions, the resulting revenues offset only a portion of the

costs incurred by those jurisdictions for providing services related to education, health care, and law enforcement. Although it is difficult to obtain precise estimates of the net impact of the unauthorized population on state and local budgets, that impact is most likely modest.

- **Federal aid programs offer resources to state and local governments that provide services to unauthorized immigrants, but those funds do not fully cover the costs incurred by those governments.** Some of the reports that CBO examined did not include such federal transfers when estimating the net effect of the unauthorized population on state and local governments. . . .

Spending by State and Local Governments

Over the past two decades, many state and local governments, as well as researchers and academics, have tried to identify and quantify the fiscal impact of immigration on state and local governments. Most of those estimates have concentrated on costs associated with unauthorized immigrants, but some include costs related to other categories of people, such as children of unauthorized immigrants born in the United States, legal immigrants, refugees, and asylum-seekers.[2] The estimates looked at a range of public services, primarily concentrating on the cost of programs over which states have limited options for controlling costs, such as those related to education, health care, and law enforcement (including incarceration).

Education

Education is the largest single expenditure in state and local budgets. Because state and local governments bear the primary fiscal and administrative responsibility of providing schooling from kindergarten through grade 12, they incur substantial costs to educate children who are unauthorized immigrants.[3] In 1982, the Supreme Court ruled that states may not exclude children from public education because of their immigration status.[4] Current estimates indicate that about 2 million school-age children (5 to 17 years old) in the United States are unauthorized immigrants; an additional 3 million children are U.S. citizens born to unauthorized immigrants. According to the most recent population data released by the Census Bureau, as of July 2006, there were 53.3 million school-age children in the United States. Thus, children who are unauthorized immigrants represent almost 4 percent of the overall school-age population. Their numbers are growing quickly in some states, adding additional budgetary pressures. For example:

- As part of a larger study on the impact of unauthorized immigrants in Minnesota, the state's Department of Administration estimated that, during the 2003–2004 school year, the state and local governments in Minnesota spent between $79 million and $118 million to educate an estimated 9,400 to 14,000 children who were unauthorized immigrants. The agency also estimated that an additional $39 million was spent for children who were U.S. citizens but whose parents were unauthorized immigrants. According to census data, Minnesota state and local governments spent about $8 billion for elementary and secondary education during the 2003–2004 school year (excluding capital costs for building maintenance and construction). The state estimated that its population of immigrant students—both legal and unauthorized—had almost doubled, from about 9,000 to more than 16,000, between 2000 and 2004.

- On the basis of a population estimate developed by the Pew Hispanic Center, analysts at the New Mexico Fiscal Policy Project reported that, for the 2003–2004 school year, total spending in New Mexico at the state and local levels for 9,200 unauthorized immigrant schoolchildren was about $67 million. The Census Bureau reports that state and local expenditures for elementary and secondary education during that period in New Mexico totaled almost $3 billion. Of the estimated 40,000 unauthorized immigrants currently living in New Mexico, 95 percent are believed to be recent arrivals, having lived in that state for fewer than 10 years.

Health Care

Immigrants in the United States, both authorized and unauthorized, are less likely than their native-born counterparts to have health insurance. As a result, they are more likely to rely on emergency rooms or public clinics for health care. The federal government requires health facilities that receive federal assistance to provide a certain level of service to residents, regardless of their ability to pay for such medical services or their immigration status. The amount of uncompensated care provided by some state and local governments is growing because an increasing number of unauthorized immigrants are using those services. According to a report commissioned by the United States/Mexico Border Counties Coalition, in 2000, county governments that share a border with Mexico incurred almost $190 million in costs for providing uncompensated care to unauthorized immigrants; that figure represented about one-quarter of all uncompensated health costs incurred by those governments in that year.

While those costs are increasing rapidly for some jurisdictions, they account for a small percentage of spending by most state and local governments. For example, in 2006, the Oklahoma Health Care Authority estimated that it would spend about $9.7 million on emergency Medicaid services for unauthorized immigrants that year, and that 80 percent of those costs would be for services associated with childbirth. The agency's actual total spending for that year was $3.1 billion. The agency also reported that, since fiscal year 2003 (the first fiscal year considered), the services provided to unauthorized immigrants have accounted for less than 1 percent of the total individuals served and cost less than 1 percent of the total dollars spent for Medicaid services.

Law Enforcement

Unauthorized immigrants who commit criminal acts or who require law enforcement services to protect them from criminal acts or behavior impose a variety of costs on state and local budgets. Although state and local law enforcement activities related to unauthorized immigrants include the same protections that ordinary citizens rely upon (such as investigating reports of criminal activity that may have targeted an unauthorized immigrant), the estimates that are currently available include only costs related to the prosecution and incarceration of unauthorized immigrants under state and local laws.

Unauthorized immigrants accused or convicted of committing crimes (other than immigration-related offenses) are not deported immediately; rather, they enter into and are processed through the local criminal justice system in the same fashion that any other suspect would be. The federal government may take custody of those who are convicted after they have completed their sentences and then begin the deportation process, but until that point, state and local governments bear the cost of investigating, detaining, prosecuting, and incarcerating such immigrants.

Researchers from Rutgers University have found that, in general, immigrants are less likely than native-born citizens to be incarcerated. However, the number of unauthorized immigrants in some state and local criminal justice systems adds significantly to law enforcement costs. For example, in 2001, the United States/Mexico Border Counties Coalition reported that law enforcement activities involving unauthorized immigrants in four states—California, Arizona, New Mexico, and Texas—cost some county governments that share a border with Mexico a combined total of more than $108 million in 1999. Of the counties included in the report, San Diego County incurred the largest cost, spending over $50 million that year, or almost half of all estimated costs incurred by the border counties. That amount represented about 9 percent of San Diego County's total spending ($541 million) for law enforcement activities that year. The report identified several factors that influenced the fiscal impact on each county, including the number of ports of entry, the population of neighboring Mexican communities, border terrain, and federal programs for deterring illegal entry.

Revenues Versus Spending

The available estimates of the budgetary impact of unauthorized immigrants vary greatly in their timing and scope. Most of the studies that include both revenues and costs for multiple programs show that state and local governments spend more on unauthorized immigrants than they collect in revenues from that population. For example:

- Recent estimates indicate that annual costs for unauthorized immigrants in Colorado were between $217 million and $225 million for education, Medicaid, and corrections. By comparison, taxes collected from unauthorized immigrants at both the state and local levels amounted to an estimated $159 million to $194 million annually.
- The Iowa Legislative Services Agency reported that the estimated 70,000 unauthorized immigrants in the state paid between $45.5 million and $70.9 million in state income and sales taxes in fiscal year 2004. The report did not quantify the costs of providing specific services to unauthorized immigrants. Rather, it estimated an average benefit of $1,534 per state resident based on total spending from the state's general fund and the number of state residents (including

unauthorized immigrants). Using that average benefit calculation, the estimated cost for providing all services to unauthorized immigrants was $107.4 million in fiscal year 2004.

Some studies estimated that states may collect more in taxes from unauthorized immigrants than they spend to provide education for children who are unauthorized immigrants, but those studies do not include costs associated with health care or law enforcement. For example:

- In 2006, the Missouri Budget Project estimated that unauthorized immigrants paid between $29 million and $57 million in state income, property, and excise taxes. That organization estimated that the state spent between $17.5 million and $32.6 million to provide elementary and secondary education for between 5,800 and 10,833 unauthorized immigrants. Local districts incurred between $26.5 million and $49.3 million in additional costs for educational services.
- The New Mexico Fiscal Policy Project estimated that the state collects about $69 million annually in individual income, property, and sales taxes from unauthorized immigrants, about $1 million to $2 million more annually than it spends on public elementary and secondary education for children who are unauthorized immigrants.

Another report—prepared by the state comptroller of Texas—estimated that, in 2006, the state collected $424 million more in revenue from unauthorized immigrants than it spent to provide education, health care, and law enforcement activities for that population. However, the state estimated that local governments incurred $1.4 billion in uncompensated costs for health care and law enforcement. . . .

Notes

1. The term "unauthorized immigrants" refers to foreign citizens residing in the United States illegally. It applies to two categories of immigrants: those who enter the country without approval of the immigration process and those who violate the terms of a temporary admission without acquiring either permanent resident status or temporary protection from removal. Members of this population are also referred to as illegal or undocumented immigrants or aliens.

2. Refugees and asylum-seekers are people who are unable or unwilling to return to their country of origin because of the risk of persecution or because of a well-founded fear of persecution. Refugees apply for admission from outside of the United States; asylum-seekers request legal admission from within the United States or at a U.S. port of entry.

3. The federal government provides about 10 percent of the total amount spent by all levels of government on kindergarten through grade 12 each year.

4. *Plyler v. Doe*, 457 U.S. 202 (1982).

Mayor Bloomberg: Right on Neighborhoods, Right on Immigration

Without its immigrants New York wouldn't be New York—and, what's more, never would have been. Ours is the ultimate immigrant city—founded by immigrants in the 17th century, sustained by immigrants over nearly four centuries, and flourishing today in part because over three million immigrants are contributing to the economy and to the rebuilding of neighborhoods. That New York is also the country's wealthiest city is no accident.

For Mayor Bloomberg, the contract between the city and its immigrants can't be denied. As he said in his Jan. 17 State of the City speech, "New York gives them unlimited opportunities, these families help make New York the nation's economic engine, its financial hub, its fashion center, its media mecca, and its cultural capital." And he's not just talking about legal immigrants. He has testified repeatedly that without its half-million or so illegal immigrants, New York's economy would be a shell of itself.

In advocating virtually open immigration, Bloomberg follows in a long line of aggressively open-minded New York administrators, beginning with the profit-oriented Dutch West India Company. "They favored admitting any settlers who would enrich the colony," says Hasia R. Diner, professor of American-Jewish History at New York University. When Gov. Peter Stuyvesant wanted to drive out the Jews, the company forced him to let them stay, noting they were good for trade. "That kind of toleration then led to real toleration. Their discourse was much like the pro-immigration arguments today: the immigrants will work hard, pay taxes, improve the whole society." And, of course, they did.

Neighbourhood Development

All over urban America neighborhoods declined after World War II, as urban dwellers moved out and very few new residents moved in. But things started turning around in the 1970s, when immigrants picked up the slack, choosing and revitalizing areas abandoned by Americans.

Immigrants saved many American cities, but perhaps none so clearly as New York. Fighting off bankruptcy in 1975, the city government soon found itself the reluctant owner of some 400,000 housing units forfeited by their owners, who refused to pay the steep property taxes. Many New Yorkers, in their despair at what seemed to be the city's inexorable decline, didn't see that their saviors were at hand. Chinese, especially from Hong Kong, and other Asians moved into Lower Manhattan; Dominicans and other Caribbeans spread through the Bronx and northern Manhattan; the Russians flooded Brighton Beach in Brooklyn; the Irish returned to northern Manhattan; Bengalis, Turks, Albanians, Uzbeks, Romanians moved to Queens. Immigrants are now even rejuvenating sections of the least urban borough, Staten Island.

What if they hadn't chosen New York? Brighton Beach would surely be as troubled financially as neighboring Coney Island; the South Bronx would have continued to burn; Flushing would have become a ghost town.

It was Flushing where the mayor, with a fine sense of neighborhood, chose to deliver his State of the City speech. A jumble of restaurants, bakeries, and cultural institutions, Flushing offers every kind of Asian food—high-end seafood in elegant settings, bubble tea cafes and fried noodles from street vendors, not to mention Vietnamese pho and Korean barbecue. Now home to 177,000 people, Flushing has minuscule commercial and residential vacancy rates. It is the impact of intense economic demand from all quarters that has neighborhood activists worried, not abandonment and decay.

What a difference a few decades make. In the 1960s those same storefronts were boarded up, the sidewalks in front of them empty. The area was so derelict it was designated in the city's 1975 federal community development block grant application as eligible for urban renewal money. Then came the Chinese immigrants, first in small numbers, then in great waves, through the 1980s and 1990s.

With Flushing's economic success as proof of the pudding, Mayor Bloomberg argued confidently, "Keeping New York City and America at the front of the pack begins with an openness to new energy, meaning immigration, and new ideas, meaning innovation. That's how I built my business, and that's the approach we've brought to a city government that was insular and provincial, and married to the conventional."

Immigrant Businesses

Because New York welcomed immigrants—both legal and illegal—its economy expanded exponentially. Immigrants opened new businesses, filled vacant jobs and moved into declining neighborhoods. Such people form "extended clans," wrote Nathan Glazer and Pat Moynihan in *Beyond the Melting Pot*.

They capture, and sometimes even invent, markets. Jewish diamond cutters, Korean green grocers, Chinese restaurateurs, Russian massage therapists, Irish bartenders and Greek coffee-shop owners aren't only stereotypes. They are the reflection of a real economic phenomenon. Immigrants sell goods and services to their own group and, once successful, to everybody else. Armed with little capital, they start labor-intensive businesses that employ friends and neighbors. The neighborhoods they settle in are decrepit, the commercial streets tired, the infrastructure overtaxed, the schools deplorable, but all that will change when immigrants reach a critical number and make an area their own.

"We've repeatedly seen immigrant succession in New York's economy," says Mitchell Moss, professor of planning and public policy at New York University. "They create businesses, especially outside Manhattan. They're willing to work long hours, investing their own human capital. And it's not just entry-level. You can't have an advanced service economy or a high-tech information economy without immigrants."

What's Next

Bloomberg, however, is looking farther afield—at New York's competitors abroad, the other world cities that hope to take New York's place at the top. "We are in a competitive struggle. And the stakes couldn't be higher," he warned in Flushing. "Over the past year, I've seen cities from London to Paris to Shanghai pushing the frontiers of progress. They are doing everything they can to attract the best and the brightest in every field: medicine; engineering; construction; and more. These cities are not putting up barriers; they're not looking inward or blaming someone else. They're not afraid of the new or the different, and we shouldn't be either. If we are, we won't have a future."

Bloomberg has spent six years strengthening New York's economy, rezoning barren land to make it developable, reforming the building code, and reducing barriers to construction. But there's one barrier to New York's competitive stance that seems to grow ever higher—and that's federal immigration policy. "No public policy is more important to cities than federal immigration policy," argues Mitchell Moss. "The immigration act of 1965 opened up the country again and did more for cities than all the HUD bureaucrats put together or all the money spent on federal housing, transportation and welfare."

But today federal immigration policy coupled with national security policy is preventing highly skilled and educated workers from coming here temporarily or permanently. Indeed, entry requirements in the U.S. are the "worst in the world," said Jonathan Tisch, chairman of NYC and Company and CEO of Loews Hotel last fall. Last spring, Bill Gates, the chairman of Microsoft, warned that restrictions on the number of skilled workers allowed to enter the U.S. put the country's competitiveness at risk.

New York wants the best and the brightest from all over the world. Only if it gets them will New York be able to stand up to London.

EXPLORING THE ISSUE

Does the New Immigration Burden Cities?

Critical Thinking and Reflection

1. What are the often unrecognized benefits that immigrants bring to the national economy and to cities?
2. Should the nation's immigration policy be based on such factors as the need of cities to find new populations to avoid property abandonment in declining neighborhoods?
3. Can you formulate a balanced policy approach to immigration, one that recognizes the importance of immigration and reaps its benefits while also responding to the legitimate concerns of opponents of immigration? What would a balanced immigration policy look like?

Is There Common Ground?

The highly contentious, emotional debate over immigration—especially over the service obligations owed illegal immigrants and their children—will not easily be resolved.

Still, there may be common ground that allows for an accommodation on a few of the narrower aspects of the immigration issue.

The United States "wins" economically if it can continue to attract highly skilled workers and entrepreneurial talent. The United States will likely "lose" economically when such talent is barred from entry into the country and winds up working overseas for the nation's competitors. Reasoned discussion of immigration should come to recognize the national importance of allowing entrance by highly skilled workers who bring their skills and talents to the United States. Technology-related workers, for instance, have contributed to the dynamism of the computer and information technology industries in San Francisco Bay/Silicon Valley communities. A policy that allows the entry of high-skilled personnel, however, does not address the larger questions related to immigration.

As we have seen, cities benefit from the arrival of new workers and immigrant entrepreneurs and from new populations that can fill housing in distressed neighborhoods. But, as we have also seen, the tax revenues generated by illegal immigrants do not fully cover the heightened costs of state and local service provision. Cities and states should not have to bear the costs resulting from national policy actions that no state or city can control. Under the Constitution, immigration remains a matter for the federal government. The federal government should compensate cities and states for the additional costs that national policy imposes on them.

17

Additional Resources

Ansley, Fran, & Jon Shefner. (2009). *Global Connections and Local Receptions: New Latino Immigration to the Southeastern United States*. Knoxville, TN: University of Tennessee Press.

Foner, Nancy, ed. (2001). *New Immigrants in New York*. New York: Columbia University Press.

Herman, Richard T., & Robert L. Smith, (2009). *Immigrant, Inc.: Why Immigrant Entrepreneurs Are Driving the New Economy (and How They Will Save the American Worker)*. Hoboken, NJ: John Wiley & Sons.

Jones, Richard C., ed. (2008). *Immigrants Outside Megalopolis: Ethnic Transformation in the Heartland*. Lanham, MD: Lexington Books.

Kotkin, Joel. (December 2000). "Movers & Shakers: How Immigrants Are Reviving Neighborhoods Given up for Dead." Reprinted in *Annual Editions: Urban Society*, 15th ed., Myron A. Levine, ed., (New York: McGraw-Hill), pp. 25–30.

Klinenberg, Eric. (2002). *Heat Wave: A Social Autopsy of Disaster in Chicago*. Chicago: University of Chicago Press.

Kloosterman, Robert, & Jan Rath, eds. (2003). *Immigrant Entrepreneurs: Venturing Abroad in the Age of Globalization*. Oxford, UK, and New York: Berg/University of New York Press.

Massey, Douglas S. (2008). *New Faces in New Places: The Changing Geography of American Immigration*. New York: Russell Sage Foundation.

Price, Marie, & Lisa Benton-Short. (2008). *Migrants to the Metropolis: The Rise of Immigrant Gateway Cities*. Syracuse, NY: Syracuse University Press.

Singer, Audrey, Susan Wiley Hardwick, & Caroline B. Brettell, eds. (2008). *Twenty-first Century Gateways: Immigrant Incorporation in Suburban America*. Washington, DC: Brookings Institution Press.

West, Darrell M. (January 2011). Creating a "Brain Gain" for U.S. Employers: The Role of Immigration. Brookings Institution Policy Brief No. 178, Washington, DC. Available at: www.brookings.edu/~/media/Files/rc/papers/2011/01_immigration_west/01_immigration_west.pdf.

Internet References

The Brookings Institution

A Washington-based think tank, the Brookings Institution has done numerous studies on how immigration is reshaping metropolitan America, on the changing shape of immigration, and possible alternative policy responses to immigration.

www.brookings.edu/topics/immigration.aspx

Center for an Urban Future

A New York City–based think tank that seeks to investigate how immigration, technological change, and other trends will affect the future of cities.

www.nycfuture.org/content/search/topicsearch.cfm?topicarea=39

Center for Immigration Studies

A research organization that stresses the fiscal consequences and security risks entailed by immigration, including the job competition and the wage losses that American workers may suffer.

www.cis.org

Partnership for a New American Economy

A bipartisan group of mayors and national leaders of business who seek to raise public awareness of the contributions that immigrants make to the U.S. economy and the importance of adopting sensible, rather than overly restrictive, immigration policies. A number of mayors were among the Partnership's founders and "featured" members, including Michael Bloomberg (New York City), Antonio Villaraigosa (Los Angeles), Michael Nutter (Philadelphia), Phil Gordon (Phoenix), Julián Castro (San Antonio), Ralph Becker (Salt Lake City), Dana Williams (Park City, Utah), and Laurent Gilbert (Lewiston, Maine).

www.renewoureconomy.org

ISSUE 2

Does Neighborhood Gentrification Benefit the Inner-City Poor?

YES: Lance Freeman, "There Goes the 'Hood: Views of Gentrification from the Ground Up" (Temple University Press, 2006)

NO: Kathe Newman and Elvin K. Wyly, "The Right to Stay Put, Revisited: Gentrification and Resistance to Displacement in New York City," *Urban Studies* (vol. 43, no.1, 2006)

Learning Outcomes

After reading this issue, you should be able to:

- Define the concepts of gentrification and displacement.
- Identify the different forces that have served to revive inner-city neighborhoods and downtown business districts.
- Identify the benefits of gentrification, explaining why city officials often favor policies that support gentrification.
- Identify the criticisms that are made of gentrification.
- Identify policies that cities can use to minimize the ill effects of gentrification.

ISSUE SUMMARY

YES: Lance Freeman, associate professor of urban planning at Columbia University, argues that most studies that have pointed to the ills of gentrification suffer from an important methodological flaw. Such studies often fail to ask the residents of poor neighborhoods how they perceive the changes that are taking place in their neighborhoods. Freeman, who is African American, worries about gentrification-related displacement. Still, he finds that the low-income African American residents in two gentrifying sections of New York City see benefits in the upgrading of their neighborhoods.

NO: Urban studies professor Kathe Newman (Rutgers) and urban geographer Elvin Wyly (British Columbia) dispute Freeman's contention that gentrification brings substantial benefits to the inner-city poor. Newman and Wyly argue that such studies understate the extent of gentrification-related displacement and the ills that such displacement inflicts on the lives of poor people. They fear that studies that overstate the benefits of gentrification will be used by developers to gain approval for new development projects that will lead to still further displacement of the poor.

In the past few decades, a number of U.S. cities have emerged from the depths of the urban crisis, experiencing new construction in downtown business districts and the "rediscovery" of once-ignored and declining inner-city neighborhoods. The new investment in cities is certainly good news for the cities. But does this new investment bring benefits to poorer residents who find that they are living in sections of the city that have newly become attractive to more upscale residents and new investment?

Gentrification is a term that is widely used when it comes to discussing the new investment activity taking place in many cities. When used quite broadly, the term refers to any new central-city activity, including the opening of new central-city hotels, indoor shopping malls, and cinema multiplexes, as well as new investment in inner-city residential areas. Used more strictly, however, *gentrification* has a more specific meaning; it refers to new residential investment and activity taking place in once-declining inner-city neighborhoods that have become increasingly attractive to upscale home seekers, especially to younger workers, professionals, and childless couples. "Urban resettlement," "urban pioneering," "neighborhood revitalization," the "back-to-the-city movement," "urban invasion," "neighborhood upgrading," and the "boutique city" are all among the terms and phrases that writers have used as synonyms for gentrification.

In the 1980s, gentrification appeared to be a relatively novel and small phenomenon, an exception to the general pattern of urban decline. To use the words of urbanist Brian Berry who wrote a classic article on gentrification in the early era, gentrification was a limited phenomenon, just "islands of renewal in a sea of decay." Yet, research in the past few decades has shown that gentrification is a much larger trend that is not confined to a few atypical city "islands." Instead, gentrification is much more all-pervasive, with cities, large and small alike, across the nation witnessing the transformation of inner-city neighborhoods as up-collar newcomers settle into core urban neighborhoods.

There are, of course, exceptions, as not all cities and inner-urban areas have experienced the sort of rebound that is associated with gentrification. Cities that lack a strong downtown job base and meaningful entertainment, cultural, and night life activities have not attracted the same degree of resettlement evident in communities that have more lively downtowns. Poorer areas in Cleveland, Detroit, Newark, and Buffalo have not experienced the same rebound apparent in core communities in New York, Chicago, Boston, Washington, D.C., and San Francisco.

But is urban resettlement good news for everyone? Certainly, cities benefit from the increase in tax yields from new construction and upgraded properties. Once dangerous portions of the inner city also tend to be safer as the newcomers alter patterns of street activity and assert their demand for heightened police protection. The appearance of street cafés, coffee shops, exercise health centers, and other such lifestyle amenities further adds to city livability and helps make a city more attractive to global firms, which will locate only in communities that can attract upscale talented workers. The gentrifiers, themselves, often comprise a higher skilled, technologically competent workforce that helps to make a city attractive to corporate headquarters and cutting-edge technology and communications firms.

But what may be good for a city and good for the physical rebuilding of a neighborhood may not necessarily be good for a neighborhood's poorer residents, especially if *displacement* results and the poor are "pushed out" of a neighborhood by the upscale new arrivals. There are a number of reasons why gentrification may lead to the displacement of the poor. When an upscale home seeker buys a large home that many years ago was subdivided into a number of small apartments, the residents of those small apartments lose their shelter when the new owner "gut-rehabs" the structure to return it to its former glory as a single-family home. A developer may tear down older and lesser attractive homes and apartment buildings, displacing poorer residents, in order to build new condominium units that will be sold to the upmarket buyers. The rise in rents in suddenly "hot" or discovered neighborhoods also may serve to make housing unaffordable for the poor. Displaced families wind up having to move to other areas of the city, often having to accept smaller or less satisfactory housing than the units they previously occupied, sometimes even having to "bunk up" with relatives. In worst-off situations, the displacees may wind up homeless.

Lance Freeman, in his award-winning book *There Goes the 'Hood,* argues that the large volume of studies over the years that stressed the ills of displacement have essentially been one-sided. Freeman interviewed residents and attended community meetings in two mostly black New York City neighborhoods undergoing gentrification—fabled Harlem in Upper Manhattan and the Clinton Hill section of Brooklyn. He found that poorer residents did indeed worry about neighborhood transformation and displacement; they generally distrusted a process that was apparently controlled by white institutions and white outsiders. Nor did gentrification produce an easy mixing of newer and long-term poorer residents, a mixing that would have built a sense of community across class and racial lines as the most enthusiastic backers of gentrification had predicted would happen. Yet, despite these problems, poorer residents did not always negatively perceive the changes taking place in their neighborhoods.

As detailed in the YES selection, *There Goes the 'Hood,* many existing residents appreciated the greater public safety and the new opportunities and new amenities—including the availability of better quality foods and produce and greater convenience and choice in shopping—that accompanied a neighborhood's upward trajectory. The poor themselves find gentrifying neighborhoods attractive, especially when compared to what their neighborhoods once were: ghettoized, unsafe, "food deserts." Consequently, Freeman and his research partner Frank Braconi have argued that the mobility rates of the poor in gentrifying neighborhoods appear to be somewhat lower than that in other poor neighborhoods. That is, the poor are less likely to move away from gentrifying neighborhoods, than they are from other poor neighborhoods, an indicator that poorer residents perceive that gentrification is bringing a number of improvements to their lives.

In the NO selection, Kathe Newman and Elvin Wyly take passionate exception to Freeman's findings and conclusions. They, too, examined the data and interviewed residents and community activists in a number of New York City areas undergoing gentrification. Their data reveal that the extent of gentrification-related displacement is much greater than what Freeman and Braconi posit. In the sections of their article that is presented here, Newman and Wyly further argue that neighborhood upgrading brings only the most meager opportunities to the poor, especially as poorer residents often cannot continue to reside for long in portions of the city that have become unaffordable. Newman and Wyly argue that any study that overemphasizes the benefits of gentrification will only serve to abet the efforts of developers to transform a neighborhood, ousting the poor.

Newman and Wyly argue for government policies to help mitigate displacement, to help assure that poorer residents will be able to continue to live in neighborhoods that are enjoying new upgrading. The authors identify a number of public policy steps that a city can initiate in an effort to minimize displacement and maintain a stock of quality affordable housing in areas experiencing the pressures of change.

YES

There Goes the 'Hood: Views of Gentrification from the Ground Up

There Goes the 'Hood

The abhorrence with which gentrification is viewed in many circles is illustrated clearly by the results of an online search of the term *gentrification*, which turned up the following:

> The term is often used negatively, suggesting the displacement of poor communities by rich outsiders.
>
> "They're pushing poor people out of the city and in the process breaking up the power bases of their struggle," he says. "It's gentrification, but you could also almost call it apartheid by both race and class."
>
> As such, gentrification is almost always a displacement of poor residents to remote and less economically favored areas with similar substandard housing, and a theft of public and private resources from other poorer neighborhoods which deserve to be improved for the people who already live there, and should be understood and resisted as such.

These snippets are illustrative of the popular wisdom of gentrification as anathema. It is a process that benefits the haves to the detriment of the have-nots. It is a continuation of the history of marginalized groups being oppressed by the more powerful. And always, gentrification leads to the displacement of poor marginalized groups.

Outside of the ivory tower, *gentrification* has become a dirty word, at least outside of real estate interests and city boosters. Although initial reports of gentrification in the 1970s tended to be favorable, this view was quickly erased by ongoing concerns about displacement and class conflict thought to be inherent in the gentrification process. Community-based organizations often sprung up to combat gentrification. For example, in my neighborhood a community-based organization sponsors an annual antigentrification block party. As early as 1985, the Real Estate Board of New York felt it necessary to take out a full-page ad in a paper defending the positive benefits of gentrification. A nonprofit research, communications, capacity building, and advocacy organization at one time had an antigentrification Web site.

The political economy approach portrays gentrification much the same way. This school of thought typically portrays moneyed real estate interests, yuppies, and government elites as the beneficiaries of gentrification. Through gentrification, the political economy critique has it, yuppies gain access to space that is conveniently located to downtown employment and cultural amenities. Real estate interests profit by speculating on previously marginal properties. Government elites see a rise in their tax base and perhaps a decline in social services needs associated with the poor. Smith and LeFaivre write:

> Thus the benefits of gentrification appear to accrue to the capitalist class, defined as those who own and control capital for the purpose of investing it for profit or interest, as well as to the middle class in general, who are the beneficiaries not only of new living space but also of profitable, if comparatively small investments.

My conversations with residents of Clinton Hill and Harlem, however, reveal a more nuanced reaction toward gentrification. If gentrification were a movie character, he would be both villain and knight in shining armor, welcome by some and feared and loathed by others, and even dreaded and welcomed at the same time by the same people.

A positive reaction to gentrification was a clear theme that emerged during my conversations with residents of Clinton Hill and Harlem. Some of the positive reactions were based on narrow economic self-interests. Especially in Clinton Hill, where many of the respondents were homeowners or cooperative owners, the escalating housing prices increased the return on their housing investment substantially. Renee grew up in a nearby public housing project and moved into a Clinton Hill coop in the mid-1990s. (The names and some identifying characteristics of the people quoted in this book have been changed to protect their anonymity.) Since then she has been considering purchasing her apartment, lamenting the opportunities lost:

> 1999, 2000 things turned around, the co-op stabilized a lot, and we began to attract, uh, what we call a different market. In 1999 apartments here sold, one-bedroom apartments, sold for maybe $35, $40, $45,000. That's when I should have made my move. Today that same apartment will sell for $160,000. Little steep for an apartment.

Or, consider the experience of James, a man in his forties who grew up in nearby Bedford-Stuyvesant and attended college for a few years before settling in East New York as an adult. He moved into Clinton Hill at the age of twenty-eight: "I paid $18,000 in cash for my apartment in 1988. Now this unit would go for a couple of hundred thousand dollars. That's because people are coming from areas that are even more expensive." For these homeowners, gentrification has been a boon. Whatever their discomfort about whites moving in, increased police protection, or other facets of neighborhood change, it would be impossible for them to ignore the economic benefits associated with gentrification.

That homeowners would stand to benefit from gentrification is an obvious if sometimes overlooked result of gentrification. Moreover, because of disinvestment in these neighborhoods, housing prices in the past were extremely depressed. Those who purchased in earlier years were not necessarily affluent but now stand to reap a considerable windfall should they decide to sell their property. To some degree this is happening for people who were fortunate to become homeowners in Clinton Hill and Harlem. Naturally some people are enthusiastic about this facet of gentrification. Barbara is a graduate student who moved to Harlem seven years ago. She was initially a renter, but her building turned into a cooperative several years ago. She summed up how the recent changes in Harlem were affecting her personally: "To sum it up I am experiencing the changes, I'm rolling with the punches. I'm excited about the possibility of making money. And I look at this as an investment—I'll be making money from my apartment."

The increase in housing values for homeowners of Clinton Hill and Harlem is clearly a good thing for these homeowners. Given the paltry homeownership rate in Harlem, however, the economic benefits of gentrification are unlikely to accrue to many Harlem residents. In contrast, in Clinton Hill, where there is a substantial presence of black homeowners, these economic benefits are meaningful. Indeed, in recent years much has been made of the vast inequalities in wealth between blacks and whites. It has been pointed out that the disparity in wealth is much larger than the income disparity, and much of this difference has been laid at the foot of unequal housing values. Oliver and Shapiro write:

> In general, homes of similar design, size, and appearance cost more in white communities than in black or integrated communities. Their value also rises more quickly and steeply in white communities. . . . Whether or not discrimination is intended, the racial housing-appreciation gap represents part of the price of being black in America.

Conley has also pointed out the costs of differences in wealth accumulation due in part to lower housing appreciation among blacks. These increases in home equity, particularly in Clinton Hill where much of the property is owned by blacks, are perhaps a long time coming.

That homeowners who moved into gentrifying neighborhoods would benefit from gentrification is perhaps not surprising even if this fact is relatively overlooked among commentators. But the economic benefits stemming from increased property values for homeowners was hardly the most prevalent source of goodwill expressed toward gentrification. More prevalent and perhaps more surprising was the reaction of some long-term residents to other aspects of gentrification. Many residents appreciated the improvements in amenities and services. Gentrification often brings to mind yuppies and the upscale specialty shops that serve them, leaving the impression that these services would do little for long-term residents. To some extent this characterization is accurate, but it is not always complete. The changes taking place in Clinton Hill and Harlem in some ways might be perceived as the normalization of commercial activity in these neighborhoods after decades of disinvestment. A supermarket with decent produce, a drugstore, and a moderately priced restaurant are amenities taken for granted in many neighborhoods but were in short supply in inner-city areas like Clinton Hill and Harlem.

Associating increased retail activity with gentrification does beg a chicken-or-egg type of question. Is the arrival of a Duane Reade drugstore really a sign of gentrification? In recent years there has been a revival of many depressed inner-city neighborhoods. When this revival occurs either in a hot market, a neighborhood with an attractive housing stock, or a neighborhood with a good location, gentrification will often accompany the revival. Certainly higher-income residents make the opening of a store like Duane Reade more attractive. Likewise, the presence of basic stores and amenities like a Duane Reade certainly make inner-city neighborhoods more attractive to those we might classify as the gentry. Although a Duane Reade certainly could open without gentrification, the arrival of higher-income residents and other kinds of investment make the arrival of these types of investment more likely to occur. Certainly residents of these neighborhoods considered all of the improvements as part of the package of gentrification.

The lack of retail amenities is not only an inconvenience but may have significant affects on quality of life. Indeed, scholars in the United Kingdom have coined the phrase *food deserts* to describe neighborhoods where affordable and nutritious food is not readily available. Instead of markets where fresh fruits and vegetables and other nutritious options are available, residents of many poor neighborhoods have to make do with corner stores with higher prices and fewer nutritious options. Some have linked residence in these food deserts to unhealthy lifestyles that contribute to morbidity and illness. Although evidence of food deserts in the United States is anecdotal, if their existence is an empirical reality, gentrification might make more nutritious food readily available and affect the health of poor residents in these neighborhoods. As will be shown shortly, several residents pointed to the improved availability of fresh produce and other grocery items as one of the more salient changes they associated with the changes in their neighborhood.

Aside from possible health implications, residents relished the options that gentrification afforded them. Juan is a mid-forties resident of west Harlem, where he has lived all of his life. He witnessed the waxing and waning of the neighborhood. The urban renewal programs, the heroin plagues, the crack epidemic, and the disinvestment that beset the neighborhood from the 1960s on. This disinvestment left the neighborhood with few satisfactory retail options. He is very cognizant of the changes in this area: "But, uh, as I was mentioning the things, there's a Fairway [a new supermarket]. You know. Uh, and that's terrific. Because the, you know they have a nice price range on things. If you want to buy something that is upscale it's there. If you wanted something reasonable it's good. But the quality is good." Tina is a single mother in her thirties native to Clinton Hill. As such she was born when the first stirrings of gentrification were beginning in parts of Clinton Hill, and when Myrtle

Avenue, the main thoroughfare up the street, was called Murder Avenue. Her overall reaction to the changes was as follows:

> I just like the change . . . and all the people. I really like the changes. You know, you get to see, different people, different stores being opened, even though those people's kind of snotty. Some of them are, some of them is kind of friendly, so . . . me and my kids go up on DeKalb Avenue to the different restaurants. Then, we went to the sushi restaurant. My son was like, what is this? I was like, let's just try it, 'cause I've never had it before.

What is particularly surprising about Tina's response was her positive reaction to amenities like a sushi restaurant. This is the type of neighborhood change that many would assume would benefit only the newly arrived gentry. Tina's response suggests that this is not always the case. Her response should not be interpreted as indicating that all long-term residents are appreciative of the more boutique type of amenities that often accompany gentrification. Most residents did not mention such amenities, instead focusing on those that impacted their daily lives, such as supermarkets. A few were even openly hostile to restaurants that they viewed as being targeted for them. Terry, native of Harlem in his fifties, said, "We don't eat there. I went in there for a piece of cake and it was like four bucks! I can get a whole cake for four bucks. Obviously they don't want too many of us in there. We don't get down like that spending four dollars for a piece of cake, know what I'm saying?" Terry lives in the same public housing project where he was born and raised and provided the comments in response to a query about some of the new restaurants that had opened in the neighborhood. The prices, though standard for restaurants in New York, seemed outlandish to him and his peer group—"we don't get down like that." But for the most part, residents were appreciative of at least some of the changes taking place in their neighborhood. Ms. James migrated to New York City from the South as a child and has been living in Clinton Hill for some forty years, since she was a teenager. She witnessed the decline of the neighborhood and is now witness to the change and seems amenable to these changes.

> Now we have um, see, a lot of things changed in that community after the, the Watts rebellion. And then you had several of the many rebellions, okay, and each time that something like that would happen, things would change. It used to be all Italian merchants on Myrtle. But after the rebellions things was real tense. Then Italian merchants left um, when it became, when Clinton Hill became all black. You know the dairy, the drugstore, and the other things changed when it became um, a black community. One of the drugstores on Myrtle put in a Plexiglas all over, so, you could no longer go behind, um, you could no longer walk through and just pick up whatever you want. Stores was leaving or hiding behind Plexiglas. But it was bad. It was bad, but, when the man is being robbed every day. And they, they had a pharmacy underneath. It was this, this was robbed twice in one day. So could you blame them? So, now I like the stores. I think um, most of us the tenants who have

been here for a long time are really delighted to see all of these things come back, because at one time when, we only had like the um, an Italian restaurant that was a, you know, and then they, when it got black they left, so, we didn't even have anything.

Carmen is a single mother of three who is native to Harlem. She expressed her appreciation of the improvements in shopping options this way: "More stores are coming, like downtown stores are in our neighborhood. Before I used to go downtown, 34th Street, 14th Street. I take the bus to 125th Street, you can find every store that you find downtown there. It's wonderful."

The convenience afforded by improved amenities and services was a constant theme in my conversations with residents of Clinton Hill and Harlem. To some degree, this speaks to the dearth of commercial activity that plagues many black communities like these. The exodus of people from many inner-city neighborhoods in the 1960s and 1970s was also accompanied by receding commercial activity. The civil unrest of the 1960s, red lining by financial institutions and insurers, and seeing their customer base steadily shrink caused commercial enterprises to flee neighborhoods like Clinton Hill and Harlem in the 1960s and 1970s. It was not uncommon for a supermarket or a video store to simply not exist in some neighborhoods. Being able to go grocery shopping or eating out in one's neighborhood are things that are available in many middle-class and mostly white neighborhoods and are often taken for granted. This was not always the case in recent years in many black inner-city communities. Juanita is a mid-thirties native of Harlem who moved out to one of the outer boroughs after attending one of the CUNY schools. She has since returned to Harlem, where she now lives in her mother's rented apartment. Juanita's narrative illustrates how living in a commercial desert might predispose one to be somewhat receptive of gentrification.

> Like the new stores, the shops and things of that nature, I appreciate that. Like I know there's a Pathmark that's opening up on 145th and 8th Avenue. That's like unheard of. I was really surprised at that, and then up the block, it's, uh, Duane Reade opening up. 'Cause we used to have the travel so far just to get prescriptions filled. 'Cause you're leaving from 8th Avenue and going, not, only ten blocks, but then you have to travel avenues further west to get to a pharmacy. So that'll be a lot more convenient.

Given this backdrop, it should come as no surprise that the respondents I spoke with often appreciated the improvements in amenities, even when they were suspicious of why additional amenities were being provided. Ms. Johnson is a native of South Carolina who migrated to Harlem in the 1940s. After living in several sections of Harlem, she now lives in an apartment building in central Harlem. Her perspective on the improving services and amenities was as follows:

> MS. JOHNSON: But to me I think it's, it's helpful, because you see more policemen. They respond faster. So here to me, I enjoy the change in the neighborhood. Okay. As I, as I said, the supermarkets are different, and

I don't see where it could hurt. I don't have no reaction, except that I think the improvement is for all the best. Well it's actually much better and since they've built it up it's much cleaner. Because with the empty lots, the people used to bring their garbage from all over, and there was all these rats would be around. Now they've built it up with new homes, so that I think the neighborhood looks better, and it's much cleaner. I don't see how it affects you know because as I've said we now have supermarkets, we always have transportation so that was one of the good thing about living in Harlem and now that we have better supermarkets and have much more umm—drugstores because I remember we went down to about one drugstore you had to walk about ten blocks to get to that one. And now we have drugstore all around the corners. So, I think it is more convenient, expensive but it is convenient.

LANCE: Okay. All right, is there anything else you think we should know about this neighborhood or how it is changing and how these changes might effect neighborhood residents?

Ms. JOHNSON: Well I—I imagine everyone don't like it because we have other people living here. But to me it helps so because you have a better source of living. For example if they weren't here we would have still had those old supermarkets with their dried out vegetable and spoiled meat—Where in now we don't have that. And they didn't do it because of us, because if they did it would have happened years ago. So to me they staying here it makes, doesn't make any difference. For us and it is better to me but then I can't speak for nobody but myself. Because I have some neighbors that despise it [laughs] but when I said to them—I said look at the supermarkets, look how nice and fresh the food, I think you go there and you can buy fresh vegetable like you can downtown. Well, we would go—and load them on the buses downtown in a better neighborhood to get fresh meat, fresh food, fresh vegetables, you don't have to do that now. But you know you can't please everybody. And so I only go and say what's best for me.

Ms. Johnson is an African American who clearly subscribes to the notion that the improvements taking place in Harlem were not for "us," meaning blacks, but for "them," meaning whites. As an African American myself, I feel confident that she was using our shared race to designate "us" in contrast to whites or "them." Certainly other racial/ethnic groups have also been moving into Harlem, notably Latinos. But given the shared history of discrimination and disinvestment, especially in New York, it is probably safe to assume that she is referring to whites. Her view is ultimately pragmatic. Although the improvement in services in her mind reflects the discriminatory treatment black neighborhoods receives, she is more than happy to take advantage of these improvements. That residents would appreciate improved amenities, in hindsight, seems like common sense. Who wouldn't appreciate better stores in which to shop? . . .

The discourse on gentrification, however, has tended to overlook the possibility that some of the neighborhood changes associated with gentrification might be appreciated by the prior residents. Even apologists or boosters for gentrification often ignored the potential for the process to benefit existing residents. Early proponents of gentrification focused on the need to bring the middle class back to the city, the improved appearance of rehabilitated neighborhoods, and the strengthening of the tax base associated with gentrification. Detractors focused on displacement almost to the exclusion of any other impact that gentrification might have. Clearly the narratives expressed here are inconsistent with this depiction of gentrification as villain and suggest benefits extend beyond improving the tax base and attracting the middle class back to the city. . . .

The positive reactions toward gentrification described here suggest a rethinking of the impacts of gentrification may be in order. Clearly there are benefits that may accrue to residents of gentrifying neighborhoods who themselves would not normally be classified as gentrifiers. The lack of even basic services in many inner-city neighborhoods means that many will welcome at least some aspects of gentrification. This does not mean, however, that gentrification did not have its downsides or detractors. As one respondent aptly stated: "What good is a nice neighborhood if you can't live there?" . . .

**Kathe Newman and
Elvin K. Wyly**

 **NO**

The Right to Stay Put, Revisited: Gentrification and Resistance to Displacement in New York City

On 23 December 1985, Neil Smith was in bed paging through the *New York Times* when he came to the paper's most prominent and pricey advertising space, the bottom right quarter of the Opinion Page. On this day, the Real Estate Board of New York, Inc., had purchased the spot for an essay appearing under a question set in large, bold type: "Is Gentrification a Dirty Word?" The essay offered a spirited defence of a process in which "neighborhoods and lives blossom," while admitting that

> The greatest fears inspired by gentrification, of course, are that low-income residents and low-margin retailers will be displaced by more affluent residents and more profitable businesses.

The Board's plea on behalf of the villainised gentry was, of course, shot through with contradictions—for instance, citing studies showing "that residential rent regulations gave apartment dwellers substantial protection against displacement" while neglecting to mention the long-standing industry campaign to liberate 'free' market forces by destroying things like rent regulation. But what Smith found most astonishing about the Board's advert was its very existence

> How did it come about that the very powerful Real Estate Board of New York, Inc.—the professional lobby for the city's largest real estate developers, a kind of chamber of commerce for promoting real estate interests—found itself in such a defensive position that it had to take out an advertisement in the *Times* for the purpose of trying to redefine one of its major preoccupations?

Almost 20 years later, we found ourselves in downtown Minneapolis for a one-day symposium attended by several hundred delegates from non-profit housing service organisations from across the US. Sponsored by the Congressionally chartered Neighbourhood Reinvestment Corporation, the event was held to discuss ways to 'manage' the effects of a decade of turbulent inner-city transformation—under the catchy title "When Gentrification Comes

From *Urban Studies*, January 2006, pp. 44–52. Copyright © 2006 by Sage Publications. Reprinted by permission via Rightslink.

Knocking: Navigating Social Dynamics in Changing Neighbourhoods." But on the morning of the symposium, hundreds of delegates opened their hotel room doors to find copies of *USA Today,* with the national section carrying a bold headline: "Studies: Gentrification a boost for everyone." The article showcased the surprising findings of several recent studies suggesting that gentrification does not, after all, cause very much displacement of low-income urban residents. The article devoted prominent coverage to several econometric studies of specialised housing and income datasets, including two studies by Lance Freeman, an Assistant Professor of Urban Planning at Columbia University who happened to be at the Minneapolis symposium. Freeman instantly became one of the celebrities of the event and played a key role in discussions of the consequences of gentrification and how to reconcile interpretations of 'official' statistics and other quantitative evidence, as opposed to the voices of residents, community activists and similar kinds of qualitative evidence. Meanwhile, debates at the Minneapolis symposium were echoed electronically when the *USA Today* piece made its way across several listservs, attracting commentary by (among others) prominent urban theorists Herbert Gans and Peter Marcuse, as well as the more neo-traditional neo-liberal urbanist John Norquist (President of the Congress for the New Urbanism and former Milwaukee Mayor). Freeman, an exceedingly careful and rigorous analyst, also circulated a clarification of several issues that had been distorted or ignored in the *USA Today* coverage.

Displacement, always a central axis of academic, policy and popular concerns over gentrification, is back on the agenda. In this paper, we report on a mixed-methods study of gentrification, displacement and low-income renters' survival strategies in New York City between the early 1990s and 2003. We begin from the premise that one answer to Smith's poignant question involves *resistance*: the powerful Real Estate Board felt compelled to defend its interests in the face of militant mobilisation drawing inspiration from the legal and political principles established in Chester Hartman's famous essay "The Right to Stay Put." After 20 years of intense gentrification and sweeping public policy changes, many of the people who would mobilise to resist displacement have themselves been displaced. . . .

Displacement: A View from the Neighbourhoods

[W]e conducted field research in neighbourhoods within the seven sub-borough areas identified by Freeman and Braconi as gentrifying (Fort Greene, Greenpoint/ Williamsburg and Park Slope in Brooklyn and the Lower East Side, Chelsea/ Clinton, Central Harlem and Morningside Heights in Manhattan). . . .

We walked through each neighbourhood and conducted in-depth field interviews with 33 respondents in those neighbourhoods. The interviews did not seek to provide objective or statistically representative estimates of the magnitude or scale of displacement. Rather, the interviews were intended to shed light on the qualitative aspects of trends identified in secondary datasets and on the perspectives of individuals and groups living through neighbourhood changes. Interviews were conducted as narrative conversations. Interviewees were not treated simply as research subjects; rather, researchers and interviewees were understood as "equal participant(s) in the interaction." . . .

Neighbourhood Gentrification in the 1990s

Interviewees from all seven study neighbourhoods described dramatic changes in their communities from the mid 1990s onwards as a tremendous surge of gentrification increased displacement pressures. Even though many of these neighbourhoods experienced some form of gentrification during earlier economic booms in the 1970s and 1980s, the transformations brought about by what Hackworth and Smith (2001) labelled post-recession gentrification or the gentrification wave that occurred in the late 1990s were different in scale and scope. Interviewees describe an influx of new residents, gentrification processes that expanded further into not yet fully gentrified parts of the neighbourhoods, dramatic demographic changes, housing revitalisation and new construction, and commercial corridor revitalisation.

The changes in Lower Park Slope are fairly typical of the changes occurring in many of the study neighbourhoods. Lower Park Slope, home to a mixture of residents including older Italian families, Latinos and longtime and more recent White residents, experienced a massive influx of gentrification that transformed 5th Avenue, a major commercial corridor, and drove up housing prices. Residents appreciate many of the changes, but fear that the changes ultimately will displace them. A Latina former resident who became a community organiser after she was displaced from the neighbourhood described her experience

> In 1999 my landlord doubled the rent in the apartment but we didn't understand why . . . My rent went from $750 to $1200. So he almost doubled it. There were five other families in the building, one from Ecuador, one from Columbia . . . worked in factories all of their lives, lived there for about 28 years; we were there for 8 years . . . My apartment was taken over by a couple and their cat. So that's what he wanted. He always said he wanted to put trees on the block. It faced a factory, which he owned. It was part of Park Slope but not very residential, more like a commercial block. He put trees on it, fixed the gates and then sends everybody a letter saying the rent doubled. It wasn't that he wanted to make it nice for us. That's where gentrification affects people. He was making it look better and fixing it up but he was doing it with a mission to put in luxury condos for other people (interview, 2003).

Like Lower Park Slope, the northern part of Brooklyn's Fort Greene neighbourhood has been rapidly gentrifying since the mid 1990s, pricing out many lower-income residents who had remained there despite the earlier rounds of gentrification during the 1970s and 1980s. Myrtle Avenue, known locally as 'Murder Avenue' because of the crack cocaine issues in the 1980s, became the site of rapid gentrification in the late 1990s and early 2000s, which transformed it from a disinvested corridor to a neighbourhood asset with fashionable restaurants, dry cleaners and an ice cream shop. The transformation brought with it higher rental prices for the units above the commercial properties and helped to set off a rapid transformation of the housing stock just north of Myrtle which had until recently been one of the few remaining affordable areas.

Central Harlem received an influx of middle-class residents throughout the 1970s and 1980s but the changes during the late 1990s and early 2000s are different. Harlem's residents report a solid flow of SUVs (sports utility vehicles) of people driving through the neighbourhood scouting for homes. One resident described the housing demand: "People are coming up while you're on the street asking who owns the building. It's a daily thing." The neighbourhood also appeals to renters seeking liveable space with manageable commutes. In less than 15 minutes, residents are whisked to midtown on a 2 or A train; in 30 minutes, they can reach jobs on Wall Street. A 20-minute cab ride gets you to LaGuardia Airport and every highway intersects with Harlem. Rents for floor-through apartments in brownstones are capturing $1 700 a month.

Many residents of gentrifying neighbourhoods like Park Slope, Fort Greene and Harlem view gentrification and the transformations it brings as a mixed blessing. A Harlem resident describes the changes on 125th Street in Central Harlem. "People love Starbucks. People who would buy 50-cent coffee now go in there and buy one for $3.00." But residents fear that their new shopping venues come with a high price tag and may help to spur the revitalisation that will ultimately displace them. One resident explained that he liked the new stores but feared displacement:

> I don't want to have to take a train to go to the Magic Johnson theatre. I live on 126th. I should be able to walk to there and when I'm done, walk back.

Longtime residents are frustrated that after years of fighting to improve their neighbourhoods during periods of severe disinvestment, now that the neighbourhoods are improving, these residents will not be able to stay. A resident of the Lower East Side explained mixed feelings about gentrification:

> I've never had a problem with it. I've welcomed it. But we feel a little bit cheated. We were here when no one wanted to be here. Landlords were selling buildings for $10 000 to 12 000. Now that it's gotten better, we want to be here too. We don't want to wind up moving. It is so unfair . . . We made it better for our community and ourselves. We are here because we had nowhere else to go (interview, 2003).

This resident's explanation highlights the irony faced by many lower-income residents. For decades, community residents of innercity neighbourhoods built organisations and fought to revitalise their communities. Now that these communities are improving, they find it increasingly difficult to remain. In the next section, we discuss displacement pressures on low-income residents.

Gentrification and Low-Income Residents

The rapid gentrification put tremendous pressure on low-income residents. Community leaders, residents and advocates revealed that displacement from the mid 1990s onwards was a tremendous problem for many population sub-groups including the poor and working class, elderly and immigrants. While it is certainly difficult to understand what happens to residents as they move, residents and community leaders report that residents often double- or triple-up with family and friends, become homeless or move into the city shelter system, or move out of the city. None of these mobility dynamics is captured in the NYCHVS dataset, suggesting that it underestimates displacement by a significant but unmeasurable amount.

According to neighbourhood informants, many displacees are moving out of the city to upstate New York, New Jersey and Long Island. Community residents and organisers in Fort Greene and Harlem described a reverse great migration with many residents returning to communities of origin in the South. A resident explains where displacees go:

> A lot of people go to the South, some to upstate New York, Schenectady; Albany historically has been very cheap and also Poughkeepsie is cheap and Orange County. A lot of people are going to where they had property, to their families in Atlanta, the Carolinas (interview, 2003).

Some groups, including seniors, find it particularly difficult to remain in the gentrifying city when housing prices increase while their incomes do not. An organiser from Brooklyn explains:

> Most of the displacement is the result of landlords tripling rents who know that a senior's income doesn't go up. It stays the same. You know she can't pay you $1500 especially when she's lived there with you for years. They have to move in with their kids; they can't go to senior housing because there aren't any—they are booked and the waiting-lists are really long. Often they go live with family or kids which is hard because they are so independent (interview, 2003).

In neighbourhoods throughout Central and Northern Brooklyn, we heard about elderly women occupying apartments for decades while paying less than market rate rent. As gentrification transformed their neighbourhoods, pressure to raise their rents increased. Landlords of rent-regulated buildings that offer below-market rents to senior citizens can receive a tax abatement called SCRIE, the Senior Citizen Rent Increase Exemption, but unregulated buildings provide little protection from the increases. There are few alternatives within the city since most senior buildings are full, with long waiting-lists. Elderly women frequently double-up or move in with family outside the city.

New immigrants face similar issues including accepting poor housing quality, overcrowding, or they leave the city to find housing. A community organiser describes the displacement choices of the people he works with:

> People we just worked with went back to Mexico. They were evicted from two unregulated places. They ran out of money and went back. Some people move to Bushwick; other people are moving in with family members. A lot of times you just don't know what happens. . . . Quite a few of the tenants I've worked with who have been evicted,

the Latino population, generally have family in the neighbourhood. One part of the generation lives in regulated housing; another lives in unregulated. They will get evicted and move in with family members who have protection from eviction (interview, 2003).

For those with no alternative, there is the city's shelter system. Community organisers described their frustration when efforts to find affordable housing for tenants failed and tenants turned to the shelter system. In 2003, community leaders in a Williamsburg nonprofit referred people to the shelter system for the first time since their organisation's founding in the 1970s. The number of people in New York City's shelter system suggests the severity of the city's current housing affordability crisis. In July 2003, more than 38 000 people, including 8249 families and more than 16 500 children, used the New York City shelter system, far exceeding the last peak of 28 737 reached in March 1987. . . .

How Low-Income Residents Stay in Gentrifying Neighbourhoods

Freeman and Braconi found that low-income residents in gentrifying neighbourhoods had lower mobility rates than similar residents in non-gentrifying areas. This seems counter-intuitive but raises important and unexplored questions about how low-income residents stay in gentrifying neighbourhoods. Certainly not all residents are displaced, but what enables them to stay? We address this question in the next section.

Public Interventions

Of the myriad forms of assistance available, interviewees identified the city's rent regulations as the single most important form of public intervention. In 2002, 49 per cent of housing units in New York City were rentstabilised, 3 percent were rent-controlled and another 17 per cent were regulated by some other form of regulation, leaving 32 per cent unregulated. Changes to rent regulation legislation over the past 10 years, however, have reduced the regulated housing stock by about 105 000 units city-wide, suggesting that the role of this important safeguard has diminished over time.

Interviewees identified problems affecting the regulated stock in gentrifying neighbourhoods. Landlords illegally charge excessive rents for stabilised units, send tenants threatening notices to leave the regulated stock, stop providing services and threaten to look at immigration papers. The Rent Regulation Act of 1997 allows landlords to increase the rent of regulated apartments by between 18 and 20 per cent upon vacancy. When the rent reaches $2000, landlords can remove the unit from the regulated housing stock. In a market with soaring market rents, and the ability to reach a rent level that enables them to decontrol units, landlords have an obvious incentive to increase rents to reach the luxury decontrol cap. In Clinton, the area in Manhattan in the west 50s, landlords are reportedly using a variety of illegal tactics to capture higher rents. In one scheme, landlords rotate tenants in rent-stabilised buildings to capture the rent increase, pushing the units more quickly towards $2000 so that they can decontrol and capture windfall profits in what one community leader describes as "the most intensely gentrified neighbourhood, right west of Midtown" (interview with community leader, 2003). For their part, tenants reportedly choose not to challenge landlords to improve housing quality or charge legal rents in rent-stabilised buildings because they are afraid that landlords will harass them. An organiser explained:

> They are happy that they have some sort of apartment even though the landlord is overcharging under rent stabilisation. In this one building, it was pretty clear that everyone in the building was overpaying at $1700. They were being overcharged but in their mentality, to have a $1700 apartment in Manhattan was great and they did not want to make waves (interview, 2003).

In Brooklyn, the story is similar.

> The only tenants we have now who are in danger are in rent-stabilised apartments. The landlord has been harassing them for a long time to try to get them out. Landlord tries to increase the rent to $2000 or beyond and deregulate (interview with a community organiser, 2003).

Staff at the Pratt Area Community Council (PACC), a CDC, related the story of a tenant in a rent-stabilised apartment whose landlord constantly files frivolous cases with city and state agencies as a form of harassment (interview with a community organiser, 2003). Community organisation staff members report a sharp increase in the number of residents seeking help to cope with landlords who file personal holdover evictions, and suggest that the process is being abused to remove tenants illegally. Tenants in designated SROs (single room occupancy units) are also facing displacement pressures even though they have eviction protection. Since 1983, landlords are required to get a certificate of no harassment before removing tenants in certified SROs. Technically, landlords cannot convert units without the consent letter, but community leaders report that landlords remove tenants by buying them out, converting the units illegally, or cutting off services with the intention of wearing the tenants down until they leave. A neighbourhood organiser in Fort Greene described one situation: "We worked with an SRO building . . . the landlord cut off heat and hot water. Now it's boarded up" (interview, 2003).

Interviewees listed assisted housing as the next most used support. Thousands of residents live in housing with some form of public subsidy, including federal public housing, housing vouchers and Section 8, or New York State's Mitchell-Lama programme. Public housing offers considerable protection against displacement for 181 000 households. Vouchers provide another critical form of support but are threatened by proposed federal cutbacks. Another 20 000 people with HIV/AIDS receive rental assistance from the city's Human Resources Administration. Even with these supports, the supply of affordable housing is inadequate to meet needs.

> Currently 224 000 households are on the waiting-list for Section 8 rental
> vouchers . . . A typical family now spends eight years on the waiting-
> list for an apartment in one of the city's public housing developments.
>
> . . .

Public interventions enable many low-income residents to remain in gentrifying neighbourhoods but they are not the only interventions. We turn next to
private strategies including community organisation production and organising, the decisions of individual landlords and resident decisions.

Private Strategies

For many low-income residents, staying in gentrifying neighbourhoods means
accepting poor housing quality, coping with high housing cost burdens and/
or sharing housing with other residents. A community leader explained the
choices in Brooklyn:

> If a unit is unregulated, there is no eviction protection; there are no
> controls of the rent. If you can't pay it, you just leave. If you move
> away from the brownstone area of Fort Greene and move closer to Bed
> Stuy, the tenants in the unregulated housing will be families pooling
> their resources, Mexican immigrant families with terrible housing con-
> ditions and overcrowding. One of the ways people cope is to crowd
> it out. You either accept sub-standard housing or pool your resources
> (interview, 2003).

Housing quality and affordability become a trade-off; residents fear that
complaining about housing quality will result in displacement. An organiser
explained that some low-income tenants in Fort Greene "are paying below
market rate, but they are in really hazardous conditions" (interview, 2003).
Some displacees, especially single parents, the elderly, immigrants and younger
families, remain in the city by doubling up with family or friends. Overcrowding is a particularly serious problem in poor immigrant communities. Poles
and Latinos in Williamsburg, Africans and Latinos in Harlem, Chinese on the
Lower East Side and an array of immigrants in Brooklyn often live in severely
overcrowded conditions merely to pay the rent.

While many low-income residents are forced to live in sub-standard
housing to find affordable rents, many other low-income residents live in
good-quality private rental housing and pay below market rents. Interviewees
throughout many of the study communities described an informal housing
market in which landlords know the tenants, in many cases for decades, and
charge rent that the tenants can afford. A community leader explains how this
works:

> Landlords are not always maximising their income. Many things affect
> the decisions of landlords. There are members of the community, there
> are thousands and thousands of disabled people and older people, for
> example, who pay far below the market rate and have been for a long
> time because the landlord knows them and has a relationship with

> them. He makes this illogical decision and that's why the old lady comes in and has been paying $600 for the last decade. There are community values that mediate the market. Not 100 per cent but in many cases, there is a community consensus that we shouldn't evict the disabled, single person; this mediates the pressure to raise the rents. As the market rate goes up and up, that consensus breaks down. One older woman was paying $500, the market was paying $800. The landlord knew she couldn't pay it and it wasn't worth it to raise the rent; he didn't really need the money. By 2002, market rate was up to $1100. It's one thing to lose $300 a month, another thing to lose $600 a month (interview 2003).

The informal housing market provides housing to many otherwise vulnerable residents but it is highly unstable. These are tenuous relationships that end as landlords pass away or sell their buildings. And gentrification itself has been chipping away at the informal housing market as landlords realise the extent of their lost income and raise rents accordingly. . . .

Community organisations play an important role in ensuring the availability of affordable housing through their organising and housing production efforts. Even though many of New York's housing units are regulated, thousands of units are not regulated and there is an important geography to the regulation. Since fewer units in Brooklyn's inner-ring brownstone neighbourhoods are regulated, community organisers have sought strategies to stem the effects of displacement. Lower Park Slope's Fifth Avenue Committee (FAC) launched an anti-displacement campaign to transform neighbourhood political culture and challenge landlords who displace residents through excessive rent increases.

Groups throughout Central and Northern Brooklyn adopted FAC's strategy. In 2001, the Pratt Area Community Council (PACC) created Brooklyn Community Action to build leadership among people who might be faced with displacement. Their initial efforts quickly expanded into Displacement Watch, a programme that "holds weekly meetings for tenants, negotiates with landlords and organises letter-writing campaigns, prayer vigils and demonstrations." The anti-displacement campaigns and organising efforts are designed to pressure landlords into reducing rents. A community leader explains an action:

> The first case we took was for a tenant who lived on Myrtle above a popular restaurant. She had a Section 8 voucher, lived there over a decade, had a kid and was very active in the neighbourhood. A new landlord took over and served 30-day eviction notices to her and another family in the building. Through a clergy campaign and threatening boycott of his store, we got her a two-year lease. This was relatively pretty easy. The other family in the building did not work with us. She ended up going into the shelter system with her son. The landlord did not call off that eviction proceeding (interview with a community leader, 2003).

Hartman and Robinson (2003) note that organisations in other parts of the country have adopted similar strategies. They describe these as useful quivers in the antidisplacement armamentarium, and even when evictions are ultimately still carried out, they serve to dramatically publicise housing problems and injustices, stressing the property rights vs. housing rights theme.

The effect of these campaigns is uncertain. It is hard to say whether a new neighbourhood norm is created in Park Slope or whether landlords are altering their behaviour beyond individual cases.

In addition to organising, the city's community development corporations and other non-profit housing developers have produced thousands of units of affordable housing. The additional production has certainly helped to relieve the need for housing but some, including those running neighbourhood non-profits, point out the limitations. First, organisations acknowledge that these efforts are a drop in the bucket compared with the housing need. Secondly, support for higher-end housing and the need for affordable home-ownership opportunities in many neighbourhoods shift the agenda of the bigger organisations to producing affordable home-ownership, leaving few organisations producing housing for very low-income residents. . . .

As Freeman and Braconi suggest, many low-income families stay in gentrifying neighbourhoods, but the interventions that enable them to do so all have serious limitations. Publicly assisted programmes are losing support and the informal private market is crumbling. Inclusionary zoning holds the most potential to capture some of the advantage of the booming real estate market.

Conclusion

For at least a generation, proponents of gentrification have argued that the process involves little or no displacement—and that, in any case, its benefits for cities far outweigh the costs imposed on a few unfortunate poor households. In recent years, some proponents have gone even further to argue that the process is inherently good, even for its victims. The new urbanist architect Andres Duany cries out in the pages of the *American Enterprise Magazine* with "Three cheers for gentrification," contending that it "rebalances" concentrated poverty while offering the improved tax-base, "ruboff work ethic" and political power of the middle class: "It is the rising tide that lifts all boats." Georgetown Law Professor J. Peter Byrne does not shout quite as loudly in his "Two cheers for gentrification," but he still contends that "gentrification is good on balance for the poor and ethnic minorities." In an era of aggressive, state-driven privatised deregulation marked by intense rivalry among cities trying to gentrify themselves, the defiant cries on behalf of the poor, hated gentrifiers are at once ironic, amusing and politically effective. Moreover, gentrification proponents have carefully selected from the evidence provided by Freeman, Braconi and Vigdor—ignoring their careful qualifications and warnings. Freeman and Braconi caution that "Even though gentrification may provide benefits to disadvantaged populations, it may also create adverse effects that public policies should seek to mitigate"; and Vigdor is careful to emphasise the enormous difficulties in answering "the question of whether gentrification harms the poor." Yet these caveats and nuances are usually lost in the press coverage of the research: "Gentrification: a boost for everyone."

Underestimating displacement involves high costs for theoretical understanding of neighbourhood change and even higher tolls for poor and working-class residents and the tattered policies in place to give them some protection. Those who are forced to leave gentrifying neighbourhoods are torn from rich local social networks of information and cooperation (the 'social capital' much beloved by policy-makers); they are thrown into an ever more competitive housing market shaped by increasingly difficult trade-offs between affordability, overcrowding and commuting accessibility to jobs and services. All of the pressures of gentrification are deeply enmeshed with broader inequalities of class, race and ethnicity, and gender. . . .

We concur with Freeman and Braconi's finding that not all low-income residents are displaced by gentrification. The historically specific web of housing supports that developed in New York City from the 1920s to the 1970s has played a key role in mediating the effects of current rounds of gentrification. If they were not already displaced in the massive housing market changes of the 1970s and 1980s, some low-income renters in gentrifying neighbourhoods of New York are protected, to a greater degree than residents in many other cities, from some of the direct displacement pressures that have accelerated in recent years. The pressures on land markets in these global cities are particularly intense. But for those cities where previous generations saw the creation of a few regulatory mechanisms, the current environment is mixed, precarious and set for dramatic change. As affordable housing protections are dismantled in the current wave of neo-liberal policy-making, we are likely to see the end-game of gentrification as the last remaining barriers to complete neighbourhood transformation are torn down.

For decades, New York has sought to attract new middle-class residents and federal priorities echo these strategies. But the recent gentrification wave has fundamentally altered the development context in many formerly disinvested neighbourhoods. Focused on market-based solutions, the neo-liberal state and even some community-based developers have neglected the housing needs of poorer residents. Inclusionary zoning, housing preservation and new construction can complement the market rate and high-end affordable housing development and rehabilitation well underway in these neighbourhoods. Community organisations, residents and organisers are strenuously working to ensure that affordable housing exists, but the urgency of the need has yet to reach policy-makers at city, state or federal levels.

US cities are at a critical turning-point and New York City, as a global city with a long history of gentrification, is facing these issues earlier than many other places. It is an instructive case that suggests the benefits of housing protections for low-income residents in gentrifying communities and the potential pitfalls of weakening these supports. The goal of home-ownership and revitalisation of mixed income/mixed race neighbourhoods will not produce the beneficial changes policy-makers seek if protections for low-income residents are not also included. Community actors and policy-makers have argued that gentrification is necessary to revitalise low-income neighbourhoods. But the context for redevelopment has changed. Gentrification is not a minor phenomenon that affects a few communities; it is evidence of vast urban restructuring. The recent wave of gentrification washed through the city with a speed and a force that few, if any, predicted. Low-income residents who manage to resist displacement may enjoy a few benefits from the changes brought by gentrification, but these bittersweet fruits are quickly rotting as the supports for low-income renters are steadily dismantled.

EXPLORING THE ISSUE

Does Neighborhood Gentrification Benefit the Inner-City Poor?

Critical Thinking and Reflection

1. Why do cities pursue gentrification?
2. Have the critics of gentrification been biased in their negative assessments of gentrification?
3. Is Freeman a bit naïve in his assessment that a neighborhood's poorer residents share in the benefits of gentrification? Does he understate the dangers inherent in gentrification?
4. Which should be of dominant concern to municipal policymakers: the good of the city or the good of the people who live in a city's poorer neighborhoods? Should cities promote new investment that adds to a city's overall economic health even at the price of displacing the poor?
5. What policies can a city enact to protect poorer residents who live in neighborhoods experiencing gentrification?
6. What is the proper role for government when it comes to gentrification and neighborhood change? Should a city essentially take a free-market "hands off" attitude when such change occurs? Or should a city attempt to put some regulations and limits on the upgrading process in order to promote fairness and racial equity?

Is There Common Ground?

Maybe, the choice is not dichotomous, that a city must stand back and allow market-led gentrification or take the exact opposite policy approach of attempting to intervene with regulations intended to slow the investment process, gentrification, and displacement. A city clearly needs rising property values and taxable resources. To be competitive economically, a city must also be able to attract the sort of talented and creative workers who often choose to reside in a "hot" core neighborhood. Such workers will help the city attract new investment by corporations. Yet, it is more than a bit unseemly to stress the benefits that gentrification brings to a city while ignoring the huge costs that displacement imposes on some of the city's most vulnerable citizens.

In the free-market "privatist" United States, where landlords and capital investors maintain so many legal rights and protections, cities will find that it is very difficult, even if they wished to do so, to enact measures that will effectively stop or even slow gentrification. The courts have largely taken a negative attitude to local anti-displacement laws that restrict the ability of inner-city property owners to sell, rehabilitate, and otherwise develop their properties. In the free-market United States, property investors and the marketplace—not government—will largely continue to determine where investment in a city will take place.

Cities cannot hope to stop gentrification. Nonetheless, governments have the ability to adopt policies that can put some limits on the extent of gentrifying activity. Governments can also undertake actions to promote the continued availability of affordable housing even in neighborhoods undergoing extensive upgrading. The choice before cities is not really either to approve or to reject gentrification. Rather, a city may pursue a middle-ground policy: allowing new investment in core neighborhoods to proceed while adopting programs that limit the ill effects that would result from unbridled, market-dictated neighborhood change.

What can a city do to limit displacement and offset some of the ill effects that accompany a neighborhood's upgrading? A partial list of possible actions would include the following measures:

1. Newman and Wyly and Freeman all agree on the importance of maintaining affordable housing in gentrifying neighborhoods. Governments need to continue to provide rental subsidies and other forms of public assistance that enable poorer tenants to stay in their home even in the face of rising rents and other gentrifying pressures.
2. Cities can help assure the availability of good-quality low-income housing units by providing assistance to *community development corporations* (CDCs), neighborhood-based groups that have established a record of success in working with bankers, government officials, and other partners in order to assemble the financing necessary for the rehabilitation or construction of housing units that remains within the reach of poor people. The federal government's *Low-Income Housing Tax Credit* (LIHTC) program is essential to the work of CDCs that are seeking to expand the supply of affordable housing in areas experiencing gentrification. The LIHTC offers tax incentives to investors who construct low-income housing projects approved by state and local officials.
3. Cities can adopt programs of *set asides,* requiring that new housing developments include a certain percentage of housing units in the affordable price range. Municipal planning approval for new developments can be made contingent upon a developer's willingness to meet affordable housing targets. Alternatively, Freeman (pp. 172–173) suggests that cities can offer a *density bonus* that will allow a developer to build additional housing units if they agree to set aside a targeted percentage of units as affordable housing.
4. Boston and San Francisco have imposed *linkage fees* on new developments, recognizing that developers will often be quite reluctant to include lower income units in a new housing project, fearing that the presence of poorer residents will depress the projects' marketability, depressing the prices that can be charged for market-rate units in the project. A linkage fee program, unlike a set-aside requirement or density bonus, does not require the construction of affordable units on the site of a new project. Instead, the developer contributes to a fund that helps to pay for affordable housing projects elsewhere in the city. While such a policy may not actually limit displacement in

a neighborhood experiencing considerable upgrading, it does help assure that development will not diminish the supply of affordable housing in a city.

5. Cities can help nurture the presence of active community associations, not just CDCs. As New York City's experience demonstrates, strong activist groups have been able to scale back the extent of a proposed new development and, at times, have led governments and developers to pay greater attention to the need to include affordable housing in their housing plans. In contrast, in neighborhoods where activist groups have been weak or nonexistent, more complete and less balanced neighborhood transformation has occurred.

6. In New York and a few other big cities, rent regulation plays a key role in maintaining housing affordability in gentrifying neighborhoods. Newman and Wyly estimate that only one out of every 15 poor renters in New York City would be able to continue to live in a gentrifying neighborhood in the absence of rent limitations. Despite this achievement, the subject of government regulation of rents remains so controversial that few cities can be expected to adopt new and strong programs of rent regulation and control.

The extent and exact pattern of a neighborhood's upgrading and transformation do not have to be dictated solely by the profit-making concerns of private developers and investors. Government programs can help assure that neighborhood voices are heard when new development projects are proposed and that a supply of affordable housing units is maintained both in gentrifying neighborhoods and elsewhere in the larger city.

Additional Resources

Brown-Saracino, Japonica, ed. (2010). *The Gentrification Debates*. New York and London: Routledge.

Lees, Loretta, Tom Slater, & Elvin Wyly, eds. (2010). *The Gentrification Reader*. London and New York: Routledge.

Maurrasse, David. (2006). *Listening to Harlem: Gentrification, Community, and Business*. New York and London: Routledge.

Smith, Neil. (1996). *The New Urban Frontier: Gentrification and the Revanchist City*. London and New York: Routledge.

Internet References

The Brookings Institution

"Dealing with Neighborhood Change: A Primer on Gentrification and Policy Choices," a 2001 discussion paper prepared for the Brookings Institution Center on Urban and Metropolitan Policy by Maureen Kennedy and Paul Leonard, provides a comprehensive and balanced overview, pointing to the pressures underlying neighborhood change and the arguments pro and con gentrification. They focus on the changes taking place in inner-city communities in Atlanta, Cleveland, Washington, D.C., and the San

Francisco Bay Area. The authors suggest pragmatic policy recommendations, ones that will allow neighborhood upgrading to continue while countering some of the ill effects of neighborhood change.

www.brookings.edu/es/urban/gentrification/gentrification.pdf

The Urban Institute

"In the Face of Gentrification: Case Studies of Local Efforts to Mitigate Displacement," a 2006 study by Diane K. Levy, Jennifer Comey, and Sandra Padilla, reviews the different levels of gentrification being experienced in communities in St. Petersburg (Florida), Sacramento, Atlanta, Los Angeles, Seattle, and Chicago. The report then does exactly what its title says: it describes policies that can assist low-income families in the face of gentrification pressures.

www.urban.org/publications/411294.html

Urban Land Institute

The Urban Land Institute (ULI) seeks balanced development. The ULI offers policies that balance the need for growth and investment with competing community concerns. *Managing Gentrification: A ULI Community Catalyst Report* (2006), prepared by Deborah L. Myerson, clearly falls within the ULI tradition.

www.uli.org/~/media/Documents/ResearchAndPublications/Reports/
Community%20Catalyst/Report%205%20Managing%20Gentrification.ashx

Issues in Urban Economic Development

*O*ver the last quarter of a century, a single issue has dominated politics in U.S. cities: economic development. The urban economy has become
increasingly competitive, with advances in transportation and communications giving firms a seeming plethora of possible location sites across
the country and around the world. In the face of such intense competition, local civic leaders have devoted considerable resources to recruiting
and keeping "good" firms. As a result, economic development priorities
have enjoyed a virtual stranglehold on the agenda of a great many cities,
with the urgency of local job creation gaining preeminence over all other
local policy concerns.

This was not always the case. In earlier eras, urban politics was
defined by numerous housing and social policy concerns, not simply by
a concern for local economic growth. In the 1930s and 1940s, local and
national officials focused on the construction of public housing to add
much-needed "livable" units to the nation's housing stock so poor families
could escape the dilapidated firetraps and rat-infested housing of the slums.
The 1950s were focused on urban renewal, an effort to bring residents and
customers back to cities that were suffering a loss of activity to the suburbs.
By the 1960s, John Kennedy's social welfare policy emphasis and Lyndon
Johnson's War on Poverty concerns dominated the urban arena. The wave
of riots that swept cities in the 1960s added to the urgency of finding solutions to the social pathologies of the inner city. By the 1970s, the flirtation
of New York City and Cleveland with bankruptcy brought a dramatic shift
in the urban arena, giving new prominence to concerns for cutback management and budget balancing, with municipal officials trying to find new
ways to live within their means, to do more with less.

Today, in city after city, the top three issues are often Jobs! Jobs!
Jobs! Municipal leaders give top priority to business recruitment and
retention. They know that jobs are the voters' number one concern.

But the tools that cities use to recruit and keep businesses have
proven to be quite controversial. Property rights groups challenge a city's
use of eminent domain powers to take land from an owner to assemble
the property that a developer—another private owner—requires for an
important large-scale economic revitalization project. City after city has
also turned to sports and new stadium construction as a means of promoting a city's "major league" image and catalyzing downtown renewal;
municipal leaders seek sports- and entertainment-related development to

replace the lost manufacturing jobs of an earlier era. Taxpayer and neighborhood groups, however, often question whether working-class citizens and small homeowners should be taxed to provide the extensive subsidies demanded by the wealthy owners of local sports teams. Citizens are especially likely to question the provision of generous subsidies to sports franchises when tight economic times demand a cutback in school funding and the provision of other essential municipal services.

Tax increment financing (TIF) arrangements are especially popular as TIF promises to be a tool that "pays for itself," with new development generating the revenues to repay the costs necessitated by infrastructure upgrading and other business-oriented improvements made in a TIF district. Here too, however, critics once again ask just who benefits and who pays when a city offers such generous tax arrangements to prospective businesses, diverting proceeds away from the public treasury.

- Should State Governments Impose Strong Limitations on the Ability of Cities to Use Eminent Domain Powers for Economic Development Purposes?

- Are Public Subsidies for Sports Stadiums a Good Investment by Cities?

- Should Cities Rely on Tax Increment Financing (TIF) as a Primary Tool in Their Efforts to Promote Local Economic Development?

ISSUE 3

Should State Governments Impose Strong Limitations on the Ability of Cities to Use Eminent Domain Powers for Economic Development Purposes?

YES: Dick M. Carpenter II and John K. Ross, from "Victimizing the Vulnerable: The Demographics of Eminent Domain Abuse," *Institute for Justice* (June 2007)

NO: Bart Peterson, "Testimony Presented to the U.S. House of Representatives Committee on the Judiciary" (September 22, 2005)

Learning Outcomes

After reading this issue, you should be able to:

- Define the concepts of "eminent domain" and a "taking."
- Identify the historic and constitutional sources of government's eminent domain authority.
- Detail how the use of eminent domain authority for local economic development purposes differs from the more traditional exercises of eminent domain authority.
- Identify the criticisms that are made of local government's use of eminent domain powers.
- Explain the view of local officials that eminent domain authority is essential to a city's well-being.
- Detail the U.S. Supreme Court's ruling in the *Kelo* decision: Can cities take private property for local economic development purposes?
- Explain why states possess the constitutional authority to put limits on the local use of eminent domain powers.

ISSUE SUMMARY

YES: Dick Carpenter is a research director and John Ross is a research associate at the Colorado-based Institute for Justice, a conservative political organization committed to protecting the rights of individuals against governmental encroachment. The Institute for Justice provided the lead lawyers in the *Kelo* lawsuit that sought to limit the use of eminent domain authority for economic development purposes. Carpenter and Ross believe that government abuses its eminent domain powers when it takes property from one owner and then transfers it to another owner who desires to build a new development project. They argue that government takings and urban renewal projects too often victimize working-class homeowners and the poor, with local governments acting on behalf of powerful corporations interested in reaping a profit from new development.

NO: Bart Peterson, then-mayor of Indianapolis, testified on behalf of the National League of Cities. He argues that public law recognizes the authority of governmental authorities to take property for public purposes, including for economic development purposes, is a long-recognized aspect of public law, with the government obligated to pay an owner just compensation for the property seized. He further argues that severe restrictions on local economic development authority would impair the ability of cities to promote new economic development and job creation, reversing a city's long-term economic decline.

Americans strongly believe in private property rights. Yet, while the protection of private property rights is very much part of the American political tradition, they are not absolute. State and local governments, for instance, have the authority to adopt zoning and land-use plans that can limit what a private owner can build on a piece of land. Governments also have the ability to seize or "take" private property for "public purposes."

The U.S. Constitution explicitly declares that the federal government has *eminent domain* authority, the ability to take property for public purposes. The *takings clause* of the Fifth Amendment to the Constitution reads ". . . nor shall private property be taken for public use, without just compensation." This wording means that the government does possess the authority to take privately owned property for public purposes, just so long as it pays just compensation to the property owner. The framers of the Constitution were drawing on an English legal tradition respecting the need of the sovereign state to effectively govern; no individual property owner possesses the ability to thwart the building of a road, bridge, or other important public project.

But what activities constitute a "public purpose" that justifies the government's taking of private property? This question is at the core of the contemporary debate over eminent domain.

Experts in the field recognize that the government clearly possesses the legal right to take property (paying the owner fair compensation, of course) in order to build such public projects as roads, bridges, airports, prisons, and university campuses—public facilities that the government would then own. But, does a government also have the right to take a piece of private property from one owner and then transfer it to a new private owner who will build a project that promises to increase the tax revenues and tax base of a community? Many Americans deem it outrageous that the government can seize a piece of land from a homeowner in order to turn it over to a private developer who will then build a shopping center, an office park, or an upscale housing project. Does local economic development and job creation constitute a sufficient "public purpose" that justified the government's taking of a piece of property?

For more than a half century, the Supreme Court has followed a more liberal interpretation of "public purposes" that allowed eminent domain to be used for wider purposes and not just for the construction of roads, bridges, and other publicly owned facilities. In its 1954 *Berman v. Parker* decision, the Court ruled that the elimination of slums and blight was a sufficient public purpose that allowed governmental authorities to seize privately owned land that could then be turned over to a new owner as part of a planned urban renewal project.

Over time, local authorities became increasingly willing to use their eminent renewal authority to assist almost any new building project that proposed to bring jobs to a city or to enhance the local tax base. No matter where in the city a new development project was to be located—even on the city's rim or in the city's downtown business district—cities argued that a new development project was a part of the effort to eliminate slums and blight, the purposes that most states required for such a taking of private property. In New York City, public authorities used their eminent domain powers to assemble the land necessary for the construction of the World Trade Center, seizing the property of small store owners opposed to the project.

New London, Connecticut, a city suffering from deindustrialization and with unemployment rates nearly twice the state average, sought to use its eminent domain authority to bring jobs and economic development back to the city. City planners sought the realization of a major development project that would include a waterfront conference hotel, prime office space, restaurants, shopping, upscale residences, and even a museum and riverside walk. The project also included space for the pharmaceutical giant Pfizer, which sought to build a new research campus. Public authorities exercised their eminent domain powers when a small handful of property owners in the project area refused to sell their homes, properties that were in good condition and clearly were not blighted. Susette Kelo and a few other recalcitrant owners sued in the courts in an effort to stop the government from taking their homes.

In its 2005 *Kelo* decision (*Kelo v. City of New London*), a sharply divided Supreme Court on a 5-4 vote ruled in favor of the local government. The Court declared that, in an economically distressed community like New London, economic rejuvenation, job creation, and the generation of new tax revenues did constitute a sufficient public purpose as the project was intended to bring benefits to the broader New London community.

But the majority opinion then went on to note that state governments also have the ability to limit just when and under what conditions a local authority may exercise eminent domain powers: "nothing in our opinion precludes any State from placing further restrictions on its exercise of the takings power." In terms of constitutional law, local governments are not mentioned in the Constitution and are only administrative subunits created by the states. Each state has the ability to determine just what powers its local governments may and may not exercise. Consequently, as the Court continued in its *Kelo* ruling, a state may enact statutes that "carefully limit the grounds upon which takings may be exercised."

The *Kelo* decision virtually invited states to put new restrictions on the local exercise of eminent domain powers. The decision spurred property rights groups to action. Politically conservative talk-radio hosts enflamed the discussion, exaggerating the prospects that, unless new restrictions were imposed, governments would use their authority to seize churches and church property.

Responding to public sentiment, more than 40 states in the post-Kelo era enacted new measures in an attempt to narrow the use of eminent domain powers by local governments. These changes more narrowed the definitions of "blight" and "slums," limiting the ability of local governments to read these terms broadly in order to take property as part of an economic development project. Some states also increased the compensation that local governments were required to pay to property owners for their property. The new state statutes also set forth more detailed and extensive public participation and appeals procedures, giving opponents greater opportunity to frustrate a property taking.

The debate in the post-Kelo era concerns the wisdom of imposing new restrictions on eminent domain authority. Are tough state and even federal restrictions on takings necessary in order to force local governments to respect private property rights? Or are such restrictions an unwise intrusion that will impede the ability of local officials to respond to the needs of their citizens on the number one issue of the day: the need to bring new economic activity and jobs to a community?

In the YES selection, Carpenter and Ross vehemently argue for the enactment of new restrictions that will curtail the abuse of local eminent domain powers. They argue that the history of property takings reveals a clear bias: that local officials have acted to assist the profit-making ventures of a powerful corporate elite with little regard to the wants of working-class homeowners and the poor. Political conservatives are not alone in this view that eminent domain powers have been used to further the interests of the wealthy, not the public interest. Susan Fainstein (2005), a liberal-left political scientist, argues that too often eminent domain has been used to uproot working-class and poor and minority families in order to enrich wealthy developers and their growth-coalition friends.

Conservatives in Congress in 2005 responded to the public outcry over the *Kelo* decision, by proposing a "Private Property Rights Protection Act" that would withdraw federal funds in instances where local authorities exercised their eminent domain powers too broadly. In his testimony before Congress (the NO selection), Indianapolis Mayor Bart Peterson, speaking on behalf of the National League of Cities, argues that such restrictions would prove hurtful to cities. Peterson admits that there have been instances where cities have misused their eminent domain authority. Yet, as Peterson argues, a city's ability to use its eminent domain authority remains essential to the economic lifeblood of a city. Peterson points to specific economic projects that have helped turn around distressed downtowns and inner-city neighborhoods, beneficial projects that would have been almost impossible to complete without the power of eminent domain.

YES

**Dick M. Carpenter II
and John K. Ross**

Victimizing the Vulnerable: The Demographics of Eminent Domain Abuse

Executive Summary

In *Kelo v. City of New London*—one of the most reviled U.S. Supreme Court decisions in history—the Court upheld the use of eminent domain by governments to take someone's private property and give it to another for private economic development. In a major expansion of eminent domain power, the now-infamous *Kelo* decision marked the first time the U.S. Supreme Court approved the use of eminent domain for purely private development under the Public Use Clause of the Fifth Amendment to the U.S. Constitution, which traditionally had been limited to taking property for unambiguous public uses, such as schools or courthouses.

In their dissents, Justices Sandra Day O'Connor and Clarence Thomas not only pilloried the five justices in the majority for this expansion of so-called "public use," but also predicted dire consequences as a result of the decision: Poor, minority and other historically disenfranchised and comparably powerless communities would be disproportionately hurt through eminent domain abuse. Although it is well documented that urban renewal projects of the 1950s and 1960s targeted the poor and minorities, some question whether such dynamics are true in contemporary redevelopment projects, as evidenced, for example, by the neighborhood at the center of the *Kelo* case—a working-class area different than those typically envisioned as in need of "renewal."

This research uses census data to test the predictions of Justices O'Connor and Thomas. It compares the demographic characteristics of 184 areas targeted by eminent domain for private development to their surrounding communities to see if such areas are, in fact, more likely to be populated by the poor, ethnic minorities and those with lower levels of educational attainment.

Taken together, more residents in areas targeted by eminent domain for private development, as compared to those in surrounding communities, are ethnic or racial minorities, have completed significantly less education, live on significantly less income, and live at or below the federal poverty

From *Victimizing the Vulnerable: The Demographics of Eminent Domain Abuse,* Institute for Justice, June 2007.

RESULTS CONFIRM THE JUSTICES' PREDICTIONS. SPECIFICALLY, IN PROJECT AREAS IN WHICH EMINENT DOMAIN HAS BEEN THREATENED OR USED FOR PRIVATE DEVELOPMENT

58% of the population includes minority residents, compared to only 45% in the surrounding communities	the median income is less than $19,000 per year, compared to more than $23,000 in surrounding communities	25% live at or below poverty, compared to only 16% in surrounding communities	a greater percentage of residents have less than a high school diploma and smaller percentages have various levels of college education compared to surrounding communities

line. Just as Justices O'Connor and Thomas predicted, eminent domain abuse is most likely to fall on the politically weak. Those often least-equipped to represent their own interests in the face of the use of eminent domain and their eventual displacement through this power inequitably bear not only an economic burden but also a socio-cultural one through the loss of social networks and support systems inherent in neighborhoods, small businesses and churches.

Expanding "Public Use"

In one of the most reviled decisions in recent history, the U.S. Supreme Court, on June 23, 2005, upheld in *Kelo v. City of New London* the government's use of eminent domain to take someone's private property and give it to another for private economic development. The *Kelo* decision marked the first time the U.S. Supreme Court approved eminent domain for purely private development under the Public Use Clause of the Fifth Amendment to the U.S. Constitution. Traditionally, the power of eminent domain had been limited to taking property for schools, roads and other unambiguous public uses.

The expansion of the eminent domain power began in earnest with the Court's 1954 decision in *Berman v. Parker*, which upheld the constitutionality of urban renewal, a massive effort by federal, state and local governments to "revitalize" urban areas by removing slums and eliminating blight. Before *Berman*, with some limited exceptions, private property could only be taken through eminent domain for public *uses*. In *Berman*, however, the Court transformed the words "public use" to mean "public purpose," thereby broadening the definition. The purported public purpose underlying the takings in *Berman* was the removal of blight, but slum clearance efforts of the 1950s and 1960s led to the demolition and destruction of many communities. Moreover, in the words of the time, urban renewal more often than not meant "Negro removal."

Over time, some state courts expanded on *Berman* and further degraded protection for property owners by declaring that mere "public benefits" from possible increased tax revenue or hoped-for job creation justified the private-to-private transfer of property through eminent domain, regardless of a property's condition. Even well-maintained properties could be taken. The trend of broadening the definition of "public use" to "public purpose" to "public benefit" culminated with *Kelo*, in which the nation's highest court held that promoting economic development is a function of the government and provides a legitimate public purpose for private-to-private transfer of property. The Court, however, was closely divided, with a narrow 5-4 vote upholding eminent domain for private development. In a strongly worded dissent, Justice Sandra Day O'Connor wrote:

> Under the banner of economic development, all private property is now vulnerable to being taken and transferred to another private owner, so long as it might be upgraded—i.e., given to an owner who will use it in a way that the legislature deems more beneficial to the public—in the process. To reason, as the Court does, that the incidental public benefits resulting from the subsequent ordinary use of private property render economic development takings "for public use" is to wash out any distinction between private and public use of property—and thereby effectively to delete the words "for public use" from the Takings Clause of the Fifth Amendment.

Justice O'Connor also predicted adverse consequences resulting from the majority's decision:

> Any property may now be taken for the benefit of another private party, but the fallout from this decision will not be random. The beneficiaries are likely to be those citizens with disproportionate influence and power in the political process, including large corporations and development firms. As for the victims, the government now has license to transfer property from those with fewer resources to those with more. The Founders cannot have intended this perverse result.

Justice Clarence Thomas also dissented, noting: "Allowing the government to take property solely for public purposes is bad enough, but extending the concept of public purpose to encompass any economically beneficial goal guarantees that these losses will fall disproportionately on poor communities." He went on to cite the disastrous effects of urban redevelopment in the middle 20th century on minority communities, concluding, "Regrettably, the predictable consequence of the Court's decision will be to exacerbate these effects."

REAL-WORLD EFFECTS OF EMINENT DOMAIN ABUSE

Reports like these, that use averages representing areas from multiple cities and states, can sometimes under-represent the real-world effects of eminent domain abuse. But residents in project areas like that in El Paso, Texas, know all too well the shadow eminent domain casts.

In March 2006, the Paso Del Norte Group (PDNG) and the city of El Paso introduced a redevelopment plan that called for the use of eminent domain to redevelop more than 100 acres of downtown. The population in this project area is almost 100 percent minority, 56 percent live at or below poverty and 80 percent have less than a high school diploma.

The working-class area will be replaced, if PDNG's vision is realized, with upscale lofts, apartments, shops and entertainment venues to lure new residents, shoppers and tourists. Not without precedent, residents fear the new neighborhood will not be as affordable as promised.

In the face of mounting criticism over the project, Mayor John Cook announced in May 2006 that the city would start the plan over again and that eminent domain would only be used as a "last resort." In October, City Council members approved the plan.

It isn't the first time city officials pushed redevelopment on the area: "There have been 53 plans in the last 50 years," said Councilman Steve Ortega, a supporter of eminent domain for the project. "Now you have a business community that is ready to finance most of the plan, whereas [before] most of the plan was left to the public sector." The public sector, however, will be in charge of conveying property to the "business community" from unwilling sellers.

In December 2006, City Council voted not to condemn any property until November 2008, a small reprieve to residents. But it also means more than 300 properties sit under the cloud of condemnation, which inevitably impacts day-to-day living, property values and any negotiations.

Urban Renewal's Legacy

For urban affairs scholars, the predictions of Justices O'Connor and Thomas represent a familiar refrain. For years, researchers have noted that the trend among urban redevelopment strategies is to attract wealthier middle classes back to the inner city, typically resulting in the replacement of one population with another. Much of the research focuses on urban renewal, which generally refers to the set of redevelopment policies and projects used during the 1950s and 1960s to make room for downtown commercial development activities, more upscale residents, or both, by leveling "blighted" neighborhoods and displacing existing populations from central-city areas. Demographically, these displaced populations were disproportionately ethnic or minority communities and/or low-income.

"ANY PROPERTY MAY NOW BE TAKEN"

Justices O'Connor and Thomas predicted that eminent domain abuse would fall hardest on the poor and minorities—as this report confirms—but they also understood that under *Kelo*, any property can be taken for private development. Indeed, neighborhoods affected by eminent domain are not exclusively those populated by residents who are poor, minority or less educated. In fact, 19 of the project areas from this sample are more accurately described as white, middle-class neighborhoods.

Take, for example, Lake Zurich, Ill., a small community of about 18,000 residents. With a population of only 7 percent minority, 8 percent with less than a high school diploma and 0.3 percent at or below poverty, the project area in this community looks nothing like the typical project areas in this report.

Yet, in 2001, consultants S.B. Friedman recommended that city officials include 36 acres of downtown in a plan that allowed for the use of eminent domain. In 2004, officials adopted the plan, drawn by Chicago architect Lucien LaGrange, which called for private developer McCaffery Interests to remake the old resort village's Swiss Alps-themed buildings into new restaurants, shops and condos.

In February 2005, residents held a candlelight vigil to protest eminent domain. "Is it public use?" asked Sarah Hudson. "I don't think so. Public use to me means a road or something like that; not condos at half-a-million dollars." "It's not for sale," said Hudson of the house her grandfather stuccoed around 1911. Her building has since been bulldozed, as have dozens of lake houses and a 130-year-old farmhouse.

Although village officials filed eminent domain proceedings in February 2005 against the owners of five houses and an apartment building, they held off acting until after the *Kelo* decision. In April 2006, the last of the remaining property owners sold after dropping a counter-lawsuit contesting the village's eminent domain authority. According to village administrator John Dixon, that meant the village had acquired 34 properties by "mutual agreement."

For example, from 1949 to 1963, urban renewal displaced an estimated 177,000 families and another 66,000 individuals, most of them poor and most of them black. Unfortunately, precise numbers are not available, and these data have been criticized for their conservatism, that is, underestimating the proportion of African-Americans affected. But of what is known of the race of 118,128 of the families relocated from 1949 to 1963, 78 percent were nonwhite. Moreover, only 48,000 new housing units were constructed during the same period, and only 20,000 of those constituted low-cost housing.

These residents did not acquiesce to displacement easily. Renewal efforts led to political battles in which poor and minority residents fought to save their neighborhoods. But they typically held little power to resist the changes befalling their neighborhoods, as strong political coalitions formed to advance an agenda of replacement. A number of historical studies have documented the role of powerful actors, such as urban mayors, federal officials and real estate representatives, in the development of post-war urban renewal and redevelopment, which left urban residents largely powerless in the process.

Eminent Domain Abuse Today

Yet, just how relevant to today's redevelopment context are the comparisons to urban renewal made by Justices O'Connor and Thomas? Given the social and economic changes that have occurred in the United States since the post-war urban renewal era, does contemporary use of eminent domain inequitably threaten specific populations as it did in the 1950s and 1960s? Some might argue it does not; contemporary redevelopment projects using eminent domain are not exclusively set in traditional urban areas. For example, the neighborhood in question in the *Kelo* case differed in several important ways from areas typically envisioned as in need of "renewal."

Therefore, we undertook this research to discern the demographic profiles of those living in areas targeted by the type of redevelopment and eminent domain at the center of the *Kelo* case and so widely used across the country. In so doing, we sought to answer: Are the predictions of Justices O'Connor and Thomas valid? Does the use of eminent domain for private-to-private transfer disproportionately affect poor, minority or other less-politically powerful populations?

To answer these questions, we used data from the 2000 census to examine the characteristics of 184 areas targeted by eminent domain for private development (called project areas hereafter) to compare them to their surrounding communities. These project areas were zones within a municipality for which the use of eminent domain for private development was designated. . . .

"Perverse Results"

As the numbers in Table 1 indicate, the predictions of Justices O'Connor and Thomas held true: Losses from eminent domain abuse "fall disproportionately on the poor," and particularly on minorities. Eminent domain project areas include a significantly greater percentage of minority residents (58%) compared to their surrounding communities (45%). Median incomes in project areas are significantly less ($18,935.71) than the surrounding communities ($23,113.46), and a significantly greater percentage of those in project areas (25%) live at or below poverty levels compared to surrounding cities (16%).

Residents of project areas are significantly less educated than those living in the surrounding communities. A greater percentage of those in project areas (34%) hold less than a high school diploma as compared to the surrounding cities (24%), and a consistently greater percentage of those in surrounding communities hold various levels of college degrees compared to the project areas.

Finally, a significantly greater percentage of residents in project areas rent their homes (58%) compared to residents in surrounding cities (45%).

Table 1

Averages for Project Areas and Surrounding Communities

	Averages	
	Project Area	Community
Minority*	58%	45%
Median Income*	$18,935.71	$23,113.46
Poverty*	25%	16%
Children	25%	26%
Senior Citizens	13%	12%
Less than High School Diploma*	34%	24%
High School Diploma	28%	28%
Some College*	22%	25%
Bachelor's Degree*	9%	13%
Master's Degree*	3%	5%
Professional Degree*	1%	2%
Doctorate*	.6%	.9%
Renters*	58%	45%

*Difference between project areas and surrounding communities is statistically significant (p<.05, which means we can be sure with 95% confidence that the differences found here in the sample data will be true in the greater population)

We found little difference in the percentages of children and senior citizens between the project areas and the communities.

Taken together, more residents in areas targeted by eminent domain—as compared to those in surrounding communities—are ethnic or racial minorities, have completed significantly less education, live on significantly less income, and significantly more of them live at or below the federal poverty line. As Justices O'Connor and Thomas predicted, "extending the concept of public purpose to encompass any economically beneficial goal guarantees that these losses will fall disproportionately on poor communities."

Of course, these data do not show or even imply that governments and developers deliberately discriminate by targeting particular areas with eminent domain *because* there are poorer, minority or less-educated residents. Yet, these results reveal such communities are disproportionately affected nonetheless, and these are typically communities less able to exert significant political influence in defense of their homes and neighborhoods. The results for such residents can be disastrous. As Justice Thomas discussed, and as researchers have acknowledged, when poor residents are displaced as a result of eminent domain, they bear enormous economic and psychological burdens that even those with middle-incomes find difficult to shoulder.

The powerlessness they experience in the process also can negatively affect their well-being. Research into the effects of powerlessness reveal distinct emotional, psychological and physiological implications for those who perceive a lack of control over their personal circumstances. Researchers find that displacement often elicits negative emotional and health reactions due to the loss of neighborhoods where residents held strong attachments to friends, neighbors, churches and local small businesses. Displaced residents further find it difficult to replicate critical community networks and culture. Justice Thomas noted these losses when he wrote, " 'urban renewal' programs provide some compensation for the properties they take, but no compensation is possible for the subjective value of these lands to the individuals displaced and the indignity inflicted by uprooting them from their homes."

Real Protections

Unfortunately, these predictions by Justices O'Connor and Thomas remain largely and remarkably unacknowledged to date. Justice Thomas called upon our past to inform present circumstances, and data in this study indicate the current effects of eminent domain for private development may mirror those of an unfortunate time when "urban renewal" meant "Negro removal." That is, the current trend of using eminent domain for private development, much like the failed urban renewal policies of decades ago, falls hardest on minorities and those of limited means—people often least equipped to defend themselves through the political process and thereby left most vulnerable to abuse by the Court's expansion of the eminent domain power.

Given the awesome nature of that power, and the inequitable effects demonstrated herein, political "quick fixes," bureaucratic tinkering, or promises of eminent domain as a "last resort" fall far short of protecting citizens who value their property as neighborhood and home from government leaders and developers who see property only for its exchange value. The only real solution is prohibiting the use of eminent domain for private development to protect the constitutional rights of all citizens, not least of which include those threatened by "Robin Hood in reverse." . . .

Bart Peterson

 **NO**

Testimony Presented to the U.S. House of Representatives Committee on the Judiciary

Good morning, Mr. Chairman, and members of the Committee. I am Mayor Bart Peterson of Indianapolis, Indiana, and I am testifying this morning on behalf of the National League of Cities ("NLC"), where I serve as its Second Vice President.

NLC is the country's largest and oldest organization serving municipal government, with more than 1,800 direct member cities and 49 state municipal leagues, which collectively represents more than 18,000 United States communities. Its mission is to strengthen and promote cities as centers of opportunity, leadership, and governance, and to serve as a national resource and advocate for the municipal governments it represents.

NLC appreciates the opportunity to present a municipal perspective on the Supreme Court's decision in *Kelo v. City of New London*. As Congress considers legislative responses, NLC urges a careful examination of the underlying premise of proposals in Congress that would severely restrict or eliminate the ability of cities to use eminent domain for economic development. NLC also urges Congress not to use the appropriations process to legislate on eminent domain. In the wake of Hurricane Katrina, proposed limits to the use of eminent domain should be studied carefully to insure that we do no harm to the efforts to revitalize our cities and regions.

I. The *Kelo* Decision Highlights the Natural Tension Public Officials Confront Daily between Individual Rights and Community Needs

The anxiety some people have with eminent domain is real. The history of how government use eminent domain is mixed, but most of it is good. Cities use eminent domain most often as a negotiating tool with property owners or to clear title where the property owner is absent. Since the release of the *Kelo* decision, the rhetoric about the use of eminent domain for economic development purposes has been one-sided. NLC is pleased to have the opportunity to speak to the position that, but for the prudent use of eminent domain, many people in our nation's cities would have few reasons to anticipate a better future.

U.S. House of Representatives, September 22, 2005.

One of the most important responsibilities of any municipal government is to provide for the economic and cultural growth of the community while safeguarding the rights of the individuals that make up that community. The prudent use of eminent domain, when exercised in the sunshine of public scrutiny, helps achieve a greater public good that benefits the entire community. Used carefully, it helps create hope and opportunity for people and communities that have little of both.

II. The *Kelo* Decision Does Not Expand Municipal Power

As a legal matter, the *Kelo* decision does not expand the use or powers of eminent domain by states or municipalities. Nor does the Court's decision overturn existing restrictions imposed at the state or local levels. In fact, the Court does not preclude "any state from placing further restrictions on its exercise of the Takings power." The *Kelo* decision, as applied to the specific set of facts in New London, reaffirmed years of precedent that economic development is a "public use" under the Takings Clause. The Takings Clause, moreover, retains its constitutional requirement that property owners receive just compensation for their property.

Some legal scholars note that the *Kelo* Court refined the eminent domain power, as applied to economic development. The majority opinion and concurrence by Justice Kennedy outline that eminent domain should only be exercised to implement a comprehensive plan for community redevelopment: (1) based on wide public consultation and input; (2) that contains identifiable public benefits; (3) with reasonable promise of results that meet an evident public need, captured in a contract like a development agreement; and, (4) with the approval of the highest political authority in the jurisdiction.

The *Kelo* majority declared that eminent domain, a power derived from state law, is one best governed by the states and their political subdivisions. The *Kelo* Court affirmed federalism and the Tenth Amendment. Since the opinion's release, more than half of the states—including Indiana—have taken the Court at its word. In my home state of Indiana, which already requires a blight finding, the legislature considered a bill last year that would further restrict the use of eminent domain. It did not pass, but instead the legislature is currently examining the issue in a study committee, and I expect it to get a lot of attention when the legislative session convenes in January 2006. Regardless of the individual state outcomes, the Court correctly concluded that eminent domain is not a one-size-fits-all power, and that states are better suited than Congress to govern its use.

III. The *Kelo* Decision Does Not Encourage Cities to Use Eminent Domain Voraciously

Eminent domain is used sparingly by cities because it often extracts a significant cost in financial, political, and human terms. With any economic development project, a city usually starts by trying to assemble the land. Cities approach landowners and offer to buy. A majority of the time, most people agree to sell, often for more than market value. Generally, just having the tool available makes it possible to negotiate with landowners. Local governments strive to avoid litigation because it costs enormous amounts of money and time. Sometimes, however, cities face property owner holdouts who make the strategic decision to wait out the process. There are also absentee property owners for whom eminent domain is necessary to clear title.

If cities did not have the tool of eminent domain, it would be impractical to undertake large economic development projects. I know that there is a success story in each of your home states, of a project that transformed an area and created jobs and home ownership opportunities, that occurred because of eminent domain. In Indianapolis, a neighborhood just north of downtown is our success story. The area, now called *Fall Creek Place,* was blighted and known for its violence and drugs. The private sector was unable to change these conditions, as it could not do anything about the abandoned homes and poorly maintained vacant lots. The city acquired 250 properties. Of those, 28 were eminent domain cases. We did not use eminent domain against any property owner's will, but only when the property owners could not be located. Today Fall Creek Place is a beautiful mixed-income neighborhood with homeowners of all backgrounds, including a majority of low-income residents, and 71 percent that are first-time homeowners. The project has spurred private development in the area, and construction will begin shortly on live-work units that feature retail stores on the first floor and residential space above. It has increased property values in every direction surrounding it. If eminent domain is unavailable to us, we simply could not do any other project like it.

Another example of the importance of eminent domain is in the case of environmental remediation. Factories in the past often located on waterfronts, for instance, where they dumped materials into the water. Today those factories have moved, leaving the property abandoned. The City of Thomson, Georgia, offers an example of how cities address this challenge. The City is using eminent domain to acquire an abandoned industrial site so that the property can be cleaned up and reused. The site, formerly the "Old Thomson Company," was a carpet recycling factory on two adjacent parcels divided by a road. A local bank foreclosed on one parcel, but could not foreclose on the adjacent 10-acre parcel because of numerous environmental problems including 2,771 tons of old used carpet. On that site are five large warehouse sites and four smaller buildings ancillary to the site with two abandoned underground tanks and one above-ground tank. The City determined that both parcels are needed to create a vital economically viable area and is in the process of initiating action to condemn the property so that it can be stabilized and put back on the market. The total project cost for cleanup, remediation, stabilizing the buildings, and putting it back into use, is more than $1.15 million dollars.

Eminent domain is also a critical tool for cities in confronting urban sprawl—the further development of cities away from the city core. Sprawl leads to abandoned property in center cities and inner-ring suburbs. Without eminent domain, that very desirable property would be off limits for redevelopment.

Philosophically, all of us instinctively feel that property rights should be preeminent—that government should not interfere with the free use of our land. Complete, unfettered freedom of property rights, however, would make it impossible, for example, to prevent an adult bookstore from locating in a residential neighborhood.

In balancing the important interests involved, please remember that the availability of eminent domain has probably led to more job creation and home ownership opportunities than any other economic development tool. If that tool vanishes, the redevelopment experienced in many communities in recent years would literally come to a complete halt. Absent redevelopment, I believe that we would have fewer people becoming homeowners, which means fewer participants in what the Bush Administration calls an "ownership society."

IV. Conclusion

Municipal officials know from experience what the Supreme Court has affirmed—that economic development is a public use. Legislation that prohibits the use of eminent domain solely to provide for private gain is understandable. However, it clouds the issue for the public when the long-standing legal principle that economic development is a public use is linked with the inappropriate tactic of taking real property from A and giving it to B, for B's sole, private benefit.

Projects that have used eminent domain ranging from Texas Ranger stadium, to Lincoln Center, to Baltimore's Inner Harbor, have all provided real public benefits to their communities. The limited use of eminent domain for economic projects designed to improve community well-being and increase new housing stock should also help increase the potential for more residents to realize their dream of homeownership.

By subjecting development projects to public debate and by planning these projects with the public welfare in mind, eminent domain allows cities and their citizens to develop the community in a way that is transparent and beneficial for all. NLC again urges Congress to avoid taking any hasty action that would undermine state and local authority with eminent domain.

Municipal leaders have a responsibility to engage in public conversation about eminent domain that can help dispel inaccuracies and stereotypes. There is, however, a delicate balance between minimizing the burdens on individuals and maximizing benefits to the community. The art of compromise is essential going forward.

EXPLORING THE ISSUE

Should State Governments Impose Strong Limitations on the Ability of Cities to Use Eminent Domain Powers for Economic Development Purposes?

Critical Thinking and Reflection

1. Should government ever have the power to take private property without the owner's consent? If so, just when should a government be allowed to do so?
2. Is the power of eminent domain critical to the revival of cities? Or can cities realize their economic goals by other means, without resorting to eminent domain?
3. What would be the consequences for cities if a state was to ban the local use of eminent domain authority to assist local economic projects?
4. Which level of government—the national government, the state government, or local government—is in the best position to decide just when a community needs to exercise its eminent domain powers in order to pursue a job or development project in the public interest?
5. What do you think is the appropriate balance that should be struck between private property rights and the need of public authorities to take land for public purposes?

Is There Common Ground?

Local governments need eminent domain powers to assure the completion of important public projects. Eminent domain authority enables a community to build roads, bridge access ramps, airports, and even critical economic redevelopment projects.

But cities have relied too greatly on their eminent domain powers. The exercise of eminent domain authority should be more the exception than the rule. Local officials have alternatives to eminent domain; they can continue to engage in bargaining with property owners, no matter how time-consuming, difficult, and expensive it is. Cities and redevelopment agencies must be willing to offer high prices to acquire necessary land parcels, in some cases even paying more than twice the fair market value of a property. Such an approach costs a city money. But that is the price a city finds that it must pay in a free society. A strategy of generous purchase offers will increase voluntary property sales, decreasing the number of property taking and the battles over eminent domain that ensue.

City leaders have also come to recognize that continued exercise of eminent domain powers risks provoking the anger of a public that tends to view property takings as illegitimate, especially when homes are taken with the property turned over to profit-oriented businesses. Too often, local governments have acted to aid powerful private interests, helping them to acquire properties without having engaged in extensive negotiations with individual owners and to pay the higher prices that will likely result.

Government must also exercise its eminent domain powers in a manner that seeks to gain the public's confidence. The taking of a property should not be the result of decisions that city officials and business interests had largely worked out in private meetings. Instead, all such decisions should be made and discussed in public forums with the full participation of affected property owners. Government leaders must also take great care to educate the public as to what exact benefits will derive from a particular public taking and how all meaningful alternatives to eminent domain have been tried and are exhausted.

Projects engulfed in controversy seldom succeed as originally envisioned. How did the *Kelo* controversy end? City of New London officials, despite their victory before the Supreme Court, recognized that the continuing public outcry over the *Kelo* decision would lead to a never-ending series of new challenges that would place new difficulties in the path of project completion. In an effort to put an end to the controversy and get the project moving, redevelopment officials sought a settlement with Susette Kelo and agreed to pay a generous price for her property. The city also paid to move her home to a new location near the city's downtown—even though Ms. Kelo chose to move to a home closer to her old neighborhood.

But the efforts at reconciliation came too late. Sadly, although the neighborhood was cleared, the project was never completed. Nothing was built on the Kelo homesite. The controversy over the years had resulted in extensive project delays and made financing for the project increasingly difficult to obtain. When the economy hit a downturn, Pfizer pharmaceutical pulled out of the project, announcing that it was leaving the city and would move 1,400 jobs to its old research campus in neighboring Groton. New London's grandiose redevelopment project lost its major tenant and collapsed. The project site remained empty, contributing neither jobs nor new tax revenues to the city. In the wake of Hurricane Irene, the city wound up using the site as a dump for storm debris.

Additional Resources

Fainstein, Susan. (December 12, 2005). "Eminent Domain Benefits Developers, Not the Public." *Gotham Gazette*. Available at: www.gothamgazette.com/article/iotw/20051212/200/1676.

Malloy, Robin Paul, ed. (2008). *Private Property, Community Development, and Eminent Domain*. Burlington, VT: Ashgate.

Porter, Douglas R. (2007). *Eminent Domain: An Important Tool for Community Revitalization*. Washington, DC: Urban Land Institute.

Internet References

The Goldwater Institute

An Arizona-based public policy institute committed to the defense of liberty, including private property rights, against the threat posed by governmental intrusion.

www.goldwaterinstitute.org

Gotham Gazette

The *Gazette*'s section on "Land Use" contains numerous articles on the controversies surrounding New York City's use of its eminent domain powers in support of various redevelopment projects.

www.gothamgazette.com

Reason Foundation

Committed to a free society and libertarian principles, the Reason Foundation has been highly critical of government's overuse and abuse of eminent domain authority.

http://reason.org/areas/topic/290.html

ISSUE 4

Are Public Subsidies for Sports Stadiums a Good Investment by Cities?

YES: Mark S. Rosentraub, from *Major League Winners: Using Sports and Cultural Centers as Tools for Economic Development* (CRC Press, 2010)

NO: Dennis Coates and Brad R. Humphreys, from "The Stadium Gambit and Local Economic Development," The Cato Institute, *Regulation* (vol. 23, no. 2, Summer 2000)

Learning Outcomes
After reading this issue, you should be able to:
• Relate the evidence presented by critics who argue that public subsidies for sports facilities are too often a "bad deal" for cities.
• Explain why public officials continue to subsidize new sports stadiums and arenas despite the seemingly negative evidence.
• Point to the benefits that San Diego derived from the public–private partnerships that built Petco Park.
• Identify the concerns that critics have regarding the development of Petco Park and the surrounding area.
• Explain how such economic concepts as "efficiency" and "substitution" are used to criticize public subsidies for sports facilities.
• Differentiate between a "good deal" and a "bad deal" for a city when it comes to funding a new sports facility.

ISSUE SUMMARY

YES: Mark Rosentraub, Bickner endowed chair and professor at the University of Michigan's Center for Sports Management, argues that cities can invest wisely in sports facilities, using new stadiums as part of a strategic plan to leverage new private investment in a declining downtown district. Rosentraub points to how planners in San Diego used the construction of a new ballpark as part of a larger project that transformed the surrounding neighborhood.

NO: Economics Professors Dennis Coates and Brad Humphreys summarize the findings of a large number of studies that all point to the same conclusion: that public subsidies for sports facilities seldom add to a region's overall wealth and in some cases may even retard economic growth. Consultant studies typically understate the costs and overpredict the benefits that a city will receive from a stadium project. They further observe how the investment in sports facilities can divert public resources from more productive uses.

Members of the local *growth coalition*—the business owners, real estate interests, and organized labor unions that gain financially from new construction projects—often push for the public funding of new sports arenas and other major new developments. These leaders argue that a state-of-the-art sports facility or convention center is necessary for the future prosperity of the city. The loss of a major sports team tells national business leaders to think twice before expanding investments in the city.

Political logic also helps to explain why elected leaders are often so willing to provide generous subsidies for new sports facilities. Elected officials fear that they will be blamed by local fans if franchise owners decide to pick up and move their team elsewhere.

Stadium projects, however, seldom deliver the full public benefits that their backers promise. The growth coalition typically hires consultants who prepare reports that seemingly demonstrate the cost feasibility of a new stadium under a variety of possible economic scenarios. In many cases, the studies argue that a stadium or convention center will be self-financing, generating sufficient revenues to pay off the costs of construction and requiring no future subsidies from the taxpayer. Few politicians can resist the appeal of a major project that promises to pay for itself. When the project is completed and revenues do not wind up covering the costs of the new facility, the taxpayers are then left with the burden of covering the difference.

In many cities, taxpayers pay considerable sums for new stadiums, while team owners are given the right to the revenues received from the sale of seat licenses and luxury boxes, parking fees, stadium concessions, and even the auctioning of naming rights to a corporation that wishes to display its name on the front of the facility. Sports franchise owners secure such advantageous terms by pointing to the "better deal" that they can get if they move their franchise to another city.

Cincinnati provides an example of a city that struck a quite disadvantageous deal in its effort to retain its major league baseball and football teams. When city officials balked claiming that they lacked moneys for the new facilities that team owners demanded, Hamilton County stepped in and agreed to build two new stadiums, a baseball stadium for the Reds and a football stadium for the Bengals. The stadiums were given valuable riverfront sites downtown, a location that could have been used for entertainment-oriented and mixed-use development. Voters approved an increase in the local sales tax to help finance the project, having been promised that the revenues would also be used for the public schools and for property tax relief. But the larger public benefits did not materialize. When the economy soured and sales tax receipts lagged, the revenues in the special fund were not even sufficient to pay off construction-related debt, never mind provide funds for new school programs and home-owner relief. County services would be cut back, but the terms of the contract insulated the teams from having to accept any cuts. Taxpayers were even obligated to pay for a modern computerized replay system for the football Bengals at a time when cutbacks were being made in the public schools and in public services throughout the county. The one-sided contract even prohibited public officials from raising the tax on admission tickets and parking, a means that the government could have used to help offset some of the burden that was placed on general taxpayers.

The competitive pressures that a city faces are real, and, as the 2008 move of the Seattle Supersonics to Oklahoma City underscores. Over the years, Minnesota voters have shown a great hesitancy to pay for professional sports facilities. But public officials eventually caved in to the threat by team owners to move the baseball Twins to Charlotte. The state agreed to finance a new home for the Twins, Target Field, but without the expensive retractable roof that the team owners had initially also sought.

Mark Rosentraub argues that stadium deals do not always have to be so one-sided. In an earlier book that he wrote, Rosentraub argued that cities were "Major League Losers" (1997) that had given vast subsidies to team owners. But, more recently, Rosentraub reports that cities have learned from their past mistakes and have been able to negotiate more even-handed deals, negotiating agreements that use stadium development as the centerpiece of a larger public–private joint plan for downtown revival. Rosentraub argues that Cleveland, San Diego, and other cities have become "Major League Winners," using stadium-related development to change the city's image and to the "creative class" (Florida 2002) and to outside investors. In the YES selection from his book, Rosentraub reports how San Diego officials forged a well-crafted public–private partnership to leverage the private investments that revitalized the entire section of the city lying beyond the walls of Petco Park, the new field for the baseball Padres. Public authorities paid the bulk of the $450 million costs for stadium construction and for land acquisition and infrastructure improvements in the surrounding area; private investors signed memos of understanding outlining the new investments that they would make that would transform the East Village area.

But not every observer agrees with Rosentraub's analysis. Even the Petco Park project has been the subject of intense criticism (Erie, Kogan, & MacKenzie 2010). Taxpayers not only paid the up-front costs of stadium construction and infrastructure improvements, they wound up having to pay for additional subsidies when the deal was renegotiated as developers confronted unexpected difficulties and the development failed to deliver the stream of revenues that its enthusiasts had predicted. Public authorities built the ballpark, but the $60 million received from the Petco retail chain for putting its name on the stadium went entirely to the ball club, not to the taxpayers. As construction the 26-block Ballpark Village project proceeded, the developers scale backed the acreage devoted to parks development and the number of affordable housing units that were built. Tax increment financing arrangements (discussed in Issue 5 in this volume) also meant that any revenue gain could only be used to pay for project-related improvements; the additional revenues could not be used to help the city's schools or improve public services elsewhere in the city.

Coates and Humphreys, in the NO selection, review studies of stadium development across the country, revealing that major subsidies for sports facilities seldom turn out to be a good investment for cities. The bias of consultant studies that overstate a project's expected revenues and understate projects costs should come as no surprise; the consultants analyzing a possible sports facility or convention center project are often hired by team owners and developers (Sanders 2005). Coates and Humphreys further emphasize the "opportunity costs" of a stadium project that are seldom fully discussed, that is, the economic gain that a city foregoes when it spends money on a stadium project rather than committing its resources to other productive uses. Coates and Humphreys contend that facilities construction is an "inefficient" means of promoting local economic growth.

Major League Winners: Using Sports and Cultural Centers as Tools for Economic Development

. . .

What Can New Facilities Do for a Region?

New sports and cultural facilities do change where people spend money. That change provides community leaders with a strategic opportunity to capitalize on the attraction of large crowds and use the new location for that economic activity to leverage development. Sports facilities, entertainment complexes, and cultural facilities that are part of large-scale redevelopment efforts involving substantial levels of private investment can renew downtown areas, creating new images, and generating real economic development. But, outcomes like that require plans and a substantial investment of private capital.

Many communities in the 1980s and 1990s invested tax money in sports, entertainment, and cultural facilities hoping improvements would follow. It was then again hoped that new buildings would attract scores of young professionals and new companies to their downtown areas. Simply put, too many cities did more "hoping" than they did planning a strategy or establishing partnerships with private capital to achieve success. Some cities, however, did just what was necessary to turn subsidies into shrewd investments. What made these cities different from others and what can community leaders and public officials learn that can turn tax dollars from subsidies to investments?

Subsidies and Strategic Investments: The Difference Defined

In some cities voters and community leaders refused to support higher taxes to pay for sports or performing arts venues without detailed redevelopment strategies or substantial private sector investments. In these communities, voters and leaders were willing to make strategic investments, but wanted to avert anything that appeared to be a subsidy. What is the difference between a strategic investment and a subsidy? A subsidy is when the public sector pays for most or all of the cost of building (and maintaining) a sports, entertainment, and cultural center while team owners, organizations, or other entrepreneurs retain all or most of the revenues from the staging of events *without* any substantial investment from these beneficiaries in redevelopment activities. An investment by the public sector, in contrast, would be defined by: (1) increased tax revenues that *substantially* offset the tax dollars spent, (2) the building of a new or revitalized neighborhood as a result of private investment, or (3) more jobs or higher salaries for residents that produces more tax revenues. To be sure there is risk for the public sector in these investments when private capital is committed. Assuming a level of risk when private investors do the same is far different from subsidizing a facility without requiring similar levels of investment and risk by private sector partners. This book is about changing public subsidies into investments in partnerships where equal and appropriate risks were assumed by the private sector.

Sports, Entertainment, and Culture for Image, Attracting Human Capital, and Economic Development

Why did voters, elected officials, and community leaders continue to raise taxes to subsidize sports and other cultural facilities when the initial warnings were that there would be no economic benefits? The reasons vary, but the themes, in every instance, are quite familiar. When it comes to sports, many argue that large cities or regions without teams did not have a "major league image" and that second-rate images meant businesses and high-skilled workers would choose to locate elsewhere. One St. Louis leader when asked why he favored a subsidy to convince the National Football League's (NFL) Rams to move from California to Missouri replied that too many people thought the city's best days were behind it (because they had lost their football team to Phoenix). The Rams would make St. Louis "big league" again in ways the St. Louis Cardinals (baseball team) or Washington University could not. By extension, smaller cities, in an effort to elevate and distinguish themselves to businesses and create an image of a higher quality of life sought to attract minor league teams, so they too were part of the sports culture of the country. And regardless of size, if a city did not have a venue to attract concerts and host shows and plays, it too risked being seen as too quaint and boring (too few concerts, shows, or other events) to attract and retain the human capital twenty-first century businesses need.

Most cities also looked to new sports facilities and cultural centers as tools to help rebuild deteriorating downtown areas or town squares. Leaders hoped the crowds and excitement of games and shows or other events would convince some people to think about living downtown and attract some of the retail and commercial businesses that were heading to expanding suburban areas. Some cities even hoped an exciting downtown could reduce the exodus of residents and businesses heading to other parts of the country or cities, such as Boston, Chicago, and New York, that seemed to have a diverse set of sports, entertainment, and cultural amenities that contributed to regional economic development. . . .

The Ballpark District: Development, Land Use, and the Best Use of Urban Land

Those opposed to the Ballpark District and the building of the Padres' new home included those who feared San Diego would again be subsidizing sports owners and those who thought the East Village should continue as a location for artists, startup businesses, and some residents. Before any conclusions are reached with regard to the fiscal merits of the project, the issue of the development strategy adopted by San Diego should be addressed.

San Diego lacked a large residential base in its downtown area and city officials were intent on anchoring a new residential flavor to the Ballpark District. Still others impressed with Jane Jacobs' philosophy suggest that the best course of action is to let regeneration occur through the reuse of properties by start-up businesses. To encourage regeneration these advocates prefer transitional areas with live/work space. By the 1990s, the East Village was an area with some artists' studios, shops, and coffee houses. There were also some fledgling business start-ups in the area. Some of the aging warehouses had been converted into live/work lofts giving the area a small residential profile. The ballpark and the Ballpark District dramatically altered the development process. The East Village was an area where these perspectives on regeneration collided. San Diego's political leadership wanted a large-scale development—a sort of new downtown area—replete with new hotels for its convention center and an accelerated timetable for commercial and residential development. Others led by Wayne Buss, an architect, focused on environmentally appropriate development, fought to sustain an alternate vision for the area as a Bohemian neighborhood, a sort of Greenwich Village for San Diego. The city's leadership from both the public and private sectors had another vision. The city wanted a downtown neighborhood anchored by hotels and the ballpark to provide a large number of market-rate homes with an appropriate concentration of houses for families with modest incomes. The city's plan did substantially increase the number of residents in the area and leadership did not believe there was a shortage of space for business start-ups or for artists. Their concern was with ensuring that the downtown area would become a neighborhood with thousands of residents, new hotels, and new commercial space that might also provide employment opportunities. In their view, development had languished and the battle between a Bohemian culture and a modern mixed-use downtown neighborhood ended with billions of dollars in new private development, a ballpark, and several new hotels. . . .

While any assessment of the Ballpark District has to look at the public's investment and taxes generated, it is also important to consider, in a qualitative sense, what was built. "Tens of thousands of condos, townhomes, and apartments have been built as part of hundreds of housing projects. Retail and entertainment projects have injected vitality into downtown. This effort has transformed downtown from its gritty past into the hottest neighborhood around," wrote the *San Diego Union Tribune*. It is now a realistic goal that as many as 50,000 people may live in the downtown area before 2020 and a new large-scale supermarket has even opened. It is also important to note that the Ballpark District has helped to preserve some older facilities. For example, the TR Produce building, built in 1934, has been refitted with two stories of office space and new condominiums:

> Completed in 1934, the TR Produce building is one of about a dozen surviving structures from around 1870 to the early 1930s in the East Village. The old produce building and the new commercial condominium complex within its walls are a novel combination of historic preservation and new construction. Under an agreement struck with a local preservationist group, the old and new buildings barely touch each other. The new structure was built within the walls of the produce building. Standing on a stilt-like structure of steel columns, the new metal-and-glass commercial condominium complex rises above the old brick walls to peer into the ballpark.

There were approximately 12 older industrial buildings that remained in the area. Bruce Coons, executive director of the nonprofit Save Our Heritage Organization, "led the negotiations that set standards for the reuse of 11 historic buildings in the ballpark area with both the developer and city officials." This led to the incorporation of the Western Metal Supply Company building as part of the left field wall in the ballpark. Chris Wahl, vice president and partner of San Diego-based Southwest Strategies LLC, and spokesman for the Downtown Residential Marketing Affiance, probably summarized things most accurately when he noted, "What the ballpark has done is opened up an entirely different part of downtown that didn't previously exist from a residential standpoint. East Village has completely taken off." In 2006, *The New York Times* reviewed the project and noted that the goal of an extraordinary level of development had indeed taken place. At the same time these accomplishments are noted, it is important to note the destruction of the Bohemian character of the East Village and the implementation of a development strategy that dramatically changed its character and image.

The Ballpark District and San Diego: Mutual Risk in a New Model for Public/ Private Partnerships

While many cities had made very extensive commitments to build sports facilities, there were never assurances or commitments from a team's owner to ensure private sector investment. Indianapolis' sports strategy was tied to a large-scale revitalization effort, but there the city essentially was responsible for facilitating additional private sector investments. Neither the Colts' nor the Pacers' ownership made any assurances for any real estate investments. The Pacers' owners, who are developers, did participate in the building and management of Circle Centre Mall, but that effort was not specifically associated with the city's investment in Market Square Arena or the Conseco Fieldhouse. In scores of other cities, even with large public sector investments in facilities, team owners were unwilling to make any commitments or assurances that real estate development would take place.

San Diego, the Padres, and JMI Realty created a new framework for a public/private partnership. Each took risks, but the potential for mutual success also existed. San Diego could realize substantial property tax revenue growth. The credit crisis of 2008/2009 could also lead to the city losing money on its investment. JMI Realty also assumed substantial risk and it too could lose money. While the bargaining position between cities and teams is uneven, the establishment of development goals and linking them to the provision of public subsidies as was done in San Diego can ensure that the public sector's development goals are a priority and, in this instance, achieved. For the first time, a city's participation in the financing and maintaining of a sports facility was directly linked to assurances provided by a team's owner that new real estate development would take place where the public sector deemed it necessary and appropriate. This accomplishment cannot be minimized.

It is also important to note that JMI Real Estate continues to assume a lead role in developing the Ballpark District, as does the CCDC. In that regard, while San Diego must continue to play a development broker role similar to the work Indianapolis must do to ensure its sports investments pay off, San Diego has a specific private sector partner that continues to lead efforts to expand and enhance the District. That work could help ensure that San Diego does indeed realize the revenues needed to repay its debt and secure a positive return on the total investment. The tax revenues earned for the development in the Ballpark District may have been new growth for San Diego, but it must be conceded that had the ballpark not been built in the East Village area, some of the development might have taken place elsewhere in the city. It is also possible that the development could have occurred beyond the city's borders. San Diego's goal was to concentrate development in the East Village area. Undeniably that goal was achieved even though it meant changing the character of the neighborhood.

The analysis of gains and losses for San Diego from the Ballpark District did not focus on other expenses, such as public safety and traffic control. Those costs would not have been any different regardless of the ballpark's location, so it does not seem to be especially relevant to include those costs. Similarly, regardless of where in the region the Padres played their home games, the team would still generate intangible benefits. Those gains might offset the costs of traffic control and public safety.

Finally, it must be recognized that the development of the Ballpark District was a decisive policy choice by San Diego to forego strategies related to Jane Jacobs' ideas and to transform the neighborhood in a relatively short period of time to a largely upscale downtown area. San Diego's leadership chose to infuse public and private money to substantially alter redevelopment patterns. The leadership wanted a new residential and commercial area to create a very different image for the downtown area. Leadership also wanted new hotels for the convention center. San Diego's leadership not only created a new model for other cities to follow when dealing with professional sports teams, but it is also secured its development goals. While it is clear some community organizations would have preferred a different strategy, with more than $1 billion in private sector investment, and more than another $1 billion poised to occur, the Ballpark District would be a welcome addition to the revitalization effort of most cities. Indeed, few mayors or city council members anywhere would not agree with an assessment that San Diego has indeed become a Major League Winner. . . .

**Dennis Coates and
Brad R. Humphreys**

 **NO**

The Stadium Gambit and Local Economic Development

"We play the Star Spangled Banner before every game—you want us to pay taxes too?"

—Bill Veeck

In recent years sports franchises have frequently used their monopoly power to extract rents from state and local governments. Typically, a franchise owner declares an existing facility unsuitable. Perhaps it is too old, or too small, or lacks enough luxury boxes or suites to raise the necessary revenues to field a competitive team. The owner reminds the local government and business community that many other cities would like to have a team, and those cities would also build a new stadium. Cities all over the country, desperate for a professional sports team, gear up to convince the owner to move. Often, the promise of a new stadium and a sweetheart lease convinces the owner to stay, but some franchises move. Regardless of whether the team stays or goes, taxpayers foot the bill for a new stadium, improvements to an existing stadium, or infrastructure needed to make the new stadium or arena as attractive as possible.

The practice of professional sports profiting at the expense of taxpayers is not new. Before the stadium gambit there was the tax shelter dodge in which the purchase and reorganization of a team could generate up to five years of losses, which could be used to offset the new owner's income from other ventures. And there is the common practice of funding stadium construction using private-purpose local bonds because their interest payments are exempt from federal income taxation and they therefore carry a lower interest rate. The net effect is that the federal government subsidizes construction of the stadiums and arenas built by state and local governments for professional sports franchises. Indeed, closing the loophole in the law that allowed this subsidy has simply been replaced by explicit state and local funding of stadiums that can be turned over rent free to franchises.

The recent spate of sweetheart stadium and arena deals is only the latest manifestation of owners of professional sports franchises getting richer at the public's expense. While not entirely new, this phenomenon has become front-page news across the country in recent years. Combined with the "build

From *Regulation,* vol. 23, no. 2, Summer 2000, pp. 15–20. Copyright © 2000 by Cato Institute. Reprinted by permission via Copyright Clearance Center.

it and they will come" attitude of many city governments, the stadium gambit has led to a marked increase in new stadium and arena construction, franchise relocations, and negotiations between teams and local governments.

Despite the beliefs of local officials and their hired consultants about the economic benefits of publicly subsidized stadium construction, the consensus of academic economists has been that such policies do not raise incomes. The results that we describe in this article are even more pessimistic. Subsidies of sports facilities may actually reduce the incomes of the alleged beneficiaries.

Trends in Stadium Ownership and Franchise Values

Public ownership of stadiums has increased over time. In 1950, the National Basketball Association (NBA) and the National Football League (NFL) had substantial public ownership of stadiums or arenas—46 percent and 36 percent, respectively. Baseball's American League had 12 percent public ownership, whereas its National League and the National Hockey League had no publicly owned stadiums. By 1991, a minimum of 65 percent of facilities in any professional sports league were publicly owned. The high was 93 percent public ownership in the NFL. The median percentage of public ownership of stadiums and arenas was 75 percent.

During the time of increased public participation in stadium ownership, franchise values have also increased dramatically. In their book *Pay Dirt: The Business of Professional Team Sports,* James P. Quirk and Rodney D. Fort report that for teams sold in the 1970s and sold again during the 1980s franchise values rose at an annual rate of 12.5 percent in baseball, 12.3 percent in basketball, and 11.5 percent in football. For teams sold twice during the 1980s, the rates of increase were 23.5, 50.2, and 19.2 percent, respectively.

The increase in the value of franchises has shown no sign of slowing in the 1990s. For example, the franchise fees charged for expansion teams in the 1990s are large and rising rapidly. In 1992 the Colorado Rockies and Florida Marlins paid $95 million in expansion fees to join major league baseball. In 1997, the Arizona Diamondbacks and Tampa Bay Devil Rays paid $130 million. That is about a 37 percent increase in five years, or about 7.4 percent per year. To (re-) join the NFL, the Cleveland Browns paid an expansion fee of $530 million in 1998; the newly awarded franchise in Houston agreed to a $700 million fee, just a 32 percent increase in one year. But the most extreme case of expansion price inflation occurred in the NBA. The fee paid for expansion by the franchises in Minneapolis and Orlando in 1989 was $32.5 million; for Toronto and Vancouver, which joined the league in 1995, the fee was $125 million. That works out to about a 285 percent increase in just six years, or about 47 percent per year.

The owners of franchises in monopoly professional sports leagues have used the real or implied threat of moving to another city to persuade state and local decision-makers and politicians to provide them with lavish new stadiums and arenas at little or no cost. The owners appear to have profited handsomely from this stadium gambit, as suggested by the triple-digit increases in franchise values. In return, taxpayers receive nonpecuniary benefits in the form of increased civic pride and image, as well as other unmeasured consumption benefits associated with living in a city with professional sports teams. Taxpayers have also been told that new teams, stadiums, and arenas create jobs and raise tax revenues and income in their city.

Do Professional Sports Produce Economic Benefits?

What justification exists for the government subsidy of professional sports? The proponents of new stadiums and franchises are always quick to point out the economic benefits of the proposed facilities and teams. Cities throughout the country have struggled to attract or keep professional sports teams in recent years, and the idea that a team brings with it large economic gains invariably arises. Part of this process is the commissioning of economic impact studies that purport to show just how much benefit the city or region will reap.

More than 20 years ago, proponents of the half-billion-dollar Skydome in Toronto claimed that this facility would generate $450 million in Canadian dollars in the first year of operation and create 17,000 jobs in the Toronto area. Half a decade ago, prospective NFL team owners in Jacksonville, Florida, claimed that a new NFL franchise would generate $340 million in new income in the city and create 3,000 jobs. In a recent case, the Baltimore *Sun* reported in April of 1999 that a new study supported tearing down the existing 36-year-old Baltimore Arena and replacing it with a new $200 million dollar facility. This investment, the study claims, will raise city taxes by $3.8 million and state taxes by $6.3 million. In addition, the facility could generate up to $100 million in new earnings for the citizens of the city of Baltimore.

Contrast these recent figures with information from the 1994 edition of the County and City Data Book. In 1990, the last year for which city and state tax collections are reported, Maryland and Baltimore collected $3.4 billion and $528 million in taxes, respectively. For the city, the tax gain from the replacement arena is, if the figures are correct, only about 0.7 percent of 1990 tax collections. For the state, the new tax collections are less than two-tenths of a percent of 1990 tax collections. Earnings in Maryland were $68 billion and personal income in Baltimore was $13.9 billion. Projected earnings from the arena are about 0.15 percent of state earnings for 1990 and about 0.72 percent of Baltimore's total personal income. Although the absolute numbers seem large and impressive, they are small compared with the existing tax revenues and local economy, even if one grants that the proponents' estimates are correct.

The Flaws in Advocacy Studies

There are strong reasons to doubt the accuracy of the estimated benefits claimed by economic impact studies. These impact studies rely upon input-output models of the local or regional economies into which the team and its new stadium will be placed and estimate the economic impact prospectively. These studies ask the question: what will happen if a new franchise and stadium enter this community? The results of these studies invariably reflect the desires of those who commission them, and advocates of stadiums and franchises typically produce impact studies that find large economic impacts, translated as benefits, from building a stadium or enticing a team to enter the city.

The Mythical Multiplier

The methodology used by impact studies has been criticized on a variety of grounds. All impact studies use multipliers to estimate the effect of each dollar spent directly on sports on the wider local economy. Critics argue that at best the multipliers used in prospective impact studies overstate the contribution that professional sports make to an area's economy because they fail to differentiate between net and gross spending and the effects of taxes. In computing the benefits of the investment in a stadium, the appropriate focus is on net benefits, that is, on benefits that would not have occurred in the absence of the stadium. Impact studies rarely consider this issue. One could think of this concern as the substitution effect. Specifically, because of sport- and stadium-related activities, other spending declines as people substitute spending on one for spending on the other. If the stadium simply displaces dollar-for-dollar spending that would have occurred otherwise, then there are no net benefits generated. To consider the spending on stadium- and sport-related activities as all benefits is, therefore, to widely overstate the value of the investment. A key issue for getting the right sense of the value of the stadium investment is, consequently, how much of stadium-related spending substitutes for otherwise intended spending and how much is net gain in spending.

An important question related to the size of these substitution effects, and on the appropriate size of sports spending multipliers, is the size of the relevant geographic area. A stadium or arena will have more added effects on a very narrowly defined community than on a largely encompassing community. The reason for this is that the more narrowly the host community is defined, the more of the spending at the stadium and the nearby restaurants, bars, and hotels will come from outside the community. However, that spending will come largely at the expense of the home communities of the fans that travel into the stadium from outlying areas. The substitution effect for the broadly defined area is quite large, but for the narrowly defined stadium community it is much smaller. What this points out is that stadiums and sports teams may be a tool for redistributing income in which the people from suburbs subsidize businesses in the city.

Efficiency Is Irrelevant

Impact studies typically do not address alternative uses of public funds. Indeed, politicians often seem to think that the means of financing the stadium generates free resources that have no alternative uses whatsoever. For example, when the state of Maryland discussed plans to lure the Cleveland Browns to Baltimore, they made clear that part of the funding for the construction of a new stadium would come from the state lottery. In state senate hearings on the issue, it was pointed out that lottery funds were essentially constant in recent years and that they were already dedicated, at least in part, to paying off the bonds issued to finance Oriole Park at Camden Yards. If lottery funds did not grow, then to add the financing of the football stadium would require that the state dip into general tax revenues either to pay interest on the baseball stadium-related bonds or to spend on the other public services supported out of lottery revenues. Alternatively, the state could choose to stop supporting other public services at all. The senators dismissed this concern out of hand. As the example makes clear, the revenues have opportunity costs.

But the issue is more than simply that there are alternative uses of the taxes used to pay for the stadium. The fundamental issue is that a stadium is a public investment in real capital. As such, the rules for sensible public investment apply to stadium finance as much as they apply to public provision of highways, schools, and airports. Specifically, the key is comparing the return on the investment in the stadium with the return on the same dollar investment in any alternative public use, including tax reduction. Efficient use of public resources requires that any given funds go into the uses that provide the highest return. This, of course, makes estimation of the return on the stadium and other investments very important. But measurement of these returns is complicated by the fact that there are substantial services of the stadium and sports franchises that do not pass through the marketplace.

Let Them Eat Civic Pride

Stadium and team advocates, for example, raise the issue of civic pride and the image of cities. According to this logic, only cities with professional sports teams are truly world class. The gain in civic pride is, of course, very difficult to measure. The benefits that accrue to individuals who never or rarely attend games at the stadium but who derive enjoyment from following the team in the newspaper or via the radio and television broadcasts are also difficult to measure. Such benefits are the result of an externality, a good or service provided by one individual or group that provides benefits to other individuals or groups and for which the latter provide no compensation to the former. The existence of these external benefits could justify some public participation in the provision of stadiums and sports franchises.

The Sordid Truth about Economic Impact

In stark contrast to the results claimed by most prospective economic impact studies commissioned by teams or stadium advocates, the consensus in the academic literature has been that the overall sports environment has no measurable effect on the level of real income in metropolitan areas. Our own research suggests that professional sports may be a drain on local economies rather than an engine of economic growth.

Many Sports, Many Cities

The difference between the impact studies commissioned by teams or cities and the academic literature is more than simply prospective versus retrospective methodology. Academic studies consider a large number of metropolitan areas with major league professional sports over a long period of time and examine other factors that are likely to predict aggregate economic activity as well as a broadly conceived view of the sports environment. In other words, these studies look specifically for the net effect of the sports environment on the economic vitality of metropolitan areas.

Our research examines all 37 U.S. cities that had one or more professional football, basketball, or baseball franchises at some point during the 1969–1996 period. This represents the universe of cities with such professional sports franchises during this period. The sample contains a wide variety of franchise moves and new stadium and arena construction. Twenty-three percent of these metropolitan areas attracted a basketball franchise, 10 percent attracted a football franchise, and 7 percent attracted a baseball franchise; 2.5 percent built a new baseball stadium, 10 percent built a football stadium, 10 percent built a new combined football and baseball stadium, and 21 percent built a new basketball arena.

Quantifying the Sports Environment

Because it is not clear whether pro-stadium studies claim that the stadium will raise the level or the growth rate of income, we focus on identifying factors that affected either the level or growth of income per person. Although attracting a new football team or building a new basketball arena might have had some effect on these variables, other factors certainly played an important role. Our approach is to quantify the sports environment, including the presence of franchises, franchise entry and departure, stadium construction and renovation, the location of new stadiums and arenas, and the "novelty" effect of a new stadium or arena for professional football, basketball, and baseball. We then estimate econometric models of the determination of the level or growth rate of income in metropolitan areas and include the variables reflecting the sports environment.

We take two different approaches to estimating the models. First, taking advantage of the time-series cross-sectional nature of our data, we are able to control for city-specific factors that affect income or income growth, including trend growth, the decline of rust-belt cities and booms in sun-belt cities, and the effect of the business cycle. The use of city-specific effects, and these other variables, means that we are able to make sure that the estimated effects of the sports environment variables are not contaminated with other historical or location-specific influences on the economic vitality of the cities.

Second, we use an event study approach to analyze the effect of professional sports on local economies. This method uses the sports environment variables as a means of explaining why a particular city differs from the average city. This technique is widely used to examine the effects of changes in laws or regulations on the market value of firms in the finance and regulation literature. This approach can also be used to examine the impact of professional sports on local economies. In this approach, one regresses the level of income in each city on the average level of income across all the cities and a set of dummy variables reflecting changes in the sports environment. If the sports environment variables are statistically significant, the difference between that city and the average of all cities is not purely random but is a function of its different sports environment. The main drawback to this approach is that city-specific variables cannot be used. That is why we place more reliance on the results of the first approach described above. But the event study is a viable alternative to the other econometric models we estimate, and the results of the event study approach serve as a check on the robustness of our other results.

Results

Our results indicate:

- The professional sports environment in the 37 metropolitan areas in our sample had no measurable impact on the *growth rate* of real per capita income in those areas.
- The professional sports environment has a statistically significant impact on the *level* of real per capita income in our sample of metropolitan areas, and the overall impact is *negative*.

The presence of professional sports teams, on average, reduces the level of real per capita income in metropolitan areas. This result differs from much of the existing literature, which generally has found no impact at all. However, we used a broader and longer panel of data and a richer set of variables reflecting the sports environment than previous studies.

Because we developed a wide variety of measures of the sports environment in metropolitan areas, many of the individual elements have a positive impact that is offset by another element that carries a negative impact. For example, the arrival of a new basketball franchise in a metropolitan area increases real per capita income by about $67. But building a new arena for that basketball team reduces real per capita income by almost $73 in each of the 10 years following the construction of the arena, leading to a net loss of about $6 per person. Similarly, in cities that have baseball franchises, the net effect of an existing baseball team playing in a 37,000-seat baseball-only stadium (the average capacity of the baseball stadiums in our sample) is a $10 reduction of real per capita income.

The results from the event study regressions are similar: sports environment variables are correlated with negative deviation from the average level of per capita income. However, the size of the estimated negative effect of the sports environment on the level of real per capita income generated by the event study regressions is considerably larger than the size of the estimated impact from the other reduced-form econometric models. The impact of an existing baseball franchise playing in a stadium of average size is a reduction in real per capita income of over $850 per year below the average level of income across the cities in our sample, based on the event study estimates. We tend to put more trust in the smaller estimated impact based on the reduced-form econometric models of income determination than in the larger impact implied by the event study regressions because the exclusion of city-specific trends and other factors from the event study regressions may force the average income variable to carry too much of the explanatory weight in these regressions.

How Sports Subsidies Reduce Income

If, as prospective team owners, developers, and politicians would have us believe, professional sports can be an important engine of economic growth, how can our estimates be correct? How can the professional sports environment reduce the level of real per capita income in a metropolitan area? A recently published volume edited by Roger Noll and Andrew Zimbalist (*Sports, Jobs, and Taxes*) contains a number of essays that examine in detail the relationship between professional sports and local economies. The essays in this volume suggest a number of possible answers to these questions, which fall into several broad categories.

Substitution in Public Spending

Public funds are often used to subsidize professional sports teams and the stadiums or arenas they play in. These public funds have alternative uses, such as maintaining local infrastructure; increasing the quality or provision of public health, safety, or education; and attracting new businesses to the area. The deterioration of local public capital or services could diminish the ability of the local economy to produce other non-sports-related goods and services, which in turn would reduce local income.

Substitution in Private Spending

Households face budget constraints; they must meet their unlimited wants with a limited amount of income. The arrival of a professional sports team in a city provides households with a new entertainment option. Households that choose to attend games will spend less on other things, perhaps going out to dinner, bowling, or the movies. If the impact of each dollar spent on these forgone alternatives has a larger effect on the local economy than the impact of each dollar spent on professional sporting events, the local economy will contract and income will be lower. Why would the impact of each dollar spent going to a professional basketball game be smaller than the impact of each dollar spent on bowling? This could easily occur if the revenue generated by the basketball team and arena, which in turn becomes the income made by the players and team owners, escapes the flow of transactions that make up the local economy to a greater extent than the income made by the owners and employees of the bowling alley or movie theater.

Compensating Differentials in Income

Perhaps professional sports do not directly reduce the level of real per capita income in a metropolitan area. Instead, our results reflect a "compensating differential" related to the presence of professional sports in some cities. Residents of cities with professional sports teams derive nonpecuniary benefits from the teams' presence and, because of those nonpecuniary benefits, are willing to accept lower income in return for living in these cities, other things being equal. This rationale implies that a recent college graduate might be willing to take a lower-paying job in a city with a professional sports franchise instead of a slightly higher-paying job in a city that has no professional sports franchises. The determining factor in the choice is whether the value of those nonpecuniary benefits is high enough. In other words, we may observe lower per capita income in cities with a professional baseball franchise because residents of those cities are willing to accept lower wages or salaries to have local access to a baseball franchise.

Negative Effects on Productivity

Productivity, broadly defined as the amount of output that a worker with a given amount of capital, experience, and education can produce, is an important determinant of income and explains much of the observed difference in per capita income across countries. The factors that affect the productivity of workers are notoriously difficult to pin down precisely, but small differences in productivity can lead to large differences in per capita income when those differences persist over time. Workers in cities with professional sports teams may spend more work time discussing the outcome of last night's game, organizing an office pool, or other similar activities than workers in cities without professional sports teams. These differences could, over a period of many years, lead to differences in income per capita.

Conclusions

The policy implications of our results are no different from those of the previous studies that found no relationship between the professional sports environment and local economies. Still, they bear repeating. The evidence suggests that attracting a professional sports franchise to a city and building that franchise a new stadium or arena will have no effect on the growth rate of real per capita income and may reduce the level of real per capita income in that city. Yet government decisionmakers and politicians continue to try to attract professional sports franchises to cities, or use public funds to construct elaborate new facilities in order to keep existing franchises from moving. According to public finance theory, the decisionmakers who attempt to attract a new franchise or build a new stadium or arena must value the total consumption benefits, including all nonpecuniary benefits, more than the total costs, including the opportunity costs. The total consumption benefits cannot be directly measured because of the nonpecuniary component of those benefits; in order for these policies to make sense, the total value of the consumption benefits associated with these policies must be larger than was previously imagined. However, regardless of the size of the nonpecuniary benefits, one thing is clear from the evidence on professional sports franchises: owners are reaping substantial benefits in the value of their teams because they are so skilled at the stadium gambit.

EXPLORING THE ISSUE

Are Public Subsidies for Sports Stadiums a Good Investment by Cities?

Critical Thinking and Reflection

1. Are subsidies for stadium construction little more than "municipal socialism" for the rich, as working- and middle-class taxpayers are made to pay for new profit-making projects desired by multimillionaire and billionaire team owners?
2. When should a city subsidize a new sports arena and when shouldn't it?
3. Can you identify different ways by which a city can come up with the funds to provide subsidies for the construction of sports facilities? Which types of taxes, fees, and revenue sources can be viewed as more fair than others when it comes to paying for the costs of a new stadium?
4. Why are team owners often so unwilling to accept balanced or two-sided agreements?

Is There Common Ground?

Public investment in a new sports facility is neither always good nor always bad. As Rosentraub has argued, much depends on the "context," the exact needs of the city and the team, the exact terms of the deal that is struck between public officials and team owners, and the exact role that a stadium will play as part of a larger strategic plan for the revitalization of a declining section of the community. Hopefully, cities will not willy-nilly engage in the folly of chasing sports franchises, building new stadiums in the hope of attracting an occupant, and of offering generous benefits to team owners without assuring the delivery of private investment and substantial public benefits in return.

Are there better as opposed to worse ways of funding new sports facilities? First of all, wherever possible, revenues for stadium construction should be drawn from a greater geographical area than just the city itself. City-subsidized sports facilities disproportionately burden the poor and working class who live in a central city. If a new sports facility will bring benefits to, and serve fans living in, an entire region, then it is unfair to make city residents bear the costs of stadium construction. Subsidies and public investment, where necessary, should be provided by the county or, better yet, by a regional authority and not by the city itself.

Second, to the extent possible, property taxes and sales taxes should be avoided as a means of funding stadium projects. Such taxes are regressive, with low-income and working-class residents (and small business owners, as well) having to pay disproportionately for a sports facility that they will seldom, if ever, use, and from which they receive almost no direct benefit. Instead, the "benefit principle" offers the possibility of fairer alternatives when it comes to financing stadium development: those persons and businesses that receive the greatest benefit from a project should bear the greatest burdens in paying for the project. Instead of paying off stadium bonds out of a municipality's general fund that is supported by taxes levied citywide, a governing authority can impose a ticket tax or additional parking fees on fans who attend stadium events. A hotel room tax and restaurant or entertainment tax could be imposed on enterprises that benefit financially from a new sports facility, especially when they are imposed on establishments located in the immediate vicinity of the arena. How about considering a tax on beer and drinks sold in the vicinity of a ballpark before and after a game?

Finally, wise public investment in sports facilities requires agreements where the obligations are two-sided, where team owners as well as the taxpayer share the burden if costs rise and if attendance and revenues do not pour in as expected. Good deals will also bind private partners to their proposed investments in a project, rather than having only public authorities legally bound to live up to the commitments spelled out in a memo of understanding. Of course, team owners and corporate officials will be quite reluctant to sign agreements that limit their flexibility to respond to changing business conditions.

Additional Resources

Delaney, Kevin J. (2003). *Public Dollars, Private Stadiums: The Battle over Building Sports Stadiums*. Piscataway, NJ: Rutgers University Press.

Erie, Steven P., Vladimir Kogan, & Scott A. MacKenzie. (2010). "'Redevelopment, San Diego Style': The Limits of Public–Private Partnerships," *Urban Affairs Review,* 45, no. 5: 644–678.

Florida, Richard. (2002). *The Rise of the Creative Class*. New York: Basic Books.

Rosentraub, Mark S. (1997). *Major League Losers: The Real Cost of Sports and Who's Paying for It*. New York: Basic Books.

Sanders, Heywood. (2005). "Space Available: The Realities of Convention Centers as Economic Development Strategies." A policy brief of the Brookings Institution Metropolitan Policy Program, Washington, DC. Available at: www.brookings.edu/metro/pubs/20050117_conventioncenters.pdf.

Spirou, Costas, & Larry Bennett. (2003). *It's Hardly Sportin': Stadiums, Neighborhoods, and the New Chicago*. DeKalb: Northern Illinois University Press.

Swindell, David, & Mark S. Rosentraub. (1998). "Who Benefits from the Presence of Professional Sports Teams? The Implications for Public Funding of Stadiums and Arenas," *Public Administration Review,* 58, no. 1: 11–20.

Weiner, Jay. (2000). *Stadium Games: Fifty Years of Big League Greed and Bush League Boondoggles*. Minneapolis: University of Minnesota Press.

Internet References

Field of Schemes

This is a large collection of newspaper articles and research reports that points to the cost overruns, economic inefficiency, extravagance, and public bailouts of sports stadium and convention center projects that seldom deliver the full public benefits that their backers had promised. The site is the work of Neil deMause, who (with Joanna Cagan) is the author of *Field of Schemes: How the Great Stadium Swindle Turns Public Money into Private Profit* (2002).

www.fieldofschemes.com

Reason Foundation

Committed to a free society and libertarian principles, the Reason Foundation has been highly critical of taxpayer subsidies for stadium development.

http://reason.org

ISSUE 5

Should Cities Rely on Tax Increment Financing (TIF) as a Primary Tool in Their Efforts to Promote Local Economic Development?

YES: Lori Healey and John F. McCormick, from "Urban Revitalization and Tax Increment Financing in Chicago," *Government Finance Review* (December 1999)

NO: Daniel McGraw, from "Giving Away the Store to Get a Store: Tax Increment Financing Is No Bargain for Taxpayers," *Reason* (January 2006)

Learning Outcomes

After reading this issue, you should be able to:

- Explain how a TIF district is created and how tax increment financing works.
- Define "base" and "increment" in property valuations in TIF districts.
- Explain why cities across the country have created TIF districts to support new economic development.
- Explain the numerous advantages that TIFs offer local governments in the pursuit of new industry and job creation.
- Detail the criticisms that are made of TIFs.
- Explain why public school officials often oppose TIF creation.

ISSUE SUMMARY

YES: Lori Healey, former Chicago Commissioner for Planning and Development and later chief of staff to Mayor Richard M. Daley, and John F. McCormick, financial manager in city's Department of Finance helped arrange many of the initial tax increment financing (TIF) projects in Chicago. These authors argue that the TIF program has been an enormous success, attracting billions of dollars in new investment to Chicago and promoting the rejuvenation of distressed sections of the city.

NO: Dan McGraw, a freelance writer living in Texas, worries that TIFs have become little more than a standard "handout" given to big and profitable businesses when such assistance is not justified. TIFs diminish the revenues available for public services, increasing the tax burden placed on homeowners and small businesses in a city.

Cities exist in a competitive environment. They must seek to attract businesses that have a choice of where to locate their offices and production facilities.

Quite commonly, cities offer large businesses *tax abatements,* reducing, for a specified period of years, the taxes and fees that the city would normally collect. Often, the abatements are given up to the maximum that state law allows.

Tax abatements, of course, suffer from an obvious problem; when taxes on one firm are reduced, a city must either raise the taxes on residents and other businesses in the city or reduce the levels of services provided its citizens. The long-term costs of tax abatements are not always understood; when a city awards a tax abatement to one business, other businesses will demand similar favorable treatment. Even businesses that have been in a city for a long number of years will demand new tax concessions.

Cities also pursue a strategy of *infrastructure improvements,* providing the upgraded roads, sewers, street lighting, water systems, and other physical supports that business expansion may require. Some cities also promise to help pay for *human infrastructure* improvements, the training programs that will provide a business with the skilled workforce it must have in order to consider relocating to the city.

The problem is that all of these strategies cost money in an age where fiscally strapped cities have little money to spare. As a consequence, cities have turned to *tax increment financing* (TIF), a development tool that seems to promise that new economic projects will pay for themselves without municipal officials having to impose new taxes on city residents.

Tax increment financing allows a city to the infrastructure improvements needed to attract businesses and then use the revenues received from that new development to pay off the costs that the city incurred. A city may issue bonds to borrow money for the road, sewer, water system, and other infrastructure improvements to attract businesses to a troubled part of a city. Business expansion increases the value of property subject to city taxation. Taxes on this "increment" or gain in property values is then used to repay the money that the city borrowed; or it can be used to pay for further zone improvements. The taxes gained from the increased property values in the zone do not go to a city's general fund to help pay for social services and projects elsewhere in the city; TIF revenues can only be used for projects within the TIF district.

Their promise of self-finance has made TIFs extremely popular with local development officials. Forty-nine of the 50 states (Arizona is the exception) and the District of Columbia authorize TIFs. Thousands of TIFs exist nationwide. California has 400 or so TIF districts; Illinois has 450 (Weber and Goddeeris 2007).

Just how does a TIF work? A city designates a targeted area, such as a run-down industrial area or a blighted portion of the downtown, in which it seeks to promote new development. Dallas created a 9.5-mile-long TIF district in the Skillman corridor, northeast of the downtown, to promote commercial renewal around the newly opened DART light-rail train stations. Indianapolis established a massive downtown TIF district, centered on the new Lucas Oil football stadium, to capture revenues that it could use to pay for sports facilities, a skywalk, and other improvements aimed at attracting tourism.

When a TIF is established, the value of the property that lies inside the district is "frozen." This constitutes the existing "base" of property valuation, and industrial and commercial owners pay taxes on this base just as they have in previous years. Any new private investment in the district above the established base or "baseline"—that is, the gains in property value due business expansion in the district—constitutes the "increment." The property taxes yielded from the increment do not go to the general public treasury. Instead, these revenues gained are used to pay for commercially related improvements in the district. Business owners know that the additional taxes they pay will be plowed back into new infrastructure and other business-related improvements.

Cities argue a TIF increases city revenues, as TIF creation serves to attract new property investment and job creation. When the authorized life of the TIF expires, the city can use and the taxes received from the new investment to support schools and other public services throughout the city.

TIFs are an amazing development tool; but they also have critics. Over the life of a TIF, business expansion does not yield revenues for a city's "general fund," revenues that governments can use to support projects outside the TIF district. The creation of a TIF district can even diminish the revenues available for public schools and other public services. When a TIF is created, schools may lose the revenues they would have received from development that would have taken place even in the absence of TIF creation. In effect, a TIF denies schools the additional revenues that they would have received from normal business growth and expansion. Not too surprisingly, school leaders are often among the most vocal opponents of TIF creation.

Numerous economists question whether TIFS really add to the regional or the national economy. Instead, TIFs may simply serve to shift the location of new development in a zero-sum game. One community may use a TIF to attract a new shopping mall that precipitates store closings in neighboring communities.

Critics also object that important TIF decisions lack transparency. An independent TIF board decides how to spend TIF funds. The general public has little knowledge and control over the actions of such a "shadow government" of business leaders and their political allies.

Chicago has been called "the town that loves to TIF" (Leher 1999). In the YES article, Lori Healey and John McCormick, city officials who worked for many years on TIF projects in Chicago, describe how tax increment financing helped the city to lure new businesses, contributing to the revitalization of a number of areas that had suffered long-term decline. They describe how TIFs can be used to promote new investment in housing and neighborhood shopping centers as well as to spark the revival of a city's aging central business district.

The article, written during the early years of Chicago's love affair with TIFs, actually understates the extent of TIF-backed renewal in the city. As of 2011, Chicago had 165 active TIF districts. The city claimed that over the life of the program, tax increment financing resulted in $7 billion in new private investments. Even though such claims are likely to be inflated, a substantial private investment would have occurred even without TIF creation, the value of the investment and the number of jobs that can legitimately be attributed to TIFs is still quite impressive.

But not everyone sees tax increment financing has been as being beneficial to Chicago and its people. Ben Joravsky, reporting for the city's alternative newspaper, *The Chicago Reader,* has written a number of investigatory pieces pointing to how TIF districts have "gobbled up" extensive sums of money, forcing the city to hike taxes and various fees in order to support service provision. In a city like Chicago, TIF districts also tend to be created in areas that politically connected businesses find attractive; more needy neighborhoods are largely bypassed.

In recent years, Chicago Mayor Rahm Emanuel and a number of aldermanic candidates won office in campaigns that criticized TIFs for having siphoned off funds that could have aided the schools and neighborhood projects. Some candidates called for a moratorium on TIF creation, questioning the wisdom of a mechanism that diverted money from community projects in order to support business expansion by automobile dealerships and a neighborhood Starbucks.

In the NO reading, Daniel McGraw, a Texas-based writer, argues that TIF creation has strayed from its original purpose of renewing blighted areas. Instead, he reports giant retailers like Cabela's and the developers of high-end housing are the primary financial beneficiaries as they play one city off against the other in order to get favorable TIF creation.

YES

Lori Healey and
John F. McCormick

Urban Revitalization and Tax Increment Financing in Chicago

Throughout the late 1800s and early 1900s, the Chicago Stockyards provided jobs for thousands of residents and fueled the local economy, earning the city the nickname "Hog Butcher to the World." But as traditional meat-packing and butchering industries declined rapidly in the late 20th century, the South Side's Stockyards closed production in 1980, leaving vast parcels of vacant and blighted land and buildings. At the time, few federal resources were available to rebuild the area's infrastructure; the soil was unstable, many roads were privately owned and unusable, and the land was divided into small lots. These factors made large-scale redevelopment for modern industries impossible.

Through a series of industrial and commercial tax increment financing (TIF) districts, the city has successfully brought this once-thriving industrial center back to life. TIFs provided the funding mechanism to clean up the stockyards and prepare land for redevelopment. The Stockyards Industrial Park is now home to modern industrial facilities for companies like Culinary Foods, Inc., Luster Products, and OSI Industries, while a new retail center has brought stores and services to a once-underserved area. In this age of dwindled state and federal funding, the Chicago Stockyards have become a national model for urban economic development.

Tax Increment Financing

Tax increment financing is a technique for financing a capital project from the stream of revenue generated by the project. It can be an important community development tool for attracting the development that will generate new taxes.

Federal economic development money available in 1997 was down 56 percent from its 1980 level, and what little funding is available usually is offered on a short-term annual basis, which makes it too unreliable to support multi-year revitalization and development programs. In response to these cutbacks, many areas began using TIF. Another advantage of using TIF over federal economic development money is that it allows for more project flexibility and local control.

From *Government Finance Review*, December 1999, pp. 27–30. Copyright © 1999 by Government Finance Officers Association. Reprinted by permission.

TIF was first enacted in Illinois in 1977 after the drastic reduction of state and federal economic development funds. For an area to be eligible for TIF in Illinois, the structures in it must have some of the following problems:

- age;
- obsolescence;
- illegal use of individual structures that are below minimum code standards;
- excessive vacancies;
- overcrowding of facilities;
- lack of ventilation, light, and/or sanitary facilities;
- inadequate utilities;
- excessive land coverage;
- deleterious land use or layout;
- lack of physical maintenance;
- lack of community planning; or
- dilapidation or deterioration.

Even though the TIF law was established in 1977 in Illinois, Chicago approached the program cautiously and did not create its first TIF district until 1984. When Mayor Richard M. Daley took office in 1989, there were only 12 TIF districts in the city. Many of them were not well monitored, and as a result, had not been generating much in terms of private investment. Mayor Daley's administration embraced TIF as a tool for reaching Chicago's economic development goals. From 1990 to 1997, the city adopted 32 more TIF districts. By the end of 1999, there will be more than 75 TIFs in Chicago.

In terms of sheer scope and scale, Chicago's use of TIF to retain and attract industry is unprecedented in urban America. Through TIF, Chicago has become one of the strongest industrial markets in the country.

TIF in Chicago

The City of Chicago works with local aldermen, community groups, businesses, and developers to identify areas not living up to their potential. The city then examines the land to determine if it is eligible to become a TIF district. If it qualifies, the city creates a TIF redevelopment plan to revitalize the neighborhood and public hearings are held to provide input. Once the redevelopment plan is completed, the City Council formally votes on the creation of the TIF district.

When the City creates a TIF district, the amount of tax revenue the area currently generates is set as a baseline that will serve as the amount local governmental taxing bodies will receive from that area for the life of the TIF, which is 23 years. As vacant and dilapidated properties are developed, with TIF assistance, the value and tax revenue from those properties increases. The "increment" above the baseline is then captured and used solely for improvements and redevelopment activities in the TIF district. After the TIF expires, or when the city's investments are repaid, all property tax revenues are again shared by all of the local taxing bodies.

Exhibit 1

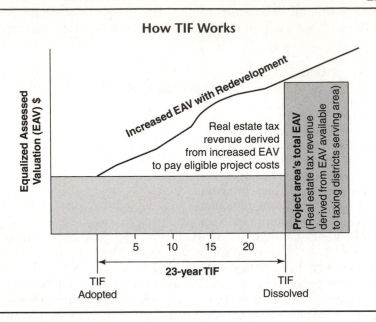

How TIF Works

Financing

The City of Chicago initially made a policy decision not to issue general obligation bonds to directly fund projects in its TIF districts. Other than four TIF Bonds issued in 1987 for commercial shopping centers that were supported by real estate tax increment, city sales tax, and state sales tax (the State of Illinois discontinued the sales tax TIF program after one year), the city was limited to offering "pay-as-you-go" TIF funding on a yearly basis for individual projects.

Because individual companies and developers often need up-front funding to make their deal complete, other initiatives needed to be taken to keep Chicago competitive with other cities and states in attracting development.

In 1992, the city allocated approximately $25 million from its larger, citywide general obligation bond issue for economic development funding. Funds from this allocation allowed the city to attract and retain large industrial companies like Culinary Foods, Luster Products, Eli's Cheesecake, National Wine Service, and Farley Candy. After completion of these projects—with their proven real estate tax increment numbers—TIF bonds were issued in the Stockyards, Reed-Dunning, and Sanitary and Ship Canal TIF districts. Proceeds from these bonds then were used to repay the funds originally allocated from the 1992 general obligation bond.

Two of Chicago's "mature" TIFs—the Near South and Central Loop TIFs—were deemed qualified for AAA-rated insurance through AMBAC. The Lincoln-Belmont-Ashland TIF was insured by ACA. The city will look to the municipal bond insurance companies in the future, realizing that the underwriters have higher requirements for the insurance (larger size, greater diversification, proven numbers, and overall higher increment coverage), rather than unenhanced TIF bonds.

The use of other forms of up-front funding, such as CD Float Loans and developer notes, provide time for projects to mature and become "bondable" (as they did in the North Side's Lincoln-Belmont-Ashland and Irving Cicero TIFs). Developer Revenue Notes place the project-completion risk upon the developer, his or her equity partners, and lenders. Here, developers enter into redevelopment agreements, complete the project, pay for eligible costs, and are then pledged incremental revenues occurring over time as a result of their project.

The developer, as holder of the securities and source of the incremental revenue stream, eliminates default risk. Costs of issuance expenses are minimal, and generally the need for a debt service reserve and capitalized interest are eliminated. Higher interest rates (equal to the developer's borrowing costs) are mitigated by the municipality's ability to call and refund these securities at any time in the future. This is especially valuable when the city wishes to issue a Tax Increment Bond for the entire district at a lower interest rate, refunding one or more high interest developer notes.

The city has been proactive in using TIF to assist financing low- and moderate-income housing revenue bonds. While Chicago's TIF funding has mainly been limited to the 30 percent interest rate write-down provided by the state TIF statutes, new legislation raised the level of assistance to 70 percent of interest rate costs, as well as 50 percent of construction costs, which could trigger even more financing in this area.

In the Near North Redevelopment Project, the most recent TIF financing of $55 million was issued on two series, had two letter of credit providers, and utilized a swap to provide an optimum interest rate. This TIF area covers Cabrini Green, once one of the poorest, most crime-infested public housing projects in the country. Tax increment to fund the TIF area is provided by a large commercial shopping center and market-rate condominiums, which were constructed in the area after the TIF was established. Project funds will be used for parks, infrastructure, new schools, and a new housing project, which will consist of a mixture of market-rate, low- and moderate-income housing, as well as replacement housing for the Cabrini residents currently in soon-to-be-demolished high-rise buildings.

TIF Programs

In order to bring some of the benefits of TIF to small businesses, homeowners, and small-scale downtown projects, the city has initiated three new lender-backed micro-TIF investment fund programs. These unique initiatives target housing and business programs in some of Chicago's most needy areas, as well as small improvements to the central business district.

The Small Business Improvement fund (SBIF) reimburses businesses and building owners for TIF-eligible investments that preserve building stock, improve neighborhood appearance or commercial value, and enable businesses to stay in the neighborhood, remain competitive, or expand. Businesses may be reimbursed for up to 50 percent of eligible costs with a maximum assistance of $50,000 per project. Businesses such as free standing fast food chains and branch banks are not eligible. Priority is given to businesses located at major intersections or major commercial corridors, projects resulting in the retention or creation of jobs, and historically significant buildings.

A pilot program in two South Side neighborhoods provides homeowners with TIF assistance for home repairs and improvements such as new roofs, entryways, windows, porches, exterior siding, and masonry work. Coordinated through the city's new TIF Neighborhood Investment Program (TIF-NIP), the program provides a maximum grant amount of $10,000 for single-family homes, $12,500 for two-flats, $15,000 for three-flats, $17,500 for four-flats, and a maximum of $50,000 for buildings with five or more units.

Two programs in the downtown "Loop" business district provide local businesses with financial assistance for projects that contribute to the area's growth as an entertainment, retail, and financial district.

The Central Loop Improvement Fund uses TIF proceeds to help property owners improve their buildings according to the standards outlined in the city's two downtown vision plans. The plans encourage building owners to install pedestrian-friendly improvements (such as new signs, awnings, facades, doors, and windows) as well as environmental remediation and upgrades to electrical and plumbing systems. The fund provides grants of up to $150,000 or 50 percent of eligible costs.

The Central Loop Loan Program, a companion to CLIF, provides low-interest loans of up to $50,000 to retail, commercial, and service-oriented businesses that are undertaking projects that benefit the city and employ Chicago residents, but do not qualify for TIF funds. Eligible projects include leasehold improvements and expenses involving inventory, working capital, equipment, and building rehabilitation. Loans last up to five years at 3 percent interest.

Special Considerations

Tax increment financing can be a controversial subject. Misinformation about TIF districts can lead to a fear of higher taxes and the perception that TIF will take money away from other entities, particularly school districts. But in fact, additional taxes created by redevelopment of blighted land goes to relieve the tax burden of other properties in the city. TIFs also work to create money for school districts and other taxing entities by developing a solid tax base that will help fund them for years to come. Local taxing bodies will realize a budget windfall after a TIF district expires. They will receive much higher revenues than they would have without the TIF-funded development. Simply put, TIF does not take a bigger piece of the taxation pie, rather, it creates a bigger pie.

While Chicago's Loop/downtown TIFs have been criticized by some as unnecessary, they have been incredibly productive for all of Chicago. Most of the downtown success stories in recent years are due to TIF: the creation and retention of thousands of jobs, providing the funds for the reconstruction of the State Street retail district, and the needed funding efforts to save and restore several historic theaters from demolition. Such projects have been

Exhibit 2

Chicago Cumulative TIF Results 1984–1998

TIF District:	64 at end of 1998 (More than 75 by end of 1999)
PUBLIC/PRIVATE INVESTMENT	
Total public investment	$ 526,925,838
Total private investment	$ 2,821,990,004
Total investment	$ 3,348,915,842
Leverage ratio	$ 5.36/$1
EMPLOYMENT	
New jobs created	9,875
New jobs retained	24,108
Total jobs	33,983
RESIDENTIAL DEVELOPMENT	
New rental units	1,506
New owner-occupied units	1,415
New student housing beds	757
New youth hostel beds	250
Total housing units	2,921
(excl. student housing/hostel)	
COMMERCIAL DEVELOPMENT	
New office space	4.73 million square feet
Rehabilitated office space	1.08 million square feet
New retail space	2.36 million square feet
Rehabilitated retail space	198,400 square feet
New parking spaces	4,615
Rehabilitated theater seats	10,920
New movie theaters	2
INDUSTRIAL DEVELOPMENT	
New industrial space	3.98 million square feet
Rehabilitated industrial space	1.03 million square feet
Total industrial space	5.01 million square feet

integral to the revitalization of Chicago's downtown and have played an essential role in the formation of a new Theater District.

Results

By the end of 1998, Chicago's TIF program had created more than 9,800 jobs and retained more than 24,000. New housing units totaled more than 3,000. New and rehabilitated office space topped 5.7 million square feet, and new and rehabilitated retail space was more than 2.5 million square feet. The city also had more than 1,300 TIF-encouraged new hotel rooms, two 10-screen movie theaters, a newly created Chicago Theater District with 11,000 seats in rehabilitated downtown theaters, 4,600 spaces in new parking facilities, and a new 250-bed youth hostel and college dormitory.

A statistic which may best illuminate the success of Chicago's TIF program is the calculation of private return leveraged from public investment. For every one dollar of public funds spent on TIF projects, the private sector has invested almost five and a half dollars. By the end of 1998, Chicago had invested a cumulative $526 million in TIF funds and benefited from $2.82 billion in private investment.

The City of Chicago has put in place an overall TIF program that not only serves its taxpayers well, but provides a model that other cities have looked to follow. This program has been successful by creating and following a policy that is aggressive and innovative in its utilization of TIF as an economic development tool, but conservative in its financing guidelines.

Many of Chicago's neighborhoods are coming alive with new development and growth. Modern industrial facilities are replacing abandoned factories, while new shopping centers are appearing in city neighborhoods that have not seen commercial or retail development in more than a generation. In most cases, these improvements would not be possible without TIF. Chicago's TIF program has become a key ingredient in rebuilding Chicago and awakening its neighborhoods.

Daniel McGraw

 **NO**

Giving Away the Store to Get a Store: Tax Increment Financing Is No Bargain for Taxpayers

If you're imagining an attraction that will draw 4.5 million out-of-town visitors a year, the first thing that jumps to mind probably isn't a store that sells guns and fishing rods and those brown jackets President Bush wears to clear brush at his ranch in Crawford, Texas. Yet last year Cabela's, a Nebraska-based hunting and fishing mega-store chain with annual sales of $1.7 billion, persuaded the politicians of Fort Worth that bringing the chain to an affluent and growing area north of the city was worth $30 million to $40 million in tax breaks. They were told that the store, the centerpiece of a new retail area, would draw more tourists than the Alamo in San Antonio or the annual State Fair of Texas in Dallas, both of which attract 2.5 million visitors a year.

The decision was made easier by the financing plan that Fort Worth will use to accommodate Cabela's. The site of the Fort Worth Cabela's has been designated a tax increment financing (TIF) district, which means taxes on the property will be frozen for 20 to 30 years.

Largely because it promises something for nothing—an economic stimulus in exchange for tax revenue that otherwise would not materialize—this tool is becoming increasingly popular across the country. Originally used to help revive blighted or depressed areas, TIFs now appear in affluent neighborhoods, subsidizing high-end housing developments, big-box retailers, and shopping malls. And since most cities are using TIFs, businesses such as Cabela's can play them off against each other to boost the handouts they receive simply to operate profit-making enterprises.

A Crummy Way to Treat Taxpaying Citizens

TIFs have been around for more than 50 years, but only recently have they assumed such importance. At a time when local governments' efforts to foster development, from direct subsidies to the use of eminent domain to seize property for private development, are already out of control, TIFs only add to the problem: Although politicians portray TIFs as a great way to boost the local economy, there are hidden costs they don't want taxpayers to know about. Cities generally assume they are not really giving anything up because the

From *Reason Magazine,* January 2006, pp. 35–39. Copyright © 2006 by Reason Foundation, 3415 S. Sepulveda Blvd., Suite 400, Los Angeles, CA 90034. www.reason.com

forgone tax revenue would not have been available in the absence of the development generated by the TIF. That assumption is often wrong.

"There is always this expectation with TIFs that the economic growth is a way to create jobs and grow the economy, but then push the costs across the public spectrum," says Greg LeRoy, author of *The Great American Jobs Scam: Corporate Tax Dodging and the Myth of Job Creation*. "But what is missing here is that the cost of developing private business has some public costs. Roads and sewers and schools are public costs that come from growth." Unless spending is cut—and if a TIF really does generate economic growth, spending is likely to rise, as the local population grows—the burden of paying for these services will be shifted to other taxpayers. Adding insult to injury, those taxpayers may include small businesses facing competition from well-connected chains that enjoy TIF-related tax breaks. In effect, a TIF subsidizes big businesses at the expense of less politically influential competitors and ordinary citizens.

"The original concept of TIFs was to help blighted areas come out of the doldrums and get some economic development they wouldn't [otherwise] have a chance of getting," says former Fort Worth City Councilman Clyde Picht, who voted against the Cabela's TIF. "Everyone probably gets a big laugh out of their claim that they will draw more tourists than the Alamo. But what is worse, and not talked about too much, is the shift of taxes being paid from wealthy corporations to small businesses and regular people."

"If you own a mom-and-pop store that sells fishing rods and hunting gear in Fort Worth, you're still paying all your taxes, and the city is giving tax breaks to Cabela's that could put you out of business," Picht explains. "The rest of us pay taxes for normal services like public safety, building inspections, and street maintenance, and those services come out of the general fund. And as the cost of services goes up, and the money from the general fund is given to these businesses through a TIF, the tax burden gets shifted to the regular slobs who don't have the same political clout. It's a crummy way to treat your taxpaying, law-abiding citizens."

Almost every state has a TIF law, and the details vary from jurisdiction to jurisdiction. But most TIFs share the same general characteristics. After a local government has designated a TIF district, property taxes (and sometimes sales taxes) from the area are divided into two streams. The first tax stream is based on the original assessed value of the property before any redevelopment; the city, county, school district, or other taxing body still gets that money. The second stream is the additional tax money generated after development takes place and the property values are higher. Typically that revenue is used to pay off municipal bonds that raise money for infrastructure improvements in the TIF district, for land acquisition through eminent domain, or for direct payments to a private developer for site preparation and construction. The length of time the taxes are diverted to pay for the bonds can be anywhere from seven to 30 years.

Local governments sell the TIF concept to the public by claiming they are using funds that would not have been generated without the TIF district. If the land was valued at $10 million before TIF-associated development and is worth $50 million afterward, the argument goes, the $40 million increase in tax value can be used to retire the bonds. Local governments also like to point out that the TIF district may increase nearby economic activity, which will be taxed at full value.

So, in the case of Cabela's in Fort Worth, the TIF district was created to build roads and sewers and water systems, to move streams and a lake to make the property habitable, and to help defray construction costs for the company. Cabela's likes this deal because the money comes upfront, without any interest. Their taxes are frozen, and the bonds are paid off by what would have gone into city coffers. In effect, the city is trading future tax income for a present benefit.

But even if the dedicated tax money from a TIF district suffices to pay off the bonds, that doesn't mean the arrangement is cost-free. "TIFs are being pushed out there right now based upon the 'but for' test," says Greg LeRoy. "What cities are saying is that no development would take place but for the TIF. . . . The average public official says this is free money, because it wouldn't happen otherwise. But when you see how it plays out, the whole premise of TIFs begins to crumble." Rather than spurring development, LeRoy argues, TIFs "move some economic development from one part of a city to another."

Development Would Have Occurred Anyway

Local officials usually do not consider how much growth might occur without a TIF. In 2002 the Neighborhood Capital Budget Group (NCBG), a coalition of 200 Chicago organizations that studies local public investment, looked at 36 of the city's TIF districts and found that property values were rising in all of them during the five years before they were designated as TIFs. The NCBG projected that the city of Chicago would capture $1.6 billion in second-stream property tax revenue—used to pay off the bonds that subsidized private businesses—over the 23-year life spans of these TIF districts. But it also found that $1.3 billion of that revenue would have been raised anyway, assuming the areas continued growing at their pre-TIF rates.

The experience in Chicago is important. The city invested $1.6 billion in TIFs, even though $1.3 billion in economic development would have occurred anyway. So the bottom line is that the city invested $1.6 billion for $300 million in revenue growth.

The upshot is that TIFs are diverting tax money that otherwise would have been used for government services. The NCBG study found, for instance, that the 36 TIF districts would cost Chicago public schools $632 million (based on development that would have occurred anyway) in property tax revenue, because the property tax rates are frozen for schools as well. This doesn't merely mean that the schools get more money. If the economic growth occurs with TIFs, that attracts people to the area and thereby raises enrollments. In that case, the cost of teaching the new students will be borne by property owners outside the TIF districts.

> "Money from the general fund is given to these businesses through a TIF, [then] the tax burden gets shifted to the regular slobs who don't have the same political clout."
>
> —Fort Worth City Councilman Clyde Picht

Such concerns have had little impact so far, in part because almost no one has examined how TIFs succeed or fail over the long term. Local politicians are touting TIFs as a way to promote development, promising no new taxes, and then setting them up without looking at potential side effects. It's hard to discern exactly how many TIFs operate in this country, since not every state requires their registration. But the number has expanded exponentially, especially over the past decade. Illinois, which had one TIF district in 1970, now has 874 (including one in the town of Wilmington, population 129). A moderate-sized city like Janesville, Wisconsin—a town of 60,000 about an hour from Madison—has accumulated 26 TIFs. Delaware and Arizona are the only states without TIF laws, and most observers expect they will get on board soon.

First used in California in the 1950s, TIFs were supposed to be another tool, like tax abatement and enterprise zones, that could be used to promote urban renewal. But cities found they were not very effective at drawing development into depressed areas. "They had this tool, but didn't know what the tool was good for," says Art Lyons, an analyst for the Chicago-based Center for Economic Policy Analysis, an economic think tank that works with community groups. The cities realized, Lyons theorizes, that if they wanted to use TIFs more, they had to get out of depressed neighborhoods and into areas with higher property values, which generate more tax revenue to pay off development bonds.

The Entire Western World Could Be Blighted

Until the 1990s, most states reserved TIFs for areas that could be described as "blighted," based on criteria set forth by statute. But as with eminent domain, the definition of blight for TIF purposes has been dramatically expanded. In 1999, for example, Baraboo, Wisconsin, created a TIF for an industrial park and a Wal-Mart supercenter that were built on farmland; the blight label was based on a single house in the district that was uninhabited. In recent years 16 states have relaxed their TIF criteria to cover affluent areas, "conservation areas" where blight might occur someday, or "economic development areas," loosely defined as commercial or industrial properties.

The result is that a TIF can be put almost anywhere these days. Based on current criteria, says Jake Haulk, director of the Pittsburgh-based Allegheny Institute for Public Policy, you could "declare the entire Western world blighted."

In the late 1990s, Pittsburgh decided to declare a commercial section of its downtown blighted so it could create a TIF district for the Lazarus Department Store. The construction of the new store and a nearby parking garage cost the city more than $70 million. But the property taxes on the new store were lower than expected, as the downtown area surrounding Lazarus never took off the way the city thought it would. Sales tax receipts were also unexpectedly low. Lazarus decided to close the store last year, and the property is still on the block. Because other businesses were included in the TIF, it is impossible to predict whether the city will be on the hook for the entire $70 million. But given that the Lazarus store was the centerpiece of the development, it is safe to say this TIF is not working very well, and Pittsburgh's taxpayers may have to pick up the tab.

If businesses like Lazarus cannot reliably predict their own success, urban planners can hardly be expected to do a better job. Typically, big corporations come to small cities towing consultants who trot out rosy numbers, and the politicians see a future that may not materialize in five or 10 years. "The big buzzwords are economic development," says Chris Slowik, organizational director for the South Cooperative Organization for Public Education (SCOPE), which represents about 45 school districts in the southern suburbs of Chicago, each of which includes at least one TIF. "The local governments see a vacant space and see something they like that some company might bring in. But no one thinks about what the costs might be. . . . They are giving away the store to get a store." Big-box retail chains such as Target and Wal-Mart seem to be the most frequent beneficiaries of TIFs. (Neither company would comment for this story, and local politicians generally shied away as well.)

Given the competition between cities eager to attract new businesses, TIFS are not likely to disappear anytime soon. "Has it gone overboard?" asks University of North Texas economist Terry Clower. "Sure. . . . But the problem is that if a city doesn't offer some tax incentives, the company will just move down the road." According to Clower, "In a utopian world, there would be no government handouts, and every business would pay the same tax rate. But if a city stands up and says they aren't doing [TIFs] anymore, they will lose out."

Instead, it's the competitors of TIF-favored businesses that lose out. Academy Sports & Outdoors, which employs 6,500 people, has about 80 sporting goods stores in eight Southern states, including a store in Fort Worth. When the Fort Worth City Council was considering the TIF for Cabela's, Academy Sports Chairman David Gochman spoke out against the tax incentives, realizing that his company is a big business, but not big enough. "This is not a nonprofit, not a library, not a school," he said. "They are a for-profit business, a competitor of ours, along with Oshman's and Wal-Mart and others."

TIFs Have Become the Standard Handout

Al Dalton, owner of Texas Outdoors, a 10,000-square-foot hunting and fishing shop in Fort Worth, echoed the sentiment that the city was favoring one business over another. "We don't have the buying power, and we don't have the advertising dollars," Dalton said. "It doesn't make any difference even if we've got the best price in town if nobody knows about it. The deep pockets, in every way, [make] a lot of difference."

And that may be the key to understanding how TIFs are now applied: The companies with the deep pockets are able to fill them with subsidies.

The Cabela's location in Fort Worth does not fit any of the blight criteria people had in mind when TIFs were first created. The 225,000-square-foot store, with its waterfalls, multitude of stuffed animals, and wild game cafe, sits on prime property just off Interstate 35. It is a few miles down the road from the Texas Motor Speedway (which has its own TIF), and the 200,000 NASCAR and IRL fans who attend races there three times a year—not to mention the fans who come to the speedway's concerts and other special events—might want to shop at Cabela's.

The area around Cabela's is affluent and has been growing for years. A half-dozen shopping centers nearby were on the drawing board well before the TIF was considered. Within a five-mile radius of the hunting/fishing megastore, 10,000 new homes have been built since 2000. That same area is expected to grow by 20,000 people in the next two years.

But the argument against the "but for" assumption is not being heard. In 2004 a state judge threw out a lawsuit against the Cabela's TIF by a Fort Worth citizens' group that claimed blight was never proven, and that the city was misusing TIFs in a prosperous area that needed no tax breaks for future development. The blight designation came from a pond and stream on the property. It was an odd designation, given that the property is in a prime development area and ponds and streams are not what one would classify as blighted.

The press releases and newspaper articles about the new Cabela's emphasize that the store is going to draw more people to Texas than visit the Alamo (the studies were done by Cabela's). The press release never mentions that a Bass Pro Shop store, part of a chain almost identical to Cabela's, is just 10 miles down the road. While Cabela's was negotiating its TIF with Fort Worth, it was also negotiating a TIF with the city of Buda, 120 miles away, outside of Austin. Cabela's got about $20 million from Buda, and the same tourist claims are being made there. If each Texas store is going to draw 4.5 million tourists, as the chain claims, that means 9 million people will be coming to Texas every year just to visit the two Cabela's stores.

"The notion that a hunting store would draw all these tourists is ridiculous," says Greg LeRoy. "But what is even more ridiculous is cities thinking that tax breaks are the primary reason businesses relocate or expand in certain areas. There are so many other factors at play—transportation costs, good employment available, housing costs and quality of life for executives—that the tax breaks like TIFs aren't very high up on their priority list. But these corporations are asking for them—and getting them—because everyone is giving them out. TIFs have become the standard handout, and the businesses have learned how to play one city off the other. Businesses would be stupid for not asking for them every time."

If TIFs continue to multiply at the present rate, we may see the day when every new 7-Eleven and McDonald's has its own TIF. That prospect may seem farfetched, but it wasn't too long ago that cities wouldn't even have considered giving up tens of millions of dollars in exchange for yet another store selling guns and fishing rods.

EXPLORING THE ISSUE

Should Cities Rely on Tax Increment Financing (TIF) as a Primary Tool in Their Efforts to Promote Local Economic Development?

Critical Thinking and Reflection

1. Are TIFs in the public's interest or in business' interest?
2. Does the creation of a TIF wind up generating new jobs and additional funds for public services, or does the creation of a TIF wind up "losing" money that a city could otherwise have used for public services?
3. What reforms and limitations should a state place on local TIF creation?

Is There Common Ground?

Wisely used, TIFs can provide a city with an important tool for attracting—or retaining—key businesses that can be critical to local economic health. In some cities, TIFs have also been valuable tools in encouraging the construction of affordable housing.

But, when TIF designations are widely awarded even to projects where the benefits they offer are not absolutely critical to the recruitment or retention of a local business, the TIF arrangement represents a reduction in the monies that a city could have used to support the public schools and other important services for city residents. When a city creates a TIF, municipal leaders will also find it difficult to resist demands from businesses located in other parts of the city that they, too, merit similar favorable treatment. TIF creation has proliferated so widely in California, a state facing serious budget difficulties, that Governor Jerry Brown called for a measure to ban TIF creation.

But such a meat-axe prohibition likely goes too far. Although many TIFs are not really necessary, in other cases, TIF creation may be critical to the revitalization of an aging shopping district or the revival of a declining manufacturing section of the city. A TIF can be part of a package of incentives that is capable of attracting new development to troubled areas.

Still, widespread TIF creation likely means that a city is paying for growth that would have taken place anyway, sacrificing general fund and school revenues in the process. A wise TIF policy would seek to be much more conservative in establishing TIFs, to limit TIF creation to those instances where a business is absolutely vital to the economic health of a community and new investment would not occur in the absence of a TIF. Also, whenever a TIF is created, its borders must be drawn as tightly as possible, so that the city's general fund and the public schools lose as little money as possible.

TIF districts also should not be allowed to exist for exceedingly long periods of time. Local governments gain the full benefit from new development only after the authorized life of a TIF district expires and the tax revenues derived from new business investment can be used for projects throughout the city. A shorter life for TIF districts will also make more money available sooner for the schools and for public service provision. A typical TIF district may be created for 20 years. In Chicago, as we have seen, a TIF district typically has a 23-year life span. A shorter life span would help to ensure that more of the revenues generated by business expansion are used to benefit the community as opposed to helping the businesses themselves.

State school aid formulas can also be changed to compensate school districts that "lose" funds as a result of TIF creation. Some states allow school districts to opt out of a TIF. In such cases, a school district is allowed to tax the full value of property in the TIF district. Businesses, of course, object that such a reform undermines the purposes of a TIF, lessening the total tax revenue that is dedicated to paying for business-related improvements in the district. In some cases, school districts have been able to negotiate agreements with the local TIF authority so that a portion of the additional funds generated from new development is shared with the schools (Weber and Goddeeris 2007).

Cities are beginning to recognize that a strategy of tax abatements and TIFs will not always prove to be an effective means to attract and retain businesses. Business firms, their executives, and technologically competent workers are drawn to communities with good schools, an educated and capable workforce, ample parks and recreational facilities, interesting cultural programs, and a pleasant living environment. To attract businesses, cities must invest in more than just physical infrastructure projects in the immediate TIF district. "Winning" cities will also find the funds to invest in human capital development and in improving the local quality of life.

Additional Resources

Johnson, Craig L., & Joyce Y. Man, eds. (2001). *Tax Increment Financing and Economic Development: Uses, Structures, and Impact.* Albany, NY: State University of New York Press.

Leher, Eli. (September 1999). "The Town that Loves to TIF." *Governing* magazine.

Weber, Rachel, & Laura Goddeeris. (2007). "Tax Increment Financing: Process and Planning Issues," a research paper of the Lincoln Institute of Land Policy, Available at: www.lincolninst.edu/subcenters/teaching-fiscal-dimensions-of-planning/materials/goddeeris-weber-financing.pdf.

Youngman, Joan M. (May 2, 2011). "TIF at a Turning Point: Defining Debt Down." *State Tax Notes.*

Internet References

The Chicago Reader

Chicago's alternative newspaper presents a series of investigative reports by Ben Joravsky that uncovers the overuse and abuses inherent in the city's extensive reliance on TIF creation.

**www.chicagoreader.com/chicago/the-chicago-reader-tif-archive/
Content?oid=1180567**

City of Chicago TIF Projection Reports

These reports detail the extent of TIF district creation, including estimates as to the value of the new investment that the city has gained as a result of its TIF strategy. Even if the figures reported by the city are overly optimistic and self-serving, the overall amount of new investment is still quite impressive.

**www.cityofchicago.org/city/en/depts/dcd/supp_info/tif_projection_
reports.html**

Council of Development Financing Agencies (CDFA)

An organization that explains the many advantages of TIF creation and why TIF districts have become, arguably, the most popular local tool for economic development.

www.cdfa.net

Lincoln Institute of Land Policy

Created to give both the general public and decision makers high-quality information about alternative policies related to land use and the taxation of land, the Lincoln Institute presents a wide-ranging collection of articles on the use of TIFs as an economic and housing development tool.

www.lincolninst.edu

Debating Changes in Urban Policy

*T*here are no perfect public policies. Policies that promote growth can jeopardize environmental values and neighborhood stability. Conversely, programs that protect the natural environment may impede new housing construction and job development. Programs of aggressive law enforcement can put civil liberties at risk. "School choice" programs may empower students with more involved families to find the schooling they want; but such programs also risk increasing racial segregation and decreasing the resources available in more traditional classrooms. Housing mobility programs that allow poor families to escape violent neighborhoods are often opposed by residents in receiving communities who fear the rise of crime and other social problems.

No urban policy produces totally good results. Policies with quite laudable objectives may often be ineffective or have unintended side effects. Programs that serve to attract new businesses may drain customers away from competing firms. Municipal actions that promote new activity in a city's downtown may require additional taxes from small business owners and homeowners located elsewhere in the city who receive no direct benefit from the new growth project. New economic development may bring benefits to a city as a whole but will be resented by low-income residents displaced from their homes and by middle-class families who face heightened levels of school overcrowding as the result of new development. These and similar tradeoffs explain why the debate over urban policies continues to be so intense.

This unit reviews the continuing debate on some of the more fundamental policy choices facing cities. "Broken windows" policing is often seen as a no-nonsense approach that sends a clear and unambiguous message that improper and criminal behavior will not be tolerated. But critics counter that the broken windows approach is overrated as a crime reduction strategy, and that such an aggressive policing posture will wind up burdening inner-city youth with criminal records for relatively inconsequential and innocuous violations of the law.

Do programs of school vouchers and charter schools give low-income families a real choice when it comes to finding schools that meet their children's needs? Critics argue that the choice is more often illusory than real and that school choice programs do not produce the educational gains for low-income students that the programs' more enthusiastic backers predicted.

Programs aimed at aiding the residents of inner-city neighborhoods, too, are often the subject of intense controversy. The HOPE VI program helped tear down the nation's worst high-rise public housing projects of hopelessness, building new and more attractive dwelling units in their place. Critics, however, question just whom the program truly serves, especially as large numbers of public housing residents were not permitted to move into the new housing that was built on site. Community activists object to the forced displacement of the poor. The residents of neighborhoods that received large numbers of Section 8 housing choice movers also argued that a reconcentration of poverty would diminish the quality of life in their neighborhoods. The Community Reinvestment Act (CRA) served to promote tens of billions of dollars in new investment in inner-city neighborhoods that banks and other investors had otherwise overlooked. But critics argue that the CRA and other regulatory programs led banks and mortgage institutions to make unwise loans that eventually served to fuel a mortgage foreclosure crisis that compounded the severity of problems of core-city communities.

Environmental programs, too, are often controversial. Environmentalists argue that the establishment of congestion zones and new investment in high-speed inner-city rail are absolutely necessary to promote sustainable development, that is, job creation that respects ecological values and preserves the livability of urban communities. Critics, however, contend that such programs entail massive waste and inefficiency and act as a "drag" on much needed economic growth.

- Does Broken-Windows Policing Reduce Crime?

- Are School Vouchers Overrated as a Strategy for Reforming Public Education?

- Do Charter Schools Improve Education?

- Should Federal Programs Seek to Deconcentrate Inner-City Poverty?

- Should Section 8 Housing Vouchers Continue to Serve as the Backbone of the Federal Government's Assisted Housing Efforts?

- Did the Government's Regulation of Lending Institutions Under the Community Reinvestment Act Lead to the Mortgage Foreclosure Crisis?

- Should U.S. Cities Adopt a System of "Congestion Pricing" to "Tame" Traffic?

- Should the United States Invest in High-Speed Intercity Rail?

ISSUE 6

Does Broken-Windows Policing Reduce Crime?

YES: William J. Bratton, James Q. Wilson, and George L. Kelling, from "This Works: Crime Prevention and the Future of Broken Windows Policing," the Manhattan Institute for Public Policy Research *Civic Bulletin* (no. 36, May 2004)

NO: Bernard E. Harcourt, from "Policing Disorder: Can We Reduce Serious Crime by Punishing Petty Offenses?" *Boston Review* (April/May 2002)

Learning Outcomes

After reading this issue, you should be able to:

- Explain the "broken-windows" concept as it applies to law enforcement.
- Explain how the broken-windows approach to policing differs from more commonplace policing approaches.
- Explain how the advocates of broken-windows policing argue that broken-windows policing led to New York City's revival.
- Evaluate the national evidence when it comes to the impact of the broken-windows on the rate of major and violent crimes in a city.
- Identify the concerns that civil rights and civil liberties advocates raise regarding the broken-windows or order–maintenance approach to law enforcement.

ISSUE SUMMARY

YES: William Bratton was Commissioner of Police in New York City under Mayor Rudolph Giuliani before he moved on to Los Angeles to serve as Chief of Police. James Q. Wilson (emeritus professor UCLA, Ronald Reagan Professor of Public Policy at Pepperdine University, and past president of the American Political Science Association) and George L. Kelling (professor of criminal justice at Rutgers University) are the academic theorists who are generally credited with publicizing the theory of broken-windows policing. These three experts talk about the importance of order maintenance and why they believe that police must respond to smaller crimes and incidents of disorderly conduct in order begin a process that will also reduce major and violent crimes.

NO: Bernard Harcourt, law professor at the University of Chicago, argues that the advocates overstate the achievements of order maintenance policing. He shows that the reduction in major crimes occurred across the nation and not just in New York and in other cities where police departments adopted a broken-windows approach to order maintenance. Harcourt further argues that the new emphasis on order maintenance poses a threat to individualism and civil rights. Minority communities will bear the costs of a more aggressive policing approach that criminalizes nonthreatening behavior.

How can a city effectively fight crime? The truth is, no one really knows. Crime has such complex roots that there is no one easy answer or "magic bullet" that will guarantee public safety in big cities.

Still, law enforcement agencies have experimented with a number of innovative strategies in the war against crime. New York's *CompStat* program (also introduced by then-chief William Bratton) is a computerized system that presents up-to-the-minute data and overlay maps to track crime patterns in a community and to compare those patterns with the deployment of police officers and other resources. CompStat does not prepare reports that sit on the bureaucracy's shelves. Instead, CompStat data presentations provide the basis for weekly meetings where higher-ups in the department (and sometimes from the mayor's office as well) review the performance of police precincts, putting relentless pressure on precinct commanders to reassign personnel and rearrange shifts as needed. City after city across the country has adopted CompStat-style systems of data-driven, real-time performance management.

Community-oriented policing (COPS) is another important innovation. Community-oriented policing is based on the recognition that the police possess only limited resources in the battle against crime. Consequently, the police must build partnerships in which members of the community help by participating in the actions necessary to reduce crime. Officers work with business owners to make sure that alarm systems are properly installed and that their property is well lighted and securely locked at night. Police participation in school programs and in athletic leagues helps to build a better relationship between youth and police officers. Citizen patrols and "positive loitering," where citizens "armed" only with flashlights and cell phones walk the streets of high-crime neighborhoods and notify officers of suspicious activity.

COPS also seeks to abridge the hierarchical, militaristic orientation of police departments where detectives and officers see themselves as experts who know best how to battle crime. In contrast, the community-oriented approach requires officers to work with citizen councils and to attend "beat meetings" where neighborhood residents direct officers to conditions (such as the prevalence of drug dealing outside a local school or of adult loiterers hanging out by a student bus stop) of concern to the community. Although many officers see the value of building community trust, more traditional officers resent the time they must spend at such meetings. These critics derisively view community activities as "social work," a diversion from more serious law enforcement activities.

Broken-windows policing is a reform that shares with COPS a sense that officers must respond to the concerns of a community. The broken-windows approach elevates the priority that law enforcement officers should give to maintain orderly behavior in a community, watching out for the many "small things" and nuisance behaviors that degrade the quality of life in a community, the sort of minor offenses that police officers in many cities often overlook.

According to broken-windows theorists, tolerance for minor infractions only serves to build an atmosphere in which persons inclined to break the law will come to believe that their criminal actions will be tolerated. By contrast, when police officers stop a person for a minor offense, such as drinking on the streets, urinating in public, singing loudly in the middle of the night, or hurdling a subway turnstile in order to avoid paying the required fare, the police reinforce expectations of proper behavior, sending a clear message that will reduce the willingness of miscreants to escalate to more serious crime.

In their classic article, Wilson and Kelling (1983) use the metaphor of an unrepaired broken window, a seemingly minor problem that, if uncorrected will soon lead to all of the windows in a building being broken. A single broken window that remains unrepaired communicates the wrong message to potential miscreants: "one unrepaired broken window is a signal that no one cares, and so breaking more windows costs nothing. (It has always been fun)." A city must take care of its own "broken windows," the small violations of the law and a neighborhood's informal rules that, if not respected, will lead potential violators to escalate their misdeeds.

A city that tolerates "taggers" who spray paint their name on buildings, or "squeegee men" who shakedown drivers at stop lights by demanding a dollar after having dragged a dirty rag across a car's windshield, or who allow unruly persons to bother people waiting at a bus stop, is not taking care of its broken windows. Instead, such a lax approach to law and order sends the exact wrong message to potential law breakers: that in this community "anything goes."

A broken-windows or order-maintenance strategy of policing requires officers to increase the number of arrests they make for minor violations. Such a law enforcement strategy not only sends a clear message, it also has a second important additional advantage: when officers hold persons for such minor matters as turnstile jumping, a check of the records will often reveal that the detainee has outstanding warrants for more serious violations. By cracking down on the "small stuff," the police gain the opportunity to remove more serious predators from the community.

New York Mayor Rudy Giuliani and police chief William Bratton claim that their reliance on broken-windows policing helped New York to escape its reputation as "fear city." Giuliani argues that the broken-windows approach not only led to a dramatic reduction in crime, but by increasing the public's sense of safety on city streets and in the subways, the new law enforcement approach also added to the city's livability and improved the city's business climate, providing the foundation for New York's economic rebirth.

Critics, however, counter that broken-windows policing is very overrated as a strategy to reduce major crimes. These critics point out the crime drop apparent in New York City in the late-1980s and 1990s was due to a number of other factors and should not be credited to the city's more aggressive policing of smaller infractions. When the crack cocaine epidemic receded, crime fell in cities across the country, not only in New York but also in cities that had not adopted the broken-windows approach.

The critics also worry that the order-maintenance approach may be too intrusive in individual lives, imposing "too great a cost to citizens" as police officers "overzealously" enforce the law against minor offenses, "criminalizing relatively innocuous behaviors" that are "relatively harmless" (Sousa 2010, p. 46). Order-maintenance police actions may even target the actions of loud and unruly teenagers who are simply "hanging out" on the streets.

Some critics further argue that an aggressive broken-windows law enforcement approach will lead officers to violate citizens' civil rights and civil liberties. Critics further worry that the broken-windows approach has an implicit class and racial bias, adopting a more aggressive posture against public drinking and other street activities that are part of the daily street life in low-income minority communities. More aggressive officers may resort to racial profiling when cracking down on small infractions and rowdy behavior, looking at a person's skin color or ethnicity in deciding just whom to stop.

In the YES article, excerpts from their presentations at a 2003 conference at the Milken Institute, Chief Bratton and Professors Wilson and Kelling argue that broken-windows policing is a strategy that works and save lives. They argue that the approach has also helped to make life in New York City more civil, helping to catalyze the city's economic turnaround after it hit bottom in the 1970s. Poor and minority communities, the victims of crime, are often among the most enthusiastic supporters of a strategy that increases the safety of their neighborhoods.

In the NO article, professor Harcourt sharply disputes a number of the claims that have been made by the supporters of broken-windows policing. He argues that a careful examination of the statistical evidence shows that the increase in the number of arrests for minor violations does not produce a clear drop in major and violent crimes. Harcourt further argues that order-maintenance policing unfairly imposes white middle- and upper-class standards on low-income minority communities, with the effect of criminalizing behavior that is an acceptable and normal part of life in the inner city.

YES    William J. Bratton, James Q. Wilson, and George L. Kelling

This Works: Crime Prevention and the Future of Broken Windows Policing

This Civic Bulletin is adapted from the transcript of a conference held at the Milken Institute in Santa Monica, CA on December 4, 2003.

WILLIAM BRATTON: Thank you all for coming. This is an exciting evening for me in that for the first time I have the opportunity to be with both George Kelling and James Q. Wilson at the same time, and they are two individuals whose writings on crime and policing tactics have profoundly influenced my career, and as a result profoundly influenced the lives of millions of others who are significantly safer today thanks to their research.

In fact, it is no exaggeration to say that there are many people who are alive today who would not be if not for the writings of these two scholars, as well as the efforts of the thousands of police officers who have taken to practicing much of what they preach. . . .

Of course, in 1990 nobody would have ever believed that New York City could become what it is today, arguably the safest large city in this country. This year, crime in New York City is down again-by almost 6 percent. Unfortunately, homicides in New York are on the rise, and they're now neck and neck with Chicago as the murder capital of the United States. Regardless, for thirteen straight years crime has gone down in New York and that is a tremendous accomplishment.

What shaped Mayor [Rudolph] Giuliani's views on crime and policing was his exposure to concepts from the two men that I have already mentioned, James Wilson and George Kelling. These two men created a true American policing innovation, an innovation that I, as chief of police, have always used as a cornerstone for all of the activities that my officers and I engage in. That innovation is "broken windows policing", a very successful, but at the same time controversial, philosophy.

And I say controversial because there are still those who don't believe that it is an essential component of making any city a safer city, and certainly not in making New York or Los Angeles the safest large cities in America. But I believe in broken windows policing as a practitioner who has been in this field for over thirty years, and as someone who practiced what they preached so eloquently about five years before they even wrote about it in the late 1970s.

From *Civic Bulletin*, No. 36, May 2004. Copyright © 2004 by Manhattan Institute, Inc. Reprinted by permission.

As a young police sergeant in Boston, Massachusetts, I was enlisted in that city's first neighborhood policing initiative, the forerunner of what came to be popularly known as "community policing" in the late 1980s and early 1990s.

In Boston in the 1970s we were developing a program called neighborhood policing, based on the unheard-of idea that police should go into neighborhoods and listen to the concerns of the residents, because up until that time police didn't invite local feedback. We thought we knew what was right for a neighborhood and we focused our energy on serious crimes: rapes, robberies, and violent assaults. Indeed, the reporting of crime, the national reporting of crime, still focuses on those serious crimes. The Universal Crime Report and the Department of Justice victimization surveys still ignore quality of life crimes.

As a young sergeant, I began to hold police and community meetings in Boston. Four nights a week we would hand out leaflets in local neighborhoods, knock on doors, and encourage people to come to police meetings. "We're the police," we said. "We want to hear from you." At the time, I was armed to the teeth with various crime statistics. I knew every murder, every robbery, and every rape. We thought that we knew that community inside out.

And what did we hear from the community? We heard complaints about prostitutes, abandoned cars, and broken windows. That was a wake-up call for me at a very early stage of my career, the formulative stage of my career as a young sergeant. I started to focus on what concerned the community, what caused them fear, and why it caused fear.

These seemingly minor crimes unnerved them because they experienced them every day. They knew before we did, before the experts did, that the so-called victimless crimes have a victim—and the victim was the entire neighborhood. Ultimately, the victim was the city, and crime was a cancer that was destroying America's cities, but we didn't really recognize that during the 1970s. We really did not recognize it in an institutional way until Kelling and Wilson wrote their "Broken Windows" article in 1982, where they put into a strong, powerful voice a concept that resonated not only with people who lived in these fear-ridden neighborhoods, but resonated with the police that patrolled them.

We had a hard time establishing community policing in the American police profession in the late 80's and early 90's, but we finally managed to institutionalize it. We succeeded because rank and file police understood that in addition to serious violent crimes, quality of life crimes were tearing apart the civic fabric of the neighborhoods they were policing. Quality of life crimes destroy the citizens' trust and confidence in government's ability to provide its first obligation, which is public safety.

This is not to say that broken windows policing is a magic solution to crime. It is more like a powerful prescription that a doctor will use to cure a sick patient. It is an essential component, in many instances the essential component, but in and of itself it is not going to solve any city's crime problem. But it can be used in a variety of ways. It is even now, 20 years later, an incredibly misunderstood paradigm and crime control tactic, because many people still don't understand that it can be applied in many different ways.

We first showed the flexibility of broken windows policing in New York when George Kelling recruited me there in 1990 when he was doing consulting work with the Transit Authority. He encouraged me to come to New York and apply broken windows policing to subway crime with the idea that, far-fetched as it seemed in 1990, if it succeeded in the subways, someone would have enough faith in us to try it on the streets of New York.

We were successful. The reduction in subway crime and quality of life crimes attracted the attention of the then-candidate Rudy Giuliani, and George and I traveled to New York in 1993 and spent a Friday afternoon with Rudy and some of his aides. The question he asked us was the central one Kelling had already anticipated: "Can you take what worked in the subways and make it work on the streets of New York?" We said we could. We continue to have confidence in broken windows policing, and we'll implement it again here in Los Angeles.

It will be a more difficult transition in Los Angeles than in New York, however, because the essential element that we had working in our favor in New York, and this is referenced in a very well-written article in *Governing* magazine on our efforts here, is that there are many people in Los Angeles who do not believe in the effectiveness of broken windows policing.

There are many people who do not believe that police count, that police can make a difference, and who believe that crime is most significantly impacted by demographics, economic circumstances, or racism. I understand that crime is influenced by all those factors, but I don't believe it's caused by any of them. I strongly believe that crime is caused by individual behavior, and since all behavior is learned, the police can do something about controlling criminal behavior, correcting that behavior, by imparting a new ethic of order to our communities—regardless of their economic, racial, or ethnic make-up. The challenge for police is to do this consistently, compassionately, and particularly in a democratic society such as ours, constitutionally.

What we showed in New York, and what we will show in Los Angeles, is that in two very different cities with two extraordinarily different police departments, both in terms of size as well as tactics, traditions, histories, and styles of policing, that the police can make an enormous difference.

We are making a difference today. This year in this city [Los Angeles, where Bratton became Chief of Police in 2002], homicides are down by over 25 percent. Overall crime is down by about 5 percent. And that's with a police force that is one-fourth the size of what I commanded in New York.

The main difficulty that we are facing here is that, unlike New York, where we had the ability by virtue of the sheer size of the department to impact the entire city at the same time, in Los Angeles the police are constantly running from fire to fire. We clamp down on one crime hotspot and then are forced to redirect our limited resources to another location. Our challenge here is very different, but we are approaching it in much the same way, with the same underpinning, that we need to focus as much attention on the signs of crime, on quality of life issues, at the same time that we focus on serious crimes. We are doing that through a variety of efforts and initiatives, Compstat for one—a program that I am sure you are all very familiar with.

But much depends on using broken windows policing or a focus on quality of life crimes to effectively influence how a city feels about itself and thereby influence actual crime. That was our great discovery on the transit system project that I worked on with George, and then again when I went into New York in 1994 and worked with one of the all-time great policemen, Jack Maple, the late, great New York City Deputy Police Commissioner, who truly understood how you could use the enforcement of quality of life crimes to enhance your ability to deal with serious crimes. While violent crimes are much smaller in number than quality of life offenses, they greatly contribute to a sense of lawlessness because those crimes are the most reported in the newspapers and FBI crime statistics. We discovered that we could impact more serious crimes through quality of life policing—through a weeding of the garden, as it were.

Let me use the example of the New York City subway system that Malcolm Gladwell used in his New Yorker magazine article "Tipping Point," an article that ultimately became the basis for his *Tipping Point* book, an extraordinary book that in many respects supports the broken windows theories of Kelling and Wilson.

Gladwell endorses the idea that you can, as fast as an epidemic spreads, just as quickly diminish the impact of that spread and in fact tip it the other way. What we did in the New York City subway system, with Kelling's guidance and a lot of great thinking by many terrific police officers, was to deal with the issue of fare evasion, an issue that nobody really wanted to do much about.

Back then, this was a $1.15 theft of service from the transit system. At the time, three and a half million people rode the New York subway system every day. However, those numbers had been declining dramatically because of a combination of fear of the system—at the time there was very little maintenance of the system, and every day there were fires on the tracks and train derailments—and every day they would encounter the subway version of the squeegee pest, or the petty criminal who vandalized the turnstiles, so that in order to get into the subway you had to go through the adjacent gate, and a beggar or petty criminal would be standing there with his hand out, intimidating you to give him money in much the same way that his counterpart at street level with a squeegee was intimidating you when you were stopped at a red light.

The system at the time was having a hard time dealing with the problem of fare evasion. Fare evasion, in the form of scruffy characters who would go under turnstiles, or over turnstiles, because it seemed that nobody was maintaining them or even cared about them, increased to 250,000 people a day and was growing worse all the time.

How did we know that? The subway system documented it. They would literally have people go out once a month, stand at every turnstile, and count the fare evaders. We had a very accurate understanding of the problem, but the subway police had a mentality that they didn't want to address minor crimes like a $1.15 fare theft.

Subway police management didn't want to deal with it because to make an arrest in New York City at that time would take approximately twelve to twenty-four hours of police administrative time—an entire day, in other words, to process a $1.15 theft of service. This meant losing an officer from the sub-way system for significant periods of time, and since they only had about 700 officers on the system at any given time, if they were making a lot of arrests there would be nobody left to police the rest of the system.

We developed a number of strategies to increase the number of arrests while still reducing arrest-processing time. We designed "bust busses," so that instead of taking prisoners twenty miles down to the central booking facility, we brought an arrest bus right to the scene. We would arrest people below ground, get them up into the bus and process them there. Those that didn't have outstanding warrants could be quickly processed and then released. Those that had warrants would be held.

And what did we find? Thanks to a very cost-effective arrest procedure, the system actually raised police morale. In a nutshell, cops like making arrests. That's what they do. But they don't want to make arrests that don't have any impact. They don't want to make arrests that keep them chained to a prisoner for twenty-four hours. They want to be part of something that they feel is going to have a demonstrable impact.

Once our program was underway, officers discovered that one out of every seven people we were arresting for fare evasion was wanted on a war-rant. Often times, these warrants would be for very serious crimes: murders, rapes, and so on. One out of every twenty-one fare-evaders, at least initially, was carrying some type of weapon—ranging from a straightedge razor on up to Uzi submachine guns. Eventually this process excited police because they had a good chance of catching significant offenders without exorbitant effort.

And, perhaps most importantly, crime began to go down. Fare evasion began to go down. Why? We were using the police in a very public, visible way to control behavior. We were going after minor types of crime, and yet we were also having a significant impact on more serious crimes. If you're a felon coming into the system to commit a robbery, you're not going to pay $1.15 to ride the subway. Criminals are very cost-efficient that way; if you are intent on stealing through theft or violence, you won't contribute to the MTA. Given that practical reality, cracking down on fare evasion provided a significant dis-incentive for other crimes as well.

Now, thirteen years later, crime in the subway system is down almost 90 percent from what it was in 1990. The MTA no longer counts fare evaders. There are so few now that it is not economically sensible to put out counters every month to keep track of them, and the MTA system now has five and one-half million riders.

It is a system also that has approximately one half the police that we had back in 1990. Why? Because there's not all that much for them to do now. We went after the broken windows, the so-called signs of crime, in a way that contributed to the reduction of serious crime.

Broken windows works. Not by itself, but as part of a master set of strate-gies. No two cities in this country, no two cities in the world are alike. This is not cookie-cutter approach. What we're designing in Los Angeles is in many respects very different than the strategies we employed in New York, and as you're going to hear from the panelists, very different in many respects from what worked in Boston.

The ailments that afflict cities seem to have a certain commonality, but when you look at it quite closely, it's like the illnesses that affect any individual. While there might be certain common elements to disease, how it impacts your particular body might be very different from how that same disease would impact the person sitting beside you. Similarly, in the policing of cities you need to be good at making broad diagnoses, but broken windows policing is an essential treatment that has to be molded to new circumstances and different environments.

When it comes to broken windows policing, I'm a practitioner of a philosophy that is no longer a philosophy. It is a reality. But it is a reality that still needs to be better understood, and I hope that in the next hour or so that you'll hear from the people who truly understand how it works and how it can be adapted.

JAMES Q. WILSON: Chief Bratton said that crime in New York City has declined for thirteen straight years. He also went on to praise quite generously George and my contribution to that development by citing the "Broken Windows" article in *Atlantic Monthly* magazine.

But I want to clarify at the outset that crime went down in New York City for many reasons, of which patrolling to deal with quality of life crimes was only one. The Compstat program, the effort to hold precinct commanders—or in Los Angeles, district commanders—accountable for individual crimes in their area on penalty of not being promoted if you failed to do so, was also a very powerful crime reduction tool, as was having more police officers to patrol the city—and, I would add, Los Angeles desperately needs more police officers. I could also note the street crime unit that Chief Bratton used to take guns off the street in order to reduce the temptation people face to use guns to commit crimes. Each of these programs, along with quality of life policing, helped bring about a tremendous reduction in crime.

What all these factors had in common, and this commonality didn't sit comfortably with many criminologists in the country, was that they were based on the common perception that the police could make a real difference. George and I had been working in this area for many decades, and when we began it was clear that hardly anyone thought that the police or even the prisons would make a difference in crime rates. The conventional wisdom of the day was that you couldn't reduce crime without addressing its "root causes." People spoke about root causes as if they knew what they were, but when pressed it turned out they weren't quite sure. It might mean changing the class structure of society, altering our culture, or eliminating the desire to join gangs—changes that, if they could be done at all, could be done only over several generations.

The view that George and I have had, and continue to share, is that the criminal justice system can make a significant difference. While society is waiting for root causes to change, and while we are building government programs to help them change, we can make our communities safer.

The police, however, need help. They cannot do this alone. They need help from other civic agencies. They need help to maintain streets, to fix stop signs. They need help from the building inspection department. They need help from the courts. They need help from all government agencies whose behavior, while they often don't see it this way, profoundly affects the quality of life in neighborhoods.

And one of the things that broken windows policing means is that the police are responsive to complaints from neighborhoods, which at first glance do not seem to be police business at all. This traffic light is out. There is garbage in the street. The building across the street hasn't been inspected and it is on the verge of collapse. Truly, broken windows policing is more than policing. We should really talk about broken windows government.

That is to say, making city government focus on local neighborhoods. There has to be a coordinated effort to bring efficiency and accountability together at the local level where citizens need it the most. And here I mean the supervisors who run schools, building maintenance programs, street maintenance, and the like. All of these agencies need to act together to identify what is important to individual neighborhoods.

Let me tell you a little bit about what broken windows policing is not. It is, first of all, not a single tactic. The tactic depends on the conditions in the city. In some cases it means getting rid of graffiti. In other places it means dealing with prostitutes hanging out on street corners or rowdy teenage gangs. In other cases it means tearing down or fixing up abandoned buildings or eliminating seedy motels that have become centers for the drug trade.

Secondly, broken windows policing is not zero tolerance, though that phrase has been hung on it, as if the police could eliminate crime by having no tolerance for any infraction however small. Even in New York City with 38,000 officers on patrol you cannot practice zero tolerance policing. What you can do is use the police to address those aspects of seemingly minor crimes that if left unattended will cause the conditions of public order in neighborhoods to deteriorate.

This doesn't mean harassing everyone. Indeed it doesn't really mean harassing anyone. It means dealing with those small signs of disorder that you believe, if left unattended, will create a problem.

And, finally, broken windows policing is not indifferent to community concerns. Indeed it is part of community-oriented policing. If you talk to people in crime-ridden neighborhoods in any serious way, they all say the same thing. They want their neighborhood repaired. And there is a broad agreement as to what that repair entails.

Broken windows policing means that you are responding, I think, to what people say are their major concerns. Broken windows policing began with an experiment done in Newark, New Jersey, orchestrated by the Police Foundation when George Kelling was its research director. The Foundation thought it would be an interesting idea to see if foot patrols would make a difference in neighborhood crime. This experiment was carried out over the objections of most police officers, which thought that foot patrol by officers would have no effect on the crime rate.

Consequently, foot patrol was instituted on an experimental basis in certain selected neighborhoods, and the behavior of people and offenders in those neighborhoods was compared with similar neighborhoods where foot patrol was not instituted.

What did we find? We found that foot patrols did not have much of an effect on crime rates, just as the police chiefs had told us. But what it did have an effect on was public confidence. What it did have an effect on was how willing people were to use the street, to feel comfortable in the street, and to feel safe in the street. Public satisfaction with the condition of their lives went up, even though the crime rate did not change. This may seem strange, but it is not.

The average person on a typical day is not the victim of a crime. The average person walking to the supermarket or going to the bus stop or passing rowdy teenagers on the street corner is, however, the subject of potential disorder or intimidation. Eliminate the disorder and the intimidation and more decent people use the streets.

George and I, in our article on broken windows, offered the speculation that if public order improved, crime rates might go down. Now there's a lively debate among social scientists as to whether the crime rates have gone down as a result of this, and like all arguments of this sort it is difficult, if not impossible, to make an absolutely non-controversial argument that we were right, but George will offer you some reasons for thinking that we could very well be right.

But even if we were wrong, even if the crime rate does not decline when you address minor offenses, public happiness undoubtedly goes up, and the police, like all civic agencies, have a responsibility to attend to public happiness.

We wanted to revive the traditional police officer's concern for public order. In the 19th and early parts of the 20th century, public order was the focus of police activity. They were the watchmen on the street corners. They would shout when they saw a fire. They would set up a hullabaloo when they saw a violent offense. They were people there to convey to the community and to those who would disturb the community that the community's preferences came first.

The police, beginning in the middle of the 20th century, became exclusively crime fighters, and by crime fighters I mean they sat in patrol cars, waited for a radio call, and then went out and tried to find, often unsuccessfully, perpetrators of a major burglary, robbery, rape or homicide. Restoring order maintenance restores the police to their older and more traditional function without at all abandoning their commitment to becoming serious crime fighters. Will this reduce crime? We think so. And in his remarks I hope George Kelling will tell you why we think so.

GEORGE KELLING: . . . When Jim first asked me if I wanted to co-author the article in *Atlantic Monthly* after the Newark foot patrol study was published, he was quick to point out to me that I would be in for some real criticism in my profession. And he also said that I was going to be called a racist, and worse. And all of that did in fact happen. But we have an obligation to publish the truth because there is a desperate need for order in the poorest neighborhoods and communities, especially in minority communities. They can't protect their own property, they can't let their children play in the streets, and as a result a culture of terror develops that diminishes those communities to the point where many of them are virtually unlivable.

But no sooner had the article come out than the police readily accepted the idea. At first it was "yes, you're right, but we have too many calls for service, we have too much serious crime that we have to concentrate on," etc. But the police knew how devastating social disorder is in poor neighborhoods and once we put quality of life in policing into an idiom that police officers could understand there was this real "Eureka!" moment among the rank and file officers. This feeling mushroomed when one day it was discovered that one in ten fare beaters either was carrying an illegal weapon or was wanted on a warrant for a serious crime. Not all fare beaters are serious criminals, but a lot of serious criminals are fare beaters.

In other words, serious criminals are busy doing a lot of bad stuff, and they're busy at it quite often, and because they have no respect for any laws at all they open themselves up to the kind of interventions that Jim has talked about and that Chief Bratton has implemented.

The criticism against broken windows policing goes something like this. Jim and I are order fanatics. We have a housekeeper's mentality, a place for everything and everything in its place, and what we want to do is to impose White Anglo Saxon Protestant values on minority communities, and that in fact we are cultural imperialists who are systematically trying to force our views of order and culture onto poor people and minorities.

Well that's an interesting argument, and it's especially interesting when I talk about broken windows policing in African American communities. Does anyone seriously think that any parent, regardless of race or culture, wants their daughters propositioned for sex on the way to school? Is that a cultural tradition that we want to preserve and pass down to future generations? If you think about it, the idea that somehow minorities and poor people revel in conditions that encourage social disorder and crime is simply an insult to the poor. It's an insult to minorities that assumes that they somehow enjoy living in broken neighborhoods. . . .

When we first started meeting with focus groups in the subway we would get, for example, different cultural groups together, including African American women, and ask them what they thought of our proposals. Surprisingly, they were disappointed in our proposals because they didn't think that we were going far enough. They lived in constant fear and were the victims of repeated insults and aggressive begging, so much so that they really wanted much more in the way of order policing. . . .

In Newark, the city has decided that it is tired of bicyclists running over and intimidating pedestrians. The first day they enforced the traffic laws regarding bicycle riding the police arrested three people who were carrying high-powered guns.

In short, we need to capitalize on the discovery by Chief Bratton, Jack Maple, and others that certain quality of life crimes are also indicators for more serious offenses. Broken windows, as I initially framed it, was focused around the idea of restoring community order, i.e. ultimately empowering the community to control itself. It turned out as we put this idea together that it also fit very well with a well-known axiom of criminology. Five percent of offenders commit over 50 percent of serious offenses. A small number of people create an enormous amount of havoc. But what researchers are discovering more and more is that habitual offenders are also committing a lot of minor offenses along the way. . . .

Bernard E. Harcourt  **NO**

Policing Disorder: Can We Reduce Serious Crime by Punishing Petty Offenses?

Punishment in these late modern times is marked by two striking developments. The first is a stunning increase in the number of persons incarcerated. Federal and state prison populations nationwide have increased from less than 200,000 in 1970 to more than 1,300,000 in 2000, with another 600,000 persons held in local jails. Today, approximately 2 million men and women are incarcerated in prisons and jails in this country. The intellectual rationale for this increase is provided by "incapacitation theory" the idea that a hardcore 6 percent of youths and young adults are responsible for the majority of crime and that locking up those persistent offenders will significantly impact crime rates.

A second dramatic development is the popularity of "order-maintenance policing," an approach to policing that emphasizes creating and maintaining orderly public spaces. This policy is driven by the "broken windows theory" the idea that tolerating such minor infractions as graffiti spraying, aggressive panhandling, prostitution, public urination, and turnstile jumping encourages serious violent crime by sending a signal that the community is not in control. The broken windows theory has ignited a virtual "revolution in American policing," also known as the "Blue Revolution." And its popularity in this country is apparently matched by its appeal abroad. In 1998 alone, representatives of over 150 police departments from foreign countries visited the New York Police Department for briefings and instruction in order-maintenance policing. For the first ten months of 2000, another 235 police departments 85 percent of them from abroad sent delegations to One Police Plaza. In New York City, where broken windows policing was introduced under the administration of Mayor Rudolph Giuliani and his first police commissioner, William Bratton, the order-maintenance strategy produced an immediate surge in arrests for misdemeanor offenses.

These two developments have common intellectual roots in the second half of the twentieth century, primarily in the writings of James Q. Wilson, and before him, Edward C. Banfield. The popularization of incapacitation theory can be traced in large part to Wilson's 1975 collection of essays, *Thinking*

About Crime, where he famously wrote: "Wicked people exist. Nothing avails except to set them apart from innocent people. We have trifled with the wicked, made sport of the innocent, and encouraged the calculators. Justice suffers, and so do we all." Like Banfield before him who, in *The Unheavenly City,* similarly advocated "abridg[ing] to an appropriate degree the freedom of those who in the opinion of a court are extremely likely to commit violent crimes." Wilson argued strenuously for increased prison sentences for hard-core offenders.

The broken windows theory can also be traced to Wilson, who, with his co-author George L. Kelling, wrote an influential *Atlantic Monthly* article in 1982 called "Broken Windows," a nine-page anecdotal essay that revolutionized policing. Wilson there spelled out and popularized the idea of cracking down on minor disorder as a way to combat serious crime.

Conservative policymakers tend to argue for both incapacitation *and* broken windows policing. . . .

What is striking, though, is that among progressives, liberals, and the full spectrum of Democrats, order-maintenance policing has been hailed as the only viable and feasible *alternative* to the three-strikes and mandatory minimum laws that have resulted in massive incarceration. The power and appeal of broken windows policing for liberals derives precisely from its *opposition* to incapacitation theory. Order maintenance is billed as a milder public-order measure. It represents, according to some progressives, one of the only "politically feasible and morally attractive alternatives to the severe punishments that now dominate America's inner-city crime-fighting prescriptions." This is precisely what makes broken windows policing "progressive."

As a result, order maintenance is popular today in a way that massive incarceration is not. Whereas the prison boom has received a lot of criticism in the media, among public officials, and in the academy, broken windows policing has received far less attention and scrutiny. With few notable exceptions, order maintenance continues to receive extremely favorable reviews in policy circles, academia, and the press.

This popularity was powerfully demonstrated during the 2001 mayoral campaign in New York City, especially before 9/11. In the early Democratic primaries, all the candidates were jockeying to be the next Giuliani on crime. The first question at the August 28, 2001 Democratic mayoral debate *what if the squeegee men come back?* had a domino effect on the candidates: they fell over each other pledging to maintain the crackdown on quality-of-life offenses. Mark Green, who ultimately won the Democratic primary, sought, obtained, and heavily publicized the endorsement of William Bratton, who appeared slated to return as police commissioner in a possible Democratic administration. As former mayor Edward Koch remarked, "Giuliani has so impacted New Yorkers by the reduction in crime that any candidate who doesn't agree with that has no chance."

After the election, the Manhattan Institute a conservative New York think tank began waging a renewed campaign in support of broken windows policing. A few days before Michael Bloomberg's inauguration as mayor, the Institute issued a new report on New York-style policing. Written by lead author

George Kelling co-author (with James Q. Wilson) of the "Broken Windows" article and of the book *Fixing Broken Windows* the report is titled *Do Police Matter? An Analysis of the Impact of New York City's Police Reforms*. The report contends that economic improvements and the end of the crack epidemic had *no* significant effect on overall drops in violent crime in New York City. In contrast, order maintenance policing exerted "the most significant influence" on violent crime trends. . . .

Two days after Bloomberg's inauguration, the Manhattan Institute caught the ear of *The New York Times,* arguing on the Op-Ed pages that broken windows policing "is not just smart policing; it's smart politics." In an editorial entitled "A Policing Strategy New Yorkers Like," Kelling emphasizes the popularity of enforcing quality-of-life laws, especially among minorities. "African-Americans, Hispanics and Asian-Americans all favor quality-of-life enforcement even more strongly than whites," Kelling claims. And for those who thought that Giuliani and Bratton were the chief architects of broken windows policing, Kelling offers a new narrative: it was Raymond Kelly, Bloomberg's new police commissioner, who, as police commissioner for former Mayor David Dinkins, started broken windows policing in the fall of 1993.

Questionable Social Science

The result is that today, broken windows theory seems more popular than ever. And the breadth of its popularity reflects the fact that it is understood as an *alternative* to the incarceration explosion we have witnessed in the latter part of the twentieth century. It has, in effect, captured the liberal imagination.

The difficulty is that there is no good evidence for the theory that disorder causes crime. To the contrary, the most reliable social scientific evidence suggests that the theory is wrong. The popularity of the broken windows theory, it turns out, is inversely related to the quality of the supporting evidence. The most recent study by the Manhattan Institute is a good illustration.

The goal of the Manhattan Institute study is to separate out "the relative contributions of police actions, the economy, demographics, and changing drug use patterns on crime" in New York City. The study's innovation is to achieve this separation by treating the city as 75 separate and comparable entities. "Rather than one city," they explain, "we view New York as 75 separate entities, corresponding to the 75 police precincts." Because economic conditions, for example, vary considerably across the 75 precincts, Kelling and his co-authors could look across the 75 cases and see if favorable economic conditions are associated with reduced rates of violent crime.

The aim of the research, then, is to determine the relative impact of four factors—broken windows policing, economic indicators, young-male population shifts, and the decline in crack cocaine consumption on violent crime in the 75 precincts of New York City. Is the decline in violent crime fully explained by an improved economy, a drop in the number of young men in the population, and reduced crack cocaine use? Or does the increase in arrests for minor offenses also play a significant role?

Naturally, the complexities in a study of this kind begin with the need to provide a precise measure of all the relevant factors. To measure broken windows policing, the authors use precinct-level reports of total misdemeanor arrests. To measure the effect of the crack epidemic, they use borough-level reports of hospital discharges for cocaine-related episodes. For the number of young males, they use precinct-level school enrollment data. And for unemployment, they use borough-level gross unemployment data. Finally, to measure violent crime, they use precinct-level reports of four violent offenses (murder, rape, felonious assault, and robbery). In all cases, they use data from 1989 to 1998.

Their findings are striking. They conclude that the "measure of 'broken windows' policing is *the strongest predictor of precinct violent crime in the model.*" Looking at the change over time, they find that neither demographics nor drug use patterns are significantly related to the drops in precinct violent crime over the ten-year study period. Unemployment *is* related to changes in crime rates, but in the *opposite* direction to what is generally assumed. As it turns out, "an *increase* in borough unemployment is related to a *decrease* in precinct violent crime," Kelling concludes.

The bottom line: "*The average NYPD precinct during the ten-year period studied could expect to suffer one less violent crime for approximately every 28 additional misdemeanor arrests made.*" Over the period from 1989 to 1998, increased rates of misdemeanor arrests therefore prevented, by their calculation, over 60,000 violent crimes or 5 percent of the overall decline. The study offers, in the authors' words, "the most-definitive possible answer to the question of whether police mattered in New York City during its intense crime-drop." It accomplishes this remarkable task with essentially one regression analysis and one page of statistical discussion. And the answer is: *Yes.*

But their case is remarkably weak and inconclusive. First, there are numerous alternative explanations that may account for the associations between the number of misdemeanor arrests and violent crime, including, for instance, the deterrent effect of police presence or even, possibly, some effect from incapacitating potential offenders. . . .

Even if we were to accept the research design, though, the authors do not have the proper data, and so could not carry through on their apparently ingenious idea. Unemployment data do not exist at the precinct level, so they instead use borough-level data: in effect, they assume that every Manhattan precinct faces the same economic conditions. Similarly, hospital discharges for cocaine-related episodes (even if that were a reliable index of crack as opposed to powdered cocaine consumption) are also borough-level data: in effect, the authors assume that every Brooklyn precinct has the same drug problem. So the report is essentially comparing apples and oranges: precinct-level data for crime, broken windows policing, and demographics, and borough-level data for gross unemployment and cocaine consumption. As Alfred Blumstein of Carnegie Mellon University recently commented, the data used to measure unemployment are too blunt and unreliable to do any damage to the idea that the economic boom and drop-off in crack cocaine use were important contributors to the national and municipal drop in violent crime. . . .

The most comprehensive and thorough study of the broken windows theory to date is Robert Sampson and Stephen Raudenbush's 1999 study entitled *Systematic Social Observation of Public Spaces: A New Look at Disorder in Urban Neighborhoods.* Their study is based on extremely careful data collection. Using trained observers who drove a sports utility vehicle at five miles per hour down every street in 196 Chicago census tracts, randomly selecting 15,141 streets for analysis, they were able to collect precise data on neighborhood disorder. Sampson and Raudenbush found that disorder and predatory crime are moderately correlated, but that, when antecedent neighborhood characteristics (such as neighborhood trust and poverty) are taken into account, the connection between disorder and crime "vanished in 4 out of 5 tests including homicide, arguably our best measure of violence." They acknowledge that disorder may have indirect effects on neighborhood crime by influencing "migration patterns, investment by businesses, and overall neighborhood viability." But, on the basis of their extensive research, Sampson and Raudenbush conclude that "[a]ttacking public order through tough police tactics may thus be a politically popular but perhaps analytically weak strategy to reduce crime."

The New York Story

If we look at the criminological evidence, the results are no more helpful to broken windows proponents. The basic fact is that a number of large U.S. cities Boston, Houston, Los Angeles, San Diego, and San Francisco, among others have experienced significant drops in crime since the early 1990s, in some cases proportionally larger than the drop in New York City's crime. But many of these cities have not implemented the type of aggressive order-maintenance policing that New York City did. One recent study found that New York City's drop in homicides, though impressive, is neither unparalleled nor unprecedented. Houston's drop in homicides of 59 percent between 1991 and 1996 outpaced New York City's 51 percent decline over the same period, and both were surpassed by Pittsburgh's 61 percent drop in homicides between 1984 and 1988. Another study looked at the rates of decline in homicides in the seventeen largest U.S. cities from 1976 to 1998 and found that New York City's recent decline, though above average, was the fifth largest, behind San Diego, Washington, D.C., St. Louis, and Houston.

A straight comparison of homicide and robbery rates between 1991 and 1998 reveals that although New York City is again in the top group, with declines in homicide and robbery rates of 70.6 percent and 60.1 percent respectively, San Diego experienced larger declines in homicide and robbery rates (76.4 percent and 62.6 percent respectively), Boston experienced a comparable decline in its homicide rate (69.3 percent), Los Angeles experienced a greater decline in its robbery rate (60.9 percent), and San Antonio experienced a comparable decline in its robbery rate (59.1 percent). Other major cities also experienced impressive declines in their homicide and robbery rates, including Houston (61.3 percent and 48.5 percent respectively) and Dallas (52.4 percent and 50.7 percent respectively).

Many of these cities, however, did not implement New York-style order-maintenance policing. The San Diego police department, for example, implemented a radically different model of policing focused on community-police relations. The police began experimenting with problem-oriented policing in the late 1980s and retrained the police force to better respond to community concerns. They implemented a strategy of sharing responsibility with citizens for identifying and solving crimes. But while recording remarkable drops in crime, San Diego also posted a 15 percent drop in total arrests between 1993 and 1996, and an 8 percent decline in total complaints of police misconduct filed with the police department between 1993 and 1996.

San Francisco also focused on community involvement and experienced decreased arrest and incarceration rates between 1993 and 1998. San Francisco's felony commitments to the California Department of Corrections dropped from 2,136 in 1993 to 703 in 1998, whereas other California counties either maintained or slightly increased their incarcerations. San Francisco also abandoned a youth curfew in the early 1990s and sharply reduced its commitments to the California Youth Authority from 1994 to 1998. Despite this, San Francisco experienced greater drops in its crime rate for rape, robbery, and aggravated assault than did New York City for the period 1995 through 1998. In addition, San Francisco experienced the sharpest decline in total violent crime, sharper than New York City or Boston between 1992 and 1998.

Other cities, including Los Angeles, Houston, Dallas, and San Antonio, also experienced significant drops in crime without adopting as coherent a policing strategy as New York or San Diego. The fact is, there was a remarkable decline in crime in many major cities in the United States during the 1990s. New York City was certainly a very high performer. But numerous major U.S. cities have achieved substantial declines in crime using a variety of different policing strategies. It would be simplistic to attribute the rate of the decline in New York City solely to the quality-of-life initiative.

A number of other factors seem to have contributed to declining crime rates in New York City, including a shift in drug use patterns from crack cocaine to heroin, favorable economic conditions in the 1990s, new computerized tracking systems that speed up police responses to crime, a dip in the number of eighteen to twenty-four-year-old males, as well as shifts in adolescent behavior. There have also been important changes at the NYPD, including a significant increase in the sheer number of police officers. Mayor Dinkins hired over two thousand new police officers under the Safe Streets, Safe City program in 1992, and Giuliani hired another four thousand officers and merged about six thousand Transit and Housing Authority officers into the ranks of the NYPD. As a result, from 1991 to 2000, the NYPD force increased almost by half, up by 12,923 police officers (including those transferred from Transit) from a force of 26, 856 police officers in 1991 to 39,779 in 2000. Excluding the Transit merger, the police force grew by almost a quarter. As a result, the NYPD now has the largest police force in the country and the highest ratio of police officers to civilians of any major metropolitan area.

Moreover, beginning in January 1994, Giuliani and Bratton instituted major changes in police management. They started relying more heavily on new computer technology to compile crime statistics, to convert the data into maps and charts that inform the police about crime patterns in different precincts, and to monitor and review police performance at the district level through regular meetings. The data and meetings allow the police to target their enforcement to changing crime trends. Bratton also shook up his management team, cut out layers of bureaucracy, aggressively promoted younger and more ambitious managers, and delegated more authority to precinct commanders. In addition, Giuliani and Bratton implemented a number of different police strategies including gun-oriented policing and enhanced drug enforcement initiatives that significantly overhauled the way the NYPD approached crime fighting.

So even if we were prepared to attribute a significant role in the drop in crime in New York City to changes at the NYPD despite comparably sharp drops in crime in cities that did not institute similar policing strategies we would still need to ask if it was the broken windows strategy that did the trick, or if instead the drop in crime owes to the increased surveillance afforded by a more aggressive policy of arrests and stop-and-frisks. The answer to this question has to be the increased surveillance. . . .

The bottom line is that the broken windows theory the idea that public disorder sends a message that encourages crime is probably wrong. . . .

The title of the new Manhattan Institute report *Do Police Matter?* asks a good question, with an obvious answer: *Yes.* . . .

But that question is too easy and is not the right one to ask. The real question is whether an agency like the NYPD needs to implement a policy of making large numbers of arrests for minor misdemeanors and public disorder violations as a primary strategy for combating violent crime. The answer to that question is equally clear: *No.* The best social scientific and criminological evidence suggests that minor social and physical disorder is not causally related to violent crime.

Troubling Consequences

. . . The trouble is, policing strategies that deliberately emphasize arresting misdemeanor and public order offenders rather than issuing warnings or implementing alternative problem-solving techniques have significant racial consequences. The fact is that in New York City, and the United States more generally, adults arrested for misdemeanors are disproportionately African-American in relation to their representation in the community. In 2000, for example, slightly over 50 percent of all adults arrested for misdemeanors in New York City were African-American (113,336 of the total 224,663 adults arrested). Slightly over 50 percent of adults arrested for disorderly conduct (19,563 of the total 38,780) and 45.6 percent of adults arrested for loitering were African-American. For prostitution and drug possession, the proportions are 40.7 percent and 51.7 percent respectively. (For DWI, interestingly, the proportion is only 22.3 percent). Yet African Americans (in 2000) represented only 24.6 percent of the New York City population. Persons of Hispanic descent represented 31.5 percent of all adult misdemeanor arrests, whereas they constituted only 25.1 percent of the city's population. In contrast, European Americans represented 48.8 percent of the population, and accounted for only 15.5 percent of adults arrested on misdemeanor charges in 2000.

These disparities hold true for large cities across the United States. In 1999, for instance, 43.4 percent of adults arrested for vagrancy in large metropolitan areas were African-American; 34.2 percent, 39 percent, and slightly over 40 percent of those arrested for disorderly conduct, prostitution, and drug abuse charges, respectively, were African-American. (Again, curiously, only 10.7 percent of those arrested for driving under the influence were black). Yet African Americans represent less than 15 percent of the total population of these metropolitan areas.

The point is not that the police are consciously targeting black misdemeanants, but simply that more blacks are arrested for misdemeanors given their proportion in the overall population. In other words, the *decision to arrest misdemeanants,* adopting that policy in preference to other policing strategies is a choice with significant distributional consequences for African Americans. Additionally, there is good evidence that New York City's policy of aggressive stop-and-frisks was in fact implemented in a racially discriminatory manner. In 1999, New York State Attorney General Eliot Spitzer, with the assistance of Columbia University's Center for Violence Research and Prevention, analyzed 174,919 stop-and-frisk "UF-250" forms the forms that NYPD officers are required to fill out in a variety of stop encounters from the period January 1, 1998 through March 31, 1999. Spitzer found that the raw number of stops was higher for minorities African Americans and Hispanics than whites relative to their respective proportion of the population. Spitzer then reanalyzed the raw numbers, this time taking account of the different crime rates and the population composition in different precincts, and found significant disparities across all precincts and crime categories: "in aggregate across all crime categories and precincts citywide, blacks were 'stopped' 23% more often (in comparison to the crime rate) than whites. Hispanics were 'stopped' 39% more often than whites." Spitzer concluded from the data that "even when crime data are taken into account, minorities are still 'stopped' at a higher rate than would be predicted by both demographics and crime rates." . . .

What does this say about order-maintenance as a police technique? First, it is an illusion to think that broken windows policing operates through increased orderliness. Second, order-maintenance probably contributes to fighting crime through enhanced surveillance. Third, broken windows policing comes at a significant cost, with negative distributional consequences for African Americans and other minorities. Fourth, there are alternative strategies of problem-solving policing.

A Broken Theory

. . . When we peel away disorder from crime, it becomes clear that the model of orderliness offers to contemporary society, first, a classic mode of enhanced surveillance. The criminological evidence suggests that it is not the order, but the surveillance associated with broken windows policing that has probably contributed to the drop in crime in a city like New York. It is the increased arrests, background checks, fingerprint comparisons, stop-and-frisks, line-ups, and informants. It is, in effect, the increased police-civilian contacts. Are they necessary? The answer is no. Many cities in the United States have experienced remarkable drops in crime during the 1990s without implementing similar order maintenance strategies. The costs are simply too steep, especially to minority communities. And there are alternatives, such as the problem-solving policing discussed, in part, in the new Manhattan Institute report.

Second, order maintenance policing provides a way to enforce an aesthetic preference, under the guise of combating serious crime. Order maintenance is a way to get homeless people, panhandlers, and prostitutes off the street. It is a way to keep the avenues clean of graffiti and litter. Broken windows policing is a way to repossess red light districts and displace street vendors, panhandlers, and ordinary street life. It is, in effect, a type of "aesthetic policing" that fosters a sterile, Disneyland, consumerist, commercial aesthetic. It reflects a desire to transform New York City into Singapore, or worse, a shopping mall. The truth is, however, that when we lose the dirt, grit, and street life of major American cities, we may also threaten their vitality, creativity, and character.

EXPLORING THE ISSUE

Does Broken-Windows Policing Reduce Crime?

Critical Thinking and Reflection

1. What does the evidence show? Is broken-windows policing an effective approach that reduces crime? Or are many of the claims made on behalf of broken-windows policing merely "hype" that is not justified by the evidence?
2. Even if there is no clear evidence that the broken-windows approach leads to a drop in serious crimes, might it still be a good idea to adopt an aggressive approach that seeks to reduce public drinking and other nuisance behaviors in a community?
3. Should big-city police departments adopt the broken-windows approach even if minority communities cry "discrimination"?
4. What alternatives are there to broken-windows policing? How can cities reduce crime without resorting to the more aggressive order-maintenance or broken-windows approach?
5. What is "racial profiling"? Is racial profiling ever justified as a law enforcement strategy?

Is There Common Ground?

It is difficult to conclusively prove whether or not the broken-windows approach actually leads to a drop in serious crime. The data will never be good enough to clearly show whether it was the broken-windows approach or some other set of factors that caused a reduction in crime. Nor can social science readily discern to what extent, if any, a city's crackdown on minor violations effects decision making by individuals who are prone to engage in violent and serious crimes. As a result, the debate over the worth of broken-windows policing will undoubtedly continue.

There is a much larger question, however, that must be addressed by cities as they explore the broken-windows approach: How can the community's "good" that can be gained from a more aggressive order-maintenance approach be balanced with a respect for individual rights and constitutionally protected civil rights and civil liberties?

Police officers who are directed to increase arrests cannot possibly arrest every violator. Police departments and the courts lack the personnel and other resources to handle the flood they would face if officers even attempted to arrest all persons who broke the law, no matter how minor or harmless the violations. Should a person be arrested for sitting on the steps, blocking the traffic flow on a subway staircase? Police officers themselves argue that they need to be allowed the discretion to use their common sense and the professional wisdom that they have gained from working in the field, that they can capably decide just when to make an arrest and when circumstances justify their overlooking a minor violation (Sousa 2010).

Broken-windows policing and the increased emphasis paid to smaller offenses should not be allowed to morph into a "zero tolerance" policy that seeks to have the police make an arrest in every situation where a violation occurs. Police officers rightly argue that they need a fair degree of discretion to do their jobs well. Also, is it really a good use of police resources to have officers arrest a nonviolent homeless person for panhandling (or even for urinating in an alley when there is no restroom nearby), especially as the courts are unlikely to give strong backing to such actions and the arrestee is soon returned to the streets? Does it really make any sense to round up youths for loud and unruly street behavior, a situation that may be a nuisance but clearly does not constitute a serious crime? A zero-tolerance law enforcement approach that seeks to eliminate police discretion will increase community order only at the cost of wasting valuable law enforcement resources and infringing on individualism.

When implementing actions aimed at preserving public order, the police themselves have an obligation to abide by the law and the U.S. Constitution. Judges, for instance, have stopped police sweeps directed against street beggars as an infringement on the constitutional free-speech rights that even panhandlers enjoy. Police departments that adopt a broken-windows posture must also adopt policies that will ensure that individual rights are safeguarded against overly aggressive police action. A broken-windows-oriented department that asks officers to increase the number of arrests for minor violations must also institute training programs and effective oversight procedures to ensure that officers are respecting constitutionally protected rights despite the new pressure to make arrests. Similarly, training and oversight programs must also be established to ensure that officers do not resort to racial profiling, looking at a person's race or ethnicity as a factor when deciding if a person's behavior should lead to further investigation or even an arrest.

Additional Resources

Harcourt, Bernard E. (2001). *Illusion of Order: The False Promises of Broken Windows Policing*. Cambridge, MA: Harvard University Press.

Kelling, George L., & Catherine M. Coles. (1996). *Fixing Broken Windows: Restoring Order and Reducing Crime in Our Communities*. New York: Touchstone.

Skogan, Wesley. G. (1990). *Disorder and Decline*. New York: Free Press.

Sousa, William H. (2010). "Paying Attention to Minor Offenses: Order Maintenance Policing in Practice." *Police Protection and Research*, Vol. 11, No. 1 (February).

Wilson, James Q., & George L. Kelling. (March 1982). "Broken Windows." *The Atlantic* magazine.

Internet References

Prof. Wesley G. Skogan Home Page: Community Policing; Crime and Disorder

Professor Skogan, one of the nation's foremost experts on the subject of community policing, maintains a website that offers a large number of his book chapters, articles, and research reports. Be sure to look at the site's numerous links to studies and reports of the broken-windows approach that emphasizes order maintenance.

www.skogan.org

The Urban Institute, Policing and Crime Prevention

This is a Washington-based "think tank" that explores a variety of urban policy initiatives, including the effectiveness of various approaches to reducing crime in the city and in public housing.

www.urban.org/center/jpc/projects/Policing-and-Crime-Prevention.cfm

ISSUE 7

Are School Vouchers Overrated as a Strategy for Reforming Public Education?

YES: Sol Stern, from "School Choice Isn't Enough," *City Journal* (vol. 18, no.1, Winter 2008)

NO: Jay P. Greene and Robert Enlow, from "Is School Choice Enough?," *City Journal* (vol.18, no.1, Winter 2008, Online Forum)

Learning Outcomes
After reading this issue, you should be able to:
• Explain how "choice" strategies seek to improve schooling.
• Identify the dangers and risks that critics charge are inherent in a system of school vouchers.
• Explain why public school teachers and administrators generally oppose school vouchers.
• Review the evidence on the impact of school vouchers in Milwaukee and Cleveland, underscoring just where vouchers have—and have not—led to educational gains.
• Explain how voucher advocates continue to defend vouchers even in the face of evidence that voucher systems have produced only the most limited educational gains.

ISSUE SUMMARY

YES: Sol Stern's "School Choice Isn't Enough" produced a considerable stir of controversy, especially in conservative political circles. Stern, a long-time advocate of school vouchers, explains why he has reassessed his position. The evidence, according to Stern, shows that school vouchers seldom lead to significant improvements in student test scores or the restructuring of public school systems. Stern argues that greater emphasis should be given to reforming and strengthening a city's public schools, rather than continuing to place so much emphasis on fighting for vouchers.

NO: Professor Jay P. Greene, professor of education policy and author of *Why America Needs School Choice,* heatedly disputes Stern's reading of the evidence. According to Greene, voucher programs produce limited but still significant educational gains. The parents of voucher children also express their great satisfaction with the schools they have chosen. Robert Enlow, president and CEO of the Friedman Foundation for Educational Choice, argues for the need to reduce state regulations that continue to insulate public school systems from the competitive pressures that a voucher system was intended to create.

Can the nation's public schools be saved? Some critics argue that the state of public education is so hopeless that radical change is required. These reformers argue for the introduction of a system of certificates or *school vouchers* that would allow dissatisfied students (and their parents) to withdraw from underperforming public schools and purchase more satisfactory schooling elsewhere.

Under a system of school vouchers, a state reduces the aid that it gives directly to a public school, and gives each student a voucher (essentially a coupon) to help the student attend the school of his or her choice. A student can use the voucher to attend the usual neighborhood school, a private school, a newly established voucher academy, or the public school in a neighboring school district. The state aid "follows" the student to the chosen school.

Voucher systems abet choice and promise to create competitive pressures that will force poorly performing public schools to "shape up." A public school would no longer be assured of enrollment; an unsatisfactory public school would lose both students and the state funding that accompanies each student in the form of a voucher. To stem the outflow of students and the loss of money, public schools will have to increase their responsiveness to students and parents.

Charter schools (which will be discussed in more detail in Issue 8) and vouchers are both "choice" strategies intended to create a competitive and performance-oriented school environment. Of the two, a system of vouchers is the more far-reaching or radical reform. Charter schools are given new flexibility but are still subject to an extensive number of state rules and regulations, including, notably, regulations that limit the ability of school administrators to dismiss teachers they find to be unsatisfactory.

A system of school vouchers, by contrast, is a more free-market approach to educational reform, intended to spur the creation of a fuller range of schools with a vast variety of instructional approaches and curricular offerings. New voucher academies are subject to fewer regulations than charter schools.

School vouchers, to a great extent, have their roots in the writings of Nobel Prize–winning economist Milton Friedman. Friedman emphasized individual freedom, and the importance of empowering citizens to make choices as opposed to accepting the one-size-fits-all systems offered by public school systems. He saw vouchers as a means of liberating students from the irresponsiveness of a "monopoly" school system.

Critics, however, charge that vouchers will worsen inequality and exacerbate the decline of the public schools. As "better" students leave to attend the school of their choice, other students are left behind in the "dumping ground" of the old public schools, now bereft of good students and with even less funding than before.

Vouchers also may not offer many students a real choice of education. Few suburban schools or top-end private schools will admit voucher students, especially when vouchers do not fully cover school costs. Schools will also maintain their selectivity in admissions, denying a place to students with a record of academic difficulty and behavioral problems.

In Milwaukee, Cleveland, and Washington, DC, vouchers have not led to a great improvement in student test scores, especially when compared to public school students who have a comparable family background. School choice advocates respond by pointing to individual cases where vouchers have clearly made a difference. They also note that voucher parents, especially minority parents in the inner city, are also quite satisfied with their children's new schools.

Voucher programs are not all the same. A targeted program that gives vouchers only to low-income students (as is the case in Cleveland and Milwaukee) will have vastly different impacts than a program that makes vouchers available to a much larger school population. Choice advocates argue for a wider program to generate the competitive pressures that will lead public schools to undertake broad reforms. But the widespread offering of vouchers also runs the risk of increasing racial segregation, as white parents will use voucher assistance to have their children escape schools undergoing racial change. The highly targeted voucher programs in Cleveland and Milwaukee did *not* exacerbate racial segregation as those programs awarded vouchers only to the most financially needy students in the city.

Public school teachers and administrators object to the unfairness of a voucher program that will allow voucher academy administrators the ability to hire nonunion teachers and to dismiss teachers who do not buy into the a school's mission. Teachers charge that the voucher programs are a veiled attempt at "union busting." Public school teachers further decry that voucher academies attempt to save money by employing unqualified teacher aides and by using computer-assisted instruction as substitutes for the teacher-led instruction. Voucher advocates respond that teacher unions are part of the problem, that unions protect undeserving teachers.

For a long time, the debate over the separation of church and state dominated the discussion of vouchers. Cleveland and Milwaukee students have largely been able to escape failing public schools by using their vouchers to attend Catholic-run parochial schools. However the question of the separation of church and state no longer dominates the voucher debate. The U.S. Supreme Court effectively resolved that matter in its 2002 *Zelman v. Simmons-Harris* decision, ruling that as long vouchers were dispensed to parents who maintained control over the choice of schools their children would attend, a voucher program does not violate the First Amendment's prohibition on the state establishment of religion.

In the YES reading presented in this issue, Sol Stern argues that school vouchers have neither improved student test scores nor led public schools to make significant reforms of their own. Rather than continuing to fight for vouchers, Stern argues that political conservatives should give greater attention to merit pay, the elimination of teacher tenure, incentives for innovative instruction, and other means of strengthening the public schools, the places where the vast majority of students continue to receive their education.

In the NO reading, Jay Greene and Robert Enlow object that Stern misreads the evidence. These authors argue that vouchers have led to significant educational gains and that there exists widespread support for school choice programs. If school vouchers have not produced the great impact that was theorized, it is only because choice has been offered to too few students to create a truly competitive and transformative educational environment.

YES

Sol Stern

School Choice Isn't Enough: Instructional Reform Is the Key to Better Schools

I began writing about school choice in *City Journal* more than a decade ago. I believed then (as I still believe) that giving tuition vouchers to poor inner-city students stuck in lousy public schools was a civil rights imperative. Starting in the 1980s, major empirical studies by sociologist James Coleman and other scholars showed that urban Catholic schools were better than public schools at educating the poor, despite spending far less per student. Among the reasons for this superiority: most Catholic educators still believed in a coherent, content-based curriculum, and they enforced order in the classroom. It seemed immoral to keep disadvantaged kids locked up in dismal, future-darkening public schools when vouchers could send them to high-performing Catholic ones—especially when middle-class parents enjoyed education options galore for their children.

But like other reformers, I also believed that vouchers would force the public schools to improve or lose their student "customers." Since competition worked in other areas, wouldn't it lead to progress in education, too? Maybe Catholic schools' success with voucher students would even encourage public schools to exchange the failed "progressive education" approaches used in most classrooms for the pedagogy that made the Catholic institutions so effective.

"Choice is a panacea," argued education scholars John Chubb and Terry Moe in their influential 1990 book *Politics, Markets and America's Schools*. For a time, I thought so, too. Looking back from today's vantage point, it is clear that the school choice movement has been very good for the disadvantaged. Public and privately funded voucher programs have liberated hundreds of thousands of poor minority children from failing public schools. The movement has also reshaped the education debate. Not only vouchers, but also charter schools, tuition tax credits, mayoral control, and other reforms are now on the table as alternatives to bureaucratic, special-interest-choked big-city school systems.

Yet social-change movements need to be attentive to the facts on the ground. Recent developments in both public and Catholic schools suggest that markets in education may not be a panacea—and that we should reexamine the direction of school reform.

One such development: taxpayer-funded voucher programs for poor children, long considered by many of us to be the most promising of education reforms, have hit a wall. In 2002, after a decade of organizing by school choice activists, only two programs existed: one in Milwaukee, the other in Cleveland, allowing 17,000 poor students to attend private (mostly Catholic) schools. That year, in *Zelman* v. *Simmons-Harris*, the Supreme Court ruled that limited voucher programs involving religious schools were compatible with the First Amendment's establishment clause. The 5–4 decision seemed like school choice's Magna Carta. But the legal victory has led to few real gains. Today, fewer than 25,000 students—compared with a nationwide public school enrollment of 50 million—receive tax-funded vouchers, with a tiny Washington, D.C., program joining those of the other two cities.

Proposals for voucher programs have suffered five straight crushing defeats in state referenda—most recently in Utah, by a margin of 62 percent to 38 percent. After each loss, school choice groups blamed the lobbying money poured into the states by teachers' unions, the deceptive ads run by voucher foes, and sometimes even voters' commitment to their children. When the Utah results came in, the principal funder of the pro-voucher side, businessman Patrick Byrne, opined that the voters failed "a statewide IQ test" and that they "don't care enough about their kids." If vouchers can't pass voter scrutiny in conservative Utah, though, how probable is it that they will do so anywhere else? And denouncing voters doesn't seem like a smart way to revive the voucher cause.

Voucher prospects have also dimmed because of the Catholic schools' deepening financial crisis. Without an abundant supply of good, low-cost urban Catholic schools to receive voucher students, voucher programs will have a hard time getting off the ground, let alone succeeding. But cash-strapped Catholic Church officials are closing the Church's inner-city schools at an accelerating rate [see "Save the Catholic Schools!," Spring 2007]. With just one Catholic high school left in all of Detroit, for instance, where would the city's disadvantaged students use vouchers even if they had them?

Even more discouraging, vouchers may not be enough to save the Catholic schools that are voucher students' main destination. Archbishop Donald Wuerl of Washington, D.C., recently announced plans to close seven of the district's 28 remaining Catholic schools, all of which are receiving aid from federally funded tuition vouchers, unless the D.C. public school system agreed to take them over and convert them into charter schools. In Milwaukee, several Catholic schools have also closed, or face the threat of closing, despite boosting enrollments with voucher kids.

During the 15 years since the first voucher program got under way in Milwaukee, university researchers have extensively scrutinized the dynamics of school choice and the effect of competition on public schools. The preponderance of studies have shown clear benefits, both academically and otherwise, for the voucher kids. It's gratifying that the research confirms the moral and civil rights argument for vouchers.

But sadly—and this is a second development that reformers must face up to—the evidence is pretty meager that competition from vouchers is making public schools better. When I reported on the Milwaukee voucher experiment in 1999, some early indicators suggested that competition was having just that effect. Members of Milwaukee's school board, for example, said that voucher schools had prompted new reforms in the public school system, including modifying the seniority provisions of the teachers' contract and allowing principals more discretion in hiring. A few public schools began offering phonics-based reading instruction in the early grades, the method used in neighboring Catholic schools. Milwaukee public schools' test scores also improved—and did so most dramatically in those schools under the greatest threat of losing students to vouchers, according to a study by Harvard economist Caroline Hoxby.

Unfortunately, the gains fizzled. Fifteen years into the most expansive school choice program tried in any urban school district in the country, Milwaukee's public schools still suffer from low achievement and miserable graduation rates, with test scores flattening in recent years. Violence and disorder throughout the system seem as serious as ever. Most voucher students are still benefiting, true; but no "Milwaukee miracle," no transformation of the public schools, has taken place. One of the Milwaukee voucher program's founders, African-American educator Howard Fuller, recently told the *Milwaukee Journal Sentinel*, "I think that any honest assessment would have to say that there hasn't been the deep, wholesale improvement in MPS [Milwaukee Public Schools] that we would have thought." And the lead author of one of the Milwaukee voucher studies, Harvard political scientist Paul Peterson, told me: "The research on school choice programs clearly shows that low-income students benefit academically. It's less clear that the presence of choice in a community motivates public schools to improve."

What should we do about these new realities? Obviously, private scholarship programs ought to keep helping poor families find alternatives to failing public schools. And we can still hope that some legislature, somewhere in America, will vote for another voucher plan, or generous tuition tax credits, before more Catholic schools close. But does the school choice movement have a realistic Plan B for the millions of urban students who will remain stuck in terrible public schools?

According to Hoxby and Peterson, perhaps the two most respected school choice scholars in the country, no such plan is necessary. In their view, the best hope for education improvement continues to be a maximum degree of parental choice—vouchers if possible, but also charter schools and tuition tax credits—plus merit-pay schemes for teachers and accountability systems that distinguish productive from unproductive school principals.

That "incentivist" outlook remains dominant within school reform circles. But a challenge from what one could call "instructionists"—those who believe that curriculum change and good teaching are essential to improving schools—is growing, as a unique public debate sponsored by the Koret Task Force on K–12 Education revealed. Founded in 1999, the Koret Task Force represents a national all-star team of education reform scholars. Permanent fellows include not only Hoxby and Peterson but also Chubb, Moe, education historian Diane Ravitch, Thomas B. Fordham Foundation president Chester Finn, Stanford University economics prof Eric Hanushek, and the guru of "cultural literacy," E. D. Hirsch, Jr. (recently retired). Almost from the start, the Koret scholars divided into incentivist and instructionist camps. "We have had eight years and we haven't been able to agree," says Hoxby. But in early 2007, members did agree to hold a debate at the group's home, the Hoover Institution at Stanford University: "Resolved: True School Reform Demands More Attention to Curriculum and Instruction than to Markets and Choice." Hirsch and Ravitch argued the affirmative, Hoxby and Peterson the negative.

Hirsch and Ravitch opened by saying that while they had no opposition to charter schools or other forms of choice, charter schools had produced "disappointing results." Try a thought experiment, urged Ravitch. Say that one school system features market incentives and unlimited choices for parents and students, but no standard curriculum. Then posit another system, with no choice allowed, but in which the educational leadership enforces a rich curriculum and favors effective instructional approaches. In the market system, Ravitch predicted, "most schools will reflect the dominant ideas of the schools of education, where most teachers get their training, so most schools will adopt programs of whole language and fuzzy math. . . . Most students under a pure choice regime will know very little about history or literature or science." The system with the first-rate curriculum and effective pedagogy, Ravitch argued, would produce better education outcomes.

Responding, Peterson and Hoxby paid respects to good curricula and instructional methods. But the key question, in their view, was who would *decide* which curricula and instructional methods were best. Here, the pro-choice debaters made no bones about it: the market's "invisible hand" was the way to go. As Hoxby put it, educational choice would erect a "bulwark against special-interest groups hijacking the curriculum."

I had supported the competition argument for school choice as a working hypothesis, but my doubts about it grew after recent results from the Milwaukee experiment, and nothing said in the Koret debate restored my confidence. And something else caught my attention: Ravitch's comment about "the dominant ideas of the schools of education, where most teachers get their training." The statement slipped by, unchallenged by the incentivist side.

While the arguments about school choice and markets swirled during the past 15 years, both Ravitch and Hirsch wrote landmark books (*Left Back* and *The Schools We Need and Why We Don't Have Them,* respectively) on how the nation's education schools have built an "impregnable fortress" (Hirsch's words) of wrong ideas and ineffective classroom practices that teachers then carry into America's schools, almost guaranteeing failure, especially for poor minority children. Hirsch's book didn't just argue this; it proved it conclusively, to my mind, offering an extraordinary *tour d'horizon* of all the evidence about instructional methods that cognitive neuroscience had discovered.

If Hoxby and Peterson were right in asserting that markets were enough to fix our education woes, then the ed schools wouldn't be the disasters that Hirsch, Ravitch, and others have exposed. Unlike the government-run K–12 schools, the country's 1,500 ed schools represent an almost perfect system of choice, markets, and competition. Anyone interested in becoming a teacher is completely free to apply to any ed school that he or she wants. The ed schools, in turn, compete for students by offering competitive prices and—theoretically—attractive educational "products" (curricula and courses). Yet the schools are uniformly awful, the products the same dreary progressive claptrap. A few years ago, the National Council on Teacher Quality, a mainstream public education advocacy group, surveyed the nation's ed schools and found that almost all elementary education classes disdained phonics and scientific reading. If the invisible hand is a surefire way to improve curriculum and instruction, as the incentivists insist, why does almost every teacher-in-training have to read the works of leftists Paolo Freire, Jonathan Kozol, and William Ayers—but usually nothing by, say, Hirsch or Ravitch?

For a good explanation, look to the concept of ideological hegemony, usually associated with the sociological Left. Instead of competition and diversity in the education schools, we confront what Hirsch calls the "thoughtworld" of teacher training, which operates like a Soviet-style regime suppressing alternative perspectives. Professors who dare to break with the ideological monopoly—who look to reading science or, say, embrace a core knowledge approach—won't get tenure, or get hired in the first place. The teachers they train thus wind up indoctrinated with the same pedagogical dogma whether they attend New York University's school of education or Humboldt State's. Those who put their faith in the power of markets to improve schools must at least show how their theory can account for the stubborn persistence of the thoughtworld.

Instead, we increasingly find the theory of educational competition detaching itself from its original school choice moorings and taking a new form. Vouchers may have stalled, but it's possible—or so many school reformers and education officials now assure us—to create the conditions for vigorous market competition *within* public school systems, with the same beneficent effects that were supposed to flow from a pure choice program.

Nowhere has this new philosophy of reform been more enthusiastically embraced than in the New York City school district under the control of Mayor Michael Bloomberg and schools chancellor Joel Klein. Gotham's schools are surging ahead with a host of market incentives, including models derived from the business world. Many of the country's major education foundations and philanthropies have boosted New York as the flagship school system for such market innovations, helping to spread the incentivist gospel nationally. Disciples of Klein have taken over the school systems in Baltimore and Washington, D.C., and Bloomberg's fellow billionaires Eli Broad and Bill Gates are about to launch a $60 million ad campaign to push the market approach during the presidential election season.

Don't get me wrong: market-style reforms are sometimes just what's necessary in the public schools. Over the past decade, for instance, I often called attention in *City Journal* to the destructively restrictive provisions in the New York City teachers' contract, which forced principals to hire teachers based solely on seniority, and I felt vindicated when negotiations between the Bloomberg administration and the United Federation of Teachers eliminated the seniority clause and created an open-market hiring system. Similarly, the teachers' lockstep salary schedule, based on seniority and accumulating useless additional education credits, is a counterproductive way to compensate the system's most important employees. The schools need a flexible salary structure that realistically reflects supply and demand in the teacher labor market.

Unfortunately, the Bloomberg administration and its supporters are pushing markets and competition in the public schools far beyond where the evidence leads. Everything in the system now has a price. Principals can get cash bonuses of as much as $50,000 by raising their schools' test scores; teachers in a few hundred schools now (and hundreds more later) can take home an extra $3,000 if the student scores in their schools improve; parents get money for showing up at parent-teacher conferences; their kids get money or—just what they need—cell phones for passing tests.

Much of this scaffolding of cash incentives (and career-ending penalties) rests on a rather shaky base: the state's highly unreliable reading and math tests in grades three through eight, plus the even more unreliable high school Regents exams, which have been dumbed down so that schools will avoid federal sanctions under the No Child Left Behind act. In the past, the tests have also been prone to cheating scandals. Expect more cheating as the stakes for success and failure rise.

While confidently putting their seal of approval on this market system, the mayor and chancellor appear to be agnostic on what actually works in the classroom. They've shown no interest, for example, in two decades' worth of scientific research sponsored by the National Institutes of Health that proves that teaching phonics and phonemic awareness is crucial to getting kids to read in the early grades. They have blithely retained a fuzzy math program, Everyday Math, despite a consensus of university math professors judging it inadequate. Indeed, Bloomberg and Klein have abjured all responsibility for curriculum and instruction and placed their bets entirely on choice, markets, and accountability.

But the new reliance on markets hasn't prevented special interests from hijacking the curriculum. One such interest is the Teachers College Reading and Writing Project—led by Lucy Calkins, the doyenne of the whole-language reading approach, which postulates that all children can learn to read and write naturally, with just some guidance from teachers, and that direct phonics instruction is a form of child abuse. Calkins's enterprise has more than $10 million in Department of Education contracts to guide reading and writing instruction in most of the city's elementary schools, even though no solid evidence supports her methodology. This may explain why, on the recent National Assessment of Educational Progress (NAEP) tests—widely regarded as a gold standard for educational assessment—Gotham students showed no improvement in fourth- and eighth-grade reading from 2003 to 2007, while the city of Atlanta, which hasn't staked everything on market incentives, has shown significant reading improvement.

One wonders why so many in the school reform movement and in the business community celebrate New York City's recent record on education. Is it merely because they hear the words "choice," "markets," and "competition" and think that all is well? If so, they're mistaken. The primal scene of all education reform is the classroom. If the teacher isn't doing the right thing, all the cash incentives in the world won't make a difference.

Those in the school reform movement seeking a case of truly spectacular academic improvement should look to Massachusetts, where something close to an education miracle has occurred. In the past several years, Massachusetts has improved more than almost every other state on the NAEP tests. In 2007, it scored first in the nation in fourth- and eighth-grade math and reading. The state's average scale scores on all four tests have also improved at far higher rates than most other states have seen over the past 15 years.

The improvement had nothing to do with market incentives. Massachusetts has no vouchers, no tuition tax credits, very few charter schools, and no market incentives for principals and teachers. The state owes its amazing improvement in student performance to a few key former education leaders, including state education board chairman John Silber, assistant commissioner Sandra Stotsky, and board member (and Manhattan Institute fellow) Abigail Thernstrom. Starting a decade ago, these instructionists pushed the state's board of education to mandate a rigorous curriculum for all grades, created demanding tests linked to the curriculum standards, and insisted that all high school graduates pass a comprehensive exit exam. In its English Language Arts curriculum framework, the board even dared to say that reading instruction in the early grades should include systematic and explicit phonics. Now a professor of education reform at the University of Arkansas, Stotsky sums up: "The lesson from Massachusetts is that a strong content–based curriculum, together with upgraded certification regulations and teacher licensure tests that require teacher preparation programs to address that content, can be the best recipe for improving students' academic achievement."

The Massachusetts miracle doesn't prove that a standard curriculum and a focus on effective instruction will always produce academic progress. Nor does the flawed New York City experiment in competition mean that we should cast aside all market incentives in education. But what has transpired in these two places provides an important lesson: education reformers ought to resist unreflective support for elegant-sounding theories, derived from the study of economic activity, that don't produce verifiable results in the classroom. After all, children's lives are at stake.

Jay P. Greene and
Robert Enlow

 **NO**

Is School Choice Enough?

For years, an uneasy truce has existed between education reformers who believe that the most important reform is expanding choice and competition and those who point instead to the adoption of a particular curriculum and pedagogy. Reinforcing the truce is the belief (which I continue to hold) that these two reform strategies are complementary. Choice and competition improve the odds that we will adopt and retain effective instructional practices, and those effective practices are the mechanism by which choice and competition bear fruit.

Sol Stern has broken this truce in the pages of *City Journal,* declaring his allegiance to "instructionist" reforms (in curriculum and pedagogy) over "incentivist" ones (choice and competition). Changing incentives through choice is neither necessary nor sufficient for widespread improvement of public schools, Stern argues, even if it may provide justice to individual students trapped in the public system. Though Stern is certainly not the first or only reformer to have adopted this view—he joins Diane Ravitch and E. D. Hirsch, among others—he differs from Ravitch and Hirsch in that they never had much enthusiasm for choice and competition. Stern's denunciation is sharper because he once believed in the power of competition to reform public schools; "facts on the ground," he tells us, have changed his mind.

But while choice is not the "panacea" claimed by scholars John Chubb and Terry Moe in a regrettable moment of rhetorical excess, it *has* produced significant improvement in public schools. And it has done so despite the very limited nature of incentive reforms adopted to date. Nothing in Stern's argument undermines the belief that incentive and instructional reforms are complementary. Stern's best chance of getting and, what's more important, keeping the instructional reforms that he desires is through incentive reforms. I would urge Stern and his fellow dissidents to restore the truce, because together, I think, we have the best chance of reforming public education.

Stern's argument consists of five points. First, he contends that "taxpayer-funded voucher programs for poor children . . . have hit a wall." Following Supreme Court approval of voucher programs in *Zelman* v. *Simmons-Harris,* Stern suggests, we expected a flood of new voucher programs, but we have added only a Washington, D.C. program to the existing ones in Milwaukee and Cleveland. This lack of political success, he argues, suggests that incentive reforms (or at least vouchers) have become a dead end and that we should move on to something else.

But looking only at vouchers for poor children doesn't prove Stern's point. If we look more broadly, we find a large and growing choice movement. According to the Friedman Foundation, there are 21 K–12 voucher or tax-credit programs in 13 states sending students to private schools at public expense. Ten of these programs were enacted after *Zelman*. To say that vouchers have run into a political roadblock is to say, oddly, that vouchers serving disabled students, vouchers serving students at chronically failing schools, and tax-credit-funded scholarships don't really count as vouchers. Sure, there have been defeats and reversals, but on the whole, taxpayer-supported private school choice has expanded significantly in the last five years.

Moreover, if we consider other incentive reforms such as charter schools, 40 states and the District of Columbia have charter laws on the books; two decades ago, none did. In total, charter schools educate about 1.1 million students, roughly as many as in New York City public schools. And if we expand the set of incentive reforms to include merit-pay programs, we see that Denver, Little Rock, Nashville, New York City, parts of Texas, and the entire state of Florida are implementing such programs. Stern's announcement of the political death of vouchers in particular, or of incentive reforms in general, is a bit premature.

Of course, even with this growth in incentive reforms, the competitive pressure that they put on traditional public school systems is quite limited. In the 13 states with vouchers or tax credits for attending private schools, the dollar value of the vouchers or scholarships is usually a fraction of what public schools receive. Also, large increases in public school expenditures have at least partly offset the financial losses that are due to these programs, insulating the public schools against competitive pressure. Incentive reforms are expanding, but we haven't seen anything close to their full potential yet.

Stern's second argument is that even if vouchers were to expand, students would have nowhere to go because Catholic schools are closing in many big cities. He cites Detroit and D.C. as examples. But the reason that Detroit's Catholic schools are under pressure is the rapid expansion of charter school options—and in Washington, Catholic schools are actually converting (so to speak) into charter schools because the financial and regulatory arrangements for charters are more attractive than for the city's voucher program. Both circumstances, then, are actually signs that incentive reforms are thriving.

In other places, where voucher programs have been more generously funded and regulated, Catholic and other private schools are flourishing. For example, in Florida, the McKay program for students with disabilities offers a voucher worth the full cost of educating a student in public school. Under those generous terms, McKay has grown to be the second-largest voucher program in the country, with about 17,000 students, and new private schools have opened to accept McKay students. We have no reason to worry that students in well-funded voucher programs will lack private options to choose from.

Third, Stern claims that "the evidence is pretty meager that competition from vouchers is making public schools better." This cuts to the heart of the matter: do competitive pressures from vouchers or other incentive reforms improve the performance of traditional public school systems? To answer that question, Stern considers whether Milwaukee and New York City, places where he suggests that different incentive reforms have been adopted, show positive results.

Since Stern's entire case hinges on this claim, it is surprising that he musters such weak evidence and neglects a considerable body of rigorous research. The crudest and least persuasive analysis of whether competition improves public school performance is simply to assess the overall performance of places where competition has been expanded, neglecting to control for other factors that influence school performance. After all, it's always possible that things would be even worse if not for competition.

For Milwaukee, Stern references his only rigorous study, by Caroline Hoxby, and acknowledges that "Milwaukee public schools' test scores also improved—and did so most dramatically in those schools under the greatest threat of losing students to vouchers." But then, Stern claims, those gains "fizzled." The only evidence that he presents on this central point is that, even after 15 years of school choice, "Milwaukee's public schools still suffer from low achievement and miserable graduation rates, with test scores flattening in recent years." But of course this neglects the question of whether things would have been worse if not for expanded competition.

A large body of research exists on this issue. Rajashri Chakrabarti, an economist at the Federal Reserve Bank of New York, extended Hoxby's initial analysis. Rather than finding that gains had fizzled, as Stern claims, Chakrabarti concludes: "Using a difference-in-differences analysis in trends and Wisconsin data from 1987 through 2002, the paper shows that these shifts led to a much larger improvement in the second phase compared to the first phase. This result is robust to alternative samples and specifications, and survives several sensitivity checks." That is, the benefits of competition on Milwaukee public school performance didn't fizzle: they *increased* after 1998, when the program expanded.

Milwaukee is not an isolated instance of incentive reforms' producing significant improvement. In Florida, where wide-ranging incentive reforms have been in place for several years, there have been four rigorous analyses of the effects of competitive pressure on the public school system. All four, from groups as disparate as the Manhattan Institute and the Urban Institute, agree that public schools made exceptional improvements in response to competitive pressure. . . . Oddly, Stern makes no mention of Florida's experience. He does not perform the crude analysis, which would show that overall Florida student achievement has been increasing since incentive reforms were under way, nor does he refer to any of the four rigorous analyses. If Stern means to conclude that competition has yielded "disappointing results," one would think he'd have to address this evidence.

Rather than discuss Florida, Stern chooses to highlight New York City to support his argument. This is especially curious because New York has only recently pursued incentive reforms (such as merit pay for principals and teachers), has no voucher program, and has only a modest-sized charter effort. The merit-pay programs haven't even been implemented yet, let alone subjected to rigorous evaluation. Stern's comparison of NAEP scores between 2003 and 2007 can't possibly speak to the effects of programs not yet in effect. Stern somehow knows the verdict not only before the jury has heard the evidence, but even before the crime has been committed.

In addition to evidence about the competitive effects of voucher programs, studies done in Arizona, Michigan, and Texas show that competition from charter schools improves the academic performance of nearby traditional public schools. A fairly large body of research also exists on the effects of public school districts' competing with each other. Clive Belfield and Henry Levin at Teachers College, no friends of school choice, conducted a systematic review of over 200 analyses in that literature, concluding: "The above evidence shows reasonably consistent evidence of a link between competition (choice) and education quality. Increased competition and higher educational quality are positively correlated."

Paul Peterson's comment in Stern's article—"It's less clear that the presence of choice in a community motivates public schools to improve"—is relative to the evidence that we have on the effects of choice on those who participate in those programs. On the latter issue, we have ten analyses of random-assignment experiments (the gold standard of research design), nine of which show significant benefits for at least some subgroups of students who get to choose private schools. Understood in context, Peterson is not denouncing the quality of evidence showing the benefits of competition for public schools. He's simply emphasizing the remarkably high-quality evidence available on participant effects.

Given multiple studies showing positive competitive effects from voucher programs in Milwaukee, several showing the same in Florida, several positive results from studies of charter competition, and more than 200 analyses of competition among public schools, Stern is simply mistaken to assert that incentive reforms fail to produce improvements by public schools—especially when he fails to discuss all but one of those studies.

Fourth, Stern thinks that the incentivist side is crippled by Diane Ravitch's "unchallenged" observation that "the dominant ideas of the schools of education" will make even schools under choice systems adopt "whole language and fuzzy math," as well as other unproductive instructional approaches. Ravitch's argument may have gone unchallenged because it's not a very cogent one. The perpetuation of ineffective instructional approaches by schools of education would appear to be a greater barrier to instructional reform than to incentive reform. Most people who select states' and districts' instructional approaches come from these ed schools; by what mechanism do Stern and Ravitch hope that they will be induced to select positive instructional reforms, instead of the "claptrap" that they acquired in their training and that most of their colleagues share? If they faced competitive pressure exposing them to the consequences of their decisions, one would think (and experience has shown) that they would be likelier to choose effective instructional approaches over foolish ones. In the absence of competitive pressure, it's not clear what would push education leaders to adopt effective curriculum and pedagogy, no matter how much Ravitch and Stern may want them to.

The "uniformly awful" schools of education provide Stern with further proof that competition fails to yield results. Students can choose any ed school and those ed schools must compete for students, so why hasn't that competition yielded better ed schools? The answer, of course, is that most of these ed schools' graduates will be employed by monopolistic public schools that suffer few if any consequences if their hires are trained badly. If the employers are indifferent or hostile to effective instructional approaches, then the students seeking jobs with them will also tend to be indifferent or hostile to those approaches, and, in turn, the ed schools that those students choose will be indifferent or hostile. (Similarly, competition among business schools wouldn't motivate them to teach effective business practices if the businesses that hired their graduates faced little or no competition.) To put it another way, competition among ed schools *is* highly effective—but it's effective at producing ed schools well-suited to the preferences of our monopolistic public school system.

Fifth, Stern invokes the Massachusetts Miracle as support for an emphasis on instructional reform. The state's overall results after it adopted instructional reforms are certainly very encouraging. But Massachusetts should also serve as a cautionary tale for those who think that they can rely solely or primarily on instructional reform. A peculiar alignment of the stars managed to make John Silber chair of the Massachusetts Board of Education, David Driscoll commissioner of education, Sandra Stotsky senior associate commissioner, Robert Costrell the governor's education advisor, and Abigail Thernstrom a member of the Board—but how often, and for how long, will we have such a team to implement and preserve instructional reforms? I'm hard-pressed to think of any other major school systems that have been similarly capable of centrally dictating effective instructional reforms. Counting on replicating Massachusetts in other states and districts is a little like counting on a solar eclipse so that you don't have to wear sunblock. You're likely to get burned.

And now that all of these key players in Massachusetts have departed the scene (Costrell and Stotsky are now my colleagues in the Department of Education Reform at the University of Arkansas), there is a great likelihood that their accomplishments will steadily be dismantled by the new governor, Deval Patrick. In the absence of competitive pressure, effective instructional reforms appear to be both rare and fleeting. Under the pressure of competition, on the other hand, I can think of many schools and school networks that have individually adopted effective instructional practices. In addition to the Catholic schools that Stern praises, I would add competitors like KIPP Academies, Green Dot Schools, Aspire Schools, K12, and many others. Incentive reforms help produce instructional reform.

Stern is unrealistic about the mechanism by which effective instructional approaches are adopted and sustained. One cannot "posit another system, with no choice allowed, but in which the educational leadership enforces a rich curriculum and favors effective instructional approaches," as Ravitch proposed in the thought experiment that Stern cites. If educational leaders and practitioners are made to experience the consequences of the curriculum and instructional approaches that they select, the odds are better that they will decide wisely. Of course, even under competition, education leaders and practitioners will sometimes make the wrong decisions, just as businesspeople sometimes make the wrong business decisions. A system of competition works by allowing people to make choices, including sometimes the wrong ones; by imposing consequences, the competitive system makes it more likely that they will make better choices over time.

Sol Stern, Diane Ravitch, and the new breed of "instructionists" have lost patience with the pitfall of choice—that people sometimes make the wrong decisions. They are confident that they know what effective practices are and would rather just tell everybody to do those "right" things. But we should all be open to the possibility that we don't precisely know the right thing to do. Perhaps even better approaches could be developed in the future. Or perhaps what is right in some circumstances is wrong in others. Closing the door to the learning that comes from competition fails to anticipate these possibilities.

In general, education reform is a very slow process, with regular setbacks and disappointments. It's a bit like the battle against cancer. Cancer may still account for almost one-quarter of all deaths. After decades of effort, there is still no universal cure, and occasionally what were thought to be promising therapies prove to be ineffective. But to conclude that cancer treatment has "hit a wall" and that we ought to try a "Plan B" would be to miss entirely the gradual but significant progress that has been made.

The same is true for incentive reforms in education. Milwaukee and other floundering school systems are not yet cured. Sometimes public school systems facing competitive pressure adopt ineffective educational strategies. Sometimes incentive reforms are defeated at the polls or overturned by courts. To dwell on these points, as Stern does, and then conclude that incentive reforms are a failure is to ignore all of the evidence of benefits that these reforms have brought.

If we didn't have a host of studies supporting the effectiveness of competition in education, or if future studies consistently failed to find those benefits, I'd agree with Stern that we should move on to more promising ideas. But those aren't the "facts on the ground." Let's keep pushing for the adoption of incentive reforms and carefully study their effects. And let's continue to recommend the adoption of effective instructional approaches. This combined approach remains the most promising avenue for improving the education of our nation's children.

   . . .

Sol Stern's article lists the familiar Greatest Hits of teachers' union talking points: school choice isn't politically viable, there aren't enough private options available, and there's no evidence that choice improves public schools. What's new is that these discredited claims appear under the byline of an author who has long claimed to be—and still claims to be—a school-choice supporter. And therein lies a tale.

First, though, let's quickly look at the claims themselves. Contrary to Stern's assertions, school-choice programs have produced significant improvements in the public schools exposed to them. A large body of scientific studies confirms this, though Stern neglects to mention it. The reason that these gains are visible only with careful scientific study is that the choice programs are limited. Choice improves public schools, but not enough schools are exposed to it. This isn't rocket science. We haven't seen wholesale, universal improvement in public schools because we haven't had wholesale, universal voucher programs.

Stern's other claims are equally unfounded. He says that private schools don't have enough capacity to serve voucher kids. In 1989, before its voucher program began, Milwaukee had about 38,500 private school students. In 2003, it had just under 138,000. If you told people in Milwaukee in 1989 that by 2003 the number of private school students would almost quadruple, they might have said: "We only have 38,500 private school seats. Where will the other 100,000 students go?" But when vouchers gave more kids the ability to attend private schools, the private school sector responded by expanding its capacity. In other words, when demand goes up, supply goes up, too. Maybe those crazy economists know something after all.

Stern says that school choice has lost its political momentum. Actually, in the last few years it has been more politically successful than ever before. In 2005, more new school-choice programs were enacted and more existing programs expanded than in any previous year. And in 2006, even more new programs were enacted and existing ones expanded than in 2005. True, vouchers lost a referendum in 2007, but that's nothing new: referendum fights have always been the strongest ground for teachers' unions. Still, despite occasional defeats, choice is growing.

I'll leave it to others to refute Stern's claims in more detail. Instead, I'd like to make two other points. First, Stern can't have it both ways. He wants to keep one foot in the school-choice boat by saying that he still favors school-choice programs, while putting the other foot in the teachers'-union boat by declaring that school choice is neither necessary nor sufficient for serious school reform. But those boats are sailing in opposite directions, and if Stern tries to straddle them, he's going to end up all wet.

He's certainly right that school choice is a justice issue, and that we should favor it regardless of whether it improves public schools. But when he denies that school choice and similar "incentivist" policies are necessary for serious educational reform, he flies in the face of common sense. How is Stern going to get the government school monopoly to adopt the pedagogical reforms that he favors if he rejects the use of incentives to pressure it? And when he denies that school choice and similar policies are sufficient for serious reform, he flies in the face of the facts—as the research shows.

Second, adding Stern's name to these union talking points doesn't make them any more credible; the facts remain what they are. The only thing that has changed is Stern. But—contrary to what is being claimed in the media—Stern has never been a leading figure in the school choice movement, nor has he been a champion of free-market ideology. The "school choice defector" storyline that made this article appear newsworthy to some is in fact groundless.

Personalities shouldn't matter. The argument for choice didn't get any weaker when Stern changed his mind, any more than it got stronger when people like Diane Feinstein and Clarence Page changed their minds and became voucher supporters. Is it too much to ask that we stick to the facts and arguments, rather than paying so much attention to bylines?

. . .

EXPLORING THE ISSUE

Are School Vouchers Overrated as a Strategy for Reforming Public Education?

Critical Thinking and Reflection

1. How do school vouchers reflect the values of individualism and freedom?
2. Explain how competition is a key element in the hopes of voucher advocates to transform public schools.
3. Do vouchers promote or undermine equality?
4. Which would you prefer: a more extensive voucher program that seeks to extend choice to middle-class students or a more targeted voucher program that restricts participation only to low-income students?
5. How does the debate between Sol Stern and his critics reveal a split in the conservative political camp as to how to best reform public education?

Is There Common Ground?

Defenders of the public schools and voucher advocates have a very difficult time in finding common ground. The defenders of public schools believe in the value of public school systems and argue for additional funding so that schools can establish new programs, attract the best teachers, and reward change. Voucher advocates, in contrast, see greater value in diversity and in creating schools that reflect values taught at home. They see no point in pouring additional monies into a public monopoly that is irresponsive to citizens and that is caught in a stranglehold by uncaring bureaucrats and self-interested teacher unions.

Yet, there may be a possible middle ground on which conservative and liberal advocates of school reform may find some room for agreement. Although a voucher program targeted on poorer students does not meet the expectations of more ideological choice enthusiasts, such a program also poses less of a threat to the public school establishment than does a much larger voucher program that serves many more students. Although political conservatives would prefer a much larger system of vouchers that would subject the public school system to the full pressures of competition, even a limited voucher program will be beneficial in offering new opportunities to students most in need of change. A targeted voucher program enables students to escape failing public schools; in the eyes of voucher advocates, a limited program is better than helping no students at all. Political liberals, despite their general antagonism to school vouchers, might be able to see the appeal that a targeted program gives new educational opportunities to inner-city racial minorities and the poor. They should also recognize the support that voucher programs have in low-income minority communities. For liberals, a targeted voucher program also entails only a small risk of promoting new school segregation, as relatively few working- and middle-class whites would receive vouchers.

The threat posed by the possible introduction of vouchers has led public school teachers and the teacher unions to look more kindly on another choice alternative, charter schools. This is the subject of the next chapter.

Additional Resources

Gill, Brian, Timpane, P. Mike, Ross, Karen E., Brewer, Dominic J., and Booker, Kevin. (2007). *Rhetoric Versus Reality: What We Know and What We Need to Know about Vouchers and Charter Schools*. Santa Monica, CA: Rand Corporation.

Henig, Jeffrey R. (1995). *Rethinking School Choice: Limits of the Market Metaphor*. Princeton, NJ: Princeton University Press.

Howell, William G., and Peterson, Paul E. (2006). *The Education Gap: Vouchers and Urban Schools*. Washington, DC: Brookings Institution.

Ravitch, Diane. (2010). *The Death and Life of the Great American School System: How Testing and Choice Are Undermining Education*. New York: Basic Books.

Internet References

Brookings Institution: School Choice, School Vouchers, Charter Schools, and Urban and Inner-City Schools

This progressive Washington "think tank" presents research reports and the transcripts of scholarly forums. These reports discuss the evidence regarding school vouchers and other reforms that aid at improving inner-city education. See their postings on the subjects of School Choice, School Vouchers, Charter Schools, and Urban and Inner-city Schools.

www.brookings.edu/topics/school-choice.aspx

www.brookings.edu/topics/school-vouchers.aspx

www.brookings.edu/topics/charter-schools.aspx

www.brookings.edu/topics/urban-and-innercity-schools.aspx

Carnegie Foundation for the Advancement of Teaching

This nationally renowned independent research center has reviewed various school reform programs, with reports that have often been quite critical of school vouchers.

www.carnegiefoundation.org/

Center for Education Reform

This advocacy group urges the expansion of school choice programs.

www.edreform.com

Center for School Reform at the Heartland Institute

The Heartland Institute is a conservative "think tank" committed to promoting individual freedom and free-market policy solutions, including choice in education.

www.heartland.org/schoolreform-news.org/index.html

Friedman Foundation for Educational Choice

Building on the work of Nobel Prize–winning economist Milton Friedman, one of the earliest advocates of school vouchers, the Friedman Foundation is committed to advancing school vouchers and other programs of choice in education.

www.edchoice.org/

National Center on School Choice, Vanderbilt University

The Center presents studies on the impacts of a variety of school choice programs, including vouchers, charter schools, and magnet schools.

www.vanderbilt.edu/schoolchoice/research-home.html

School Choice, Wisconsin

A collection of news articles and more scholarly studies that analyze the impact of school choice programs, with a special focus on both the Milwaukee voucher program and the city's use of charter schools.

www.schoolchoiceinfo.org

Thomas B. Fordham Institute

A think tank committed to the advancement of school choice and other educational reform measures.

www.fordhaminstitute.org/template/index.cfm

ISSUE 8

Do Charter Schools Improve Education?

YES: Stéphane Lavertu and John Witte, from "The Impact of Milwaukee Charter Schools on Student Achievement," The Brookings Institution, *Issues in Governance Studies* (no. 23, March 2009)

NO: Gary Miron, from "Testimony Prepared for the Hearing of the Committee on Education and the Workforce, U.S. House of Representatives" (June 1, 2011)

Learning Outcomes

After reading this issue, you should be able to:

- Differentiate charter schools from a city's more traditional public schools.
- Differentiate charter schools from voucher schools.
- Explain the limitations that states often put on charter schools.
- Evaluate the evidence regarding the performance of charter schools.

ISSUE SUMMARY

YES: Stéphane Lavertu is a member of the faculty at the John Glenn School of Public Affairs at The Ohio State University. John Witte, nationally renowned education policy analyst, is professor of political science at the University of Wisconsin and former evaluator of the Milwaukee Parental Choice Program. Lavertu and Witte assess the performance of Milwaukee charter schools, observing both their achievements and their disappointments in the all-important area of student educational gains.

NO: Gary Miron, an expert in policy evaluation and professor in the College of Education at Western Michigan University, testified before Congress, noting the many flaws in charter school performance. He observes mediocre student performance, lax accountability standards, and the dominance of concerns for business-like efficiency in schools run by educational management corporations.

$\mathbf{A}$s observed in Issue 7, educational vouchers are so controversial that only a handful of states and cities have turned to the voucher approach. The creation of *charter schools* represents a more popular and more politically acceptable choice strategy.

Charter schools are arguably the most important reform to reshape K-12 education over the last half decade. Forty states permit the establishment of charter schools, and 5000 have been created across the country. Arizona, a hotbed of school choice, has 500 charter schools serving 100,000 students. After Hurricane Katrina, New Orleans made charter schools the central focus in an effort to recast the city's problem-ridden public schools, with the result that 70 percent of New Orleans' students attend charter academies.

A *charter school* is a public-funded school that emphasizes a nontraditional or innovative approach to education. Unlike voucher academies, charter schools charge no tuition. Just like any public school, a student can attend without paying tuition.

The governing body of a proposed charter school applies to the state for permission (that is, for a state charter) to establish the new public school with a specified mission or philosophy. Each charter school is typically allowed a great deal of flexibility to develop its own curriculum, teaching approach, and attendance and disciplinary policies. Yet, as public schools, charter schools are still subject to considerable regulation, including rules and laws that limit the ability of charter school operators to abridge teacher tenure or to hire instructors who lack state certification. A charter school is not given total free rein but instead works under the sponsorship and supervision of a state-approved educational authority, such as the education department at a major state university, a local community college, or even the local public school board.

There exists a great variety of charter arrangements across the nation. A charter school may require student uniforms, mandate parental assistance in classroom and extracurricular activities, or require frequent teacher–parent meetings. A charter school may set a longer school day or lengthen the school year beyond the normal public school calendar. Some charter schools serve college-bound students, stressing AP courses. Others may focus on providing an educational alternative for students who have had academic and disciplinary problems in their former schools. Many charter schools utilize a computer-assisted approach to supplement—in some cases, to replace—classroom-based instruction. More conservative charter schools may emphasize a values-based education and strong discipline. Some charter startups occupy brand new buildings with glorious theater facilities and science laboratories; other charter schools occupy former industrial buildings or may even share part of a building with a traditional public school.

Charter schools vary considerably in terms of quality. Some, like New York City's Harlem Success Academy and the KIPP (Knowledge Is Power Program) college-prep schools in Houston, Dallas, East Los Angeles, New York, and the District of Columbia, are truly excellent. Yet others are disappointing. Some charter schools have been so mismanaged that they soon closed, in some cases forcing students to scurry in the middle of the academic year to find a school that would admit them.

Critics fear that the creation of charter schools will reinforce social tribalism and separatism, with schools that serve different racial, ethnic, and religious constituencies, each teaching students a different version of U.S. history. As a charter school is a public school, it cannot engage in religious instruction. Still, a charter academy created by more fundamentalist religious groups may teach biology classes that undermine the credence given to Darwinian evolution.

Do charter schools improve student performance? Although a number of charter academies have been quite successful, charter schools on the whole have not produced the dramatic increases in student achievement that charter advocates had argued would result from establishing schools with a strong sense of mission and innovative pedagogy. In city after city, the test scores of students enrolled in charter schools differ only slightly, if at all, from the scores of equivalent students in a city's more traditional public schools. The prestigious Carnegie Foundation, reviewing the disappointing results of an earlier wave of charter (and voucher) school formation, concluded in its volume *School Choice: A Special Report* (1992) that "many of the claims for school choice have been based more on speculation than experience."

In 2009, the Center for Educational Research Outcomes (CREDO) at Stanford University examined performance data in 15 states and the District of Columbia and found the results to be largely disappointing. As CREDO reported in *Multiple Choice: Charter School Performance in 16 States*:

> The group portrait shows wide variation in performance. The study reveals that a decent fraction of charter schools, 17 percent, provide superior education opportunities for their students. Nearly half of the charter schools nationwide have results that are no different from the local public school options and over a third, 37 percent, deliver learning results that are significantly worse than their students would have realized had they remained in traditional public schools.

Many students attending charter schools would have done better had they remained in the more traditional public schools.

Public school teachers and administrators have largely opposed the expansion of charter schools. The National Education Association (NEA), the largest association of teachers in the country, supports the creativity that charter schools nurture. But the NEA seeks to place charter academies under the purview of local school boards—the very governmental authority from which choice had sought to free the schools! The NEA also seeks to ensure that charter school creation will not lead to the diversion of resources from traditional classrooms. The NEA further insists that the teachers hired in charter schools must meet the same state certification requirements and enjoy the same protections and bargaining rights as other public school teachers. Public school teachers and administrators further argue for a "cap" or ceiling that will limit the number of charter schools permitted to operate in a state. A cap serves to reduce the potential for mismanagement that can accompany the creation of a large number of charter academies that cannot be properly staffed or supervised. A cap also serves to limit the competition that the charter approach offers more traditional classrooms.

In the YES article, Stéphane Lavertu and John Witte attempt to give an even-handed assess the performance of charter schools in Milwaukee, a city that offers both charter and voucher "choice" programs. They compare the educational gains of charter school students with those of students from comparable backgrounds who continue to attend the city's traditional public schools. The authors find generally positive, but not overwhelming, results as charter school students exhibit relative gains in math but not in reading. The educational advantage of charter schools also seems to be concentrated in the initial years in which a student attends a charter school, years when the change in pedagogy is exciting. The educational advantages that accompany charter school enrollment decrease with the number of years that a student attends the school. Overall, according to Lavertu and Witte, charter schools are a reform worth pursuing.

In the NO article, Professor Gary Miron, in his testimony to Congress, asks: "Who Stole My Charter School Reform?" Miron cites his concerns over student achievement, the racial and class stratification of charter school enrollments, and the unwillingness of oversight agencies to close schools guilty of education failure. Miron worries that charter schools have strayed from the original vision of nurturing from the bottom-up the creativity of teachers as for-profit educational management corporations have standardized charter school operations.

YES

**Stéphane Lavertu and
John Witte**

The Impact of Milwaukee Charter Schools on Student Achievement

As part of a multi-state evaluation project on the impact of charter school attendance on student achievement, we put together and analyzed panel data on Milwaukee Public School (MPS) students spanning the 2000–01 through 2006–07 school years. Specifically, we employed "fixed effects" models to estimate the impact of charter school attendance on student gain scores on mathematics and reading achievement tests. We found that:

1. charter school attendance is associated with higher scores on mathematics exams than attendance at traditional public schools, but there is no statistically significant relationship between charter school attendance and performance on reading exams;
2. positive results in mathematics are due to student performance in the initial years of the program—the performance of charter schools and traditional public schools is statistically indistinguishable for the most recent years of our study;
3. the positive impact of charter schools on achievement (relative to traditional public schools) declines as the number of years a student has attended a charter school increases;
4. charter schools that have operated for a number of years and those that had been traditional public schools drive the positive charter school results;
5. student mobility has a negative effect on performance and it is a more robust predictor of student performance than the organizational factors we consider;
6. there is no evidence that the presence of charter schools induces better student performance in traditional public schools.

We conclude that while charter schools overall may help the education of urban youth, our study of Milwaukee indicates that they should not be expected to be the silver bullet that some reformers seek. We also suggest that it is important to better understand and deal with instability in school attendance in urban school districts, as it proves to be the most significant determinant of student achievement in all of our statistical models.

From *Issues in Governance Studies*, No. 23, March 2009, pp. 1–10. Copyright © 2009 by Brookings Institution. Reprinted by permission.

Introduction

Charter schools are public schools that have been "chartered" by an authorizing organization (such as a school board, non-profit organization, or university), usually to provide a specific form of education to a minimal number of students within a specific budget. If schools meet their accountability standards, their charters are renewable after a period of years. Although their charters often specify the organization of the school, personnel practices, and accountability measures, charter schools operate without some of the regulations that bind traditional public schools. In addition, charter schools provide parents with affordable alternatives to traditional public schooling. These features are popular and charter schools have proliferated as a result.

Reformers posit that the greater autonomy afforded to charter schools should enable them to educate students more effectively than traditional public schools. Some also contend that the mere presence of charter schools should induce traditional public schools to better educate their students, as traditional public schools must compete with nearby charter schools for students. On the other hand, critics question the notion that greater autonomy necessarily yields academic benefits, and they sometimes counter that charter schools could have a negative impact on the academic achievement of students in traditional public schools by robbing them of their funding and of strong students with motivated parents.

Our research seeks to address these disputes using student-level data obtained from the Milwaukee Public Schools. . . .

We also limited our analyses to mathematics and reading achievement, as the district tested students in grades 3-10 on these subjects for most years of the panel. . . .

Table 1 summarizes the number of traditional public schools and charter schools that appear in our panel every year, as well as the number of students who took tests in those schools. (The counts fluctuate as schools come and go and as new testing is phased in and out.) . . .

Table 1

Tradition Public and Charter School Observations in Panel

	Schools		Students	
	TPS	Charters	TPS	Charters
2000–01	177	4	10,394	79
2001–02	183	16	38,667	3,696
2002–03	182	17	35,005	4,404
2003–04	181	23	36,105	5,165
2004–05	177	33	34,195	5,837
2005–06	173	38	32,835	5,998
2006–07	166	35	26,572	4,741

That many charter schools now have been in operation for a number of years provides this study with advantages over earlier ones (Witte, *et al*, 2007). . . .

Our statistical models employed yearly student gains on normalized test scores as the dependent variable. We normalized the test scores across test-taking cohorts to account for differences in the tests from grade to grade and from year to year. We estimated value-added (i.e., "gain score" or "growth") models to account for selection bias, which occurs because charter schools do not enroll a random sample of traditional public school students. Gain scores control for student performance prior to attending a charter school. . . .

Results

There is controversy over whether or not charter schools provide a better education than traditional public schools, as well as whether or not the presence of charter schools improves education in traditional public schools by providing competitive pressures. These controversies continue in part because empirical research yields mixed results. The empirical results we present below contribute another set of findings to the accumulating empirical literature. They also reveal a trend which suggests that the initial positive results for charter schools that some prior studies detected were temporary.

Achievement in Charter Versus Traditional Public Schools

Consistent with past research on Milwaukee Public Schools (Witte *et al*, 2007), we found that, between the 2000–01 and 2006–07 school years, charter schools outperform traditional public schools in mathematics and that they perform about as well as traditional public schools in reading (i.e., the reading gains are not statistically significant). The last pair of bars in Figure 1 illustrates the average advantage of attending a charter school across the years of the panel. But the figure also reveals that the positive results overall are due in large part to initial gains in the early years of the panel, which are the years to which existing studies are limited. The results clearly reveal a downward trend in terms of the "advantage" that charter school attendance provides with respect to student performance on achievement tests. In fact, in 2005–06 there is an advantage for students in *traditional public schools* in reading.

Models that account for the number of years that a student has been in a charter school yielded results that are consistent with the notion that the positive effects of charter schools ebb once the initial enthusiasm of participants subsides. As Figure 2 reveals, the positive charter school gains reported in Figure 1 come from students who have just started attending charter schools (controlling for the negative impact that switching schools has on a student). However, as the figure also shows, the positive effects come largely from students for whom we could not determine the years of attendance.

One also must be careful about how much one reads into this trend. Just as the initial positive effects of charter schools were temporary, so may be the non-positive (perhaps negative) effects found for recent years. One reason is that many charter schools are new; and, as Figure 3 illustrates, the positive

Figure 1

Student Performance Associated with Charter School Attendance Compared with Student Performance Associated with TPS Attendance

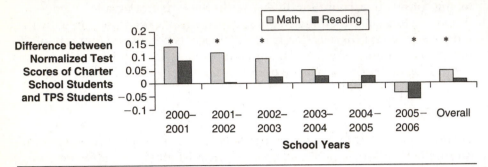

Figure 2

Student Performance Associated with Charter School Attendance Compared with Student Performance Associated with TPS Attendance, Broken Down by the Number of Years a Student Has Been in a Charter School

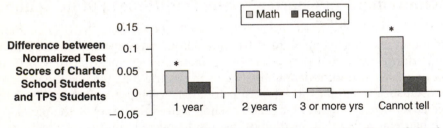

Figure 3

Student Performance Associated with Charter School Attendance Compared with Student Performance Associated with TPS Attendance, Broken Down by the Number of Years a Charter School Has Been in Operation

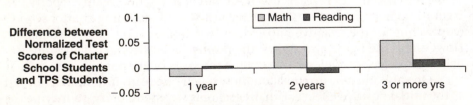

Figure 4

Student Performance Associated with Charter School Attendance Compared with Student Performance Associated with TPS Attendance, Broken Down by Charter School Type (MATHEMATICS)

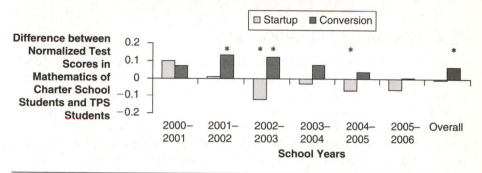

Figure 5

Student Performance Associated with Charter School Attendance Compared with Student Performance Associated with TPS Attendance, Broken Down by Charter School Type (READING)

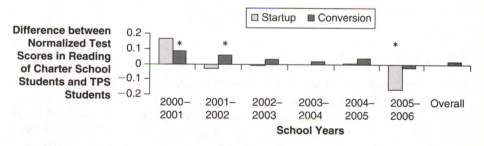

charter school effects we report in Figure 1 are driven by charter schools that have been in operation for a number of years.

Additional models we estimated that distinguish between "conversion" charter schools—those created out of existing traditional public schools—and "startup" charter schools also yielded results that point to the importance of organizational maturity. As Figure 4 and Figure 5 indicate, "conversion" charter schools drive the positive charter school results, while traditional public schools sometimes outperform "startup" charter schools.

It also is worth mentioning that student stability is an important predictor of student achievement. One of our key statistical controls, which indicates whether or not a gain score is observed immediately after a student has switched schools, yielded the most substantively and statistically significant results. Switching schools has a strong, *negative,* and significantly significant impact on all students, whatever type of school from which and to which they switch. This factor is more robust a predictor of performance than charter school attendance, and its impact is consistent and strong across all years of the panel. One of the policy implications of this study is that it is important to better understand and deal with instability in school attendance in urban school districts.

Charter School Competitive Effects

Finally, we estimated a number of statistical models in an effort to uncover the effect that the presence of charter schools may have on the performance of students who attend traditional public schools. Specifically, we estimated models that seek to identify a relationship between the number and distance of charter schools from the traditional public school that a student attends—again employing the controls we identify above. Using a number of model specifications, we found no relationship between the proximity and concentration of charter schools and the performance of students in traditional public schools.

These findings are not too surprising, however, as Milwaukee is relatively saturated with school choice options. Milwaukee options include charter and magnet schools, a voucher program that sends 20,000 students to private schools, and extensive open enrollment that allows students to go to other school districts. Distances between schools are also relatively small compared to those in geographically larger urban districts.

Conclusion

Our research indicates that there is a positive relationship between attending a charter school and performance on achievement tests in mathematics, but that there is no statistically significant relationship between charter school attendance and performance in reading. The positive impact of charter school attendance on mathematics achievement is due mostly to student performance in the charter school program's initial years. In the most recent years of our study, the performance of charter schools is statistically indistinguishable from the performance of traditional public schools. Moreover, the analysis yields no statistically significant relationship between the concentration and proximity of charter schools and the performance of students who attend traditional public schools.

In addition, we found that the achievement advantage associated with charter school attendance disappears after students have been in charter schools for a number of years, which may help explain the decline in charter school performance overall. One should be cautious about extrapolating from the negative charter school trend that we identify, however. Doing so requires that one understand better the causal factors that drive it. Moreover, our analysis suggests that there are forces at work that could counteract it. For example, we found that performance improves as charter schools mature. Consistent with this notion, we found that the positive charter school effects associated with student performance on mathematics exams are driven by schools that had been traditional public schools, not "startup" charter schools.

Our analysis also indicates that whether or not a student switches schools has a strong, negative, and statistically significant correlation with student performance on reading and mathematics achievements tests, and that the magnitude of this factor's impact exceeds that of the organizational factors on which our study focuses. Put differently, our results are consistent with the notion that stability in a student's life is a better predictor of academic performance than organizational factors. One of the policy implications of this study is that it is important to better understand and deal with instability in school attendance in urban school districts.

The impact of charter schools on student performance on reading and mathematics achievement tests is not the only factor one should consider when assessing the value of charter schools. One might be more concerned about the relationship between charter school attendance and college enrollment rates, for example. And choice options often are associated with higher levels of parental engagement and satisfaction, regardless of student performance on achievement tests. However, for the many policymakers who consider achievement test results to be of primary importance, our study indicates that charter school attendance in Milwaukee at best has a modest positive affect on such achievement. In other words, charter schools may contribute positively to improving the education of urban youth, but they should not be expected to be the silver bullet that some reformers seek.

References

Bifulco, Robert and Helen F. Ladd. 2006. The Impacts of Charter Schools on Student Achievement: Evidence from North Carolina. *Education Finance and Policy* 1 (1), 50–90.

Booker, Kevin, Scott M. Gilpatric, Timothy Gronberg, and Dennis Jansen. 2008. "The Effect of Charter Schools on Traditional Public School Students in Texas: Are children Who Stay Behind Left Behind?" *Journal of Urban Economics*, 64, 123–145.

Sass, Timothy. 2006. "Charter Schools and Student Achievement in Florida." *Education Finance and Policy*, 1, 91–122.

Witte, John F., David Weimer, Arnold Shober, and Paul Schlomer (2007). "The Performance of Charter Schools in Wisconsin." *Journal of Policy Analysis and Management*: 26 (Summer), pp. 557–574.

Gary Miron

 **NO**

Testimony Prepared for the Hearing of the Committee on Education and the Workforce, U.S. House of Representatives, June 1, 2011

Background Information Relevant to My Testimony

I am a professor of evaluation, measurement, and research at Western Michigan University. Over the last 2 decades I have had extensive experience evaluating school reforms and education policies in the United States and Europe. I have conducted 9 comprehensive evaluations of charter school reforms commissioned by state education agencies and have undertaken dozens of other studies related to charter schools and private education management organizations (EMOs) that have been funded by the US Department of Education, state agencies, private foundations, as well as advocates and critics of charter schools. In addition to my direct research or evaluation work related to charter schools, I have provided technical assistance to charter schools in Connecticut, Hawaii, Michigan, New York, Ohio, and Pennsylvania. This assistance has largely focused on developing accountability systems and helping schools to collect and report data.

In Europe, I have studied the national voucher reform in Sweden and conducted research on school restructuring in four other countries. For the Organisation for Economic Co-operation and Development (OECD), I have been serving as an external expert and over the past few years I have worked with a network of OECD countries to develop international indicators related to school choice, parent voice, and school accountability.

In recent years, my research has increasingly focused on education management organizations and efforts to create systemic change in urban schools in Michigan and rural schools in Louisiana. Prior to coming to Western Michigan University in 1997, I worked for 10 years at Stockholm University. Aside from a long list of technical reports, I have authored or edited eight books and has published more than 3 dozen articles or chapters in books.

U.S. House of Representatives, June 1, 2011.

Original Goals of Charter Schools

Charter schools were created as a new form of public school that—in exchange for autonomy—would be highly accountable. They would improve upon traditional public schools in two ways: by developing and sharing innovative practices, and by promoting competition. Charter schools have received considerable bipartisan support and have become one of the most prevalent and widely debated school reforms visible in the last several decades. Today there are around 5,000 charter schools in 40 states and the District of Columbia, enrolling close to 1.5 million students.

While I looked favorably upon the original intent of charter schools, I am increasingly concerned that after two decades and substantial growth, the charter school idea has strayed considerably from its original vision.

A growing body of research as well as state and federal evaluations conducted by independent researchers continue to find that charter schools are not achieving the goals that were once envisioned for them.

Charter schools are nonsectarian public schools of choice, free from many regulations that apply to traditional public schools. The specific goals for charter schools are typically found in legislative acts. Let me identify these goals and comment on the related research evidence:

- *Empower local actors and communities.* Involvement of local persons or groups in starting charter schools is shrinking, replaced instead by outsiders, particularly private education management organizations (EMOs), which steer these schools from distant corporate headquarters. Claims that EMOs can make charter schools more effective have not been substantiated by research.
- *Enhance opportunities for parent involvement.* Parents who choose schools can be expected to be more engaged, presumably leading to higher student achievement and other positive outcomes. Evidence suggests that parent satisfaction is one of the strengths of charter schools. Most of this evidence, however, is based on surveys of parents whose children remain in charter schools and excludes parents whose children have left these schools. Nevertheless, the fact that charter schools are growing in size and number is a strong indication of the demand that still exists for charter schools.
- *Create new opportunities for school choice with open access for all.* Charter schools are schools of choice. With few exceptions, they are open to students from any district or locale. Advocates argue that the very act of choice will spur students, parents, and teachers to work harder to support the schools they have chosen. Evidence, however, suggests that charters attract and enroll groups sorted by race, class, and ability. Increasingly, charter schools are using admissions or placement tests. Last year, research conducted by Western Michigan University found that only one-quarter of charter schools have student populations that are similar to local school districts in terms of ethnic composition and the proportion of low-income students. When it came to student composition based on students with disabilities or students classified as English language learners the findings were even more stark.

- *Develop innovations in curriculum and instruction.* Proponents argued that charter schools could function as public education's R&D sector, and their benefits would extend to traditional public schools that adopted and emulated their innovations. Evidence to date, however, suggests that charter schools are not more likely than traditional public schools to innovate.
- *Enhance professional autonomy and opportunities for professional development for teachers.* Allowing teachers to choose schools closely matching their own beliefs and interests was to create school communities that spent less time managing stakeholder conflicts and more time implementing effective educational interventions. Although some charter schools have created and fostered professional opportunities for teachers, the overall evidence on this goal does not suggest that this has been realized. High levels of teacher attrition suggest teachers are not finding suitable professional learning communities in charter schools.
- *Create high performing schools where children would learn more.* Notwithstanding pressure for performance on state assessments, the growing body of evidence indicates charter schools perform similar to demographically matched traditional public schools on standardized tests. This is so despite the existence of some exceptional charter schools in every state.
- *Create highly accountable schools.* In exchange for enhanced autonomy over curriculum, instruction, and operations, charter schools agree to be held more accountable for results than other public schools. Schools that fail to meet performance objectives can have their charter revoked or not renewed (performance accountability); schools that don't satisfy parents may lose students and, in theory, go out of business (market accountability). Yet closure rates are relatively low, and most charter schools that close do so because of financial mismanagement, rather than performance or market accountability. The burden of producing evidence regarding charter school success has shifted to external evaluators or authorizers. Charter schools—on the whole—have not been proactive with regard to accountability; instead of being "evaluating" schools, they have become "evaluated" schools.

Reasons Why Goals for Charter Schools Have Not Been Achieved

Why this overall lackluster performance?

- *Lack of effective oversight and insufficient accountability.* Many authorizers lack funds for oversight and some of them are unprepared and—in some cases—unwilling to be sponsors of charter schools. A key factor that undermines effective oversight is that objectives in charter contracts are vague, incomplete, and unmeasurable. Between 2002 and 2008 more attention was given to the role and importance of authorizers, however, this seems to receive less attention today.
- *Insufficient autonomy.* Re-regulation and standardization driven by NCLB and state assessments are limiting autonomy. Requirements

that charter schools administer the same standardized tests and have the same performance standards as traditional public schools means that they cannot risk developing and using new curricular materials.

- *Insufficient funding.* The financial viability of charter schools is dependent on the state, on how facilities are funded, and on the particular needs of the students served. Some charter schools maintain large year-end balances thanks to less costly-to-educate students or extensive private revenues; others are clearly underfunded for the types of students they serve or because they lack social capital to attract outside resources, or both. Funding formulae vary by state, but it is fair to say that if charter schools are expected to innovate, they need more funding, not just greater autonomy.
- *Privatization and pursuit of profits.* The increasing numbers of private operators may bring expertise or experience, but they also glean high management fees and tend to spend less on instruction—and reports continue to show that EMO-operated schools perform less well than non-EMO operated schools. There are some emerging nonprofit EMO models that may prove to be more effective.
- *Strong and effective lobbying and advocacy groups* for charter schools quickly reinterpret research and shape the message to fit their needs rather than the long-term interests of the movement. They attack evidence that questions the performance of charter schools and offer anecdotal evidence, rarely substantiated by technical reports, in rebuttal. Such lobbying has undermined reasoned discourse and made improving charter schools more difficult.
- *High attrition of teachers and administrators,* ranging from 15 to 30 percent, leads to greater instability and lost investment. Attrition from the removal of ineffective teachers—a potential plus of charters—explains only a small portion of the annual exodus.
- *Rapid growth of reforms.* In states that implemented and expanded their charter school reforms too quickly, charter schools have faced a backlash as shortcomings in oversight and other neglected aspects of the reform become apparent. The states that have grown their reforms more slowly have been able to learn from early mistakes and establish better oversight mechanisms.

Questions Policy Makers Should Be Asking

Can we create better public schools through de-regulation and demands for greater accountability? How are charter schools using the opportunity provided them? The answers to these questions require comprehensive evaluations—resisting the dodge that every charter school is its own reform and should be looked at separately. More specific questions that policy makers should be asking include:

- How can charter school laws be revised to create more accountable schools?
- Can funding formulae be revised to ensure that charter schools serving the neediest students receive sufficient funding, motivating more

charters to attract and retain more-costly-to-educate students, such as high school students, those with special needs, and those living in poverty?
- How can incentives and regulations be used to ensure poorly performing charter schools will be closed?
- Are there better uses for public resources than charter schools—smaller class size, increased teacher remuneration or incentives, increased oversight of public schools, support to restructure struggling or failing district schools, etc.?

Who Stole My Charter School Reform?

Even as the original goals for charter schools are largely ignored, charter schools fulfill other purposes.

- *Promote privatization of public school system.* Charter schools have provided an easy route for privatization; many states allow private schools to convert to public charter schools, and increasing the use of private education management organizations is increasingly being seen as the mode for expanding charter schools.

  Today, one-third of the nation's charter schools are being operated by private education management organizations (EMOs) and this proportion is growing rapidly each year. In states such as Michigan, close to 80% of charter schools are operated by private for-profit EMOs. Claims regarding privatization remain rhetorical and unsupported by evidence. The recent economic crisis has shown that our economy requires greater public oversight and regulations, a finding that can be reasonably extended to markets in education.
- *Means of accelerating segregation of public schools while placing the "Private Good" ahead of the "Public Good."* State evaluations find that charter schools seem to accelerate the re-segregation of public schools by race, class, and ability, instead of creating homogeneous learning communities based on particular learning styles or pedagogical approaches.

If privatization and accelerated segregation are not outcomes that the federal government wishes to achieve with charter schools, then it would be wise to consider how federal funding can be used to persuade states to revise their charter school reforms.

Federal and state policy makers need to revisit the goals and intended purpose of charter schools, clearly articulating values and anticipated outcomes.

Quality Versus Quantity

Once dedicated to educational quality, today's charter school movement is increasingly dominated by powerful advocates of market-based reform and privatization in public education.

As the federal government considers how it wishes to steer and develop charter schools, it would be wise to articulate a new—or renewed—vision for chartering that focuses on quality over quantity. Then, as US Department of Education wields its influence, it can persuade states to make revisions in their charter school laws that reflect those goals and values. Most importantly, such guidance should reward states that create successful charter schools, rather than states that simply expand the charter school market.

Finally, authorities need to move more aggressively to close poorly performing charter schools. This will strengthen charter reforms in four ways: lifting the aggregate results for charters that remain; sending a strong message to other charter schools that the autonomy-for-accountability tradeoff is real; redirecting media attention from a few scandal-ridden schools to successful schools; and opening up space for new, carefully vetted charters.

Although these suggestions may be seen as antagonistic by the charter school establishment, we believe they will help improve and strengthen such schools in the longer run. The charter school idea was to create better schools for all children, not to divide limited public resources across parallel systems that perform at similar levels and suffer from similar breaches in accountability. Rapid proliferation in the charter sector appears to be interfering with the original vision for the schools: to serve as a lever of change, spurring public schools to improve both by example and replication.

The only way to ensure quality may be to get off the expansion express. Rapid proliferation in the charter sector appears to be interfering with the original vision for the schools: to serve as a lever of change, spurring public schools to improve both by example and replication.

Charter schools can be returned to their original vision: to serve as a lever of change, spurring public schools to improve both by example and through competition. But if they are to do so, they must be better than traditional public schools, and they must be held accountable for their performance.

EXPLORING THE ISSUE

Do Charter Schools Improve Education?

Critical Thinking and Reflection

1. On balance, should states and communities seek the creation of a wider network of charter schools?
2. What state regulations do you consider necessary when it comes to the creation and operation of charter schools? What state regulations intrude on charter schools and impede their operation?
3. Do you feel that the creation of public schools will ultimately serve to generate pressures that will lead more traditional public schools to revise their own curriculum and educational approach? Or, alternatively, do you think that the creation of public schools serve to accelerate the decline in the quality of education at a city's more traditional public schools?
4. Should the number of charter schools in a state be capped?

Is There Common Ground?

Choice advocates and public school advocates are not likely to agree on the bigger issues regarding charter school creation. Choice advocates want to remove the caps that limit charter school creation and remove regulations that impede creativity and constrain a school's adopting new cost savings and effective teaching strategies. Choice advocates are especially critical of regulations that limit their freedom in hiring and firing of teachers and in using lower-cost alternatives, such as student interns or a volunteer from the private sector who can teach the use of computers, for certain functions instead of certified teachers. Defenders of traditional public schools, by contrast, insist on stringent caps and regulations to limit charter school formation, prevent mismanagement and educational failure, and prevent the hiring of unqualified personnel.

The public school establishment needs to recognize that there exists a large number of very fine charter schools that respond to student and parent needs. There is a clear demand for charter schools that will not go away. The defenders of traditional public schools also need to recognize the successes that charters have had in serving low-income and minority students, offering at-risk students individualized instruction and new opportunities to succeed.

The advocates of charter schools, in turn, should recognize the waste and human costs involved in charter school mismanagement. They should be willing to accept the need for greater oversight of what Stanford's CREDO has termed the disturbingly large minority of charter schools that are performing poorly. In such cases, state oversight agencies should insist on plans for school improvement with deadlines and benchmarked performance standards. States and localities must demonstrate a greater willingness to close charter academies that have not made measurable progress and are failing to fulfill the terms of their charters. Even choice advocates should recognize that not all schools are successful and that some startup or new schools are poorly run. By closing schools that are unable to meet the needs of students, more resources can be devoted to creating charter schools that work.

The restructuring of the nation's public schools will not by itself solve the problem of poor student performance. Freeing educators to pursue innovative pedagogy is a very worthwhile goal. But, as we have seen, part of the success of the best charter schools lies in their ability to raise the money that they need to provide a quality education. Schools—charter schools and traditional neighborhood schools alike—need adequate resources. But will those resources be available in the "new normal," the troubled economy of postindustrial America? The structural reform of public schools, however meritorious, does not fully substitute for the need of the nation to invest in quality education. Some choice advocates will accept the need to provide adequate public funding to support charter formation and reward teacher creativity. Other choice advocates, however, view privatization and competition as strategies for restraining growing school budgets and teacher salaries; these choice advocates will be unlikely to accept the need to maintain a high level of taxpayer support for schools—for charter, voucher, and traditional public schools alike.

Additional Resources

Buckley, Jack, & Mark Schneider. (2010). *Charter Schools: Hope or Hype?* Princeton, NJ: Princeton University Press.

Gill, Brian, et al. (2009). *Charter Schools in Eight States: Effects on Achievement, Attainment, Integration, and Competition.* Rand Corporation.

Lubienski, Christopher A., & Peter C. Weitzel. (2010). *The Charter School Experiment: Expectations, Evidence, and Implications.* Cambridge, MA: Harvard Education Press.

Merseth, Katherine K. et al. (2009). *Inside Urban Charter Schools: Promising Practices and Strategies in Five High-Performing Schools.* Cambridge, MA: Harvard Education Press.

Ravitch, Diane. (November 11, 2010). "The Myth of Charter Schools." *New York Times Review of Books.*

Internet References

Brookings Institution: Charter Schools

This progressive Washington "think tank" reviews the evidence on charter schools and other educational reform programs.

www.brookings.edu/topics/charter-schools.aspx

Carnegie Foundation for the Advancement of Teaching

This highly respected and nationally renowned independent research center presents a large number of articles on charter schools and various other alternative educational reforms.

www.carnegiefoundation.org/

Center for Education Reform

This advocacy group urges the expansion of charter schools and other educational choice programs.

www.edreform.com

Center for Research on Educational Outcomes (CREDO) at Stanford University

CREDO's16-state study reveals considerable variation in the performance of charter schools. Although one-fifth are providing superior education, a larger number of charter schools are performing poorly. CREDO's site presents the national report, the state-by-state findings, and the debate over the study's methodology.

http://credo.stanford.edu/research-reports.html

Center for School Reform at the Heartland Institute

The Heartland Institute is a conservative "think tank" that promotes individual freedom and free-market policy solutions, including choice in education.

www.heartland.org/schoolreform-news.org/index.html

National Alliance for Public Charter Schools

The Alliance attempts to "debunk" what it sees at the "myths" that opponents use in their attempts to discredit charter schools.

www.publiccharters.org

National Center on School Choice, Vanderbilt University

The Center presents studies on the impacts of charter schools and other educational reform programs.

www.vanderbilt.edu/schoolchoice/research-home.html

National Educational Association (NEA)

The largest teachers' organization and the country presents its views of charter schools, underscoring studies that point to the lack of educational gains at charter academies.

www.nea.org/charter

School Choice, Wisconsin

A collection of news articles and scholarly studies that analyze the impact of the state's voucher and charter school programs.

www.schoolchoiceinfo.org

Thomas B. Fordham Institute

A think-tank committed to the advancement of school choice.

www.fordhaminstitute.org/template/index.cfm

ISSUE 9

Should Federal Programs Seek to Deconcentrate Inner-City Poverty?

YES: Susan J. Popkin, from "Testimony Prepared for the Hearings on HOPE VI Reauthorization, Committee on Financial Services, Subcommittee on Housing and Community Development, U.S. House of Representatives" (June 21, 2007)

NO: Sheila Crowley, from "HOPE VI: What Went Wrong," in *From Despair to Hope: HOPE VI and the Promise of Public Housing in America's Cities* (Washington: The Brookings Institution, 2010)

Learning Outcomes

After reading this issue, you should be able to:

- Explain the concept of "displacement" and why the urban renewal programs of the 1950s and 1960s are often characterized as "Negro removal."
- Identify government policies that helped to create and expand urban ghettoes.
- Define "concentrated poverty" and explain its ill effects.
- Explain why tenants in the Gautreaux mobility program seemed to fare better than tenants in the Moving to Opportunity (MTO) dispersal program.
- List the goals of the HOPE VI program.
- Evaluate the evidence on HOPE VI, pointing to the program's successes and failures.

ISSUE SUMMARY

YES: Susan J. Popkin is senior fellow at the Urban Institute and lead researcher on the *HOPE VI Panel Study* that looked at the fate of families displaced by the demolition of aging public housing projects. She reports that HOPE VI families moved to safer neighborhoods with lower concentrations of poverty and greater economic opportunity.

NO: Sheila Crowley is president of the National Low Income Housing Coalition, sharply criticizes the extensive demolition and displacement that were part of the HOPE VI effort. She questions just who are the real beneficiaries of the HOPE VI program.

Sociologist William Julius Wilson, in his landmark writings, underscored the ill effects of *concentrated poverty,* where the residents of core urban neighborhoods "jobless ghettos" with little daily connection to the mainstream outside world. The residents of these neighborhoods lacke the skills demanded by the new post-industrial economy and are further victimized by a *spatial mismatch* where new jobs are increasingly located in far-off suburban and exurban sites that are inaccessible to the inner-city poor. In "vulnerable" inner-city neighborhoods, bored youth, lacking a clear path to conventional success, turn to drugs, crime, early sex, and other problematic social behaviors.

As Wilson argued, concentrated poverty served to reinforce dysfunctional behavior. Public policy could help break the cycle of poverty by assisting low-income families in their efforts to flee the inner city for better areas of the metropolis that offered greater public safety, functioning schools, and an abundance of job opportunities.

Concentrated poverty is not purely a "natural" phenomenon created by a free market. Government policies actually played a prominent role in segregating the poor into urban ghettoes and public housing.

Local governments in the 1950s and 1960s, used *urban renewal and public housing* to shape and extend ghetto boundaries. Driven by the demands of local merchants and property developers, the programs *displaced*—that is, pushed out—the residents of low-income neighborhoods to make way for the new commercial projects. In big cities, displacees were often relocated to newly built high-rise public housing structures where social conditions. Conditions in the new high-rises quickly deteriorated, creating a living environment that in many cases was much worse than the low-rise communities that urban renewal had demolished. The program also gained the ugly epithet of *Negro removal,* as local governments pushed poor African Americans out of areas desired by developers, merchants, and major civic institutions.

In Chicago and other cities, public authorities used their control over public housing siting and tenant selection to reinforce racial segregation. Historian Arnold Hirsch uses the term *second ghetto* to underscore the fact that local governments, responding to the concerns of development interests and white voters, often made a conscious decision to reinforce racial separatism, creating an enlarged ghetto of high-rises on the edges of a city's already-existing "first" ghetto. The Chicago Housing Authority (CHA) color-coded housing applicants; African Americans were consigned by the government to housing projects built inside the ghetto. Chicago built a "wall" of high-rise housing projects on the city's South Side to house the displacees of urban renewal, to prevent low-income black families from spilling into nearby white areas of the city.

Civil rights activists challenged the government's segregative actions. The U.S. Supreme Court in its 1976 *Gautreaux* decision ruled that Chicago was guilty of state-endorsed (that is, *de jure*) segregation in its housing programs, denying residents the "equal protection" of the laws guaranteed by the 14th Amendment of the U.S. Constitution.

In response to the Court's decision, Chicago agreed to deconcentrate public housing by leasing new units in predominantly white areas of the city and the suburbs. Each year until 1998, the city held a public lottery offering public housing residents a chance at a new life in better parts of the metropolitan area. From 1976 to 1998, the Gautreaux deconcentration program enabled 7100 poor black families to leave Chicago public housing for new homes in better areas of the city and in more than 150 suburbs.

The Gautreaux dispersal effort offered researchers a unique opportunity to measure the impact of poverty concentration efforts. As DeLuca and Rosenbaum (2010) report, the Gautreaux mobility program produced impressive results. Movers to "opportunity-rich communities" took advantage of new employment opportunities. Their children were able to adjust to the demands of the suburban schools. Compared to public housing families, Gautreaux children were less likely to be involved in gangs and more likely to graduate from high school and attend college.

The Gautreaux program enjoyed a number of advantages the program enjoyed. Program participants were a self-select and motivated group that desired to escape distressed public housing. The program also provided tenants with extensive tenant counseling, with counselors working hard to find landlords in better areas of the city who would be willing to rent to public-housing residents.

The success of the Gautreaux program led the federal government to establish the *Moving to Opportunity* (MTO) demonstration program to determine if deconcentration efforts could achieve similar results when applied to the general public housing population, not just the self-selected Gautreaux applicants. The MTO results were rather disappointing. MTO movers did not exhibit the gains in employment and education on the scale of those observed in the Gautreaux program. Few tenants used their MTO vouchers to move to the suburbs and to areas with above-average school districts. Many MTO movers simply found housing close to their old neighborhoods.

The MTO effort ran into a firestorm of resistance from the residents of the neighborhoods that were to receive the MTO movers (a matter that will be discussed in greater detail in Issue 10). In the face of such fierce opposition, federal officials decided not to expand the MTO effort beyond the five initial demonstration cities.

But the goal of poverty deconcentration continued to influence federal housing policy. The 1992 HOPE VI program began a process of demolishing the nation's most dilapidated public housing structures. Some of the residents displaced by demolition were rehoused on site in attractive low- and mid-rise buildings constructed according to New Urbanism design principles (which we describe in further detail in Issue 17). HOPE VI offered other residents extensive relocation assistance, with the goal of helping the poor to move to better

186

neighborhoods—even suburbs—that offered improved public safety and new jobs and schooling opportunities.

HOPE VI allowed cities to tear down problem buildings that were costly to maintain. HOPE VI also sought to improve the livability of neighborhoods that were in the shadow of the old housing projects. In cities where the city built new mixed-income developments that included attractive market-rate units, public officials sought to use HOPE VI demolition and new construction to facilitate the gentrification and the transformation of neighborhoods lying near the downtown.

Do programs that deconcentrate poverty serve to improve the lives of the inner-city poor? Housing analyst Susan Popkin has tracked the lives of residents relocated by various poverty deconcentration programs. In her testimony to Congress (excerpted in the YES selection), she argues that the housing moves made under the HOPE VI program have largely been for the better. HOPE VI movers appreciate the safety of their new neighborhoods and express their satisfaction with children's schools.

The HOPE VI moves were not an unqualified success. Many voucher users chose locations that were fairly close to their old neighborhoods and to extended family and friends. The new neighborhoods seldom exhibited extensive racial integration. HOPE VI displacees often wound up moving to other low-income neighborhoods in a city, neighborhoods that offered little in terms of improved employment opportunities.

Critics like Sheila Crowley, president of the Low-Income Housing Coalition, argue that HOPE VI demolition actually diminished the supply of affordable housing available to the poor. The forced relocations of inner-city residents by HOPE VI were reminiscent of the old urban renewal program; poor residents were displaced to make way for new development that the city desired.

Crowley questions why decision makers ignored the fundamental lesson of the urban renewal experience, that the residents of redevelopment areas should have an important voice in decisions that will intrude on their lives.

Crowley shares much of the perspective of critical urban theorists (see the essays in Davies & Imbroscio, 2010) who argue that the true driving motivation behind HOPE VI was to remove the inner-city poor from sites desired by private developers and their political allies.

YES

Susan J. Popkin

Testimony Prepared for the Hearings on HOPE VI Reauthorization, Committee on Financial Services, Subcommittee on Housing and Community Development, U.S. House of Representatives, June 21, 2007

The views are those of the author and do not necessary reflect those of the Urban Institute, its board of trustees, or its sponsors.

The HOPE VI program targeted some of the most beleaguered housing in this country—dilapidated public housing developments that had failed to deliver on the promise of decent housing for the poor. The goals of the HOPE VI program are ambitious and include "improving the living environment for residents of severely distressed public housing" and "providing housing that will avoid or decrease the concentration of very poor families." If successful, the program has the potential to dramatically improve life circumstances for the families who endured the terrible conditions in distressed public housing. The policymakers who created the program hoped that these improvements in the quality of residents' neighborhoods would also help residents in other ways, particularly in becoming self-sufficient.

The HOPE VI Panel Study is the only national study of outcomes for HOPE VI families and was intended to address basic questions about where residents move and how HOPE VI affects their overall well-being. The study was initiated in 2000; at that time, seven years into the HOPE VI program, there was little reliable evidence about what had happened to original residents. Many critics were asserting that relocation and involuntary displacement would inevitably leave residents worse off, sending them to communities that were little better than the distressed developments where they started, while housing authorities were claiming great successes with their new developments.

The study has tracked the experiences of a sample of 887 original residents from five developments slated for revitalization in 1999 and 2000 (Shore

U.S. House of Representatives, June 21, 2007. The footnotes and references accompanying the original report have been omitted.

Park, Atlantic City, NJ; Wells/Madden, Chicago, IL; Easter Hill, Richmond, CA; Few Gardens, Durham, NC; and East Capitol, Washington, DC). Respondents were surveyed at baseline in 2001, prior to relocation, and followed up in 2003 and again in 2005. At baseline in 2001, survey respondents at all five sites reported intolerable conditions, with a substantial proportion reporting hazards like peeling paint, mold, inadequate heat, and infestations of cockroaches and other vermin. Crime was rampant; virtually all (90 percent) of the residents reported serious problems with drug trafficking, drug use, and gang activity. Even worse, about 75 percent viewed violent crime (shooting, assaults, and rape) as "big problems." The surrounding neighborhoods were equally troubled—extremely high poverty, predominantly minority neighborhoods with high rates of unemployment, welfare recipiency, and other ills.

After tracking residents through the relocation process, the HOPE VI Panel Study is able to address effectively the question of whether HOPE VI has succeeded in its goal of improving residents' life circumstances or whether the critics' predictions have been realized. We find that for the most part, former residents are living in neighborhoods that are dramatically safer and offer a far healthier environment for themselves and their children. However, a substantial minority continue to live in traditional public housing developments that are only marginally better than the distressed developments where they started. These findings demonstrate the ways in which HOPE VI has improved the quality of life for many original residents, while underscoring the need to continue to seek solutions for the problems that have kept too many from being able to take advantage of new opportunities.

Most Residents Have Not Moved Back

By 2005, 84 percent of the families in the HOPE VI Panel Study had relocated from the five HOPE VI sites. The remaining 16 percent of the respondents still living in their original developments were from either Atlantic City's Shore Park or Chicago's Wells, where the housing authorities were doing staged relocation. The largest number of families—43 percent—had received Housing Choice Vouchers, and 22 percent had moved into other traditional public housing developments. Another 10 percent were renting in private-market units with no assistance, and 4 percent had become homeowners. Approximately 1 percent of the HOPE VI Panel Study respondents were either homeless or in prison in 2005.

Redevelopment was under way in all of the sites by 2005, although none were completed. Therefore, it is not surprising that only 5 percent of the Panel Study respondents had moved into a newly remodeled HOPE VI unit by the 2005 follow-up. Atlantic City's Shore Park, where the housing authority was building a revitalized unit for every household that wanted one, had the greatest share of original families (14 percent) who had moved back into redeveloped HOPE VI units. Other research suggests that return rates to HOPE VI sites overall have varied considerably from less than 10 percent to 75 percent, with the largest numbers returning to sites that were rehabilitated rather than demolished and rebuilt—not the case in any of these five sites. Based on this evidence, it seems likely that the final figures for returning for the HOPE VI Panel Study sites will increase somewhat over time, but will remain relatively low.

The reasons for this low rate of return are both positive and negative. With the shift to mixed-income developments, there are simply fewer public housing units on site. Some sites have imposed relatively stringent screening criteria that have excluded some former residents. And, on the positive side, many former residents who have received vouchers are satisfied with their new housing and are not interested in returning. Finally, at a few more troubled sites, long histories of mismanagement and neglect mean that residents do not trust the housing authority's promises of better conditions and choose not to return. With low rates of return, the program has not met its initial vision of residents coming back to live in revitalized developments; for most original residents, the major impact of HOPE VI is relocation.

Most Residents Are Living in Substantially Better Housing

Residents who have moved to the private market or mixed-income developments reported substantial improvements in the quality of their housing. We asked families to rate their current housing as "excellent, good, fair, or poor." In 2005, 68 percent of voucher holders and homeowners rated their housing as excellent or good, as did 64 percent of unassisted renters. More than three-fourths (85 percent) of families living in the new HOPE VI units gave their units high ratings. In contrast, a much smaller share of households in public housing rated their housing as excellent or good. Only 39 percent of those in the original public housing (those that had not yet been relocated) gave their units high ratings in 2005. And only about half of those relocated into other public housing (49 percent) rated their housing as excellent or good.

At baseline in 2001 and at each of the follow-ups, we asked respondents about a series of specific housing problems, such as broken heating units, insect and rodent infestation, broken toilets, and peeling paint. Those who moved to the private market or to mixed-income developments reported significantly fewer problems. In contrast, those who remained in traditional public housing—either their original development or a different one—experienced virtually no improvement in housing quality over time; about 40 percent of those living in other public housing and about 60 percent of those in the original public housing units reported having two or more problems at the baseline and at the 2005 follow-up.

Residents Are Living in Dramatically Safer Neighborhoods

Fear of crime has profound implications for residents, causing stress and social isolation. At the final follow up in 2005, relocation had brought about a profound impact in residents' life circumstances. Those residents who left traditional public housing—voucher holders and unassisted renters and homeowners—were

Figure 1

HOPE VI Panel Study Respondents Reporting that Drug Selling in Their Neighborhood Is a "Big Problem," by Housing Assistance (percent)

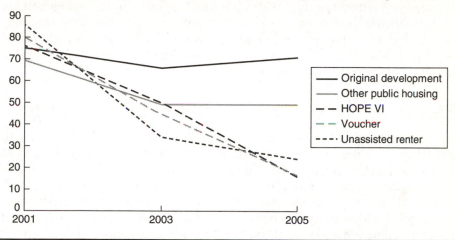

living in neighborhoods with considerably lower poverty. Further, these movers and those living in mixed-income developments reported conditions far safer than in their original developments. For example, the proportion of respondents reporting "big problems" with drug sales dropped from 78 percent at baseline to 47 percent in 2003, and declined even further to 33 percent in 2005—a drop of 45 percentage points. The trends for virtually every measure of neighborhood safety showed the same dramatic decline.

The trends for respondents who had moved to mixed-income developments or to the private market (with vouchers or on their own) were even more striking. Figure 1, which shows the trends in respondents reporting big problems with drug trafficking by housing assistance status, dramatically illustrates the "safety benefit" these relocatees have gained from moving out of distressed public housing. These respondents report extraordinary improvements in their conditions. For example, while about 80 percent of voucher holders and HOPE VI movers had reported big problems with drug trafficking in their original neighborhoods at baseline, only 16 percent reported the same problems in their new neighborhoods in 2005.

The trends for perceptions of violent crime were the same—at baseline, more than two-thirds of the respondents reported big problems with shooting and violence in their developments; in 2005, just 17 percent of voucher holders reported big problems in their new communities. The trends for the relatively small numbers of HOPE VI movers, unassisted renters, and homeowners were identical.

These improvements in safety have had a profound impact on residents' quality of life. Relocatees' comments reflected a wide range of life improvements, including allowing their children to play outside more frequently, less fighting among neighborhood children, sleeping better, and generally feeling less worried about drug dealing and shootings in the neighborhood. Our statistical analysis shows that those who have moved with vouchers report less worry and anxiety and have lower depression scores than those who remain in traditional public housing. With such small numbers of respondents living in mixed-income, we cannot see accurate statistical trends, but given that they experienced the same improvements in housing quality and neighborhood safety, it is likely that they have experienced the same benefits in terms of quality of life as those who received vouchers.

Children in Voucher Households Are Better Off

Children are particularly vulnerable to the effects of HOPE VI relocation. On one hand, children are the most likely to benefit in important ways from improved housing quality—and reduced exposure to risks like lead paint or mold—and from safer, less distressed neighborhoods. On the other hand, moving can disrupt their education and friendships and even put older youth at risk for conflict with local gangs. The HOPE VI Panel Study sample included questions on parental reports of children's behavior—an indicator of children's mental health—to see how relocation affects children. Overall, we find that children whose families received vouchers are faring better after relocation than those who moved to other traditional public housing developments. Parents of children in families that relocated with vouchers report lower rates of behavior problems in 2005 compared with their children's behavior in 2001, prior to relocation. In 2001, 53 percent of children in voucher households demonstrated two or more behavior problems, but by 2005, this proportion dropped to 41 percent. Although the pattern held for both boys and girls in voucher households, only the decline for girls was statistically significant. Again, because the numbers are small, we cannot see statistically accurate trends for households who moved to mixed-income developments, but given the similar trends for housing and neighborhood quality, their outcomes are likely similar to those for voucher holders.

However, while children who moved to the private market are doing better, those whose families moved to other public housing are not faring as well. In 2005, children in voucher households were more likely than children in other public housing to exhibit five out of six positive behaviors (62 versus 43 percent). They were also marginally less likely to exhibit two or more delinquent behaviors (3 versus 12 percent). The trends for delinquent behavior for the children still living in traditional public housing are especially disturbing. The incidence of delinquent behaviors has increased for youth still living in their original development (by 12 percentage points) and youth in other public housing (by 10 percentage points), while it has changed in no significant way for youth in the voucher households. And our analysis shows that the incidence of delinquent behaviors has skyrocketed (by 24 percentage points since 2001) for those girls still living in their original development, waiting for relocation. This spike is primarily driven by increasing rates of school suspensions (28 percentage points) and going to juvenile court (24 percentage points). This finding suggests that girls, in particular, are suffering from the ill effects of being left behind in developments that are becoming increasingly dangerous and chaotic as vacancies increase. . . .

HOPE VI Did Not Affect Employment

In addition to providing residents with an improved living environment, the HOPE VI program seeks to help them attain self-sufficiency. However, we find that while there have been dramatic improvements in quality of life, there have been no overall changes in employment. At baseline, 48 percent of the working-age respondents were not employed—the same share as at the 2003 and the 2005 follow-up. Our analysis suggests that HOPE VI relocation and voluntary supportive services are unlikely to affect employment or address the many factors that keep disadvantaged residents out of the labor force.

As discussed above, HOPE VI Panel Study respondents are in extremely poor health; these health problems are by far the biggest barrier to employment. Among working-age respondents, nearly a third (32 percent) reported poor health, and most of them (62 percent) were unemployed. The strongest predictor of not working was having severe challenges with physical mobility. Forty percent of respondents reported moderate or severe difficulty with mobility; less than half (38 percent) of these respondents were employed in 2005. As figure 2 shows, a typical respondent with no employment barriers

Figure 2

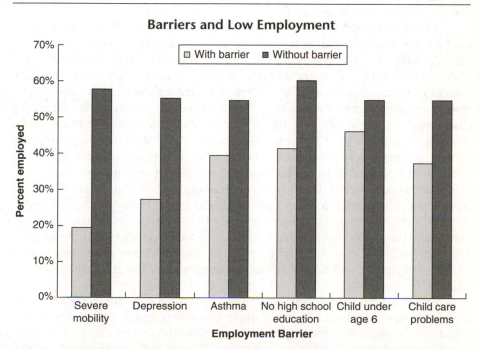

Barriers and Low Employment

Source: Authors' calculations from the 2005 HOPE VI Panel Study.

had a roughly 82 percent chance of being employed; severe mobility problems lowered this probability by 40 percentage points. Depression also substantially reduced the probability of being employed, as did having been diagnosed with asthma. Obesity did not have a direct effect on employment but rather was associated with other serious health problems. Relative to nonobese respondents, obese respondents were more likely to report having mobility difficulties, asthma, and an overall health status of "fair" or "poor."

While health was clearly the biggest obstacle to obtaining—and keeping—a job for HOPE VI Panel Study respondents, other factors affected employment as well. Specifically, not having a high school diploma, having children under age 6, and having problems with adequate child care also reduced the probability of employment for working-age respondents.

HOPE VI Did Not Cause an Increase in Homelessness

A main criticism of the HOPE VI program is that intentionally relocating residents—even temporarily—increases the likelihood that some residents will end up homeless. Housing authorities have been accused of "losing" residents and not providing them with the relocation assistance to which they were entitled; critics in some cities have claimed increases in shelter populations. However, most of the evidence has been anecdotal, and while there has been much rhetoric on both sides, there has been no hard evidence to support or disprove critics' claims that HOPE VI increases homelessness.

To address this concern, we used the HOPE VI Panel Study data to conduct a systematic analysis, first identifying residents who report experiencing homelessness or are doubled up with other households (and considered "precariously housed") and then, second, looking at the available data on nonrespondents in our sample—that is, those we were unable to interview—to see if we could determine their housing status. The results of this analysis indicate that there is no evidence that HOPE VI caused an increase in homelessness. Less than 2 percent (or 12 of the 715 respondents to the follow-up survey in 2005) reported experiencing homelessness at some point during the four years since relocation started in 2001. Another 5 percent of respondents were "precariously housed"—that is, they were doubled-up with friends or family. These figures are comparable to those from other studies of public housing populations. We are able to account for nearly all of the respondents whom we were not able to interview at the two follow ups. Our analysis shows that these "nonrespondents" were probably slightly more likely (about one percentage point) to have become homeless than those we interviewed, but the differences are likely to be small.

Families who live in distressed public housing typically have very low incomes, health problems, and are likely to have complex family situations. Our analysis, particularly the comparison to other public housing populations, suggests that financial vulnerability, rather than HOPE VI relocation, places these families at risk for housing insecurity.

HOPE VI Is Not the Solution for the "Hard to House"

Hard-to-house residents—families coping with multiple complex problems such as mental illness, severe physical illness, substance abuse, large numbers of young children, weak labor-market histories, and criminal records—are less likely than other residents to realize significant improvements in their quality of life as a result of HOPE VI revitalization. Our earlier work showed that these residents make up a substantial proportion of the population at all five sites and more than two-thirds of the households in Chicago's Wells and Washington's East Capitol developments. In 2005, we found that, at every site, hard-to-house families were more likely to end up in traditional public housing than in the private market, and so ended up little better off than they were at baseline. Placing them in other traditional developments—or, as in Atlantic City's Shore Park and Chicago's Wells, leaving them in the parts of the development awaiting revitalization—may well have kept them from becoming homeless. But concentrating multiproblem families in a few traditional developments may well mean that those developments rapidly become as—or even more—distressed than the developments from which these families came. Clearly, we need to continue to search for solutions for families who have long relied on distressed public housing as the housing of last resort.

Where Do We Go From Here?

For most original residents, the major HOPE VI intervention has been relocation; only a small number returned to revitalized HOPE VI communities. Many critics predicted that relocated residents would end up concentrated in other very poor, minority communities that would leave them little better off—and perhaps worse off—than they were in their original developments. But results from the HOPE VI Panel Study show that, in fact, relocation has meant profound benefits for their quality of life. For residents who have moved to the private market with vouchers, become homeowners, moved off assistance, or moved to new mixed-income developments, the HOPE VI program has more than met its goal of providing an improved living environment. There is no question that the enormous improvement in safety and consequent reduction in fear of crime is the biggest benefit for many original residents. With these major improvements in life circumstances, it is possible that living in these safer neighborhoods may have long-term benefits for the mental and physical health of adults and children. . . .

HOPE VI: What Went Wrong

HOPE VI was initiated with the best of intentions, but it is a case study in how badly a government program can run amok. While HOPE VI has resulted in the removal of blighted buildings and the development of some lovely new homes, it also has resulted in the involuntary displacement of tens of thousands of poor, predominantly African American families from their homes and communities, made the housing situation for some of the nation's most vulnerable citizens even more precarious, and exacerbated the shortage of affordable homes for people in the lowest income brackets. The promise (and rhetoric) of HOPE VI as a means of improving opportunities for residents of distressed public housing never matched the reality. Many more displaced residents were promised improved housing *and* economic uplift than have actually received both or are ever likely to.

Those who have examined HOPE VI refer to "winners and losers," with one study concluding that "the effects have been mixed, with some former residents . . . better off . . . and . . . others at risk" and another asserting that "HOPE VI enhances only a small number of public housing residents." Overall, more people who lived in public housing communities redeveloped under HOPE VI were hurt by the program than helped. Thus, the core tenet of government intervention in the lives of its citizens—"First, do no harm"—has been violated.

Evaluation scholar Egon G. Guba of Indiana University asserts that public policy must be examined and understood from three perspectives: what the policy intended, how the policy was implemented, and what happened to the people whom the policy was supposed to affect. . . .

Actual impacts and experiences are continually fed back into the policy-making loop to improve the policies in order to better meet the needs of the intended beneficiaries.

It is in that spirit that this critique of the HOPE VI program is offered, trusting that indeed the intended beneficiaries of HOPE VI are the residents of "distressed" public housing and not the developers, lenders, public housing officials, and politicians who are the program's most loyal advocates. This chapter examines the implementation of the HOPE VI program from the vantage point of the intended beneficiaries and other low-income people in need of affordable homes in their communities. The thesis of the critique is that the implementation was more about the real estate than it was about the people.

The chapter closes with recommendations for reform to best address the failings identified and with thoughts about the future of public housing.

For Residents, Displacement and the Loss of Home

The number of public housing households relocated under HOPE VI has now [through 2008] reached more than 72,000. All of those families—even the small number that have or will return to the redeveloped sites—were removed from the place that was their home.

The importance of "home" to the physical and mental health of human beings cannot be overstated. Shelter is one of the most essential human needs. One's house is where one's life is centered and where family life is conducted. One's house is connected to other houses, creating the structure for communal life and the organization of human society. The disruption of a home that occurs when a move is not freely chosen by the people who must move is one of the most serious consequences of any action that a public authority can take, and *forced relocation should be approached with extreme caution.*

Forced Relocation

In the United States, poor and disenfranchised people are disproportionately forced from their homes. Urban renewal in the United States is the story of poor people "pushed out of their neighborhoods to make room for various forms of 'progress' . . . no other group will allow itself to be displaced." So, too, the vast majority of homes that were lost to the construction of the interstate highway system belonged to poor and black people. The displacement of 72,000 families from their homes by HOPE VI is another chapter in this sad history.

Decision makers justify forced relocation by defining the community to be demolished as distressed and by marginalizing the people who live there. In a three-stage process, residents are diminished, then they are dispersed, and then their homes and institutions are destroyed to make way for new development that those in power find preferable.

Forced relocation, under any conditions, always causes trauma to those who are displaced. People who are uprooted against their will experience "root shock, the traumatic stress reaction to the destruction of all or part of one's emotional ecosystem." Place attachment is deeply felt, with place including one's actual dwelling and a neighborhood populated with people and services on which one can rely. The longer one has resided in a home and community, the more attached one becomes.

Despite being dismissed as dysfunctional by policymakers and the general public, poor communities nonetheless have intricate webs of social connections that offer communal support and sustain their members through difficult times. In a 2004 article, Sudhir Venkatesh and Isil Celimli introduce the reader to Lee-Lee Henderson, who lived in Chicago's infamous Robert Taylor Homes and left in 2002 under HOPE VI redevelopment. A year later, she wanted to move back. She was glad to be rid of the gang activity but missed the child care and mutual financial support in her old neighborhood. As she explained, "poor people help poor people. They have no one else, so they know how to help each other get by."

Venkatesh and Celimli report that three-quarters of the social network of a public housing resident is composed of other public housing residents. In an interview with the Center for Community Change, a resident who was displaced by HOPE VI in Detroit expressed her loss: "I get real sad sometimes when I know I can't go back to Herman Gardens. It makes me want to cry. I think because I lived there so long . . . I just felt safe there. At Herman Gardens, we just knew everybody."

Elderly people are among the most vulnerable to physical and emotional damage when they are uprooted from their homes and their support systems. The HOPE VI Panel Study found that the mortality rate among black women fifty-five years of age or older displaced by HOPE VI was, shockingly, twice than of older black women in general and higher among HOPE VI Panel Study participants than in a comparison group of public housing women. Although the comparison was imperfect and an overwhelming majority of HOPE VI women had illnesses or chronic health needs before moving, the findings raise serious questions about the impact of the stress of moving on people who already are in frail condition.

Relocation can also have a harmful effect on school-age children, who risk falling behind in their studies when they must move during the school year. It is not just the children who move who are affected. With the churning of students through classrooms over the school year, all students are subject to disruption of the learning process. During a planning meeting for one HOPE VI project, a school official was observed begging the housing authority staff to hold off on relocating residents of the site slated for demolition until the end of the school year. The plea fell on deaf ears; housing authority staff said that the demolition had to go ahead as planned. HOPE VI Panel Study participants who moved to private market housing with or without vouchers experienced significant rates of residential mobility, with half moving twice in two years. It is likely that the children in those households also changed schools during that time.

Is the "Cure" Worth the Pain?

In the case of HOPE VI, the severing of ties to communities and schools may have been justified if the people who were displaced were guaranteed to be better off as a result. The one improvement that studies of HOPE VI outcomes have consistently shown is that people feel safer. While increased security is an extremely important outcome, the improvements were experienced primarily by residents who relocated with vouchers to better neighborhoods or who were able to reestablish themselves without housing assistance, not by people who were relocated to other public housing. At best, these voucher or unassisted movers constitute little more than half of the affected families.

Residents relocated from HOPE VI sites have not improved their economic and employment status. While families that relocated with vouchers are in safer neighborhoods and higher-quality housing, they also face higher levels of economic hardship and housing instability because, with the addition of utilities to their monthly costs, their housing costs have increased. Indicators of well-being of school-age children in the HOPE VI Panel Study referenced earlier are inconclusive about positive effects on children's health, school engagement, and behavior. And as already noted, the health status of many residents displaced by HOPE VI may have actually deteriorated.

The HOPE VI Panel Study is the only analysis to date to examine the extent of homelessness among people displaced by HOPE VI. The researchers found that just 2 percent had become homeless and concluded that the rate was insignificant. That anyone became homeless as a result of government-initiated forced relocation from their homes is unacceptable. At a minimum, any homelessness of former residents should have been prevented under any HOPE VI project.

Moreover, the analysis includes only families from five HOPE VI sites. Other studies that do not specifically raise the question of homelessness nevertheless show that the whereabouts of some displaced residents was unknown. According to HUD data on HOPE VI households relocated as of June 30, 2003, 20 percent were not able to be assessed. The Miami-Dade Housing Authority cannot account for more than half of the residents displaced by the Liberty City HOPE VI project. After initially relocating with vouchers, many of the Miami families lost their vouchers at the end of the first lease and became homeless when they could not find another home to which to move. In a remarkable example, researchers studying the Atlanta Smith Homes HOPE VI site four years after the relocation of residents received a contact list from the Atlanta Housing Authority for 493 relocated households. A stunning 90 percent of the heads of household could not be reached. Eventually, researchers were able to find just 116 households by word of mouth among former residents.

As noted by the National Housing Law Project in 2002's *False Hope,* the most definitive analysis to date of the flaws of HOPE VI, there is an astonishing lack of data about what has occurred as a result of the program. In the early years, no one was required to track the outcome for each resident, making it impossible to assert that HOPE VI did not contribute to the continued crisis of homelessness in the United States in the 1990s. The number of residents who were simply "lost" should be of enormous concern to the architects of HOPE VI and those who want to continue redevelopment under the program. The failure to plan and carry out the least harmful relocations possible and to follow residents to ensure their well-being is a permanent stain on the HOPE VI record. It certainly supports the thesis that the well-being of public housing residents was not the principal focus of those charged with redevelopment.

Flaws in the Intervention Lead to Disempowerment

Although overused and misused in the discourse of anti-poverty programs, empowerment remains a crucial goal for interventions to improve the social and economic well-being of low-income people. At its core, empowerment is the redistribution of power in a socially and economically stratified society to create greater equality and fairness. Empowerment practice seeks collaboration between the implementers and beneficiaries of social programs to produce both personal and social transformations. It presumes that all people even the most disadvantaged, have strengths and resources. The most beneficial transformations occur through interventions that are based on maximizing people's gifts. . . .

As implemented, HOPE VI did not seek the empowerment of residents; its emphasis was on transforming neighborhoods, not the people who lived in them. HOPE VI has been disempowering in at least three ways. First, resident participation in the planning and implementation of HOPE VI redevelopment has been weak and ineffectual. Second, many residents feel that they were misled to believe that the redevelopment was really for them and that they would benefit from new services and other opportunities. Third, HOPE VI failed to accurately assess the serious challenges faced by many public housing residents for whom any improvement in social and economic well-being would require much more support than HOPE VI has ever offered.

Weak Resident Participation

Since their inception, public housing programs have included more than housing; they also have focused on creating community with the encouragement and support of tenant councils and other forms of resident participation. Resident participation in its ideal form involves residents of public housing collaborating with the staff of public housing agencies in order to improve the lives of individuals and the community. Although that goal was reaffirmed in the HOPE VI rules requiring residents to be active participants in the decision to apply for a HOPE VI grant and in the preparation of the application, implementation was weak.

A GAO study of resident participation in the twenty HOPE VI sites that received grants in 1996 found considerable variation across sites. All held informational meetings, but some engaged residents in actual decisionmaking while others complied with resident participation requirements only after they were threatened with litigation. . . .

Residents reported in the Center for Community Change study that the meetings in which the most important decisions were made were the least accessible; for example, they would be held at the central office of the housing authority during regular business hours. At the meetings that they did attend, residents experienced their role as that of passive recipients of information who were expected to rubber-stamp whatever decision officials had decided to make. In the words of one resident, "instead of residents developing information, the City gives us information and wants us to agree with it." A frequent complaint voiced in the Center for Community Change report was that public housing authorities co-opted selected residents who would go along with the plans and gave them special favors in return. . . .

Lies and Deceit

A repeated theme in resident complaints about HOPE VI is that they were deceived by the housing authorities and the numerous consultants who were engaged in the HOPE VI projects. Residents report that they were deceived even in the application process, when sign-in sheets for informational meetings about HOPE VI were used as documentation that the people who attended the meeting supported the application.

The most egregious lie was that public housing residents would someday live in the new homes and have new opportunities for economic betterment if they supported a HOPE VI application. Seduced by charettes in which architects flashed sketches of idyllic settings and housing with modern amenities, many residents believed that those sketches represented their future. A resident in Jersey City, New Jersey, said that "at the beginning, they showed us the townhouses that they were going to build, showing us how pretty they were going to be. But they did not tell us that we would be kicked out." A Richmond, Virginia, resident reports that the housing authority told her, "You'll be the first to come back." But, the resident said, "Everything that has been said has been a lie . . . When they sent me the letter that told me I was not able to come back, I was tore up."

Residents who have returned to new homes developed under HOPE VI constitute less than a third of those who were displaced. A primary reason is that the people who are displaced cannot afford most of the new units. For example, the Atlanta Housing Authority's redevelopment of Techwood–Clark Howell Homes displaced 998 households whose median household income was $3,960 a year, and planners did not intend for the vast majority of original residents to return. Reserving only 360, or 40 percent, of the planned 900 units at the new Centennial Place as public housing, authorities targeted households with a minimum income of 40 percent of the area median, much higher than the income of the former residents, to occupy those units. The other 540 units were intended for families with even higher incomes. What actually happened at Centennial Place is an improvement over the plan; about 40 percent of the 738 units built are public housing–assisted units, predominantly serving households with incomes of less than 30 percent of AMI. Nonetheless, there was a significant reduction in units that the people who were displaced could afford. Overall, just over a third of the total units appear to serve extremely low-income households.

Other reasons for permanent displacement include not passing new screening requirements such as credit checks and new units not having the same number of bedrooms as the ones that were demolished. In some cases, the lapse of time between relocation and redevelopment has been so prolonged that residents just give up hope.

Some former residents cannot or will not meet the requirements of residency in redeveloped units, which range from work requirement to restrictions on certain kinds of outdoor activities, like barbequing. Anticipating that she would not be able to return, a resident in Washington, D.C., said that she had heard from a former resident of an earlier HOPE VI project that "a lot of residents there didn't try to return because they were afraid if they moved in, the rules were so strict that they would probably be evicted."

In addition to new homes, HOPE VI is supposed to include supportive and community services for residents such as child care, job training and counseling, education, substance abuse treatment, and recreation centers. Indeed; the initial HOPE VI statute allowed up to 20 percent of the HOPE VI grant to be used for such services; in 1998, the amount was capped at 15 percent. Public housing authorities have not spent anywhere near the amount allowed for services for residents, despite the fact that those services have been considered a distinguishing feature of the program. HUD guidelines indicate that services are to be provided to original residents of a project that is redeveloped under HOPE VI, but for the most part, the new residents of a redeveloped site are the ones who will benefit, not the residents who were displaced. . . .

How could there be such a disconnect between what was intended and what happened? It is rooted in the failure to answer this basic question: Is the program about building buildings or about improving lives and building communities? The buildings are not an end in themselves; they are a means to the end of helping people maintain stable homes and improve their social and economic well-being.

Adding to the Housing Shortage

When HOPE VI was first authorized in 1992, public housing law still required a new unit to be built for every public housing unit that was demolished, a practice known as one-for-one replacement. As long as one-for-one replacement was in force, HOPE VI projects had to abide by it. But within a few years, the long-standing failure of Congress to properly fund public housing had forced a change in policy. Evidence that public housing agencies could not keep their stock in good repair and lacked the funds to replace uninhabitable units prompted Congress to rescind the one-for-one rule in 1995. Public housing agencies were now free to pursue plans that would result in a net loss of federally assisted units in their communities.

Remarkably, while the U.S. Department of Housing and Urban Development was requiring state and local jurisdictions that received federal housing and community development funds to identify their housing needs and propose how they would meet them, the department's HOPE VI program was causing the loss of the very housing that was most needed in every jurisdiction—housing that the lowest-income families could afford. HUD also was routinely issuing its own reports on the country's shortage of affordable rental housing. The enthusiasm with which HOPE VI was touted by HUD officials, the housing industry, and politicians created considerable dissonance for those who were examining the data on housing needs. It seemed that HOPE VI supporters were ignoring the reality of waiting lists for housing assistance, poor families with unsustainable housing costs, and homelessness.

There is widespread agreement that the United States has an acute shortage of rental housing that extremely low-income households can afford. There are more than 9 million extremely low-income renters, 25 percent of all renters in the country, but there are only 6.2 million rental housing units that these households can afford, according to the standard of affordability that allots no more than 30 percent of household income to housing. The result is a shortage of more than 2.8 million homes. Moreover, many of the units that extremely low-income households can afford are rented by higher-income people, so that the real shortage is 5.6 million units. . . .

Because of the shortage, the majority of extremely low-income families pay substantially more for their homes than they can afford. Seventy-one percent of such households pay more than half of their income for shelter, forcing them to forgo other basic necessities and putting them at high risk of eviction and homelessness. No other income group comes close with regard to the percent of income consumed by housing.

Public housing is one of the few sources of rental housing that extremely low-income households can afford. Of the 1,282,099 public housing units available in 2000, 69 percent were occupied by extremely low-income households; 45 percent of those households had incomes of less than $10,000 a year. Because public housing residents pay 30 percent of their income for their homes, they are among the lucky minority of poor families that do not have unsustainable housing costs.

HUD and public housing officials frequently cite the number of units demolished and the number of units that have been or will be rebuilt through HOPE VI. An uninformed reader can be left with the impression that eventually most, if not all, of the units that are demolished will be replaced. This sleight of hand masks the reality that a minority of the new units are actual public housing units that families in the same income group as those that lived there before can afford. HOPE VI developers actually plan for one-for-one replacement of public housing so infrequently that those who do so call special attention to their efforts.

Supporters of HOPE VI will argue that the condition of the public housing that has been demolished under the program was so deplorable that HOPE VI could not wait for Congress to come up with the money to replace all lost housing and address the rental housing shortage. The public housing originally envisioned for HOPE VI probably had deteriorated so badly that it could not be saved. . . .

Unfortunately, neither Congress nor HUD has ever concretely defined "severely distressed" or identified the units that would meet such a definition if one existed. The National Housing Law Project cited several different definitions in its 2002 study, noting that the lack of a clear definition of "severely distressed public housing" has allowed the demolition and redevelopment of far more public housing than was originally intended.

The number of units demolished through HOPE VI has now reached more than 91,000, and calls for expanding the program continue to come from the housing industry and elected officials. Some charge that HOPE VI has become a vehicle by which local officials can tear down public housing that stands in the way of new development considered more desirable. HOPE VI likely has caused and in the future certainly will cause the loss of public housing that could have remained viable with proper upkeep and sufficient investment in programs to improve the social and economic well-being of current and future residents. In the absence of reform to once again require one-for-one replacement, public policy will continue to contribute to the scarcity of homes for the poorest people in the United States. . . .

Going Forward

. . . The task at hand is much greater than simply seeking compromise on changes to the HOPE VI program. The task is to figure out how the country will ensure good housing for everyone who resides here and what role the federal public housing program will play in meeting the challenge. How does the nation ensure that elderly and disabled residents of public housing will be able to age in place in decent and safe homes in the communities that they know best? How does it ensure that public housing is improved and preserved as a viable option for the generation of aging baby boomers whose future housing needs will not be met by the housing market?

While the myriad questions that arise in examining the future of public housing are beyond the scope of this chapter, the fundamental principles that should guide the analysis can be articulated:

- Funding must be sufficient to do the job right, in terms of providing both human services and housing.
- The best interests of all current and future residents, collaboratively determined and accurately assessed, must be paramount.
- Policy must be informed by both practice and the felt experiences of those most affected.

But first, do no harm.

EXPLORING THE ISSUE

Should Federal Programs Seek to Deconcentrate Inner-City Poverty?

Critical Thinking and Reflection

1. Should people be forced to move against their will, even for the goal of moving people to communities with greater economic and educational opportunities?
2. What can be done to improve the conditions of public housing neighborhoods if resident objections are allowed to thwart the demolition of dilapidated housing structures?
3. Should redevelopment efforts emphasize the construction of mixed-income housing developments, even if the construction of such housing requires that a city devote extensive subsidies to attracting better-off citizens, reducing the number of new residential units that are made available to the poor?
4. Is the ideal of integrated residential neighborhoods and housing still an ideal worth pursuing? Would the abandonment of dispersionist programs represent a return to an "American apartheid," where the ghettoization of low-income minority populations is allowed to continue unchallenged?

Is There Common Ground?

Perhaps the wishes of the poor themselves should play a greater role in deciding just when relocation should occur. There is considerable difference between voluntary and forced relocation. Participation in the Gautreaux program was voluntary; it worked as it assisted families who wished to escape public housing and start anew in a safer and more opportunity-rich community. Residents who valued their old neighborhood were not forced to move. HOPE VI, in contrast, lacked voluntarism. Wide-scale demolition left public housing residents with no choice. As a result, HOPE VI families, like MTO movers, did not exhibit the full range of gains that were apparent in the Gautreaux mobility program.

As much as possible, government programs should emphasize voluntary mobility programs that assist families in escaping violent neighborhoods and improving their lives. The thousands of residents who applied for Gautreaux housing and MTO assistance show that there exists a large number of public housing residents who are quite willing to participate in voluntary mobility programs.

When programs like HOPE VI entail extensive demolition, the number of families forcibly relocated against their will can be minimized by providing new

205

housing on site or in the immediate vicinity. HOPE VI did not adequately provide such housing. Instead, the program tore down problem housing structures before new housing units were finished. Residents temporarily relocated grew tired of waiting for the completion of the new housing, with many eventually giving up on their dream to return to the old neighborhood. As a result, even residents who were temporarily relocated, were residents who expressed the desire to return and move back into the old neighborhood. Such displacement can be minimized by completing the construction of replacement units on-site (or nearby) *before* a distressed public housing structure is torn down. A "build first" approach can minimize forced displacement.

Intensive housing counseling and more generous housing certificates will also enable more residents to find good housing and neighborhoods. As seen in the Gautreaux program, the work of housing agency staff is essential to developing good relationships with landlords, overcoming their reluctance to rent to the former residents of public housing.

One other potential area for common ground concerns the development of mixed-income communities. Mixed-income residential areas represent the integrationist ideal. But they are very expensive to build, as they require extensive subsidies for relatively well-off citizens. Even when such housing is finished, there is little guarantee that tenants from different backgrounds will interact and build a true "community." Mixed-income development is unlikely to deliver the payoffs that its backers promise. Conservatives and liberals may be able to find common ground in limiting the waste of taxpayer money that occurs when governments give vast subsidies in an attempt to attract well-off buyers to mixed-income projects. For liberals, the money can be directed to the construction of additional affordable units that will house low-income families.

Additional Resources

Bennett, Larry, Janet L. Smith, & Patricia A. Wright, eds. (2006). *Where Are Poor People to Live? Transforming Public Housing Communities.* Armonk, NY: M.E. Sharpe.

Briggs, Xavier de Sousa, Susan J. Popkin, & John Goering. (2010). *Moving to Opportunity: The Story of an American Experiment to Fight Ghetto Poverty.* New York: Oxford University Press.

Cisneros, Henry G., & Lora Engdahl, eds. (2010). *From Despair to Hope: HOPE VI and the Promise of Public Housing in America's Cities.* Washington, DC: The Brookings Institution, 2010.

Davies, Jonathan S., & David L. Imbroscio, eds. (2010). *Critical Urban Studies: New Directions.* Albany NY: SUNY Press.

DeLuc a, Sefanie, & James E. Rosenbaum. (2010). "Residential Mobility, Neighborhoods, and Poverty: Results from the Chicago Gautreaux Program and the Moving to Opportunity Experiment," pp. 185–197 in *The Integration Debate*, op cit.

Hartman, Chester, & Gregory D. Squires, eds. (2010). *The Integration Debate: Competing Futures for American Cities.* New York: Routledge.

Hirsch, Arnold R. (1998). *Making the Second Ghetto: Race and Housing in Chicago, 1940–1960*. Chicago, IL: University of Chicago Press, 2nd ed.

Massey, Douglas, & Nancy Denton. (1993). *American Apartheid: Segregation and the Making of the Underclass*. Cambridge, MA: Harvard University Press.

Polikoff, Alexander. (2006). *Waiting for Gautreaux: A Story of Segregation, Housing, and the Black Ghetto*. Evanston, IL: Northwestern University Press.

Turner, Margery Austin, Susan J. Popkin, & Lynette A. Rawlings. (2008). *Public Housing and the Legacy of Segregation*. Washington, DC: Urban Institute Press.

Wilson, William Julius. (1987). *The Truly Disadvantaged: The Inner City, the Underclass, and Public Policy*. Chicago, IL: University of Chicago Press.

Wilson, William Julius. (1996). *When Work Disappears: The World of the New Urban Poor*. New York: Vintage.

Internet References

Brookings Institution

This Washington-based think tank has produced an extensive number of reports on the HOPE VI program and other poverty deconcentration efforts.

www.brookings.edu

National Low-Income Housing Coalition

The National Low-Income Housing Coalition pursues socially just housing policies and fights to maintain the public commitment to affordable housing.

www.nlihc.org

Shelterforce Online

Published by the National Housing Institute, the journal explores a wide range of housing policy topics, including vouchers, HOPE VI, and other poverty deconcentration efforts. The journal's articles also seek to describe ways by which low-income residents can challenge plans that seek to relocate them from development sites. The November/December 2004 issue of *Shelterforce* took a largely critical perspective on the HOPE VI program.

www.shelterforce.org

Urban Institute

This Washington-based think tank has produced a large number of reports on HOPE VI and other policy efforts aimed at deconcentrating poverty and transforming public housing. See, in particular, *A Decade of HOPE VI: Research Findings and Policy Challenges* (2005) and *HOPE VI Panel Study: Baseline Report, Final Report* (2011).

www.urban.org

ISSUE 10

Should Section 8 Housing Vouchers Continue to Serve as the Backbone of the Federal Government's Assisted Housing Efforts?

YES: Margery Austin Turner and Susan J. Popkin, from *Why Housing Choice and Mobility Matter* (The Urban Institute, August 17, 2010)

NO: Christopher Swope, from "Section 8 Is Broken," *Governing* magazine (May 2002), reprinted by NHI, *Shelterforce Online*, 127 (January/February 2003)

Learning Outcomes

After reading this issue, you should be able to:

- Explain how housing vouchers work.
- Differentiate between Section 8 housing vouchers (now renamed Housing Choice vouchers) and Section 8 new construction.
- Detail the advantages of housing vouchers has compared to a program that seeks to build new housing for low-income families.
- Evaluate the evidence on the impact of vouchers, explaining their achievements and shortcomings.
- Explain why some critics oppose the continuing "voucherization" of U.S. housing policy.
- Explain how opponents use the concept of a "reconcentration" of poverty to object to criticize housing vouchers.

ISSUE SUMMARY

YES: Margery Austin Turner and Susan Popkin, housing researchers for the Urban Institute, review the many benefits of housing vouchers. They argue that evidence shows that vouchers add to the life chances of poor people, increasing the job prospects and educational opportunities available to low-income families.

208

NO: Christopher Swope edits the website *Stateline* and previously served as the managing editor of *Governing* magazine, a publication devoted to the analysis of state and local policy issues. Swope argues that the housing vouchers have wound up creating new concentrations of the poor in vulnerable neighborhoods, speeding the decline of fragile but otherwise stabile working-class communities.

$\mathbf{A}$s we saw in the preceding chapter, housing vouchers (also often referred to as housing certificates) were an important part of the Gautreaux, MTO, and HOPE VI mobility programs. Each of these programs distributed vouchers to a relatively small population. This chapter looks at a much wider program, the Housing Choice voucher program (commonly referred to as Section 8 vouchers, the program's older name), the nation's largest program of housing assistance to low-income people.

Vouchers are the primary tool by which the United States assists families who cannot otherwise afford decent housing. In 2011, housing vouchers were awarded to 2.1 million families at an annual cost of $16 billion (2009 HUD figures). The program was fairly well targeted to need; the mean family income of voucher recipients was only $13,100, well below the national poverty line.

As large and expensive as the program is, the Housing Choice voucher program does not serve all people with housing needs. According to the Center on Budget and Policy Priorities, only one-fourth of the families who qualify for housing assistance actually receive voucher assistance. There simply is not enough money (or political will) to subsidize the housing choices of all families in need. As a consequence, many cities and counties have long waiting lists of families seeking voucher assistance.

The voucher approach represents a fundamental shift away from the approach that dominated United States housing policy for much of the twentieth century. Initially, the government built *public housing* for people who could not find quality affordable units in the private market. Public housing units were government owned and operated. Beginning in the 1970s, the government also offered *Section 8 new construction* assistance (a program that is different from Section 8 vouchers) to encourage private developers to build affordable housing. A Section 8 new construction agreement typically obligates a public housing agency for two decades or even longer (sometimes for 40 years!) to fill a specified number of housing units in the building with low-income residents.

In more recent decades, the construction of low-income housing has slowed to a snail's pace. Except for populations with special needs (such as the elderly, the disabled, and homeless persons who require "assisted" housing with on-site social services), the government no longer seeks to promote the construction of new housing for the poor. Instead, the government awards *housing vouchers* (previously called *housing certificates*) to help low-income families to rent units that already exist. The voucher program pays a landlord the portion of the monthly rent that the low-income renter cannot afford to pay (with the tenant's share capped at 30 percent of a family's monthly adjusted gross income).

A system of housing vouchers serves to increase a tenant's choices. Housing vouchers are *portable;* the subsidy "follows" the tenant and is not tied to a specific building or project. Renters who receive voucher assistance, of course, are not forced to relocate. Many recipients "lease in place," using their certificates to help pay the rent of an apartment in which they already reside.

Vouchers have a second very important advantage: they provide housing at a cost that is dramatically less per unit than the cost of new construction. Vouchers do not require the government to pay the full cost of construction, only the portion of the monthly rent that a tenant cannot afford (the "gap" between the "fair market rent" of a unit and the 30 percent of a family's income that the tenant contributes). Unlike Section 8 new construction, vouchers do not saddle a government with a 20- to 40-year financial obligation. Nor are vouchers an *entitlement* program where a person has a legal right to a benefit. Instead, vouchers are a *nonentitlement* program, with the government setting the amount that will be spent on the program each year. Budget cutters can curtail housing expenditures simply by voting to reduce the annual appropriations or funding given to vouchers.

In recent years, political conservatives have sought to reduce voucher assistance, a program that in their eyes has grown way too large. Liberals, in contrast, have leapt to the defense of a program that extends help to so many vulnerable families, usually female-headed families with children.

Initially, political conservatives were the advocates who pushed for the adoption of a voucher program as a better alternative to public housing. Vouchers held out the promise of empowering tenants who could threaten to move elsewhere, maybe even putting new pressures on landlords to pay greater attention to a building's upkeep.

Over the years, as the program proved to be a quite successful and relatively cost-efficient way of provide assistance, Liberal Democrats and poor people's advocates, including the Low Income Housing Coalition (LIHTC), became the program's chief defenders.

In big cities with "tight" housing markets (where there are few vacant units), recipients often face considerable difficulty in finding quality housing for the fair market rent as established by the voucher program. Many landlords are also reluctant to accept vouchers, preferring to rent to nonvoucher tenants and to avoid the hassles of dealing with Department of Housing and Urban Development inspection, reporting, and paperwork requirements. As a result of these problems, a sizeable number of voucher users have great difficulty in finding apartments. Only 70 percent of certificate holders are actually able to find a suitable apartment where a landlord is willing to accept voucher payment. In cities with "tight" housing markets, the success rate for voucher users is even lower. Large families, in particular, have difficulty in being able to use vouchers to find apartments of appropriate size (Schwartz 2006).

Vouchers enhance housing mobility, allowing inner-city families to move to neighborhoods that are less impacted by poverty and less racially segregated.

Of course, wealthier suburbs (where rents are generally higher than what the voucher program allows) wind up with relatively few voucher tenants. Working- and lower-middle-class neighborhoods, by contrast, can become the site of new concentrations of voucher-assisted moves.

In the YES selection, Urban Institute researchers Margery Austin Turner and Susan Popkin argue that the evidence shows that vouchers can help bring significant improvements to the life chances of poor families, affording greater safety and new opportunities at work and in school. In the NO selection, Christopher Swope, however, changes the focus of the discussion, by pointing to the potential harm that a voucher program can inflict on transitional neighborhoods that become the new home to large numbers of low-income residents. For vulnerable neighborhoods, according to Swope, vouchers are a "bigger housing problem" than public housing.

However, national data show that in many communities, fears of poverty reconcentration may be greatly exaggerated. In only a small handful of communities do voucher users even comprise as much as 10 percent of a neighborhood's population. As Peter Dreier and Xavier de Souza Briggs (2008) point out, "Section 8 voucher holders comprised 10 percent or more of all households in only 5 percent of the census tracts. That is, in only 1 in 20 neighborhoods do voucher holders make up even 1 in 10 of the households." Still, the "clustering" of voucher users in certain working-class neighborhoods does occur (Turner, Popkin, & Cunningham, 2000).

YES

**Margery Austin Turner and
Susan J. Popkin**

Why Housing Choice and Mobility Matter

HUD's proposal for transforming federal rental assistance program expands subsidy recipients' freedom to choose where to live. Today, low-income households living in public housing and in federally assisted projects lose their subsidies if they move. These programs tie rental assistance to particular housing units, and qualifying families must remain in place or forgo the housing assistance.[1] Typically, the waiting lists for these projects are long, so households have a very strong incentive to stay once they've gained admission.

The proposed Preservation, Enhancement, and Transformation of Rental Assistance Act of 2010 (PETRA) would allow residents of subsidized projects to move—with a portable housing voucher—after living in the project for at least two years. The vacated housing unit would still be subsidized, opening up an opportunity for another low-income family from the waiting list. And the voucher for the departing household would be drawn from the locality's available pool of "turn over" vouchers.[2] So the administration's proposal leaves the total number of subsidized housing units and the number of assisted households unchanged. What's new is that all households receiving assistance would have more choices about where to use their assistance. Allowing all federally subsidized renters the freedom to choose where to live can contribute to better outcomes for families.

This essay summarizes research evidence showing that

- project-based programs limit families' choices about where to live,
- families benefit when they move with vouchers,
- assisted housing mobility programs further expand families' options, and
- "opportunity moves" can improve families' life chances.

Project-Based Programs Limit Families' Choices About Where to Live

Both public housing and federally assisted housing projects are clustered in low-income, central-city neighborhoods, while vouchers give low-income households access to a wider range of locations (figure 1). Public housing is the most geographically concentrated of the federally subsidized rental housing

Figure 1

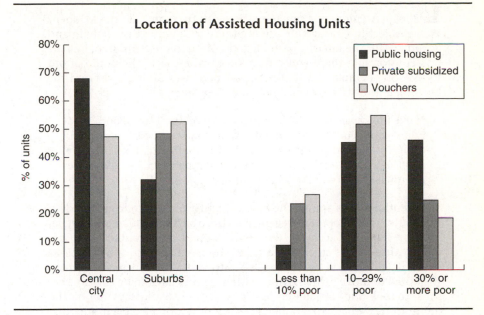

Location of Assisted Housing Units

Source: Preliminary UI tabulations of data from HUD's 2008 Picture of Subsidized Housing.

options; over two-thirds of the public housing units in the top 100 metropolitan areas nationwide are in central cities, and almost half are in neighborhoods with high poverty rates.[3] Federally subsidized projects that are privately
owned are somewhat more widely dispersed. Just over half the units located in
the top 100 metropolitan areas are in central cities and a quarter are in high-
poverty neighborhoods. However, most suburban units are designed to serve
elderly residents, not families with children.

Voucher recipients live in a much wider range of neighborhoods, including suburban and low-poverty communities. As of 2008, slightly less than
50 percent of voucher holders in the top 100 metropolitan areas lived in central cities, and 18 percent lived in high-poverty neighborhoods. Moreover,
while only 9 percent of public housing units are located in low-poverty neighborhoods, 27 percent of voucher holders live in such communities.

The voucher program has the potential to expand families' choices about
where to live even further. Based on analysis of 2000 Census data, HUD estimates
that almost all census tracts in the 50 biggest metropolitan areas nationwide have
at least some rental housing units affordable for housing voucher recipients. And
83 percent are home to at least one voucher household.

Families Benefit When They Move with Vouchers

Families that have used vouchers to relocate from public housing enjoy substantial improvements in housing quality and satisfaction and dramatically
reduced exposure to drug trafficking and violent crime. The Urban Institute's
research has tracked housing and neighborhood outcomes for residents of

In 2001, Gwendolyn, a single mother with two sons, left the Madden/ Wells project in Chicago after living there for many years (Popkin and Buron 2010). She knew it wasn't a good place to raise children, but she was comfortable there and didn't know where else she could afford to live. She complained that her apartment was falling apart and the housing authority never made requested repairs:

> "I like [my] apartment, the fact that it's up on the 11th. [floor]. What I don't like about the apartment is that they won't come up and fix things the way they should . . . . like the plumbing, the electricity, and the wiring in the walls. It's all like falling apart. . . . Sometimes the tub backs up and the toilet stops up. . . ."

Gwendolyn was among the first residents to relocate from Madden/ Wells after redevelopment began. She chose a Housing Choice Voucher and, by her own account, was both "scared and excited." She has moved three times since. For a time, she lived in a low-poverty, low-crime neighborhood on Chicago's Southwest Side, but most recently, she opted to move further east to a higher-crime area to be closer to her sons' school. She was able to rent a small house and says she has no desire to move back to a public housing development, even now that it's been redeveloped. She feels at home in her house—and has a land-lord who fixes things when they are broken:

> "I feel comfortable here. I'm happy.... I wanted to make sure the house wasn't in foreclosure, because you find out a lot of landlords don't tell you that the housing is in foreclosure. So, once I found out that it's not in foreclosure, I'm going to do little things to fit it up and make it more homey."

HOPE VI developments who used vouchers to relocate. These families generally moved to neighborhoods with lower poverty rates than their original public-housing neighborhoods. Specifically, while poverty rates in the original projects were extremely high—averaging around 40 percent—after relocation, half the voucher relocatees were living in census tracts with poverty rates lower than 20 percent, and only 11 percent remained in high-poverty communities.

These HOPE VI voucher relocatees live in much higher quality housing than the projects they left behind. For example, less than 25 percent now report having two or more serious problems with their housing, down from more than 50 percent in their original public housing units. Even more striking, these relocatees reported dramatic reductions in fear of crime (figure 2). For example, the proportion of respondents reporting "big problems" with drug sales and use in their neighborhood dropped from about 80 percent before relocation to 33 percent in 2005 (Popkin, Levy, and Buron 2009).[4]

Low-income families that have used vouchers to leave public housing place high value on these changes, seeing them as significant improvements in their quality of life.

Figure 2

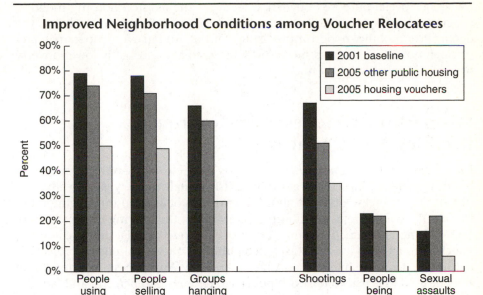

Improved Neighborhood Conditions among Voucher Relocatees

Source: Popkin and Cove (2007), table 2.

Assisted Housing Mobility Programs Can Further Expand Families' Choices About Where to Live

Some low-income families have volunteered for programs offering mobility counseling along with housing vouchers, so they can move to dramatically better neighborhoods. Over the past two decades, assisted housing mobility programs have been implemented in many communities across the country, providing counseling and search assistance in conjunction with special-purpose housing vouchers for families that want to move to lower-poverty or less segregated neighborhoods.

These local programs have mainly been implemented as part of litigation settlements or as research demonstrations. Many of them include restrictions on the types of neighborhoods where the vouchers can be used. The services offered by these mobility programs vary widely but typically include some combination of outreach to landlords with properties in desirable neighbor-hoods; individual or group counseling to help families plan and prepare for their search; information about unfamiliar neighborhoods, schools, shopping, and transportation access; hands-on help with housing search; and follow-up counseling and supports.

Many of these programs have had far more volunteers apply to participate than available slots. For example, 5,300 families from targeted housing devel-opments in five cities (25 percent of project residents) applied to participate in the Moving to Opportunity program and 13,000 households have applied for 2,000 special-purpose vouchers offered by the assisted housing mobility program operating in the Baltimore region. This evidence suggests that the demand for mobility opportunities is substantial. And in every program, many (though not all) volunteers successfully move to a dramatically lower-poverty or less segregated neighborhood.

"Opportunity Moves" Can Improve Families' Life Chances

Families that move from distressed housing projects to low-poverty neighborhoods experience substantial gains in housing quality, safety, and health (figure 3). The strongest evidence about the impacts of assisted housing mobility for families comes from the interim evaluation of the Moving to Opportunity (MTO) demonstration. In the mid-1990s, MTO offered special-purpose housing vouchers to families living in distressed public and assisted housing projects in Baltimore, Boston, Chicago, Los Angeles, and New York. These vouchers could only be used in census tracts with poverty rates below 10 percent, and families received counseling and search assistance to help them find and lease qualifying homes and apartments.

Figure 3

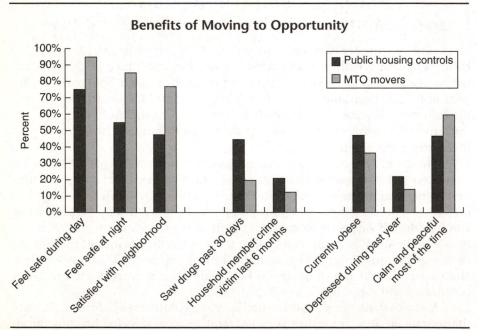

Sources: Orr et al (2003), exhibits 3.5 and 4.2.

MTO families moved to neighborhoods that were dramatically less poor than where they started—and considerably less poor than those occupied by similar families receiving conventional vouchers (with no search assistance). The MTO families also enjoyed dramatic gains in neighborhood safety—their main reason for enrolling in the program. For example, roughly five years after their initial move, the share of mothers reporting that they saw drugs being sold or used in the neighborhood was 20 points lower among MTO movers than among comparable families that remained in public housing. And MTO families described their neighborhoods as dramatically quieter, more secure, and less stressful than those they had left behind.

Women and girls who moved with MTO vouchers experienced significant improvements in mental and physical health, probably stemming from their reduced exposure to violence, disorder, and harassment. The interim MTO evaluation showed girls in the experimental group reported significantly lower rates of psychological distress and anxiety than those in the control group. For adult women, psychological distress and depression were reduced by 3.5 percentage points, or over one-fifth, relative to the control group. To put this in perspective, reductions of this magnitude are comparable to that achieved by some of the most successful drug treatments for depression and related disorders. The significance of MTO's impacts on safety, stress, and women's health should not be understated. Maternal depression is recognized as a major risk factor for the healthy emotional development of young children (Popkin, Leventhal, and Weisman 2010). However, the interim evaluation found no evidence that MTO contributed to significant educational, employment, or earnings gains, as had been hoped. And MTO boys had not shared in the benefits enjoyed by MTO girls.

Ongoing experimentation with mobility counseling programs offers the potential to help low-income families achieve even greater gains by moving to opportunity-rich neighborhoods. Although MTO families moved to low-poverty neighborhoods, few moved to the suburbs or to majority-white neighborhoods. And few MTO families stayed long in their new neighborhoods; instead, most moved several times over subsequent years, ending up in moderate-poverty, central-city neighborhoods.

Evidence from the earlier Gautreaux mobility program suggests that if families move to suburban neighborhoods with high-quality schools and other resources, they may achieve meaningful gains in education, employment, and—over the longer term—earnings. The latest generation of mobility programs, like the one operating in the Baltimore metropolitan area as part of a litigation settlement, encourages families to move to opportunity-rich neighborhoods throughout the region, and provides ongoing assistance to help movers stay in their new neighborhoods and take advantage of resources offered there.

In sum, many families living in federally subsidized housing projects will choose to stay, especially if new investments improve the quality and safety of these communities. But opening up opportunities for families to move—to live closer to work, or in a safer neighborhood, or near a high-performing school—strengthens federal rental housing policy by improving the well-being of assisted households.

Notes

1. Several federal housing programs provide deep, gap-filling rent subsidies—paying the difference between a rent contribution that is considered affordable (currently set at 30 percent of monthly income) and the actual rent for a house or apartment. Families receive this kind of "gap-filling" subsidy if they live in public housing (owned and managed by a local public housing agency) or in privately owned developments that have long-term subsidy contracts with the federal Department of Housing and Urban Development (HUD). In both cases, the subsidy is "project based"— attached to the house or apartment; if the family moves, it loses its subsidy.

2. The Housing Choice Voucher program provides the same kind of deep, gap-filling subsidy as the project-based programs, but these subsidies are used to supplement what households can afford to pay for rental homes and apartments in the private market. Even in periods when funding isn't available to expand the total pool of Housing Choice Vouchers, vouchers regularly become available as recipients lose eligibility, move away from an area, or give up their vouchers for other reasons. PETRA specifies that only one in every three turnover vouchers would have to be available to households wishing to leave assisted projects. The remaining two thirds of turnover vouchers would be available for households on the waiting list for assistance.

3. Census tracts where more than 30 percent of the population has incomes below the poverty level are considered high poverty and particularly susceptible to disinvestment and distress. Living in these high-poverty neighborhoods has been shown to undermine the well-being and long-term life chances of children and adults.

4. Similarly, families that volunteered to participate in the MTO demonstration (discussed further below) and received unrestricted vouchers moved to lower-poverty neighborhoods with lower crime rates than the public housing developments they left behind.

NO

Section 8 Is Broken

When badly managed, the voucher program doesn't deliver housing choice for low-income residents—and may even undermine revitalization efforts.

The Patterson Park neighborhood, on the East Side of Baltimore, stands perched precariously between renewal and collapse. A mixed-income population, almost evenly divided between white and black, lives here in nearly identical blocks of rowhouses, clad in red brick and drab formstone. Some of the poorer blocks look ragged, and residents complain about drugs and crime. But unlike so many neighborhoods in Baltimore, Patterson Park has never tipped to the point of severe blight. There are encouraging signs. Every so often, a young professional couple moves in, encouraged by the cheap real estate, close proximity to downtown and the wide patch of green that gives the neighborhood its name.

A fragile balance holds Patterson Park together. Sometimes, it seems the poor residents might force the richer ones out; other times, a reverse pattern of gentrification seems likely. Yet in recent years, a government program has been throwing off this delicate balance and quietly creating an outcome. It is the federal government's Section 8 housing program, and it has been dragging Patterson Park down. Section 8—known officially now as the "housing choice vouchers" program—subsidizes housing for some of Baltimore's most impoverished residents, mostly African-American women with children. In theory, these families can use their vouchers to rent apartments anywhere in the Baltimore metro area. In practice, their options are limited to a few low-income and transitional neighborhoods. Patterson Park is one of them. Hundreds of voucher-holders are finding their way to its rowhouses, including many refugees from the high-rise public housing projects that Baltimore began demolishing seven years ago.

Ed Rutkowski, who heads a community development corporation working to revitalize the neighborhood, bluntly calls Section 8 "a catalyst in neighborhood deterioration and ghetto expansion." Every day, Rutkowski says, he finds himself fighting the program's unintended consequences: neglected properties, persistent crime and a continual influx of dysfunctional families, some of whom have never lived outside of public housing.

Section 8 is supposed to deconcentrate poverty, but in Rutkowski's view, it actually reconcentrates it—in struggling neighborhoods such as his. At best, this has a destabilizing effect. At worst, it can drive middle-class residents out

and turn the entire area into a slum. "Once a neighborhood has some problems," Rutkowski says, "Section 8 accelerates those problems."

Rutkowski's concerns are echoed in transitional neighborhoods of other
cities as well, notably Chicago and Philadelphia. In Chicago, where more than
a dozen public housing high-rises are coming down, residents with vouchers
have clustered in working-class black neighborhoods such as South Shore, on
the South Side, and Austin, on the border with affluent suburban Oak Park.
Suburbs south of the city have taken in so many voucher families that local
officials there have asked for a Section 8 moratorium. "Left to its own devices,
Section 8 will always seek out the softest housing markets," says Christine
Klepper, director of Housing Choice Partners in Cook County. "And it will
often be in a transitional or poor neighborhood."

A Variety of Results

Grassroots concerns do not often make their way up to the higher policy-
making levels, where the recent response to the clustering problem has been
quite simple: Reduce the pressure by increasing the supply of vouchers. In fact,
Congress and the U.S. Department of Housing and Urban Development have
come increasingly to view vouchers as the answer to housing the nation's poor
(see Shelterforce #94). With little fanfare, vouchers have become a bigger housing program than traditional public housing. And the pendulum swings a little
further each time an old housing project gets the wrecking ball. To be sure, the
most decrepit projects needed to be demolished, but critics of Section 8 say
that the result of this shift to vouchers is little more than the replacement of
vertical ghettos with horizontal ones.

HUD is working hard to challenge this idea. A report issued by the agency
in 2000 argued that voucher families typically end up in better neighborhoods
than the ones they leave behind. Nationally, it said, Section 8 families live in
far less impoverished neighborhoods than public-housing families, and, on
average, the housing conditions of voucher-holders are comparable to those
of renters generally. "Neighborhood problems directly related to the Section 8
program are extremely rare, if they exist at all," the report said.

Indeed, from a bird's-eye view, Section 8 does work pretty well. With
vouchers, thousands of families each year do exactly what the program expects:
They migrate out of poor neighborhoods and into places with better schools
and more job opportunities. But the results vary substantially from city to
city, because the rental housing market is different in each one. In fact, the
success of Section 8 can vary from neighborhood to neighborhood and even
from block to block. And it is at these highly localized levels where patterns of
concentration emerge.

Section 8 is commonly described, and endorsed by both Democrats
and Republicans, as a "free-market" program. But there is no free market in
rental housing the way there is for shoes or airline tickets. Local laws concentrate the supply of such housing in lower-income areas due to zoning
restrictions, and in some cases to racial discrimination. Even where race is
not a major issue, landlords in more prosperous areas often do not want to

rent to single mothers with children, or simply don't like dealing with the Section 8 bureaucracy.

But the most important difference between Section 8 and any real free-market process is that the market doesn't set the prices—HUD does that. The agency decides what a voucher is worth by setting a "fair market rent" for each metro area. This sensibly takes into account the fact that housing costs more in New York City, for example, than it does in Lincoln, Nebraska. The formula is readjusted each year. But it is very hard for HUD to keep up with variations in rental prices from one neighborhood to the next in a given city. Lately, HUD has been offering local housing authorities more flexibility to adjust rents, but the market shifts faster than the economists can sharpen their pencils. If the voucher is worth too little for a "good" neighborhood, landlords won't take it and the poor get locked out. If the voucher is set too high in a marginal neighborhood, landlords milk it, and the door, perhaps, opens a bit too wide.

To conservatives such as Howard Husock, Section 8's problems are irreparable. Husock, a housing expert at Harvard University's John F. Kennedy School of Government, says that it's time to end the 30-year voucher experiment altogether. "We can't just end it tomorrow," Husock explains, "but we could really improve the character of the voucher program if there were time limits. Our housing policy is now completely out of sync with our welfare policy. If your rent is paid forever, then you don't have an incentive to improve your living situation."

Section 8's defenders, of course, draw a different conclusion. With good management and a few tweaks, they say, the program's disruption of transitional neighborhoods can be minimized. The underlying problem, housing activists argue, is that housing vouchers are being asked to take up too much of the housing burden. "Section 8 is not a bad program, but the federal, state and local governments want to see it as a panacea," says Barbara Samuels, a housing attorney with the ACLU of Maryland. "It's an important piece of our overall housing policy, but when you expect it to be the mainstay of that policy, it just collapses."

The "Tipping Point"

Driving around East Baltimore, Rutkowski offers a tour of the dilemma facing his community. Patterson Park is wedged tightly between two neighborhoods, one a gleaming success and the other a glaring failure. To the south, down a slope toward the city's waterfront, is Canton. Young couples are buying two-story row-houses here for as much as $250,000. Nearly every block has at least one house covered in scaffolding, with workmen busy making repairs. To the north, however, is a neighborhood called Middle East. Here, entire blocks of houses much like the ones in Canton have simply been abandoned. Instead of the scaffolding, plywood boards cover the windows and doors to keep out squatters and drug dealers. Patterson Park forms something of a buffer between these two areas. "We're trying to pull a little bit of Canton up here," Rutkowski says.

Patterson Park is in transition in all sorts of ways: racial, economic and generational. Historically, it was a modest bedroom community for blue-collar white families whose breadwinners worked in the nearby steel factories and canning companies. But many of those residents moved when the plants closed, and others from that generation who stayed have been passing away. As middle-class and then lower-class blacks moved in to take their place, more whites left. The neighborhood now is about as integrated as you'll find in Baltimore, where all-white and all-black neighborhoods are the norm.

During the past decade, speculators saw an opportunity in Patterson Park—and in the loopholes of the voucher program. They found they could snap up vacant rowhouses for as little as $10,000, give them a fresh coat of paint, pass Section 8 inspection, and start to rake in vouchers worth $700 a month, much more than the rentals would be worth on the private market. As groups of out-of-town investors got in on the deal, Section 8 families flooded into as many as 700 of Patterson Park's rowhouses. The neighborhood became visibly poorer and shabbier as the landlords ignored maintenance. "The people buying here were not experienced property managers," Rutkowski says. "They were accountants and lawyers in the suburbs."

Rutkowski has written a book about Patterson Park with Marcus Pollock, another Baltimorean active in community development. The Urban Transition Zone, now out of print, talks a lot about "tipping points" for declining neighborhoods. After a certain point, the theory goes, middle-class flight accelerates, intense poverty and blight follow and a neighborhood becomes unsalvageable. Lots of forces have been pushing Patterson Park toward its tipping point, including a spate of house "flipping" and predatory lending (see Shelterforce #113). But Rutkowski and Pollock believe Section 8 is the most serious. "We would hardly claim that the Section 8 program is single-handedly responsible for the problems of transitional neighborhoods," they write. "But it may well be the straw that breaks the camel's back."

It might not have to be. Properly managed, a Section 8 program could monitor where its voucher-holders have settled and avoid concentrating too many in any one neighborhood. This is a simple task for modern mapping software. Yet management of Baltimore's voucher program has been so abysmal that HUD threatened to take it over after a scathing audit in 2001. (The computers at Baltimore's housing authority are among the only ones in the world that actually suffered Y2K problems.) It is a situation that Paul Graziano, the housing commissioner, and Michael Kramer, the Section 8 chief, are working hard to fix.

Throughout the authority, managers are being replaced, new computer systems are being set up, and there is an emphasis on such nuts-and-bolts tasks as getting rent checks out on time. Meanwhile, Graziano is stepping up oversight of landlords and trying to better synchronize Section 8 rents with the market. The last thing he wants is to continue luring droves of absentee investors to Patterson Park and similar transitional neighborhoods. "We were facilitating speculation, facilitating shoddy management practices and encouraging those who frankly should not be in the business of property management to come into our program," he says. "We paid them top dollar without regard to any kind of reasonable rent determination process and asked for little in return."

Still, Graziano is in a Section 8 squeeze. If he wants to avoid filling transitional neighborhoods with voucher families, he must find landlords in wealthier neighborhoods who will take them. And those landlords shun Section 8, not merely because of its bad reputation but also because they can get higher rents from the private market.

Graziano and Kramer have their fingers crossed that a recent change will help on the supply side. Last year HUD gave Baltimore permission to increase its rental ceiling in tighter markets. Higher rents, it is hoped, will attract new landlords throughout the city. An independent market analysis is also underway to determine how much of the rental market—if any—remains untapped by Section 8. Kramer, however, doesn't expect it to turn up many units outside the usual voucher zones. It's a matter of geography, he says: "You really only find multi-family rental housing along three corridors out of the city. That's where the housing is. In neighborhoods where house prices far exceed the median, I wouldn't expect to see any renter moving there, Section 8 or not."

Opportunity Areas

The forces working against Section 8 are so complex and interconnected that focusing on market rents and luring landlords may sound a bit simplistic. If housing authorities really want to deconcentrate poverty, some argue, perhaps it is time they try something radically different. Like investing in buses or light rail systems.

You might come to this conclusion if you talk with Richard Doran. Doran runs a nonprofit in suburban Baltimore County whose counselors go apartment hunting with voucher-holders throughout the metro area. The counselors try to open them to the idea of looking in so-called "opportunity areas," while trying to persuade landlords in those areas to take Section 8 tenants. As Baltimore defines it, an opportunity area is one that has a poverty level below 20 percent, is less than one-quarter minority, and has fewer than 5 percent of its households in subsidized housing. In the end, of course, it is the voucher-holder's choice where to move. Yet some 350 families who have gone through the counseling—65 percent—have moved to opportunity areas.

There are lots of available apartments in opportunity areas all over the Baltimore region, Doran says. The problem, for people who can't afford to own cars, is that there's no public transit to get there. "A lot of great opportunity areas are not on a public bus line," Doran says. "There's a lot of housing available out there that makes absolutely no sense for our families to live in."

It may be a stretch for municipal housing authorities to fund mass transit. But increasingly, they are turning to the sort of counseling that Doran's group does. The goal is to create Section 8 demand outside the inner city. Some voucher-holders, it seems, end up in impoverished neighborhoods not because they want to be there but because they never dreamed they could go anywhere else. "It's amazing," Doran says. "There were people in Baltimore who had never been beyond North Avenue"—one of the city's racial and economic dividing lines. "They didn't know what other parts of the city or the suburbs looked like, that there are nice neighborhoods with good rental units."

Information technology may also have a role to play in closing the gap between Section 8 supply and demand. In Minnesota's Twin Cities, HousingLink is a computerized housing referral service. The database includes listings of available Section 8 apartments in a seven-county area. This makes it easier for housing agencies to match voucher-holders, most of whom are from Minneapolis or St. Paul, with landlords, who tend to be in the suburbs. The regional approach is important, says HousingLink president Colleen O'Brien. "In the Twin Cities area, we have 13 different housing authorities managing Section 8. It had gotten so fragmented that they had a hard time finding any apartments outside their own jurisdictions."

Meanwhile, in Patterson Park, the Section 8 influx is slowing down. But not for very encouraging reasons. Some of the Section 8 investors, it seems, had also engaged in mortgage fraud. Several have gone bankrupt and had their properties foreclosed on. "Some of the Section 8 tenants are having to move out," says Rutkowski. "I feel badly for them because it is a hardship. Where are they going to go?"

Rutkowski hopes to add some of the newly foreclosed properties to his portfolio. In just six years of working to turn Patterson Park around, his grassroots group has fixed up 285 homes in the neighborhood and filled them with stable homeowners and renters. The strategy is paying off, if a recent Baltimore Sun headline is to be believed: "Improvement: Patterson Park Is Drawing the Attention of Young Couples, Families and Developers."

Most important, Rutkowski's complaints have made the housing authority aware of what's at stake with Section 8 and the very real prospect of sloppy voucher programs destroying fragile but viable neighborhoods. "This problem isn't about poor people," Rutkowski says. "It's not about whether or not we help the poor. It's not about poor people's behavior, and it's certainly not about race. It's really about management. If the housing authority manages the program well and the people who manage the properties do it properly, a ton of our problems disappear."

EXPLORING THE ISSUE

Should Section 8 Housing Vouchers Continue to Serve as the Backbone of the Federal Government's Assisted Housing Efforts?

Critical Thinking and Reflection

1. Do communities have legitimate concerns regarding the concentration of so many low-income newcomers? Or, are such concerns more an expression of class and racial prejudices and fears?
2. Should there be a cap or ceiling that limits the concentration of voucher users in a geographic area?
3. Should housing voucher applicants be "screened" according to such factors as their job history, their enrollment in college or training programs, their children's truancy record, and their past run-ins with the law? What would be the consequences of such screening measures?
4. How should policy makers balance the needs of voucher users, who may likely gain from a move to a safer and better neighborhood, with the needs of existing residents who fear that the arrival of large numbers of voucher users will accelerate a community's decline?

Is There Common Ground?

The debate over vouchers and poverty deconcentration can turn quite fiery and emotional. In Essex and Dundalk, Maryland, working-class suburbs in Baltimore County, residents exploded in anger when they discovered that HUD was using the MTO program to relocate former public housing residents to their neighborhood. The residents of these areas objected to the unfairness of a Section 8 assistance that seemingly targeted their communities while other communities in the region housed so few Section 8 tenants. Confronted by politicized and angry constituents, prominent Democratic officials joined Republicans and put the brakes on MTO expansion.

To maintain the political sustainability of voucher programs, public officials may wish to consider taking steps that will minimize the perceived threat that voucher-assisted moves may bring to a community. Housing authorities can avoid overwhelming more vulnerable working-class communities by using extensive housing counseling in an effort to have families use their vouchers in communities across a metropolis, especially in communities that have relatively small voucher populations. Longer-distance relocations will require more intensive support from housing agencies, especially as low-income tenants may be fearful of moving into unfamiliar communities. Where a family's lack of transportation poses a barrier to relocation in more distant and automobile-dependent opportunity-rich communities, a local housing agency may partner with a nonprofit agency that can help a "carless" family find an automobile.

Counseling and tenant screening can also help soothe the fears of receiving communities. Conservatives like Howard Husock point to the utility of work requirements, such as those in Atlanta where voucher users are required to work 30 hours or more per week or to continue their enrollment in full-time school and training programs. The Gautreaux program in Chicago (reviewed in the preceding chapter) worked quite well largely because participants were highly motivated and effectively screened, with chosen applicants possessing the history and attitudes indicating that their move to a new neighborhood would likely be a success. Housing Choice vouchers, dispensed much more widely, however, have not been as selective and have often lacked intensive screening and counseling. Although poor-peoples advocates argue against the cultural biases of screening and selection criteria, local housing authorities may still consider it prudent to avoid recruiting voucher users as tenants whose behavior can wind up being the source of controversy that can drain public support for future voucher efforts. Not all low-income families are "ready" for voucher-assisted moves to new communities.

Local housing agencies may also consider measures to help limit new voucher-approved moves to neighborhoods where a large numbers of voucher users already reside and where there exists a risk of poverty reconcentration. GIS technology and computer-assisted mapping can make it relatively easy for local housing authorities to spot neighborhoods that already have dense concentrations of Section 8 arrivals, allowing housing counselors to steer new voucher users to other communities.

But such steps, as sensible as they may seem to be, may wind up limiting the number of families who can be assisted by vouchers. Affordable housing units available within the price guidelines set by the voucher program are more likely to be found in a city's working- and lower-middle-class neighborhoods. Suburbs often use zoning and land-use ordinances to restrict the number of rental units that can be built within their borders. In many communities, those rental units that do exist have monthly rents beyond what voucher program guidelines allow. If a cap or other rationing instrument serves to limit the number of poor families that can move into areas of the city where landlords are willing to rent to voucher users, just where will poor people live?

Additional Resources

Dreier, Peter, & Xavier de Souza Briggs. (July 22 2008), "Memphis Murder Mystery? No, Just Mistaken Identity," *Shelterforce*, Web Only article. Available at: www.shelterforce.org/article/special/1043/P0/.

Hays, R. Allen. (1995). *The Federal Government and Urban Housing: Ideology and Change in Public Policy*, 2nd ed. Albany, NY: State University of New York Press.

Schwartz, Alex F. (2010). *Housing Policy in the United States*, 2nd ed. New York: Routledge.

Turner, Margery Austin, Susan J. Popkin, & Mary Cunningham. (2000). *Section 8 Mobility and Neighborhood Health. Washington*, DC: Urban Institute.

Internet References

Brookings Institution

Brookings' in-depth studies explore numerous aspects of housing voucher programs.

www.brookings.edu

City Journal

A publication of the Manhattan Institute, a conservative "think tank" concerned with urban policy, *City Journal* has been critical of the short-comings of vouchers, especially their impact on receiving neighborhoods. See, in particular, the writings of Howard Husock.

www.city-journal.org

National Low-Income Housing Coalition

This advocacy group presents studies pointing to the continuing need for housing assistance. The NLIHC examines various reform measures that seek to "reform" the operation of vouchers and other low-income housing programs.

www.nlihc.org

Urban Institute Metropolitan Housing and Communities Center

This Washington-based think tank has produced a voluminous number of reports on Section 8 vouchers as well as on other housing and mobility programs.

www.urban.org

ISSUE 11

Did the Government's Regulation of Lending Institutions Under the Community Reinvestment Act Lead to the Mortgage Foreclosure Crisis?

YES: Peter J. Wallison, from "Cause and Effect: Government Policies and the Financial Crisis," *American Enterprise Institute for Public Policy Research* (November 2008)

NO: Philip Ashton, from "Cry Wolf Policy Brief: Community Reinvestment Act and Responsible Lending" (February 2011)

Learning Outcomes

After reading this issue, you should be able to:

- Explain why the CRA was enacted.
- Identify the requirements that the CRA places on mortgage lenders.
- Explain why supporters of the CRA see it as one of the most essential governmental programs for improving the conditions of inner-city neighborhoods.
- Detail the criticisms that business leaders and political conservatives make against the CRA.
- Explain how the deregulation policies of the Reagan years wound up narrowing the scope of the CRA.
- Define "predatory" lending.

ISSUE SUMMARY

YES: Peter J. Wallison, former general counsel at the United States Department of Treasury holds the Arthur B. Burns Chair in Financial Market Studies at the American Enterprise Institute (AEI). A political conservative, he is critical of governmental intrusion in the free market. Wallison argues that the CRA helped to undermine the industry's normal standards for home loans, leading mortgage institutions to make loans to persons who were not good credit risks.

NO: Philip Ashton, associate professor of Urban Planning and Policy at the University of Illinois-Chicago, argues that it is unfair to blame the CRA for a home foreclosure crisis that occurred three decades after the act's passage. Ashton observes that the lending industry has been critical of the CRA since its very beginning and has used the recent mortgage crisis as a pretense to launch yet one more attack on the CRA. The greatest abuses did not occur in CRA-covered loans but in loans made by institutions that were exempted from CRA requirements. Ashton argues that it was deregulation, not regulation, that contributed to the home foreclosure crisis.

How much governmental regulation of the private sector is desirable? Is governmental regulation necessary to protect citizens against abuses by rogue private businesses? Or does governmental regulation too often represent unwise and costly interference in decisions that are best left to the private sector?

For most of the country's history, lending institutions set their own loan policies with little government oversight. In a practice known as *redlining*, banks and other credit institutions dismissed entire neighborhoods as "bad" for business. At its crudest form, banks had a map on which they drew a red line around large portions of the inner city; no loans were approved within that perimeter.

Critics argue that redlining represented a very crude approach to protecting loan portfolios, an approach that virtually guarantees the *disinvestment* in, and the accelerated decline of, inner-city communities. Under redlining, even credit-worthy business owners and home seekers with exemplary job and loan repayment histories were denied investment capital if they come from a part of town that banks and insurance companies deemed to pose too great a risk for loans.

The Fair Housing Act of 1968 prohibits discrimination in the sale or rental of housing on the basis of a person's race, ethnicity, religion, or country of origin. Lending institutions clearly cannot discriminate against an individual home buyer. Redlining, however, entails the denial of credit to an entire neighborhood, not discrimination against a particular individual.

The *Community Reinvestment Act* (CRA) of 1977 responded to the problem by banning redlining and by imposing an "affirmative" obligation on banks and depository institutions to make loans in low- and moderate-income communities within their service area. A bank, for instance, with depositors from the South Side of Chicago cannot ignore the credit "needs" of that poor community as it prefers to make loans in the growing suburban portions of the metropolis. To meet their CRA obligations, banks advertise their services in underserved portions of the community. Lending institutions also often work in partnership with community groups to seek out worthy loan applicants in poorer communities.

The CRA has been quite successful in promoting new investment in inner-city communities and in extending credit to minority residents. The National Community Investment Coalition estimates that, since its inception, the CRA has leveraged trillions of dollars (by some estimates in excess of $4 trillion) of investment in lower income neighborhoods.

But critics charge that the CRA has essentially forced banks to make unwise loans that the banks would otherwise have sensibly turned down. The CRA leads banks to "waste" money by aggressively marketing their loan products in inner-city areas where they are likely to find few customers. Banks pay community groups to help search out credit-worthy loan applicants in low-income communities, an expense that many lending institutions would not normally undertake.

The most severe critics view the CRA as legalized "extortion," giving community groups the ability to block government approval of bank mergers in cases where institutions fail to expand their loan portfolios in inner-city communities. The Association of Community Organizations for Reform Now (ACORN) and other activist groups used the threat of opposing bank mergers to force banks to commit millions of dollars in loans to inner-city businesses and affordable housing projects.

Defenders of the CRA respond that the critics exaggerate the coercive nature of CRA regulation. As Mara Sidney (2003) has shown, when the CRA was enacted, legislators took special care to minimize the burdens placed on lenders. As a result, the act contained no explicit sanctions for noncompliance. Reporting requirements were also kept to a minimum. Few banks have difficulty in earning a "satisfactory" rating or better from the CRA.

No provision in the CRA requires a bank to make a loan to an individual who is undeserving of credit. Instead, the act merely requires banks to go out and seek worthy loan applicants in low-income communities, rather than simply shift their lending activities to the suburbs.

The continuing complaints by the industry against the CRA led Republican administrations in Washington to relax CRA coverage. Amendments passed during the Reagan years exempted a number of smaller lending institutions from CRA requirements. Reagan pursued a *deregulation* policy that sought to free business and the nation's economy from the debilitating effects of over-regulation. Reagan believed that the relaxation of government oversight and rules would lead to the expansion of the economy.

The Gramm-Leach-Bliley Act of 1999 narrowed the coverage of the CRA, exempting smaller banks, savings institutions, and mortgage companies from CRA requirements. A decade later, the George W. Bush administration exempted and even greater number of savings-and-loan and other lending institutions from CRA coverage. As a result of these deregulatory initiatives, more than half of the home loans made in the United States originate in independent mortgage companies and nondepository institutions that are *not* subject to CRA regulation.

Critics of deregulation argued that the relaxation of government oversight enabled unscrupulous private lenders to engage in *predatory lending practices* (Immergluck, 2009; Schwartz, 2006; Squires and Kubrin, 2006) that deceived borrowers, convincing home owners of the affordability of subprime loans by hiding the true costs and risks that accompanied the more exotic lending instruments. Home owners wound up losing their homes when, after having made years of affordable monthly payments, the contract required a huge final *balloon payment* that would cover all of the outstanding loan principal and remaining accrued interest. Other predatory practices entailed charging borrowers excessively large loan placement fees, high premiums for insurance policies, and exorbitant prices for unnecessary home repairs.

In the YES selection, Peter Wallison argues that the CRA was one of a number of government programs that virtually forced the lending industry to relax their lending standards, compromising normal good business practices. Wallison points to the Clinton administration's use of performance-based measures to track just how well lending institutions were meeting CRA goals. According to Wallison, this imposition of *de facto* lending quotas led to an urgency among lending institutions to improve their CRA numbers. Institutions approved loans to applicants who lacked strong conventional work and credit histories and who could not make a reasonable downpayment. Middle- and upper-income buyers demanded similar liberal credit terms, and, in too many cases, wound up buying bigger homes than was otherwise wise. When housing prices plummeted, numerous owners found that they owed more money than their home was worth. Not anchored in their investment by a significant downpayment, many owners simply walked away from their obligations.

In the NO selection, Philip Ashton responds that such criticisms are part of a "cry wolf" strategy where policy conservatives and industry leaders have unfairly tried to blame the CRA for problems it did not cause. As Ashton underscores, loans made by CRA-covered institutions were *not* at the heart of the foreclosure crisis. Loans advanced by independent lending companies exempted from CRA regulation actually suffered a higher rate of default than did loans initiated by CRA-covered institutions. Smaller lenders, exempt from CRA oversight as a result of Republican deregulation efforts, were also more likely to engage in predatory practices that deceived home buyers.

YES

Peter J. Wallison

Cause and Effect: Government Policies and the Financial Crisis

Although the media are full of talk that we face a "crisis of capitalism," the underlying cause of the financial meltdown is something much more mundane and practical—the housing, tax, and bank regulatory policies of the U.S. government. The Community Reinvestment Act (CRA), Fannie Mae and Freddie Mac, penalty-free refinancing of home loans, tax preferences granted to home equity borrowing, and reduced capital requirements for banks that hold mortgages and mortgage-backed securities (MBS) have all weakened the standards for granting mortgages and the housing finance system itself. Blaming greedy bankers, incompetent rating agencies, or other actors in this unprecedented drama misses the point—perhaps intentionally—that government policies created the incentives for both a housing bubble and a reduction in the bank capital and home equity that could have mitigated its effects. To prevent a recurrence of this disaster, it would be far better to change the destructive government housing policies that brought us to this point than to enact a new regulatory regime that will hinder a quick recovery and obstruct future economic growth.

The current financial crisis is not—as some have said—a crisis of capitalism. It is in fact the opposite, a shattering demonstration that ill-considered government intervention in the private economy can have devastating consequences. The crisis has its roots in the U.S. government's efforts to increase homeownership, especially among minority and other underserved or low-income groups, and to do so through hidden financial subsidies rather than direct government expenditures. The story is an example, enlarged to an American scale, of the adverse results that flow from the misuse and manipulation of banking and credit by government. When this occurs in authoritarian regimes, we deride the outcome as a system of "policy loans" and note with an air of superiority that banks in these countries are weak, credit is limited, and financial crises are frequent. When the same thing happens in the United States, however, we blame "greedy" people, or poor regulation (or none), or credit default swaps, or anything else we can think of—except the government policies that got us into the disaster.

Expansion of homeownership could be a sound policy, especially for low-income families and members of minority groups. The social benefits of homeownership have been extensively documented; they include stable families and neighborhoods, reduced crime and delinquency, higher living standards, and less depreciation in the housing stock. Under these circumstances, the policy question is not whether homeownership should be encouraged but how the government ought to do it. In the United States, the policy has not been pursued directly—through taxpayer-supported programs and appropriated funds—but rather through manipulation of the credit system to force more lending in support of affordable housing. Instead of a direct government subsidy, say, for down-payment assistance for low-income families, the government has used regulatory and political pressure to force banks and other government-controlled or regulated private entities to make loans they would not otherwise make and to reduce lending standards so more applicants would have access to mortgage financing.

The two key examples of this policy are the CRA, adopted in 1977, and the affordable housing "mission" of the government-sponsored enterprises (GSEs) Fannie Mae and Freddie Mac. As detailed below, beginning in the late 1980s—but particularly during the Clinton administration—the CRA was used to pressure banks into making loans they would not otherwise have made and to adopt looser lending standards that would make mortgage loans possible for individuals who could not meet the down payment and other standards that had previously been applied routinely by banks and other housing lenders. The same pressures were brought to bear on the GSEs, which adapted their underwriting standards so they could accept the loans made under the CRA and other loans that did not conform to what had previously been considered sound lending practices. Loans to members of underserved groups did not come with labels, and once Fannie and Freddie began accepting loans with low down payments and other liberalized terms, the same unsound practices were extended to borrowers who could have qualified under the traditional underwriting standards. It should not be surprising that borrowers took advantage of these opportunities. It was entirely rational to negotiate for a low-down-payment loan when that permitted the purchase of a larger house in a better neighborhood.

Many culprits have been brought before the bar of public humiliation as the malefactors of the current crisis—unscrupulous mortgage brokers, greedy investment bankers, incompetent rating agencies, foolish investors, and whiz-kid inventors of complex derivatives. All of these people and institutions played their part, of course, but it seems unfair to blame them for doing what the government policies were designed to encourage. Thus, the crisis would not have become so extensive and intractable had the U.S. government not created the necessary conditions for a housing boom by directing investments into the housing sector, requiring banks to make mortgage loans they otherwise would never have made, requiring the GSEs to purchase the secondary mortgage market loans they would never otherwise have bought, encouraging underwriting standards for housing that were lower than for any other area of the economy, adopting bank regulatory capital standards that encourage bank lending for housing in preference to other lending, and adopting tax policies that favored borrowing against (and thus reducing) the equity in a home.

As a result, between 1995 (when quotas based on the CRA became effective during the Clinton administration) and 2005, the homeownership percentage in the United States moved from 64 percent, where it had been for twenty-five years, to 69 percent; in addition, home prices doubled between 1995 and 2007. In other words, the government is responsible for the current crisis in two major respects: its efforts to loosen credit standards for mortgages created the housing bubble, and its policies on bank capital standards and the deductibility of interest on home equity loans made the current crisis inevitable when the bubble collapsed. This *Outlook* will explore the strong relationship between the intervention of the U.S. government in the housing market and the worldwide financial crisis that has resulted.

The Community Reinvestment Act

As originally enacted in 1977, the CRA was a vague mandate for regulators to "consider" whether an insured bank was serving the needs of the whole community it was supposed to serve. The "community" itself was not defined, and the act stated only that it was intended to "encourage" banks to meet community needs. It was enforced through the denial of applications for such things as mergers and acquisitions. The act also stated that serving community needs had to be done within the context of safe and sound lending practices, language that Congress probably inserted to ensure that the law would not be seen as a form of credit allocation. Although the act was adopted to prevent "redlining"—the practice of refusing loans to otherwise qualified borrowers in low-income areas—it also contained language that included small business, agriculture, and similar groups among the interests that had to be served. With the vague compliance standard that required banks only to be "encouraged" and their performance to be "considered," the act was invoked relatively infrequently when banks applied for permission to merge or another regulatory approval, until the Clinton administration.[1]

The decisive turn in the act's enforcement occurred in 1993 and was probably induced by the substantial amount of media and political attention that had been paid to the Boston Federal Reserve Bank's 1992 study of discrimination in home mortgage lending.[2] The study concluded that while there was no overt discrimination in the allocation of mortgage funds, more subtle forms of discrimination existed in which whites received better treatment by loan officers than members of minorities. The methodology of the study has since been questioned,[3] but it seems to have been highly influential with regulators and members of the incoming Clinton administration at the time of its publication. In 1993, bank regulators initiated a major effort to reform the CRA regulations. Some of the context in which this was occurring can be gleaned from the following statement by Attorney General Janet Reno in January 1994: "[W]e will tackle lending discrimination wherever and in whatever form it appears. No loan is exempt, no bank is immune. For those who thumb their nose at us, I promise vigorous enforcement."[4]

The regulators' effort culminated in new rules adopted in May 1995 that would be phased in fully by July 1997. The new rules attempted to establish objective criteria for determining whether a bank was meeting the standards of the CRA, taking much of the discretion out of the hands of the examiners. "The emphasis on performance-based evaluation," A. K. M. Rezaul Hossain, an economist at Mount Saint Mary College, writes, "can be thought of as a shift of emphasis from procedural equity to equity in outcome. In that, it is not sufficient for lenders to prove elaborate community lending efforts directed towards borrowers in the community, but an evenhanded distribution of loans across LMI [low and moderate income] and non-LMI areas and borrowers."[5] In other words, it was now necessary for banks to show that they had actually made the requisite loans, not just that they were trying to find qualified borrowers. In this connection, one of the standards in the new regulations required the use of "innovative or flexible" lending practices to address credit needs of LMI borrowers and neighborhoods.[6] Thus, a law that was originally intended to encourage banks to use safe and sound practices in lending now required them to be innovative and flexible—a clear requirement for the relaxation of lending standards.

There is very little data available on the performance of loans made under the CRA. The subject has become so politicized in light of the housing meltdown and its effect on the general economy that most reports—favorable or unfavorable—should probably be discounted. Before the increases in housing prices that began in 2001, reviews of the CRA were generally unfavorable. The act increased costs for banks, and there was an inverse relationship between their CRA lending and their regulatory ratings.[7] One of the few studies of CRA lending in comparison to normal lending was done by the Federal Reserve Bank of Cleveland, which reported in 2000 that "respondents who did report differences [between regular and CRA housing loans] most often said they had lower prices or higher costs or credit losses for CRA-related home purchase and refinance loans than for others."[8] Much CRA lending after 2000 occurred during a period of enormous growth in housing values, which tended to suppress the number of defaults and reduce loss rates.

The important question, however, is not the default rates on the mortgages made under the CRA. Whatever those rates might be, they were not sufficient to cause a worldwide financial crisis. The most important fact associated with the CRA is the effort to reduce underwriting standards so that more low-income people could purchase homes. Once these standards were relaxed—particularly allowing loan-to-value ratios higher than the 80 percent that had previously been the norm—they spread rapidly to the prime market and to subprime markets where loans were made by lenders other than insured banks. The effort to reduce mortgage underwriting standards was led by the Department of Housing and Urban Development (HUD) through the National Homeownership Strategy published in 1994 in response to a request by President Clinton. Among other things, it called for "financing strategies, fueled by the creativity and resources of the private and public sectors to help homeowners that lack cash to buy a home or to make the payments."[9] Many subsequent studies have documented the rise in loan-to-value ratios and other indicators of loosened lending standards.[10]

After 1995 and the adoption of the new CRA regulations, homeownership in the United States grew rapidly. Having remained at 64 percent for almost twenty-five years, it grew to 69 percent between 1995 and 2005.[11] The increased availability of credit under CRA requirements probably also spurred housing demand, which doubled home prices between 1995 and 2007.[12] The key question, however, is the effect of relaxed lending standards on lending standards in non-CRA markets. In principle, it would seem impossible—if down payment or other requirements were being relaxed for loans in minority-populated or other underserved areas—to limit the benefits only to those borrowers. Inevitably, the relaxed standards banks were enjoined to adopt under CRA would be spread to the wider market—including to prime mortgage markets and to speculative borrowers. Bank regulators, who were in charge of enforcing CRA standards, could hardly disapprove of similar loans made to better qualified borrowers. This is exactly what occurred. Writing in December 2007 for the Milken Institute, four scholars observed: "Over the past decade, most, if not all, the products offered to subprime borrowers have also been offered to prime borrowers. In fact, during the period from January 1999 through July 2007, prime borrowers obtained thirty-one of the thirty-two types of mortgage products—fixed-rate, adjustable rate and hybrid mortgages, including those with balloon payments—obtained by subprime borrowers."[13]

Sure enough, according to data published by the Joint Center for Housing Studies of Harvard University, from 2001 through 2006, the share of all mortgage originations that were made up of conventional mortgages (that is, the thirty-year fixed-rate mortgage that had always been the mainstay of the U.S. mortgage market) fell from 57.1 percent in 2001 to 33.1 percent in the fourth quarter of 2006. Correspondingly, subprime loans (those made to borrowers with blemished credit) rose from 7.2 percent to 18.8 percent, and Alt-A loans (those made to speculative buyers or without the usual underwriting standards) rose from 2.5 percent to 13.9 percent. Although it is difficult to prove cause and effect, it seems highly likely that the lower lending standards banks were required to adopt under the CRA influenced what they and other lenders were willing to offer to borrowers in prime markets. Needless to say, most borrowers would prefer a mortgage with a low down payment requirement, allowing them to buy a larger home for the same initial investment. There is nothing immoral about this; if the opportunity is there, most families can think of better uses for their savings than making a large down payment for a home.

The problem is summed up succinctly by Stan Liebowitz of the University of Texas at Dallas: "From the current handwringing, you'd think that the banks came up with the idea of looser underwriting standards on their own, with regulators just asleep on the job. In fact, it was the *regulators* who relaxed these standards—at the behest of community groups and 'progressive' political forces. . . . For years, rising house prices hid the default problems since quick refinances were possible. But now that house prices have stopped rising, we can clearly see the damage done by relaxed loan standards."[14] The point here is not that low-income borrowers received mortgage loans that they could not afford; that is probably true to some extent but cannot account for the large number of subprime and Alt-A loans that currently pollute the banking system. It was the spreading of these looser underwriting standards to the prime loan market that encouraged the huge increase in credit availability for mortgages, the speculation in housing, and ultimately the bubble in housing prices. . . .

Conclusion

A review of the key housing, tax, and regulatory policies pursued by the U.S. government over many years connects these policies very directly to the rise of a housing bubble, a decline in the quality of mortgages, and a reduction in the home equity and bank capital that would have protected the economy in the event of a bubble's collapse.

Preventing a recurrence of the financial crisis we face today does not require new regulation of the financial system. What is required instead is an appreciation of the fact—as much as lawmakers would like to avoid it—that U.S. housing policies are the root cause of the current financial crisis. Other players—"greedy" investment bankers; foolish investors; imprudent bankers; incompetent rating agencies; irresponsible housing speculators; shortsighted homeowners; and predatory mortgage brokers, lenders, and borrowers—all played a part, but they were only following the economic incentives that government policy laid out for them. If we are really serious about wanting to prevent a recurrence of this crisis—rather than increasing the power of the government over the economy—our first order of business should be to correct the destructive housing policies of the U.S. government.

Notes

1. See the extensive discussion of the Community Reinvestment Act's development in A. K. M. Rezaul Hossain, "The Past, Present and Future of Community Reinvestment Act (CRA): A Historical Perspective" (working paper 2004-30, Department of Economics, University of Connecticut, Storrs, CT, October 2004), available at www.econ.uconn.edu/working/2004-30.pdf (accessed November 21, 2008).

2. Alicia H. Munnell, Lynn E. Browne, James McEneaney, and Geoffrey M. B. Tootell, "Mortgage Lending in Boston: Interpreting HMDA Data" (working paper 92-7, Federal Reserve Bank of Boston, 1992), available at www.bos.frb.org/economic/wp/wp1992/wp92_7.pdf (accessed November 21, 2008).

3. See discussion in Vern McKinley, "Community Reinvestment Act: Ensuring Credit Adequacy or Enforcing Credit Allocation?" *Regulation* 17, no. 4 (1994): 32, available at www.cato.org/pubs/regulation/regv17n4/vmck4-94.pdf (accessed November 21, 2008).

4. Ibid., 30.

5. A. K. M. Rezaul Hossain, "The Past, Present and Future of Community Reinvestment Act (CRA): A Historical Perspective," 54.

6. Ibid., 57.

7. See, for example, George J. Benston, "The Community Reinvestment Act: Looking for Discrimination That Isn't There" (Policy Analysis 354, Cato Institute, Washington, DC, October 6, 1999), available at www.cato.org/pub_display.php?pub_id=1213 (accessed November 21, 2008).

8. Robert B. Avery, Raphael W. Bostic, and Glenn B. Canner, "The Performance and Profitability of CRA-Related Lending," *Economic Commentary, Federal Reserve Bank of Cleveland* (November 2000), available at www.clevelandfed.org/research/Commentary/2000/1100.htm (accessed November 21, 2008).

9. Quoted in Joseph R. Mason, "A National Homeownership Strategy for the New Millennium." The National Homeownership Strategy, referred to in the Mason article, was removed from the Department of Housing and Urban Development website in 2007.

10. See, for example, Yuliya Demyanyk and Otto Van Hemert, "Understanding the Subprime Mortgage Crisis" (Social Science Research Network, August 19, 2008), available at http://ssrn.com/abstract=1020396 (accessed November 21, 2008); and Robert Stowe England, "Giving It 100 Percent," *Mortgage Banking,* February 1, 2002.

11. Polina Vlasenko, "Home Ownership in the United States" (commentary, American Institute for Economic Research, Great Barrington, MA, September 2008), available at www.aier.org/research/commentaries/533-home-ownership-in-the-united-states (accessed November 21, 2008).

12. Economagic.com, "Economic Time Series Page: US: Average Price of Houses Actually Sold," available at www.economagic.com/em-cgi/data.exe/cenc25/c25q07 (accessed November 21, 2008). The average price of homes sold increased from $153,500 in the fourth quarter of 1995 to $322,100 in the first quarter of 2007.

13. James Barth, Tong Li, Triphon Phumiwasana, and Glenn Yago, "Surprise: Subprime Mortgage Products Are Not the Problem!" (Milken Institute, Santa Monica, CA, December 6, 2007), available through www.milkeninstitute.org/publications/publications.taf?function=detail&ID=38801030&cat=Papers (accessed November 21, 2008).

14. Stan Liebowitz, "The Real Scandal: How Feds Invited the Mortgage Mess," *New York Post,* February 5, 2008.

Philip Ashton  **NO**

Cry Wolf Policy Brief:
Community Reinvestment Act
and Responsible Lending

Introduction

The Community Reinvestment Act (CRA) has been critical to the expansion of responsible credit for low- and moderate-income borrowers since its passage in 1977. Designed to address low levels of lending activity in low- and moderate-income neighborhoods, it has helped spur a growing range of successful affordable loan programs that reduce barriers to credit and increase responsible lending. Despite consistent evidence that the Act produces modest increases in access to capital and is an important incentive for bank investments to profitably tap new opportunities in community economic development, it has been a convenient scapegoat for journalists, academic economists, banking industry lobbyists, and their allies in Congress.

Opponents' have shifted their arguments over time, but have consistently associated the Act with a number of doomsday scenarios that accompanied greater regulation of bank lending activity. These have alternated between dry, academic arguments—for instance, that the Act "promotes the concentration of assets in geographically non-diversified locations, encourages banks to make unprofitable and risky investment and product-line decisions, and penalizes banks that seek to reduce costs by consolidating services or closing or relocating branches" (Macey & Miller 1993: 295); and ferocious accounts by journalists and pundits manufacturing stories about "diabolically brilliant" conspiracies to compel banks to loan money (Schweizer 2009). In one recent revisionist history of the Act:

> The solution to their problems, they believed, lay in forcing lending institutions to make risky loans in urban areas and set aside funds for selected socioeconomic or racial groups. Egged on by a media with an appetite for stories about racism, class warfare, and rising income disparities, the activists would increasingly demand a say in how mortgage loans were made. Using fear and intimidation and the megaphone of a sympathetic press, they would begin to chip away at lending standards, weaken underwriting rules, and push banks away from their traditionally conservative practices (Schweizer 2009: 29).

Republican control of Congress after 1994 provided a platform for these critiques. As prominent opponents (including Republican Senators Alphonse D'Amato, Phil Gramm, Connie Mack, and Richard Shelby) tried to roll back key provisions of the Act as part of broader financial reform, they associated the Act with systemic instability—in the words of Richard Shelby (R-AL), "the Community Reinvestment Act is nothing more than a Government-mandated credit allocation, much like the mandated credit allocation in East Asia that has caused the currency crisis, among other things." In the wake of the growing mortgage crisis after 2006, this "cry wolf" strategy gained momentum, as conservative commentators have uniformly pushed the argument that government "mandates" forced banks to load their portfolios with risky loans, exposing the banking sector to heightened losses.

As policymakers and Congress consider not only new regulations for CRA, but also an entirely new architecture for housing finance, this is an important opportunity to review the historical record on CRA's accomplishments and identify the thin grounds for these criticisms of the Act.

Legislative History

The roots of the Community Reinvestment Act of 1977 (CRA) lie in the civil rights struggles of the 1960s and the enactment of landmark federal legislation outlawing discriminatory treatment in housing and lending (the Fair Housing Act of 1968 and the Equal Credit Opportunity Act of 1972) and expanding consumer access to information (the Home Mortgage Disclosure Act of 1975). Complementing those earlier initiatives, CRA addressed problems of poor credit access by low-income borrowers and neighborhoods by affirming the obligation of chartered banks to meet the credit needs of the communities in which they do business. The Act directed federal banking regulators to assess each bank on its "record of meeting the credit needs of its entire community, including low- and moderate-income neighborhoods, consistent with the safe and sound operation of such institution," and permitted sanctions for institutions with weak records.

Initially, the Reagan administration marginalized community reinvestment regulations; the first denial of a bank application on CRA grounds did not come until 1989. . . .

The Clinton administration embraced FIRREA's [Financial Institutions Reform, Recovery and Enforcement Act of 1989] reforms, and codified them in 1995 amendments to the regulations governing implementation of CRA. Among other changes, these amendments shifted the emphasis of CRA exams from process (proper record-keeping, setting goals and other good faith efforts) to quantitative assessment of community reinvestment performance and outcomes. Changes to CRA regulations also enabled public opinion through a set of right-to-know provisions; in particular, regulators are supposed to solicit and review public commentary about bank performance when making decisions about applications for charters, FDIC insurance, relocation, merger, acquisition or consolidation.

These reforms moved the CRA exam process out of the margins of the banking system and into the center of the financial transformations of the 1990s. As damaging public criticism during the application process could cause regulators to delay approval of expansions or mergers, "CRA ratings appear to have an impact on the share prices of institutions in the process of merger or takeover, with poor ratings lowering prices" (Macdonald 1995). This pressure and the need for speedy approvals mean that many banks have opted to negotiate with their critics, spurring an estimated $4.2 trillion in bank commitments or agreements aimed at increasing lending and service in historically underserved markets between 1992 and 2005 (NCRC 2007).

As the Act gained additional teeth after 1989, however, and regulators signaled their intent to enforce its provisions through new regulations, a chorus of industry trade groups joined with Congressional opponents to attempt to water down its provisions. In 1991, Rep. Paul Kanjorski (D-Pa) and Sen. Connie Mack (R-Fl) introduced separate bills that would have exempted a significant proportion of lenders from CRA; similar proposals providing "safe harbor" from the regulations for selected groups of banks were advanced by the Bush administration in 1992. These initiatives, though unsuccessful, began a two-decade struggle over the scope and enforcement of the Act.

With Republicans taking control of Congress in 1994, attempts to repeal CRA or roll back significant portions of the Act were periodically surfaced within discussions of broader financial legislation by influential members of the Senate Banking Committee. They successfully pressured the Clinton administration to exempt small banks—those independent banks with assets under $250 million—from expanded examinations under new regulations in 1995, requiring only that they pass a simple lending test. Similar attempts to further water down the bill advanced with consideration of the 1999 Financial Modernization Act, which reduced the frequency of exams for small banks with good records, and created a set of "sunshine provisions" requiring disclosure of any bank-community agreements negotiated pursuant to CRA.

This climate was picked up in the Bush administration, which appointed former Texas and California small bankers to head the Federal Deposit Insurance Corp. and the Office of Thrift Supervision. They spearheaded new CRA regulations in 2005 that changed the definition of "small bank" to any institution with assets less than $1 billion, reducing the number of institutions subject to the full CRA examination process and incentivizing banks to recharter. More importantly, these banks would be considered "small" no matter what the size of the organization or holding company that owns them—"even banks and thrifts that are part of mammoth holding companies would be considered small as long as the bank or thrift itself held less than $1 billion in assets" (Barr 2004). These new regulations sent a signal to the banking community that CRA enforcement was a secondary issue for Bush Administration regulators.

Crying Wolf: CRA's Supposed Deleterious Effects on the Banking System

Arguments about the inefficiency of CRA have been present since its enactment in the 1970s, as banking industry groups complained about the extra costs of compliance. As the Act gained additional teeth after 1989, and regulators signaled their intent to enforce its provisions through new regulations, a chorus of industry trade groups and academic economists began attacking the theoretical premises of CRA. With Republican control of Congress after 1994, these attacks were taken up within a variety of House and Senate proposals that served to amplify opposition to the Act. Throughout, these attacks have consistently followed three major themes. . . .

CRA Is Unnecessary Due to an Efficient Banking Market

The major academic argument against the Act has emphasized how CRA-induced lending would have happened anyways under efficient market conditions; in other words, there are no market failures justifying CRA-style intervention. . . .

Throughout the late 1990s, academic economists and conservative analysts consistently pointed to the rising subprime mortgage market as evidence that an efficient market could deliver credit to all deserving customers. As nonbank lenders not covered by CRA were leading the expansion of that market, analysts interpreted this as evidence of CRA's redundancy. They also pointed to critical developments such as risk-based pricing, the use of information technology—including automated underwriting and geo-demographic targeting—and the growth in private label securitizations as evidence that banking markets no longer needed the kinds of intervention represented by CRA.

CRA Is a "Drag" on Profitability

Claims of lower profit rates or enhanced operating instability for CRA-covered institutions have persisted since the early 1990s. This has been based on several arguments. One argument has focused on regulatory burdens, arguing that the costs imposed by CRA—including extra reporting and paperwork, the need to dedicate staff time to the examination process, or even an imagined requirement that banks "pay out" money to silence community critics—are anti-competitive, amounting to a discriminatory tax that forces differentially high costs onto chartered banks relative to nonbank financial firms not covered by CRA. Industry sponsored studies in the early 1990s identified CRA as "the single most costly regulation" and a major contributor of an estimated $10.7 billion in compliance costs in 1990 (as quoted in Macey & Miller 1993: 325). . . .

A second argument interprets CRA as a mandate that banks increase their output of "marginal" loans. According to this interpretation, under efficient market conditions lenders would be making all profitable loans; any new loans spurred by the Act must have a higher probability of loss and a lower margin of profit than lenders would normally make. As banks must then set aside more funds to cover loan losses as a part of risk-based capital rules, CRA also hampers their ability to compete with their non-bank counterparts. The net result, it is argued, is that banks must absorb increased losses and reduced profit margins onto their balance sheet, potentially jeopardizing their viability.

CRA Increases Systemic Risk

. . . According to these arguments, CRA directs banks into high risk market segments, producing greater financial fragility as the banking system becomes more loaded with risky loans (Wallison 2008). Focusing specifically on loosened underwriting standards, CRA is tied to both the explosion in credit issuance during the mid-2000s, and to the run-up in housing prices during the same period. A typical formulation is as follows:

> Although it is difficult to prove cause and effect, it is highly likely that the lower lending standards required by the CRA influenced what banks and other lenders were willing to offer to borrowers in prime markets. Needless to say, most borrowers would prefer a mortgage with a low down payment requirement, allowing them to buy a larger home for the same initial investment (Wallison 2009).
>
> . . .

Responding to the Critics: CRA's Role in Building a More Efficient Banking System

Quantitative assessments of CRA have consistently confirmed that the Act produces positive outcomes in the form of increased credit availability for low- and moderate-income borrowers and neighborhoods, even while noting that the marginal effects of CRA were quite small. The Joint Center for Housing Studies at Harvard University estimated that in 2000 CRA expanded the supply of mortgage loans to targeted groups by 2.1 percentage points; they noted that, in the context of declining market share for chartered banks, this probably represented the "peak" of CRA's impact. In the wake of the subprime mortgage crisis, a wide range of scholars and advocates have called for CRA's expansion as a means to ensure wider availability of responsible credit (Quercia et al. 2009; Seidman 2009).

Taken as a whole, the existing body of research studying the effects of CRA exposes critics as relying heavily on a mixture of abstract economic assumptions, sloppy data analysis, and ideology when they "cry wolf."

CRA Produces a More Efficient Banking System

CRA's positive impacts can be seen in increased capacity to tapped underserved markets; one measure here has been increased innovations in the way that banks deliver responsible credit to low- and moderate-income markets. A Federal Reserve survey found that 73% of responding banks had at least one initiative to increase lending to historically underserved areas; common innovations include special loan programs to meet lending targets, community outreach and marketing initiatives, partnerships with community organizations for homeownership counseling and credit remediation, and the creation of special units and affiliates, such as community development departments or bank-owned CDCs. These help to reduce "process barriers" to credit availability, increasing the overall efficiency of the banking system by tapping opportunities to lend to eligible borrowers in historically underserved areas (Quercia 1999). It is on this basis that bankers have consistently voiced their support for the Act:

> "It's not just the right thing to do, it is the smart thing to do in a pluralistic and highly competitive marketplace," said Richard M. Rosenberg, chairman and CEO of BankAmerica Corp. (Cummins 1993).
>
> The CRA has convinced us that when businesses invest in distressed communities, they are much more likely to return to health (Fisk 2007).

CRA Does Not Hamper Bank Profits

Even as long ago as 1993, when the profitability arguments were gaining ground, banking industry analysts failed to find any connection between CRA and lower profit margins:

> No bank ever failed because of the Community Reinvestment Act. In fact, the act specifically states that any activities should be consistent with the safe and sound operation of the institution. Certainly, if all loans to low-income and moderate-income areas are considered CRA loans, not all them are risky. After all, 40% of American households are in this income range, and loans to 40% of America can't all be risky (Thomas 1993).

More recent studies have used detailed survey data to arrive at the same conclusions. Studies of bank lending programs by researchers at the Federal Reserve found few differences in return on equity for CRA loans relative to non-CRA loans, and that lending programs developed specifically to improve a CRA rating were almost as profitable for home mortgage lending and more so for home improvement. These findings have been complemented by recent work assessing foreclosure losses, which has found that "loans made by CRA lenders within their assessment areas, which receive the greatest regulatory scrutiny under the CRA, are significantly less likely to be in foreclosure than those made by independent mortgage companies that do not receive the same regulatory oversight" (Laderman & Reid 2009: 122). . . .

CRA Did Not Promote Excessive Risk-Taking

Here, the evidence is consistent: there is little causal connection between CRA and the subprime mortgage crisis. CRA regulations and enforcement have seen little change since 1995, and the explosion in mortgage lending took place as the Bush administration further diminished the Act's coverage (Bhutta & Canner 2008).

Moreover, data has consistently confirmed that the majority of subprime loans were made by independent mortgage lending companies not covered by CRA (Bhutta & Canner 2008; Laderman & Reid 2009). With the advent of

HMDA data on high-interest mortgages from 2004 onwards, researchers have determined that, controlling for income, loans made by CRA-covered lenders typically carried lower interest rates than subprime loans and were less likely to end up securitized into the private mortgage-backed security pools that have caused the greatest losses (Traiger & Hinckley 2008). CRA loans (loans by covered institutions within their assessment areas) accounted for only 9% of higher-priced loans to lower-income borrowers and neighborhoods, while independent mortgage companies accounted for over 50% (Park 2008).

Claims that CRA somehow initially spurred an erosion of underwriting standards, or otherwise indirectly spurred irresponsible lending, are hampered by a poor understanding of the history of the subprime market. Research into this question has determined that "less than 2 percent of the mortgage origi-nations sold by independent mortgage companies in 2006 were higher-priced, CRA-credit-eligible, and purchased by CRA-covered banking institutions" (Bhutta & Canner, 2009). This is not to say that there was not excessive risk-taking by CRA-covered institutions; rather, the majority of that lending took place outside of CRA's purview (Ashton 2010). Here, the problem was not CRA's regulations but their lack of extensive coverage across all of a lender's lines of business. High-cost lending by CRA-covered lenders was more prevalent outside of their assessment areas (Laderman & Reid 2009) and amongst mortgage affiliates and subsidiaries—both areas where lenders are not subject to full-scope CRA review (Ashton 2010).

The message that emerges from this body of research is consistent and clear: CRA was a channel for responsible lending, and the mortgage crisis might have turned out differently if its scope had been wider and its enforce-ment more rigorous (Quercia et al., 2009; Seidman 2009). The primary issue on the table for mortgage market reform is how to modernize the Community Reinvestment Act to better address the growth of the shadow banking system and the growing need for responsible credit.

Appendix A: Additional Sources

Organizations

- National Community Reinvestment Coalition. www.ncrc.org.
- Center for Responsible Lending. www.responsiblelending.org.
- Woodstock Institute. www.woodstockinst.com.
- Joint Center for Housing Studies, Harvard University. www.jchs .harvard.edu.
- Federal Reserve Bank of San Francisco, Community Affairs. www.frbsf .org/index.html.
- Center for Community Capital, University of North Carolina. www .ccc.unc.edu.

Statistics/Reports on CRA & the Mortgage Crisis

- Ashton, Philip. 2010. CRA's 'blind spots': Community reinvestment and concentrated subprime lending in Detroit. *Journal of Urban Affairs* 32 (5): 579–608.

- Bhutta, Neil, and Glenn Canner. 2009. Did the CRA cause the mortgage market meltdown? Community Dividend, Federal Reserve Bank of Minneapolis (March). Available at www.minneapolisfed.org/research/pub_display.cfm?id=4136.
- Ding, Lei, Quercia, Roberto G., Ratcliffe, Janneke, and Wei Lei. 2008. Risky Borrowers or Risky Mortgages: Disaggregating Effects Using Propensity Score Models. Chapel Hill, NC: Center for Community Capital, University of North Carolina. Available at www.ccc.unc.edu/abstracts/091308_Risky.php.
- Kroszner, Randall S. 2009. The Community Reinvestment Act and the recent mortgage crisis. In P. Chakrabarti, D. Erickson, R. S. Essene, I. Galloway & J. Olson (Eds.), *Revisiting the CRA: Perspectives on the Future of the Community Reinvestment Act* (pp. 8–11). Boston/San Francisco: Federal Reserve Bank of Boston/Federal Reserve Bank of San Francisco. Available online at www.frbsf.org/publications/community/cra/cra_recent_mortgage_crisis.pdf.
- Laderman, E., & Reid, C. 2009. CRA lending during the subprime meltdown. In P. Chakrabarti, D. Erickson, R. S. Essene, I. Galloway & J. Olson (Eds.), *Revisiting the CRA: Perspectives on the Future of the Community Reinvestment Act* (pp. 115–133). Boston/San Francisco: Federal Reserve Bank of Boston/Federal Reserve Bank of San Francisco. Available online at www.frbsf.org/publications/community/cra/index.html.
- Park, Kevin. 2008. Subprime Lending and the Community Reinvestment Act. Working Paper N08-2. Cambridge, MA: Joint Center for Housing Studies, Harvard University. Available at www.jchs.harvard.edu/publications/governmentprograms/n08-2_park.pdf.
- Quercia, Roberto, Ratcliffe, Janeke, and Michael Stegman. 2009. The Community Reinvestment Act: Outstanding, needs to improve. In P. Chakrabarti, D. Erickson, R. S. Essene, I. Galloway & J. Olson (Eds.), *Revisiting the CRA: Perspectives on the Future of the Community Reinvestment Act* (pp. 47–58). Boston/San Francisco: Federal Reserve Bank of Boston/Federal Reserve Bank of San Francisco. Available online at www.frbsf.org/publications/community/cra/cra_outstanding_needs_improve.pdf.
- Ratcliffe, Janeke. 2010. CRA services test: Leverage changes to qualifying criteria and take advantage of some old ones too. Comments at the CRA & Fair Lending Colloqium, Las Vegas, NV, November 10. Available at www.ccc.unc.edu/documents/CRA.Colloquim.11.2010.pdf.
- Seidman, Ellen. 2009. A more modern CRA for consumers. In P. Chakrabarti, D. Erickson, R. S. Essene, I. Galloway & J. Olson (Eds.), *Revisiting the CRA: Perspectives on the Future of the Community Reinvestment Act* (pp. 105–114). Boston/San Francisco: Federal Reserve Bank of Boston/Federal Reserve Bank of San Francisco. Available online at www.frbsf.org/publications/community/cra/more_modern_cra_consumers.pdf.
- Traiger & Hinckley LLP. 2008. *The Community Reinvestment Act: A Welcome Anomaly in the Foreclosure Crisis. Indications that the CRA Deterred Irresponsible Lending in the 15 Most Populous U.S. Metropolitan Areas.* New York, NY. Available at www.traigerlaw.com/publications/traiger_hinckley_llp_cra_foreclosure_study_1-7-08.pdf.

Historical Resources [cited in this article]

Barr, Michael S. 2004. Community investing, under attack. Urban Institute *MetroView,* October 28.

Cummins, Claudia. 1993. Banks see CRA as opening door to new markets. *American Banker,* September 2.

Fisk, Lawrence K. 2007. The democratization of credit. *The Washington Post,* December 3. Available at www.washingtonpost.com/wp-dyn/content/article/2007/12/02/AR2007120201512.html.

MacDonald, Heather. 1995. The politics of mortgage finance: Implementing FIRREA's reforms. *Journal of Planning Education and Research* 15 (1): 3–15.

Macey, Jonathan R., and Geoffrey P. Miller. 1993. The Community Reinvestment Act: An economic analysis. *Virginia Law Review* 79 (2): 291–348.

NCRC. 2007. CRA Commitments 1977–2005. Washington: National Community Reinvestment Coalition.

Schweizer, Peter. 2009. *Architects of Ruin: How Big Government Liberals Wrecked the Global Economy.* New York, NY: Harper.

Thomas, Kenneth H. 1993. Arguments against CRA don't stand up against scrutiny. *American Banker,* November 5.

Wallison, Peter. 2008. Cause and effect: Government policies and the financial crisis. *AEI Online,* November. Available at www.aei.org/outlook/29015.

Wallison, Peter J. 2009. The true origins of this financial crisis. *American Spectator*, February 6. Available online at http://spectator.org/archives/2009/02/06/the-true-origins-of-this-finan.

EXPLORING THE ISSUE

Did the Government's Regulation of Lending Institutions Under the Community Reinvestment Act Lead to the Mortgage Foreclosure Crisis?

Critical Thinking and Reflection

1. How do the benefits of the CRA point to the importance of government regulation of private sector institutions?
2. What arguments can be made against government regulation? How do the criticisms of the CRA point to the ills and costs of government regulation of private sector institutions?
3. What is your overall assessment? On balance, is government regulation justified when it comes to forcing mortgage institutions to make loans in underserved inner-city neighborhoods? Or, are such regulations unwise and unnecessary?
4. Did government regulation cause the mortgage finance crisis of the early twentieth century? Evaluate the evidence. What does the evidence reveal?

Is There Common Ground?

Business leaders and equality-oriented liberals will continue to clash over the need for government regulation. Some reformers will argue for the desirability of bringing small lenders and independent nonbank lenders under the CRA umbrella, so that all lenders in the industry face the same set of lending rules. The lending industry and free-market conservatives, however, will likely object that such a measure represents a retreat from the promises of deregulation. They do not wish to extend, but to restrict, CRA coverage.

There may be common ground for agreement in one minor area where reform is needed. The CRA rates a bank according to the steps it takes to meet the credit needs of communities in the geographic service area in which a bank and its branches are physically located. Advances in communication technology, however, make such a spatial definition of a bank's service seem quite antiquated; e-technology now enables lending institutions to reach consumers who reside well beyond a community's spatial borders. Perhaps supporters and critics of the CRA can both agree that a bank should be judged favorably for extending loans to underserved communities throughout a metropolis, even when a loan goes to an applicant from a community that lies outside the more narrow geographic service area in which the bank and its branches are located.

Although the clash over the CRA will continue, there appears to be greater consensus that discrimination against individual buyers on the basis of race, ethnic origin, and religion should not be tolerated. "Fair housing" is the law of the land. Principled free-market conservatives and political liberals may be able to find common ground when it comes to enforcing fair housing laws designed to eliminate odious discrimination based on an individuals' race, ethnicity, or religion.

There may also be the potential for agreement when it comes to banning some of the most abusive predatory lending practices. Free-market advocates may continue to argue for desirability of allowing businesses the freedom to develop a variety of exotic loan products that can meet a variety of consumer needs. But the American public, seeing stories of hard-working families who have been duped out of their homes, will not be easily convinced. Although Americans oppose costly overregulation, they nonetheless support regulations that protect individuals from abusive and deceptive practices. Safeguards can protect consumers against aggressive, high-pressure marketing practices and against contracts that burden the consumer with excessively high prices for unnecessary, unwanted, and costly extras. Americans sense that something is very wrong when a family loses its home after a mortgage agent has earned a lucrative sales commission by having manipulated the homeowner to refinance a home with a new contract that saddles the home owner with a number of costly hidden high fees and a final balloon payment cannot be met. Faced with the heart-breaking stories of hard-working families who have lost their homes and savings as a result of unfair contracts and hidden costs, only the most hard-hearted individualist will cry *caveat emptor*, let the buyer beware. Even principled free-market conservatives should be willing to curtail deceptive and predatory practices as a violation of the "perfect information" requirements of a true free-market where customers act as fully informed free agents.

Additional Resources

Immergluck, Dan. (2009). *Foreclosed: High-Risk Lending, Deregulation, and the Undermining of America's Mortgage Market.* Ithaca, NY: Cornell University Press.

Schwartz, Alex F. (2010). *Housing Policy in the United States,* 2nd ed. New York: Routledge.

Sidney, Mara S. (2003). *Unfair Housing: How National Policy Shapes Community Action.* Lawrence, KS: University of Kansas Press.

Squires, Gregory D., ed. (1992). *From Redlining to Reinvestment: Community Responses to Urban Disinvestment.* Philadelphia, PA: Temple University Press.

Squires, Gregory D., and Kubrin, Charles E. (2006). *Privileged Places: Race, Residence, and the Structure of Opportunity.* Boulder, CO: Lynne Rienner.

Internet References

American Enterprise Institute

A moderate-conservative "think tank" explores the economic impact of the CRA.

www.aei.org

Cato Institute

The website of this "think tank" committed to the ideal of liberty and limited government, contains a number of articles critical of the CRA and critical of various government policies that have been proposed in response to the mortgage foreclosure crisis.

www.cato.org

Center for Responsible Lending

An advocacy group that seeks to promote compliance with the CRA and continued investment in low- and moderate-income communities that might otherwise be bypassed by private lending institutions.

www.responsiblelending.org

Community Reinvestment Network

A passionate advocate of programs that support lending in low-income communities, the CRN reports that the CRA has helped infuse more than $4 trillion in investments in low-income and minority communities.

www.communityinvestmentnetwork.org

Joint Center for Housing Studies, Harvard University

In particular, see K. Park, "Subprime Lending and the Community Reinvestment Act." JCHS Working Paper N08-2 (2008).

www.jchs.harvard.edu

www.jchs.harvard.edu/publications/governmentprograms/n08-2_park.pdf

National Community Reinvestment Coalition

An advocacy group that supports the CRA and other policies designed to promote reinvestment in underserved communities.

www.ncrc.org

ISSUE 12

Should U.S. Cities Adopt a System of "Congestion Pricing" to "Tame" Traffic?

YES: Environment Defense Fund, from "Road Pricing Makes Sense: Taming Traffic in London, Singapore, and Norway," www.edf.org

NO: The Keep NYC Congestion Tax Free Coalition, from *Congestion Pricing in the Manhattan Central Business District: Let's Look Hard Before We Leap* (May 2007)

Learning Outcomes

After reading this issue, you should be able to:

- Explain how a system of "congestion pricing" works.
- Explain how a system of congestion pricing is more "flexible" than a regulatory approach to reducing pollution.
- Identify the various forms that road pricing can take.
- Identify the successes and problems of congestion zones in London, Singapore, and other cities around the world.

ISSUE SUMMARY

YES: A public interest group with a formidable record of lobbying for clean air, the Environmental Defense Fund (EDF) is a strong advocate of congestion zones. Case studies of London, Singapore, and cities in Norway demonstrate how a toll system can reduce traffic congestion and enhance the livability and economic attractiveness of the center city.

NO: The Keep NYC Congestion Tax Free Coalition is an alliance of businesses, labor organizations, and ideological groups that organized to oppose to Mayor Michael Bloomberg's effort to have New York City adopt a London-style congestion zone. The Coalition emphasizes the potential harmful impact that a congestion zone would have on the city economy as well as the burden that a congestion zone would impose lower-income and working-class citizens.

Traffic congestion is associated with serious respiratory and cardiovascular health problems, including childhood asthma. The Harvard Center for Traffic estimates that, in 2005 alone, tailpipe emissions resulting from congested traffic were associated with approximately 3,000 premature deaths (Levy, Buonocore, & von Stacklberg, 2010) also diminishes the quality of community life and can even pose a barrier to future economic growth. Firms that face difficulty in getting supplies, customers, and workers to their door may simply choose more accessible locations elsewhere.

Economist Anthony Downs (2002) explains why road building and other policies aimed at relieving congestion often have such minimal effect. Even where road improvements are undertaken to reduce clogged arteries, the increase in traffic speeds is almost surely to be short-lived. An unclogged roadway attracts drivers who had been taking other routes, quickly returning a roadway to its previous congested state.

Still, certain policies have produced results. Policies aimed at reducing the usage of diesel fuel—for instance, by banning such fuel consumption by city trucks and bus fleets—have lessened the incidence of childhood asthma in inner-city neighborhoods. Los Angeles, fearing that avoided the prospect of monumental traffic tie-ups at the 1984 Summer Olympics by taking strong steps to keep trucks off major freeways during rush hours. Los Angeles' planners also gave renewed emphasis to ramp metering, and the creation of temporary one-way flows to move high volume traffic. After the Olympics ended, however, truckers and others were no longer willing to submit to changes that disrupted their driving habits.

Policy analysts have begun to search for traffic reduction remedies that are more flexible than regulatory restrictions that ban specified activities. A flexible approach seeks to reduce congestion while allowing each driver—not the government—to make the final decision of whether or not to make a trip by car. Advances in technology enable cities to experiment with more flexible approaches.

Traffic planners in the United States have already begun to experiment with *road pricing systems* that seek to expedite traffic flow by charging drivers for privileges that are denied to other drivers. When driving on SR-91 in Los Angeles, I-15 in San Diego, or I-394 in Minneapolis, a motorist who is tired of being mired in traffic can choose to pay an extra toll (billed electronically) to enter the High Occupancy Vehicle (HOV) express lanes normally reserved for cars with multiple persons. The HOV lanes effectively become High Occupancy Toll (HOT) lanes. Drivers who are unwilling to pay the extra toll remain in the slower lanes of the highway. The drivers who pay the toll save substantial travel time. By leaving the normal lanes, their choice also helps to ameliorate congestion in the slow lanes.

The Netherlands is using satellite technology as part of a road pricing system that will impose a fee on every automobile trip made in the country. The charge imposed on motorists will vary according to the mileage driven, the time of day (with a higher charge for trips during peak hours), and the fuel efficiency of the vehicle. The goal of the program, targeted for implementation beginning 2012, is to halve the number of traffic jams in the country and to encourage commuting by bicycle and mass transit.

A *congestion zone* (also known as a "cordon" system) can similarly be set up to discourage automobile entry into congested sections of a city during peak hours. Compared to a regulatory ban, the cordon system maintains a degree of flexibility; if entry to the city by car is important enough, the individual driver will pay the charge.

Advocates argue that a congestion zone can serve to improve a city's economy, freeing streets for deliveries. Major corporations benefit when meetings can proceed with executives losing less work time while stuck in traffic. A congestion charge system should also lead a number of travelers to use mass transit, improving the financial viability of public transit. Stockholm, Sweden, uses a large portion of the proceeds gained from its congestion charge system to fund new bus routes.

In the YES selection reprinted below, the Environmental Defense Fund describes how congestion pricing in city centers has been tried in Singapore, Oslo, Bergen, Stockholm and other cities around the world to apparently good results.

The London congestion charge system, established in 2006, is perhaps the most analogous case for a U.S. city. The zone originally covered London's financial center (or "The City," as the British call it) and the immediate surrounding vicinity. The zone was later extended to fashionable Kensington and Chelsea, just to the west. Drivers typically prepay for passes to enter the zone between 7:00 A.M. to 5:00 P.M. Monday through Friday. Drivers who have not prepaid are allowed a short grace period to go online and submit the required payment. Drivers can also pay at designated retail outlets and Internet payment booths located inside the zone. A vast network of cameras records the license plate numbers of vehicles as they cross into the zone; readers review the tapes to spot vehicles where owners have failed to pay the required fee.

In 2011, London charged drivers entering the city center £10 (about $16) for the day. Certain discounts are offered to the drivers of "green" vehicles. Drivers who live in the zone receive a 90 percent discount. The fine for non-payment of the required fee is quite steep, £120 (about $190), which is halved if payment is made within 14 days.

London's congestion charge system led to an immediate reduction in central London congestion. The policy also resulted in "significant shifts of commuters to transit, particularly to buses." With fewer cars on the city's streets, bus delays in central London dropped 50 percent (Federal Highway Administration 2008, p. 8.). In the years that ensued, however, traffic times in the zone crept back up to their older levels.

Critics, however, contend that the pricing system has had a deleterious impact on small businesses that faced declining patronage as customers were reluctant to pay the price of entry into the zone. In the face of such criticisms, the geographic area covered by congestion pricing was halved in 2010, removing the western extension area; drivers entering Hyde Park, Kensington, and Chelsea no longer pay the congestion zone fee.

New York Mayor Michael Bloomberg sought to bring a version of the London congestion zone to his city. His plan sought to impose a charge of $8 on each automobile, $21 on a small truck, and $42 on a large truck for entering Manhattan below 60th Street during peak hours. For trips originating in the zone, drivers would pay half that amount. Approximately 1,000 cameras would record traffic movement to help to enforce payment.

Bloomberg's proposal ran into a firestorm of criticism from business owners who feared a loss of customers. Suburban commuters and the residents of poorer sections of the city also voiced their opposition. The Mayor succeeded in getting the city council to approve of the zone. But the New York State Legislature, responding to the outpouring of opposition, refused to give the city the necessary authorization to establish such a system of fees.

The Keep NYC Congestion Tax Free Coalition (in the NO selection) argues that a system of congestion pricing would inflict grievous economic harm on the city, especially on small business entrepreneurs. The Coalition further argues that a congestion zone is a regressive tax that will impose a disproportionate burden on the poorer and working-class residents who drive into the downtown.

Civil libertarians also raise concerns over the possible threat to privacy that such a system entails with its extensive network of cameras. They worry about the possible misuse of a massive data base that contains extensive photographic files that record the traffic movements of law-abiding individuals.

Finally, it should also be noted that New York's fee, proposed at only $8 per car (about half that of London), might not have been large enough to have had a great impact, especially as the normal bridge and tunnel tolls for entering the city were to be deducted from the congestion charge. To have a significant impact, the congestion charge and penalties will have to be much higher.

YES

Road Pricing Makes Sense: Taming Traffic in London, Singapore, and Norway

Road pricing (also called congestion pricing) is based on common sense supply and demand principles. When demand for the road is high, the value placed on using the road—a toll—is higher than other times of the day.

This pricing signal encourages drivers to reschedule trips, use alternative travel modes (like transit), or pay a higher fee for driving. The greatest environmental benefit accumulates when revenues generated by the tolls are used to improve local transit service.

How Road Pricing Works

An electronically-collected toll system charges drivers more to use the most congested roads at the busiest times. As with airline tickets, the prices are cheaper at off-peak times.

Cities around the world are beginning to use congestion pricing systems to cut traffic in their urban centers and along busy corridors. In London, motorists are charged when they drive into the central business district, encouraging them not to drive during peak times or to use alternative means of transportation.

Road Pricing in the U.S.

Road pricing has been employed in a limited basis at high-occupancy toll lanes on a number of highways in the U.S. Just how much these HOT lanes have helped the environment is uncertain. A number of these lanes have increased capacity and the number of cars on the road without substantially offsetting the new pollution those cars generate.

A more promising form of congestion pricing is like that demonstrated in cities like London and Stockholm where entry points into congested urban centers are priced and revenues are dedicated to improving cleaner forms of transportation.

New York City came very close to getting a congestion pricing plan in spring 2008. An extraordinary majority of New Yorkers supported

From *Road Pricing Makes Sense: Taming Traffic in London, Singapore, and Norway,* Environmental Defense Fund, August 8, 2007.

congestion pricing, but the state legislature nixed the plan, despite City Council approval.

San Francisco received a federal grant to study the possibility of deploying a congestion pricing plan similar to those in London and Stockholm. The study was completed in December 2010, and the San Francisco County Transportation Authority, which developed the study, is now taking steps to prepare an environmental impact report that could lead to a cordon pricing pilot in 2015.

Taming Traffic in London

The cordon charge has helped London to reclaim places like Trafalgar Square for pedestrian use.

In 2003, London embarked on a remarkable experiment: a large-scale introduction of congestion pricing in the central business district of a major financial and world capital city. Singapore and several cities in Norway have also implemented similar programs. The results in London, as in these places, are extraordinary.

Less Congestion

Two years after implementation of the cordon pricing system in London, congestion has decreased by an average of 30 percent in the tolled zone. The average speed of traffic has increased 25 percent, from 8 miles per hour to 11 mph. Congestion has also decreased during the "shoulder" periods prior to and following the charging times.

Cleaner Air

Inside the cordon, emissions of smog-forming nitrogen oxide (NOx) and particulate matter (PM10), or soot, declined by 18 percent and 22 percent, respectively. Fossil fuel consumption and carbon dioxide (CO_2) emissions are estimated to have declined by 20 percent. Air quality tests show NOx concentrations decreasing across the city. Region-wide concentrations of PM10 are also falling.

More Revenue

London quickly invested toll revenue in transit, especially bus service, which is now more viable because of decreased congestion. As a result, 37 percent more people are riding buses into the city during charging times than before cordon pricing. Bus delays have been cut in half. Excess waiting time, a measure of the time passengers wait at bus stops, has decreased by 24 percent across London, and by 30 percent in the cordon area during charging times. Overall, 85 percent of people entering the capital during tolling times are now taking public transit.

The system is expected to make a net profit of £97 million ($174 million) in 2004/2005 that can then be reinvested in the public transit system to further improve service.

Strong Public Support

Mayor Livingstone enjoys high approval ratings and is now planning to expand the cordon pricing zone to other London neighborhoods.

The start of the cordon charge coincided with an economic slump (the most serious since the early 1990s) and the temporary closure of two subway lines, making it difficult to evaluate the charge's initial effect on businesses and retail outlets. Many businesses, though, have benefited from reduced travel times, improved air quality, and easier city access afforded by enhanced public transit. According to a 2003 poll by London First, a coalition of 300 major companies in London, 71 percent of businesses reported that congestion pricing has not hurt business, 49 percent are happy with the system and 35 percent were still unsure.

Addressing a Real Problem

Before the implementation of cordon pricing, vehicles in the central business district were estimated to spend 50 percent of their time stuck in traffic. About 250,000 motor vehicles, or 25 lanes of traffic, enter central London every day. Due to the severity of the traffic, London Mayor Ken Livingstone made congestion reduction a major part of his successful campaign platform in 2000. On February 17, 2003 Livingstone implemented an ambitious cordon pricing scheme (with the help of traffic expert Robert Kiley from New York City) in order to unclog the city's streets.

Smart Implementation

This cordon pricing system is run by Transport for London (TfL), the unified agency responsible for carrying out the Mayor's transit strategy. London's system uses cameras with automatic number plate recognition (ANPR) technology to capture the license plates of drivers entering and driving within the central business district. Due to privacy concerns, license plate images are erased from the system each evening.

There are cameras at the 174 entry points to the central business district, as well as approximately 50 cameras throughout the zone. The system covers an eight square mile area (1.3 percent of Greater London). Originally, it cost £5 (about $9 US) to enter the district on weekdays from 7 am to 6:30 pm. In July 2005, the charge was increased from £5 to £8 (from $9 to $14 US). This was done to achieve additional reductions in congestion as well as to fund further public transit improvements. The revenue raised will first go toward paying for the system, and then toward improving public transit.

Singapore: A Pioneer in Taming Traffic

Singapore's congestion pricing system dates to 1975, when it introduced an Area Licensing Scheme (ALS) that charged drivers a flat rate for unlimited entries into Singapore's central area. In 1998, Singapore replaced the system with the Electronic Road Pricing (ERP) program which uses modern technology. The

ERP is also more expansive than ALS, tolling drivers each time they enter the charging zone. Both systems produced immediate benefits.

Congestion Is Under Control

The ALS system led to an almost immediate 45% reduction in traffic and a 25% decline in vehicle crashes. Average travel speeds increased from 11 mph to 21 mph. After the institution of the ERP system, traffic levels decreased a further 15%. This has helped Singapore to maintain ideal travel speeds of 30 to 40 mph on expressways and 12 to 19 mph on arterial roads. In addition, 65% of commuters now use public transportation, an increase of nearly 20%.

The Air Is Cleaner

Air quality in Singapore meets health-based standards set by the United States EPA. It also meets the long-term goals of the World Health Organization. According to Singapore's National Environment Agency, this shows that "measures adopted to control vehicular emissions, which include both land transport and environmental policies, have worked well in Singapore." Reduced traffic in the charging zone led to an 176,400 pound reduction in CO_2 emissions and a 22 pound reduction in particulate matter (soot).

The System Generates Revenue

Implementation of the ERP system, including in-vehicle technology and installation, cost approximately $125 million in U.S. dollars ($200 million Singapore dollars (SGD)). Annual revenue from the program is $50 million ($80 million SGD), much higher than the program's $10 million ($16 million SGD) annual operation costs.With approximately $40 million ($64 million SGD) per year in net profits, ERP has already paid for itself.

Officials Built Public Support

Before the ERP started, the Land Transport Authority (LTA) outfitted 98% of vehicles with the necessary electronic transponders free of charge. Officials also launched a public education campaign and held a demonstration period during which motorists were allowed to drive through the gantries to test their devices but were not charged a toll. This helped boost drivers' familiarity with and confidence in the system. The Land Transport Authority also established outlets around Singapore where short-term visitors can purchase transponders.

The System Is Flexible

Toll rates change throughout the day, with charges ranging from about 30 cents ($0.50 SGD) to $1.90 ($3.00 SGD) for passenger vehicles. Tolls for large vehicles like trucks and buses can be as much as $3.80 ($6.00 SGD).The prices are raised and lowered gradually to prevent a build-up of traffic trying to get into the RZ before the start or after the end of the most expensive periods. Every three months, LTA officials review toll levels to ensure that traffic keeps flowing smoothly. Seven months after implementation, for example, the LTA did away with all Saturday tolls because it found that roads were not congested on that day.

> *Congestion is under control, with the help of the ERP system.*
> Singapore Prime Minister and Finance Minister Lee Hsien Loong

Singapore's system is flexible in other ways as well. For example, when traffic decreased during tolling hours but increased in the shoulder periods, the cordon tolling hours were extended. The boundary of the cordon in Singapore also expanded as the central business district grew. Changes like these allowed the cordon pricing system to be more effective, so that tolls were subsequently lowered.

The System Uses Advanced Technology

Vehicles enter the charging area, or restricted zone (RZ), by passing through one of more than 25 overhead tolling gantries that form the cordon around Singapore's central area. Through electronic communication with these overhead gantries, the price of the toll is deducted from a CashCard inserted into an in-vehicle unit. In-vehicle units with CashCards inserted into them communicate electronically with overhead gantries to deduct the price of the toll. CashCards are essentially refillable debit cards that are transferable between vehicles. The in-vehicle units feature a small liquid crystal screen to display the CashCard balance.

Because tolls vary based on vehicle type (for example, trucks are charged more than cars), the in-vehicle units are color-coded according to vehicle class. This is meant to discourage drivers from illegally using an in-vehicle unit for a vehicle type that would be charged less. Video cameras are used to enforce the ERP program. If drivers pass through the gantries without an in-vehicle unit, a CashCard, or sufficient funds to pay the toll, a photo of the license plate is sent to a control center and the violator is billed an administrative penalty charge plus the cost of the toll.

Norway: Rings Around Cities Reduce Traffic

By Creating Toll Rings Around Its Large Cities, the Country Has Reduced Traffic and Reaped Economic Benefits

Bergen's toll ring decreased congestion. Revenues have helped fund improvement projects.

In 1986, Norwegian officials created the country's first toll ring around Bergen, Norway's second largest city. This was followed by cordon rings around other Norwegian cities, including the nation's capital Oslo in 1990, and Trondheim, a city in the center of Norway, in 1991.

Congestion Is Under Control
Tolling reduced congestion in all three cities. In Trondheim, traffic has dropped by more than 10 percent within the charging ring. Bergen has seen a 6 to

7 percent decrease in traffic. The toll ring in Oslo helped reduce traffic by 6 to 10 percent. However, revenues from the toll ring were used for large-scale road improvements throughout Oslo, increasing traffic on many suburban highways.

The System Generates Revenue

Until recently, Norwegian law allowed tolling programs only if they were designed to raise revenues for transportation infrastructure. As a result, Bergen, Oslo and Trondheim implemented cordon pricing for the specific purpose of financing improvements to their aging transportation systems. In Oslo, for example, 20 percent of toll revenues are dedicated to public transportation projects. In 2002, cordon pricing helped Oslo raise $169 million (1,046 million Norwegian krones—NOK). Operational costs were only 10 percent of the total revenue.

In Trondheim, revenue has helped pay for 60 percent of the cost of the city's planned transportation and environmental improvements. Projects funded with toll revenues in Trondheim include public transportation improvements, the construction of bicycle paths, and the provision of 200 free bicycles for public use.

The System Uses Advanced Technology

The toll rings in Bergen, Oslo and Trondheim all operate in slightly different ways. The Bergen toll ring, for example, is in effect from 6 am to 10 pm on weekdays, and has eight toll stations. Oslo's toll ring is much larger, with 19 toll stations, and tolls are in effect at all hours. In Trondheim, tolls are charged on weekdays from 6 am to 6 pm at 12 toll stations. While the tolls in Bergen and Oslo are a flat rate during all operating hours (heavy vehicles are charged more), the toll rates in Trondheim vary by time of day.

Each system, however, enables drivers to use electronic transponders, known as AutoPasses, to pay the toll. AutoPass use is widespread—in Trondheim, for example, 95 percent of people entering the charging area during peak periods used AutoPasses. Drivers without transponders can still pass through the tolls, either through manual collection toll stations, stations with video cameras that take photographs of vehicle license plates and send invoices for the toll, or booths with automatic payment collection machines that allow motorists to pay with cash or cards.

The Systems Are Regional and Renewable

The systems are regional and renewable: Norway requires political consensus between parties on formal agreements to implement toll rings. Each of the toll rings was established at the local level as a temporary fundraising mechanism and was set to expire after a predetermined number of years. In Bergen, the toll ring expired in 2001, but was renewed for another ten years. The Oslo toll ring will expire in 2007.

According to an official at the Norwegian Public Roads Administration, Oslo's toll will be extended to finance more road projects, including a tunnel under the Bjørvika Bay in the center of Oslo, which will connect two other tunnels and provide room for a new city district close to Oslo's main rail-way station and new opera building. In Trondheim, the toll ring expired on December 31, 2005, and was not renewed because of political promises that no toll project would run longer than 15 years. Also, the city had already financed all of its planned transportation projects through the original toll ring. Parts of the cordon may be reopened at a later date in connection with the financing of new local road projects.

Congestion Pricing in the Manhattan Central Business District: Let's Look Hard Before We Leap

Executive Summary

Auto travel and truck transport are essential to a vibrant economy.

- Auto travel is critical to New York City's economy. About 31 percent of the 3.6 million people who come into the Manhattan central business district every day—and about 55 percent of all domestic business and leisure visitors to the city—travel by car.
- The importance of auto and truck transportation to New York's economy means that it is vital to keep traffic moving as efficiently as possible. Concern about traffic congestion has recently led Mayor Bloomberg to propose that the City establish a "congestion pricing" system—similar to one now operating in London—in Manhattan below 86th Street.
- The City's goal should not be simply to reduce the total volume of traffic in the Manhattan CBD. Rather, it needs to make all of its transportation systems work together more efficiently, so that it can simultaneously reduce congestion and accommodate the increased demand for travel that a growing economy and a growing population will inevitably produce.

Despite continued growth in the City population and its economy, the number of vehicles being driven into the Manhattan CBD each day has actually declined.

- Between 1998 and 2004 (the last year for which data are available), the number of automobiles and trucks driven into the Manhattan CBD each day declined by 3.4 percent, while the number of people using mass transit to travel to the CBD rose by 10 percent.
- During the last decade, mass transit ridership has increased City-wide by 36 percent, far outpacing the growth of population and jobs during that period.

- The New York Metropolitan Transportation Council forecasts that even with continued population and job growth through 2030, congestion will be less severe than it was in 2005.
- Since the number of cars entering the Manhattan's CBD is not rising, we need to look elsewhere for the major causes of congestion—double-parked vehicles, blocking the box, poor construction site management, etc.—and for practical ways to reduce it.

The debate over congestion pricing risks diverting attention away from the very real need to invest more in our mass transit system.

- In part because ridership has grown by 36 percent during the last ten years, many of the City's bus and subway lines are overcrowded.
- At the same time, many residents and businesses located in the outer boroughs are underserved and lack convenient mass transit options.
- Congestion pricing would lead 90,000 people to switch to an already overburdened mass transit system. Many will have to travel substantial distances to get to an overcrowded subway.
- The money which would be spent building a flawed congestion pricing system would be better spent directly on mass transit improvements.

London's congestion pricing system should not be seen as a success.

- Advocates for congestion pricing point to the "success" of London's system. But London's congestion charging system has been successful only in the sense that it has reduced the number of cars traveling into central London each day. By many measures, London's system is a major failure.
    - It is expensive and highly inefficient. The initial set-up of the system cost £190 million (about $376 million); and even with a daily charge of £8 (about $15.81), annual operating and administrative costs in 2005–06 ate up 42 percent of total revenues.
    - Businesses within the charging zone have been hurt.
    - Even with reduced traffic volumes, congestion in central London is once again getting worse.
    - In the wake of Mayor Livingstone's decision, despite strong local opposition, to go ahead with expansion of the congestion charging system, residents and leading London business groups have become increasingly vocal in their criticism of the system.
    - Based in part on dissatisfaction with congestion pricing in London, 1.8 million people have petitioned Prime Minister Tony Blair urging that the government not adopt a proposed road pricing program.

The costs associated with the proposed congestion pricing system would far outweigh the benefits.

- *In New York City, the costs associated with the proposed congestion pricing system would far outweigh the gains from reduced congestion.* The congestion pricing scheme proposed for Manhattan would reduce the costs that excess congestion now imposes on the City's economy by approximately $140 million annually. The costs incurred to achieve this rather modest economic benefit would be substantial. They can be measured in the following ways:

- Initial set-up costs that—given the more complex system that has been proposed for New York City, and the fact that it would have to handle many more vehicles and payment transactions per day than London's—could significantly exceed the $376 million set-up cost of London's system. (The City intends to seek federal funding to offset some of these up-front costs—but that funding is by no means guaranteed.)
- The direct cost of $620 million in congestion charges paid by people who live, work, do business in or visit New York City.
- Approximately $100 million annually in "compliance costs," the value of time motorists and businesses will have to spend paying congestion charges (or appealing fines for late payment, etc.)
- A reduction in overall economic activity in the City of as much as $690 million, and a loss of as many as 8,700 jobs.
- The cost of longer commuting times experienced by people who switch from autos to transit ($77 million or more).
- The cost of increased congestion in certain areas where the volume of traffic is likely to increase—such as the Cross-Bronx Expressway—as a result of diversion of traffic away from the CBD.

Congestion pricing is an inefficient way to raise new revenues for mass transit.

- As a means of generating new revenues for mass transit, congestion pricing is extraordinarily inefficient.
  - In London, operating and administrative costs eat up 42 percent of all revenues generated by the City's congestion charging scheme.
  - In New York City, the Office of Long-Term Planning and Sustainability estimates that the proposed system's annual operating costs would total $240 million annually—39 percent of estimated gross revenues. People who live, work, do business in and visit New York would be paying $620 million each year to generate $380 million for regional transit improvements.

Congestion pricing fees could rise quickly, as they did in London.

- The system's high operating costs, could quickly lead—as they did in London—to a sharp increase in charges.
- In London the fee started at $9.89 (£5) in 2003, and rose to $15.81 (£8) in 2005. In 2007, the size of the zone in which the congestion charge applies was doubled, and now the Mayor of London seeks to raise the charge to $49.43 (£25) on certain vehicles.

Congestion pricing is an unfair flat tax on small businesses and working people.

- London-style congestion pricing also raises serious issues of fairness. Commuting to the CBD by car is not necessarily a sign of affluence. In 2000, the average income of Brooklyn, Queens, Bronx and Staten Island residents who commuted to Manhattan by car was $43,300. For many of these New Yorkers, mass transit commuting options are limited.

Claims that congestion pricing will significantly reduce greenhouse gas emissions are misleading.

- According to data published by the City, the total volume of greenhouse gases generated in New York City by on-road vehicles declined by 5.6 percent between 1995 and 2005, while those generated by all other sources rose by 12.8 percent.
- Congestion pricing would reduce City-wide traffic by only 2 percent. Vehicular emissions, moreover, are only one source of greenhouse gases. PLANYC2030 acknowledges that 79 percent of all such emissions come from buildings, and only 20 percent from on-road vehicles. Even if the system is as effective as its proponents claim, it will reduce emissions by only 0.4 percent.
- The claim that the proposal will make a significant impact on the reduction of greenhouse gas emissions—or that it will significantly reduce the severity of asthma in the City's poorer neighborhoods thus appears to be somewhat disingenuous.
- Congestion pricing could lead to a decline in air quality in those parts of the City where congestion would increase as a result of diversion of traffic away from the CBD—for example, along the Cross-Bronx Expressway or the Staten Island Expressway.
- In the long run, it would make far more sense to focus on speeding the transition to cars and trucks that produce fewer emissions. The City might consider what types of incentives it might provide to encourage that transition.

There are fairer and more effective ways to mitigate congestion.

- There are more effective, more efficient and fairer ways to reduce congestion in the Manhattan central business district—without hurting the City's economy. They include, for example:
  - More active enforcement of existing traffic and parking rules;
  - More intensive use of information technology to manage traffic—as in Lower Manhattan; and
  - Improving mass transit options—for example, through the use of bus rapid transit and ferries, and through carefully-planned expansion of the subway system.

Congestion pricing fails the test of equity, efficiency and economic sense.

- Any initiative that aims to reduce traffic congestion or to provide additional funding for mass transit has to be judged in terms of efficiency, equity and the need to minimize any adverse effects on the City's economy. By all three tests, the proposed congestion pricing system fails. . . .

Transport for London (TfL), the city's transportation agency, has now been operating a congestion pricing system in central London for more than four years. Does its experience suggest that New York should follow suit?

Part Two: London's Experience

In 2003, London instituted a new system of "congestion charging," aimed at relieving traffic congestion in the city's commercial core. The congestion charging scheme has been widely hailed for its success in reducing the volume of automobile traffic in the center of the city, and for the resulting decline in congestion. But before we conclude that London's congestion charging system offers an example that New York City should follow, we need to look carefully at what London's experience has been, what its system costs, and how it has affected the City's economy.

How London's Congestion Charging System Works

London's congestion charging scheme initially imposed a daily charge of £5 (about $9.89 at recent exchange rates) on most private vehicles traveling in a 22-square-kilometer area in central London between 7 AM and 6:30 PM. (In 2005 the charge was increased to £8—about $15.81 at recent exchange rates.) The system operates through a network of cameras located along the perimeter of the charging zone, and at intersections throughout the zone, that record the registration numbers of vehicles traveling into or within the area.

Drivers are offered a number of payment options—paying on-line, by phone, at kiosks, by mail or at selected retail stores and service stations. They can pre-pay the charge for a week, a month or a year. Those who have not pre-paid are expected to pay the £8 ($15.81) charge before midnight on the day they travel within the zone—or the following day, in which case the charge rises to £10 ($19.76).

After one day, those who have not paid are subject to a penalty of £50 ($99) if paid within 14 days, £100 ($198) if paid in 15 to 28 days or £150 ($297) if paid later than 28 days.

London's system offers a variety of exemptions and discounts.

- Disabled drivers are exempted from the charge, as are those who drive alternative-fuel vehicles;
- Residents of the zone pay only 10 percent of the full charge;
- Fleet-owners pay £7 ($13.84) per vehicle per day; and
- Those who pre-pay on a monthly (or annual) basis get a 15 percent discount.

While TfL has sought to make the process of paying congestion charges as easy as possible, the system still imposes significant "compliance costs" on drivers in the form of time and effort involved in paying the charge. Moreover, data on the penalties TfL levies for late payment of charges suggest that—four years after it was launched—many people are still having difficulty with the system. In 2005–06, fines accounted for about 31 percent of all system

A congestion charge of $8 per day ($2,000 per year) would be equal to a tax of 3.2 percent on the gross earnings of City residents who commute to the Manhattan CBD by car.

revenues (£65 million, or about $128 million). Putting it another way—for every £100 that TfL collected in congestion charges, it levied £46 in fines on people who failed to pay on time, or who otherwise violated the system's rules.

As originally designed, one of the primary purposes of the congestion charging scheme was to generate revenues that could be used to improve transit services. However, the system's costs have proven to be substantially higher than originally anticipated. During the first few years, operating costs consumed most of the system's revenues; and as a result, many of the improvements in bus service that have followed the imposition of congestion pricing have in fact been financed from other sources.

High operating costs remain one of the system's most difficult problems. In 2005–06, operating and maintenance costs totaled £88 million (about $174 million); and net revenues—£122 million (about $241 million). The system's high operating costs—42 percent of total revenues in 2005–06—continue to be a target of criticism. . . .

Congestion Pricing in New York City . . .

An Issue of Fairness

In addition to the damage that it would inflict on New York City's economy, and its gross inefficiency as a means of raising revenue to finance mass transit investments, London-style congestion pricing presents serious issues of fairness. As noted above, commuting by car from Queens, Brooklyn, the Bronx and Staten Island to Manhattan is not necessarily a mark of affluence—according to the Census Bureau, the earnings of these New Yorkers averaged about $43,300.

Yet it is these New Yorkers—as well as small businesses throughout the City—who would bear a substantial part of the cost of the proposed congestion charge. Assuming that those who commute by car average 1.45 persons per vehicle, and that they earn an average of $43,300, a congestion charge of $8 per day ($2,000 per year) would be equal to a tax of 3.2 percent on the gross earnings of City residents who commute to the Manhattan CBD by car.

Working and middle-class residents of other parts of the City would thus be required to pay $8 to drive into Midtown or Lower Manhattan during the hours when the congestion charge is in effect. Those who live below 86th Street, in contrast—an area that includes some of the City's most affluent neighborhoods—would be charged only $4 to drive within the zone. In 2005, according to the Census Bureau, the median household income of car-owners living in the area of Manhattan roughly corresponding to the proposed congestion pricing zone was $138,500. . . .

EXPLORING THE ISSUE

Should U.S. Cities Adopt a System of "Congestion Pricing" to "Tame" Traffic?

Critical Thinking and Reflection

1. Do people have a "right" to drive?
2. At what level would you set the fee for an automobile's entry into a city's central business district during peak business hours? Is your charge high enough that it will lead a large number of people to switch to carpools, bicycles, and mass transit?
3. Is a congestion zone a form of regressive taxation?
4. Which people or activities do you feel should be exempted from having to pay the congestion charge? Who should be charged only a reduced fee rather than the full congestion charge? Do such exemptions and discounts undermine the impact of a congestion charge?
5. Does a congestion zone system pose a danger to individual privacy rights? What safeguards would help to reduce the possible dangers that such extensive use of cameras and photographic records poses to individual privacy?

Is There Common Ground?

Congestion pricing has a clear record of success in reducing congestion in cities where it has been implemented. Still, the opposition to congestion zones in the United States can be expected to be quite overwhelming. Motorists resent the charge. People in general oppose being forced to pay for something (in this case, the privilege of driving into a city center) that in the past they have been able to do for free. Although major corporations may see benefits in being located in a city center where traffic congestion has been eased, smaller businesses and retailers will resist the imposition of a system that threatens to chase away potential customers. The residents of poor and working-class neighborhoods will also object having to pay to enter adjacent parts of the city.

If a congestion zone is adopted, steps can be taken to ensure that the fees do not impose a burden on residents who can least afford to bear them. Zone administration can allow exceptions or discounts for low-income residents, the elderly, and residents of neighborhoods located immediately adjacent to the zone. Alternatively, lower-income residents can be given a credit to reimburse them for the new costs they incur. The tax credit can ensure that grievous financial harm is not inflicted on poorer families, even while a per-trip charge serves to discourage entry by automobile into high-congestion areas of the city.

Given such widespread opposition to congestion zones in the U.S., the European experience points to some possible key steps that can be taken to increase the system's political feasibility. First, the boundaries of a congestion zone must be drawn as narrowly as possible to minimize the inconvenience to drivers and the disruption to business. Even London wound up narrowing the boundary of its central cordon, removing the western extension, targeting the congestion charges to "the City," London's financial center.

Second, although objections from motorists can be expected, their sense of outrage can be lessened if a road pricing program promises motorist benefits, not just hundreds, and in some cases even thousands, of dollars in new charges. A road pricing system can replace annual automobile annual registration fees (similar to the Dutch system). A large portion of the revenues generated can be dedicated to road improvements and not just solely to mass transit projects as environmental activists demand.

Any congestion charge system must also have accompanying rules that ensure the safeguarding privacy—including strict procedures regarding records management and destruction. Traffic records can use generic identifiers with any indication of a vehicle owner's name, address, and other personal information, which can all be kept on separate files. A strict policy can also require the erasure or destruction of the records after a very short period of time where no violation has been recorded, so that no central storehouse of citizen travel records is maintained.

Congestion zone pricing is not suitable for all cities. Congestion zones are most appropriate in cities that truly suffer from clogged streets and in cases where a city's attractiveness to global corporations, tourists, and conventioneers is so great, that local businesses can be expected to weather the inconveniences that accompany the imposition of a congestion charge. Congestion pricing also has a greater chance of delivering its promised goals where a city already has effective mass transit alternatives in place.

With or without a congestion zone, cities also need to continue to take steps to reduce diesel emissions that are responsible for health problems such as childhood asthma. Appropriate measures can curtail idling by buses and trucks, require the use of alternative fuels in city fleets, and impose extra fees on trucks that continue to rely on diesel fuel.

Additional Resources

Downs, Anthony. (2002). *Stuck in Traffic*. Washington, DC: Brookings Institution.

Federal Highway Administration, United States. (2008). *Congestion Pricing—A Primer: An Overview*. Washington, DC: U.S. Department of Transportation.

Levy, Jonathan I., Jonathan J. Buonocore, & Kathleen von Stackelberg. (2010). "The Public Health Costs of Traffic Congestion: A Health Risk Assessment," Cambridge, MA: Harvard Center for Risk Analysis. Available at www.transportationconstructioncoalition.org/Docs/TCC-Harvard-Traffic-Congestion-Report-Final.pdf

Schaller, Brad. (2010). "New York's Congestion Pricing Experience and Implications for Road Pricing Acceptance in the United States," *Transport Policy*, vol. 17: 266–273.

Small, Kenneth A., & Erik T. Verhoef, Erik T. (2007). *The Economics of Urban Transportation*. New York: Routledge.

Internet References

Business First

A self-proclaimed "influential business membership organisation (sic) with the mission to make London the best city in the world in which to do business," London First supports congestion pricing as a necessary tool to improve the business climate of London.

www.londonfirst.co.uk

City of Stockholm: "Congestion Tax Monitoring Report"

This detailed report, available in English, assesses just how well Stockholm's congestion zone is working when it comes to reducing traffic and congestion. The report shows no negative influences on businesses located inside the congestion zone, that the zone actually created a positive climate for business.

http://international.stockholm.se/-/News-from-the-City-of-Stockholm/News/Congestion-tax-monitoring-report/

International Transport Forum

The International Transportation Forum has 52 member countries. Its website describes a variety of policy approaches that countries utilize to reduce traffic congestion while promoting economic development and social inclusion.

www.internationaltransportforum.org

London (England) Chamber of Commerce

The Chamber has produced numerous studies that show that congestion pricing has been "bad for business," especially smaller retailers.

www.londonchamber.co.uk/lcc_public/home.asp

Reason Foundation

Committed to a free society and libertarian principles, the Reason Foundation generally looks favorably upon road pricing but urges cities to proceed quite cautiously before importing the London congestion zone with its imperfections.

http://reason.org

Transport for London

Transport for London (TfL) is the governmental body responsible for transit policy and operations, including management of the centrals congestion zone. The TfL website describes the operation of the congestion zone and how the zone has been modified over the years. TfL also seeks to evaluate the impact that the zone has had on transportation usage and the environment.

www.tfl.gov.uk/roadusers/congestioncharging/default.aspx

Victoria Transportation Policy Institute

This independent organization advocates congestion zones and other regulatory and taxing strategies to improve transportation and protect the environment. In particular, see the work of Todd Litman.

www.vtpi.org

ISSUE 13

Should the United States Invest in High-Speed Intercity Rail?

YES: U.S. PIRG Education Fund, from *A Track Record of Success: High-Speed Rail Around the World and Its Promise for America* (2010)

NO: Robert Poole, from "Questions Legislators Should Ask About High-Speed Rail: Testimony to the National Conference of State Legislators" (April 2010)

Learning Outcomes

After reading this issue, you should be able to:

- Explain how a high-speed rail system differs from more conventional fast trains.
- Identify high-speed rail systems around the world.
- Explain the environmental benefits of high-speed rail.
- Explain how high-speed rail can be a catalyst for the economic development of cities.
- Articulate the criticisms of investing in high-speed rail.
- Identify the various opponents of high-speed rail.

ISSUE SUMMARY

YES: U.S. Public Interest Research Group (PIRG) advocates stronger governmental action in such policy issues as environmental protection. PIRG looks at the high-speed rail systems of other countries and argues that the United States can similarly build a high-speed rail that can reduce pollution while promoting both national economic growth and local urban revitalization.

NO: Robert Poole is a policy analyst who, over the years, has questioned a number of the more orthodox big-spending solutions to urban problems. Poole questions whether high-speed rail in the United States is capable of attracting a great number of riders. He argues against investing so heavily in a transportation system that ultimately will accomplish so little.

For Americans who travel abroad, the discovery of high-speed trains, such as France's TGV and Japan's Shinkansen or "bullet" train, often comes as quite a surprise. The United States does not have anything close to these marvels. France's TGV bullet trains can reach speeds of 200 mph outside built-up areas, halving the time of a comparable automobile trip. A Eurostar rail trip from London to Paris via the "Chunnel" (the tunnel under the English Channel) takes only 2.5 hours. High-speed rail can pose a viable alternative to intercity air travel, alleviating congestion at airports. High-speed rail (HSR) can provide an energy-efficient and less polluting alternative to both jet travel and the automobile.

The stations that serve high-speed trains are the new entry doorways to a city. Mayors and city business leaders point to the potential of high-speed rail to stimulate high-density mixed-used development around centrally located stations.

Construction of a high-speed system would be the government's largest and most expensive job creation program since the completion of the interstate highway system more than a half century ago. The California High-Speed Rail Authority claims that construction of an HSR network would create more than 600,000 jobs in the state over the life of the project. An HSR system would also generate the need for new rail cars, stimulating the emergence of a new manufacturing industry in the United States.

HSR will improve the connectivity of cities, aiding economic growth by enabling executives and labor to move quickly from one important location to another. An executive will be able to board a train and quickly travel to a business' operations in another city. China has invested heavily in high-speed rail in an effort to open seemingly distant or "back water" sites to new investment. In the United States, an HSR system can similarly be expected to have similar economic effects. A California HSR system with trains traveling at speeds approaching 220 mph would reduce the travel time from San Francisco to Los Angeles to a little more than two-and-half hours, helping to combine the Bay Area and southern California into a single, integrated economic region. A Tampa-Orlando-Miami high-speed network, including a stop near Disney World, would enable tourists as well as executives and laborers to move more easily from one destination to the next.

The U.S. Conference of Mayors argues that HSR will enhance the development of "technology clusters," the pivotal cauldrons of interrelated industries that are critical to the nation's future economic growth. An HSR network can enable executives and scientists in a region to meet more frequently, with face-to-face collaboration leading to important industrial breakthroughs. An HSR network in the Northeast would enable researchers in New York to meet more frequently with colleagues from Boston. A Midwest HSR network would allow university scientists from Cleveland, Detroit, St. Louis, Madison, and Minneapolis to gather in Chicago.

But critics argue that an American HSR system faces much lower prospects of success as a result of business and residential settlement patterns that are much more sprawled than in Europe. In the United States, where commercial activity is spread out more widely over a vast suburban expanse, a downtown-oriented HSR train station may not be a really good economic "fit." Indeed, the major train stations that dominated United States cities during the industrial age all faded with suburbanization. U.S. metropolitan areas also generally lack the density of population to make trips by rail truly convenient. In the United States, travelers will generally have to journey by car to reach an HSR station and wait for a train; many travelers will simply find it more convenient to complete the entire trip by car. The United States also has a stronger car culture than Europe. With lower ridership levels, high-speed rail in the United States will require continued subsidies.

The Republican governors of Ohio, Wisconsin, and Florida turned down Obama administration federal funds for HSR development, fearing that taxpayers in their states would wind up having to pay for the seemingly endless costs of an HSR system that are not covered by federal grants. Even after the construction of an HSR system is finished, high-speed rail is likely to require continuing operating subsidies, as the price of an HSR trip still must be kept low enough to compete with automobile and air travel alternatives.

Critics further contend that many of the economic benefits claimed for HSR are highly inflated. Many of the jobs that will be created by HSR will only be temporary and will continue to exist once construction is completed.

It may be somewhat inaccurate to characterize much of the evolving U.S. systems as "high speed." In Europe and China, HSR trains can reach top speeds as they travel across the great rural expanses between cities. In the United States, however, trains will seldom be able to travel at top speeds as they must wind their way through already built-up suburban areas, where concerns for safety and the local quality of life will require that trains run more slowly. In numerous built-up areas, HSR will share tracks with conventional freight and passenger trains, again forcing reductions in speed. The inclusion of intermediary stops will further add to travel times, with trains slowing to enter a station, waiting to pick up passengers, and then picking up speed when exiting a station. When such factors are considered, the overall time of an HSR trip may not be that much better than that of a comparable automobile trip.

California has already been forced to modify its HSR plans. Advocates of HSR had envisioned a futuristic rail network where, even in populated areas, trains would be able to whiz by on exclusive tracks built on overhead aqueducts or passing through deep tunnels. The residents of suburban areas, however, mobilized to protest the harm that such a project would inflict on their communities. In the Peninsula area south of San Francisco, residents objected to the property takings that HSR construction would require. Local residents further objected that even track laid at ground level would divide communities and lower property values. In response to these concerns, legislators from affected communities sought to alter the design of the system: high-speed trains would run through the Peninsula on existing Caltrain commuter tracks, with tunneling and the construction of an elevated rail system needed only at major intersections. The proposed modifications in HSR design promised to save billions of dollars in construction costs. But, by running on existing tracks, HSR trains would be able to reach only a speed of

90 mph, not the 125 mph that had initially been envisioned for trains on this segment of the route.

To minimize displacement, costs, and voter outrage, California decided that its initial HSR line would not run into the centers of Los Angeles and San Francisco. Instead, the initial HSR route that would run from Fresno, far to the south of the Bay Area, to Palmdale, a rapidly growing exurban area far to the northeast of Los Angeles. In Florida, similar concerns led planners to envision a Tampa-Orlando-Miami route with a western terminus located 80 miles from downtown Tampa. HSR systems that do not allow passengers to arrive near the center city cannot be expected to have strong positive impacts on center-city economies and job creation.

In California, the state Legislative Analyst's Office (LAO) questioned whether the state, given its fiscal difficulties, had the funds to pay the $43 billion costs of constructing the San Francisco-to-Los Angeles "first phase" of the state's HSR system, never mind the Phase Two extension to San Diego, Sacramento, and Oakland. The LAO further contended that the official estimates vastly understated the system's real costs. The LAO estimated that Phase One construction costs would exceed $67 billion.

U.S. PIRG and Robert Poole capably present the competing sides in the debate over HSR. In the excerpts of its *Track Record for Success* report that are reprinted in the YES selection, PIRG reviews the experience of high-speed rail in other countries, showing how HSR contributes to energy independence and environmental protection, while enabling local economic development and providing the "eased connections" that are critical to a nation's future economic growth.

In the NO selection, Robert Poole responds that HSR in the United States cannot be expected to greatly alter patterns of transportation use. He further suggests that many of the claims made regarding HSR's impacts on pollution reduction and energy independence are based more on faith than on solid evidence. He also stresses the "opportunity costs" of such a steep investment, that the huge monies invested inefficiently in HSR will not be available to support other more critical public programs.

YES    U.S. PIRG Education Fund

A Track Record of Success: High-Speed Rail Around the World and Its Promise for America

Executive Summary

As America moves toward construction of new high-speed rail networks in regions throughout the country, we have much to learn from experiences abroad. High-speed rail lines have operated for more than 45 years in Japan and for three decades in Europe, providing a wealth of information about what the United States can expect from high-speed rail and how we can receive the greatest possible benefits from our investment.

Indeed, the experience of high-speed rail lines abroad, as well as America's limited experience with high-speed rail on the East Coast, suggests that the United States can expect great benefits from investing in a high-speed passenger rail system, particularly if it makes steady commitments to rail improvements and designs the system wisely.

High-speed rail systems in other nations have been able to dramatically reduce the volume of short-haul flights between nearby cities and significantly reduce inter-city car travel. In the United States, similar shifts would ease congestion in the skies and offer alternatives to congested highways, reducing the need for expensive new investments in highways and airports. Short-haul plane trips are the least efficient in terms of time and fuel, and replacing those trips allows air travel to be more efficient and focused on long-haul trips. High-speed rail service has almost completely replaced short-haul air service on several corridors in Europe, such as between Paris and Lyon, France, and between Cologne and Frankfurt, Germany.

- The number of air passengers between London and Paris has been cut in half since high-speed rail service was initiated between the two cities through the Channel Tunnel.
- In Spain, high-speed rail service between Madrid and Seville reduced the share of travel by car between the two cities from 60 percent to 34 percent. The recent launch of high-speed rail service between Madrid and Barcelona has cut air travel on what was once one of the world's busiest passenger air routes by one-third.

- Even in the northeastern United States, where Amtrak Acela Express service is slow by international standards, rail service accounts for 65 percent of the air/rail market on trips between New York and Washington, D.C., and 52 percent of the air/rail market on trips between Boston and New York.

High-speed rail saves energy and protects the environment. In the United States, high-speed rail could cut our dependence on oil while helping to reduce air pollution and curb global warming.

- *Continual improvement*—Japan's Shinkansen system is estimated to use one quarter the energy of air travel or one-sixth the energy of automobile travel per passenger. The energy efficiency of Shinkansen trains has continually improved over time, such that today's trains use nearly a third less energy, while traveling significantly faster, than the trains introduced in the mid-sixties.
- *More efficient*—On Europe's high-speed lines, a typical Monday morning business trip from London to Paris via high-speed rail uses approximately a third as much energy as a car or plane trip. Similar energy savings are achieved on other European high-speed rail lines.
- *Replacing oil with electricity makes zero emissions possible*—Energy savings translate into reduced emissions of pollutants that cause global warming or respiratory problems—particularly when railroads power their trains with renewable energy. In Sweden, the country's high-speed trains are powered entirely with renewable energy, cutting emissions of global warming pollutants by 99 percent.

High-speed rail is safe and reliable. In the United States, reliable service via high-speed rail could be an attractive alternative to oft-delayed intercity flights and travel on congested freeways.

- *High-speed rail is safe*—There has never been a fatal accident on Japan's Shinkansen high-speed rail system or during high-speed operation of TGV trains in France, despite carrying billions of passengers over the course of several decades.
- *High-speed rail is reliable*—High-speed rail is generally more reliable than air or car travel. The average delay on Japan's Shinkansen system is 36 seconds. Spain's railway operator offers a money-back guarantee if train-related delays exceed five minutes.

High-speed rail can create jobs and boost local economies. A U.S. high-speed rail system could help position the nation for economic success in the 21st century while creating short-term jobs in construction and long-term jobs in ongoing maintenance and operation.

- Construction of high-speed rail lines creates thousands of temporary jobs. For example, about 8,000 people were involved in construction of the highspeed rail link between London and the Channel Tunnel.
- Well-designed high-speed rail stations located in city centers spark economic development and encourage revitalization of urban areas:

- A study of the Frankfurt-Cologne high-speed rail line in Germany estimated that areas surrounding two towns with new high-speed rail stations experienced a 2.7 percent increase in overall economic activity compared with the rest of the region.
- Office space in the vicinity of high-speed rail stations in France and northern Europe generally fetches higher rents than in other parts of the same cities.
- The city of Lyon experienced a 43 percent increase in the amount of office space near its high-speed rail station following the completion of a high-speed rail link to Paris.
- Property values near stations on Japan's Shinkansen network have been estimated to be 67 percent higher than property values further away.
- Several cities have used high-speed rail as the catalyst for ambitious urban redevelopment efforts. The city of Lille, France, used its rail station as the core of a multi-use development that now accommodates 6,000 jobs. The new international high-speed rail terminal at London's St. Pancras station is the centerpiece of a major redevelopment project that will add 1,800 residential units, as well as hotels, offices and cultural venues in the heart of London.

- High-speed rail has increased overall travel in corridors in Spain and France and the number of one-day business trips in South Korea. Increases in overall travel indicate that high-speed rail is having an impact on broader economic decisions and improve the chances that high-speed rail lines can recoup their overall costs.
- High-speed rail can expand labor markets and increase the potential for face-to-face interactions that create value in the growing "knowledge economy." A British study projects that the construction of the nation's first high-speed rail line will lead to more than $26 billion in net economic benefits over the next 60 years.

High-speed rail lines generally cover their operating costs with fare revenues. In the United States, a financially sustainable high-speed rail system will likely not require operating subsidies from taxpayers (although public funding is essential to getting the system up and running).

- High-speed rail service generates enough operating profit that it can subsidize other, less-profitable intercity rail lines in countries such as France and Spain, as well as in the U.S. Northeast.
- Two high-speed rail lines—the French TGV line between Paris and Lyon and the original Japanese Shinkansen line from Tokyo to Osaka— have covered their initial costs of construction through fares.

Properly planned high-speed rail can encourage sustainable land-use and development patterns. In the United States, focusing new development around high-speed rail stations can reduce pressure to develop in far-flung areas, reducing other infrastructure costs such as for sewers and electricity. By creating new centers of commerce and activity, high-speed rail stations can create new opportunities for riders to travel by public transportation, by bike, or on foot.

- Cities throughout Europe have paired the arrival of high-speed rail with expansion of local public transportation options—in some cases, using new high-speed rail lines to bolster local commuter rail service.
- Proper land-use policies in areas that receive high-speed rail stations, coupled with effective development of station areas, can ensure that high-speed rail does not fuel new sprawl.

To obtain the economic and transportation benefits experienced by other nations, the United States should follow through on its decision to invest in high-speed rail, while taking actions to maximize the benefits of that investment. Specifically, the United States should:

- Follow through on its decision to build a national high-speed rail system akin to the commitment to build the Interstate Highway System in the 1950s. Doing so will create thousands of jobs and position the United States to meet the economic, transportation, energy and environmental challenges of the next century.
- Use high-speed rail to focus future development by locating stations in city centers and planning for intensive commercial and residential development near stations.
- Make high-speed rail stations accessible to people using a variety of transportation modes, including automobiles, public transit, bicycling and walking. The United States should follow the lead of other nations and pair high-speed rail with expansion of local transit networks. . . .

High-Speed Rail: Experiences from Around the World

Nations throughout the developed world (and increasingly, the developing world) have seen the value of high-speed rail in addressing transportation, energy and environmental challenges and boosting economic development. The experience with high-speed rail abroad both underscores the potential benefits of express rail service to the United States and suggests important lessons America can learn in the design of its high-speed rail system.

High-Speed Rail Replaces Short-Haul Air Travel

Everywhere high-speed rail lines have been built, rail travel quickly replaces a significant share of air travel between the cities being served, demonstrating the strong demand for clean, fast and efficient travel between metropolitan areas, and freeing up capacity in the aviation system for long-haul and international flights.

The United States has several reasons to shift short-haul travelers from air to rail. Airport congestion contributes to delays that frustrate passengers, waste fuel, and hamper effective travel between cities. Flights of 500 miles or fewer—a distance increasingly served by high-speed rail in other countries—accounted for almost half of all flights in the United States and for 30 percent of all passengers in the 12-month period starting in April 2008, according to the Brookings Institution. The nation's second-busiest air travel corridor—between San Francisco and Los Angeles—is only 347 miles and carries 6.3 million passengers every year. Other short-hop trips, such as between Dallas and Houston (232 miles; 2.9 million passengers), and Chicago and Minneapolis (342 miles; 2 million passengers), also clog airports and skies with trips that could easily be served by high-speed rail.

The need to move people between nearby cities by air contributes to congestion in airports and can cause flight delays. As air traffic increases, so do delays. Congestion-related delays plague the nation's busiest airports, with New York, Chicago, Philadelphia, Miami, Atlanta and San Francisco this year reporting more delays and longer delays than average for both arrivals and departures. Nearly half (45.8-48 percent) of the delays at the nation's largest air traffic hubs can be attributed to the nation's air traffic system. These delays are directly related to the heavy traffic volume and tight schedules that characterize these airports; in fact, airports with the largest share of flights of less than 500 miles were the source of 42.2 percent of all departure delays in the United States, according to the Brookings Institution.

Substituting rail for air trips would also save energy and protect the environment. Short-haul flights are more energy intensive than longer flights, since much of the energy consumed in any air journey is used on take-off. Trips of 155 miles consume approximately 40 percent more energy per seat-mile than trips of more than 625 miles in the same aircraft. . . . In addition, electric high-speed rail service can provide an economical alternative for airline passengers during periods of high jet fuel prices, when airlines often impose ticket surcharges to recover costs from consumers.

High-speed trains around the world effectively replace air travel for precisely the kind of high-frequency, short- to middle-distance trips that would be served by the regional high-speed rail networks connecting cities in the United States. . . .

High-Speed Rail Saves Energy and Protects the Environment

Transportation in the United States is heavily dependent on oil and is a major contributor to both global warming and air pollution problems in cities throughout the nation. Although home to a mere 4.5 percent of the world's population, the United State emits nearly one-fifth of the world's global warming emissions. In the United States, the transportation sector is responsible for 33 percent of these emissions. In Europe, however, transportation only accounts for about 19 percent of total emissions.

Transportation also contributes heavily to the nation's air pollution problem. Despite decades of improvement in air quality, more than half of Americans—about 175 million—suffer pollution levels that are often "too dangerous to breathe" and can lead to reduced lung function and even premature death, according to a 2010 report by the American Lung Association. Of the hazardous, smog-forming pollutants produced nationally in the United States, 27 percent are emitted by cars and trucks.

Reducing Oil Dependence with High-Speed Rail

The transportation system in the United States is highly dependent on oil. Fully 95 percent of all energy used for the nation's transportation comes from petroleum. That dependence on oil—not only for cars but also for airplanes, trucks and trains—leaves Americans and U.S. businesses at the mercy of volatile world oil markets, erodes our energy independence, and hurts our economy. By building high-speed rail, the United States will reduce its dependence on oil for transportation—a sound, long-term investment in the nation's economic future.

Rail travel—particularly on electric trains—has some inherent energy-saving advantages compared with cars or airplanes. Both cars and airplanes are, at the moment, completely reliant on oil, whereas trains can be powered by electricity generated from a variety of fuels, including renewable energy. Electric motors are also inherently more energy efficient than the internal combustion engines used in cars and trucks, which dissipate much of the energy in their fuel as heat. High-speed rail also competes favorably in terms of energy consumption with short-haul aircraft, which expend much of their energy on takeoff. . . .

High-speed rail may also have secondary energy-saving impacts by encouraging patterns of development—including greater concentration of residential or business activity near high-speed rail stations—that reduce the distance of trips made in day-to-day travel.

Assessing the energy savings delivered by high-speed rail is challenging, and researchers come to different conclusions. The degree of energy savings depends on a complex interaction of speed, ridership, the source of energy used, and many other factors—as well as the emissions assumed to come from competing modes of travel. For example, a train that moves at high speeds might consume more energy per *seat* than a slower train. But if the higher speeds mean that the service is more attractive and more of the seats on the train are filled, the faster train may be more energy efficient on a *per-passenger* basis and may deliver a larger total energy savings.

Energy Savings on European High-Speed Rail Lines

Europe's high-speed rail lines deliver significant energy savings when compared to flying or driving. Passengers traveling on high-speed trains for a typical Monday morning trip from London to Paris use one-third as much energy as traveling by automobile and 30 percent as much energy as flying, according to a trip evaluation model developed by the Institute for Energy and Environmental Research in Heidelberg, Germany. Passengers traveling on high-speed trains between Madrid and Barcelona use 28 percent as much energy traveling by automobile and 30 percent as much energy as flying. (See Figure 1.)

Energy Savings in Japan

Even greater energy savings are achieved in Japan, whose Shinkansen system is estimated to consume one-quarter the energy of air transportation and one-sixth the energy of automobiles on a per-passenger basis. Japan has continually improved the energy efficiency of the Shinkansen, with the latest, most energy-efficient trains consuming 32 percent less energy than the original

Figure 1

Energy Consumption of Trains, Cars, and Aircraft Traveling Between European Cities, Monday Morning Trip

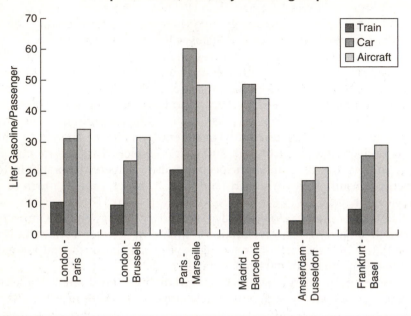

Shinkansen trains, even though they are capable of traveling 43 miles per hour faster.

Emission Reductions from High-Speed Rail in Europe and Japan

High-speed rail systems around the world also reduce emissions of harmful pollutants compared to other forms of travel. Because high-speed rail is more energy efficient and can use electricity generated from less polluting forms of energy, it often delivers large reductions in air pollutant emissions.

High-speed rail lines in Europe produce dramatic reductions in emissions of carbon dioxide—the leading contributor to global warming—compared to other forms of travel. For a typical Monday morning business trip, emission reductions compared with air travel range from 77 percent for a trip between Frankfurt and Basel, Switzerland, to 96 percent for a trip from Paris to Marseille. (See Figure 2.)

The carbon dioxide emission reductions from high-speed rail can add up quickly. Spain's national railway estimates that the Madrid-Barcelona high-speed rail line averted a quarter-million metric tons of carbon dioxide in its first year of operation, the equivalent of taking more than 45,000 of today's American cars off the road.

High-speed rail also curbs emissions of air pollutants that contribute to the formation of smog and cause human health problems. Factoring in emissions from generation of the electricity used to power the trains, the high-speed train

Figure 2

Carbon Dioxide Emissions of Trains, Cars, and Aircraft Traveling Between European Cities

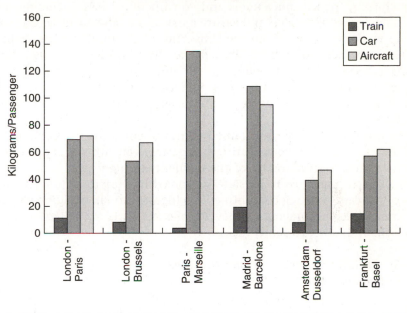

between Frankfurt and Basel emits approximately 18.1 times less particulate matter per passenger than automobiles and 6.5 times less particulate matter per passenger than aircraft. France's high-speed TGV between Paris and Marseille emits approximately 46.2 times fewer nitrogen oxides per passenger than automobiles and 31.9 fewer nitrogen oxides per passenger than aircraft. . . .

High-Speed Rail Boosts the Economy

The arrival of high-speed rail alters the economic geography of a region. Places that had once been difficult to reach—due to distance, congestion or lack of an efficient transportation link—suddenly become easily accessible. The calculus behind countless individual and business decisions—where to locate, how to travel, when to travel—is changed dramatically. As a result, high-speed rail has broad, and often difficult to quantify, economic impacts.

To begin to understand the impact of high-speed rail on the economy, it is best to start from the center and work outwards, beginning with job creation in construction of the line, then addressing economic growth in areas with stations, and looking finally at the broader economy. . . .

High-speed rail systems require vast amounts of labor to create—from the professional services required to plan, design and finance the system right down to the workers who pour the concrete and lay the rails. Perhaps the biggest source of job creation is in the actual construction of the system.

Rail construction is more labor-intensive than highway construction, meaning that investments in rail can create more jobs than investment in highways. The construction of a high-speed rail line will create thousands of jobs, both in the short and long terms, starting with urban planners, rail engineers and architects, then manufacturers and construction crews (including skilled professionals such as welders and electricians), and finally operators and maintenance workers. A report from the University of California, Irvine, estimates 127,000 permanent jobs will be brought to the Los Angeles-Orange County region by 2035 with the completion of the California high-speed rail project. . . .

In addition to the creation of short-term construction jobs, high-speed rail investments can spark the development of companies to manufacture rail cars and other equipment. . . .

In the United States, a sustained commitment to high-speed rail could energize the nation's manufacturing base. American firms already have the capacity to manufacture many of the elements of high-speed rail cars, with 249 manufacturing firms in 35 states involved in the production of various types of rail cars. A strong commitment to high-speed rail could benefit these industries while encouraging the development of parts of the high-speed rail supply chain the U.S. currently lacks.

High-Speed Rail Creates New Opportunities for Development Near Stations

High-speed rail stations bring with them the potential for economic development, serving as an attractive location for stores and offices and increasing land values in the near vicinity. The success of development near high-speed rail stations, however, depends on where the stations are located and the quality of planning for station-area development. A high-speed rail line built in a lightly traveled corridor, or with stations far away from existing centers of development, for example, is going to have less of an economic impact than a well-designed line with busy, accessible stations in the midst of bustling, economically vibrant cities.

High-speed rail can create new opportunities for economic growth, while also shifting development that would have happened elsewhere toward areas near high-speed rail stations, particularly city centers. The United States would clearly benefit from more intensive development in many center-city areas. In cities that have experienced dramatic growth in recent years, high-speed rail stations can focus development in ways that reduce sprawl and the costs of farther flung infrastructure. Meanwhile, in cities, especially older industrial cities, where center-city populations have declined dramatically but suburban populations have continued to increase, high-speed rail infrastructure can provide a critical shot in the arm to encourage renewed investment in downtown areas and reverse patterns of sprawl.

Extensive study of the experience with high-speed rail in Europe and Japan leads to several conclusions: First, high-speed rail can act as a powerful magnet, drawing economic activity toward areas with access to the high-speed rail network—generally helping to focus development in city centers rather than in exurban areas. Second, well-planned high-speed rail stations can serve as a major catalyst for economic growth in an area. Finally, high-speed rail can contribute to a vibrant tourism economy.

Japan   With Japan's massive rail ridership, development opportunities around Shinkansen stations have abounded. Studies have shown that population growth and employment in several industries increased faster in cities with high-speed rail stations than in those without. Property values near high-speed rail stations increased by 67 percent. Many high-speed rail stations have become city centers, with intensive mixed-use development and strong connections to local transit networks.

High-speed rail stations have proven to be such drivers of economic activity that the railroads themselves have sought to get in the act by intensively developing their rail stations. Central Japan Railway has built a complex with two 50-story high-rises above Tokyo's Nagoya Station, including a 780-room hotel, department store, offices and Japan's largest indoor garden. The Tokyo example shows that the revenues brought in by development of high-speed rail station areas can be an important part of the business model for making high-speed rail an economically self-sustaining enterprise.

France   France has had mixed experience with generating economic development near high-speed rail stations, depending chiefly on whether it invested the necessary funds to bring high-speed rail into city centers or placed stations far from city centers to save money. Some of these more remote stations, known colloquially as "beet field" stations, because they were built in agricultural areas, have failed to draw significant numbers of travelers or spark significant economic development.

In other locations, the arrival of high-speed rail service has sparked dramatic development near rail stations:

- The city of Lille along the France-Belgium border used its location at a junction of high-speed rail lines linking London, Brussels and Paris as a basis for economic revitalization. The Lille-Europe high-speed rail station is at the core of a multi-use development including a shopping mall, residences, office buildings and entertainment venues. Office rents in the station area are higher than in other parts of the city, and its location along the high-speed rail line has led to an increase in tourist visits to the city.
- Lyon, which was connected with Paris via the first TGV line in 1981, has experienced dramatic growth around its TGV station, which was newly built specifically for high-speed rail. By 1990, the area surrounding Lyon Part Dieu station was attracting 60 percent of new development projects in the city. The amount of office space in the area increased by 43 percent. Currently, the area surrounding Part Dieu station hosts 5.3 million square feet of office space, 1,000 hotel rooms and 20,000 jobs.
- Cities with more recent access to high-speed rail have experienced similar development. Office space near high-speed rail stations in cities such as Le Mans, Nantes and Vendome attracts a 20 percent rent

premium compared to areas farther away. In Le Mans, the new high-speed rail station was integrated into a business center development that now hosts 80 companies and 2,500 jobs.

- Strasbourg will soon be at the center of a high-speed rail connection linking France to Germany and Eastern Europe, and the city is looking to capitalize on its position by redeveloping several areas of the city, planning to add at least 6,000 housing units as well as commercial development. . . .

High-Speed Rail, Transit and Land Use

The United States faces important decisions about the future growth of its cities. It can continue to encourage sprawling forms of development that take up vast amounts of open space and commit residents to dependence on the automobile for most daily trips. Or it can encourage compact communities where most travel can be done on foot or by public transportation, reducing the nation's dependence on oil and its contribution to global warming.

High-speed rail, in and of itself, cannot change land-use patterns in the United States. In fact, high-speed rail is better understood as putting an exclamation point on whatever vision of future development that is promoted by local, state or federal government. As one study of development around French TGV stations put it: "The TGV accelerates or amplifies what are already favorable or unfavorable factors. It does not create them from nothing."

If the United States opts to pursue a future of automobile dependence and sprawl, it can design high-speed rail systems that accelerate that vision—locating stations in undeveloped areas, with access only by automobile, and surrounding those stations with low-density bedroom neighborhoods. (Even then, high-speed rail would be a better alternative than expanding highways, which generate sprawl along their entire length, rather than only at stations located many miles apart.)

But, high-speed rail can also be used to accelerate more sustainable forms of development, creating vibrant new centers of activity and commerce, and anchoring well-planned new neighborhoods that include a walkable mix of residential and commercial uses that are well-connected to the rest of the region via public transportation.

The question of how to integrate high-speed rail into the transportation and land-use vision of a region has been important everywhere that high-speed rail lines have been built. The competitive success of high-speed rail depends on the easy accessibility of high-speed rail stations via both automobile and transit. And high-speed rail's value as an economic development tool depends on stations being well integrated into the fabric of their cities. As the United States builds its high-speed rail systems, it is important that it does so in ways that promote sustainability and facilitate mobility in its cities. . . .

High-Speed Rail, Commuting and Land Use

One concern about high-speed rail in parts of the United States is that it could contribute to further suburban sprawl, which consumes vast amounts of land and leads to increased automobile use and oil consumption. In the worst-case scenario, high-speed rail stations would be located in undeveloped areas, accessed primarily by car, and surrounded by low-density development.

In some ways, the experience abroad is reassuring. While there are some examples (see below) of outlying cities becoming "commuter towns" for major metropolitan areas, there is little evidence that high-speed rail has contributed to sprawl.

In addition, high-speed rail has some characteristics that make it less likely to produce sprawl than alternative transportation options such as freeways. First, unlike freeways, which have multiple exits, often spaced a few miles apart, there will be very few access points for each of the nation's high-speed rail networks. While there are 38 exits along Interstate 4 between Orlando International Airport and Tampa, for instance, there are only five proposed stations on the high-speed rail line between the two cities. As a result, any new development sparked by high-speed rail is likely to be more concentrated than that created by new freeway construction. Second, depending on the pricing policy followed, commuting via high-speed rail could be expensive, and therefore out of the reach of many would-be commuters.

Indeed, to the extent that high-speed rail attracts *existing* long-distance commuters, it may actually help to address some of the problems associated with sprawl. According to the U.S. Census Bureau, 3.4 million workers now travel more than an hour-and-a-half to work and back, a 95 percent jump since 1990. There are many long-distance commuters, particularly those traveling between cities and their bedroom communities—sometimes more than 100 miles away—who could potentially switch to high-speed rail for at least part of their journeys. Evidence from around the world suggests that high-speed rail can facilitate commuting, but that commuters make up a small share of high-speed rail travelers. It will be vital for land-use planners to ensure that the arrival of new high-speed rail service in the United States is accompanied by land-use policies that ensure sustainable development in communities with new stations.

South Korea and Japan   South Korea and Japan have both taken steps to encourage commuters to use high-speed rail via the sale of discounted passes. In South Korea, regular users of commuter passes account for 2.4 percent of total ridership on the KTX system, but for some sections of the line, the share of commuters is as high as 37 percent.

In Japan, an estimated 47,000 business people and students commute using the Shinkansen high-speed rail. While commuters make up less than 10 percent of the ridership on the Shinkansen system, the number of commuters has increased steadily over time, and the railway has added double-decker cars to accommodate demand during rush hours.

France and Spain   In France, the existence of the TGV has led to an increase in the number of people commuting from formerly distant provincial cities and towns to the capital, Paris. In some cases, as with the cities of Le Mans and Tours, which are about an hour away from Paris by TGV, the overall number of commuters has not changed, but the nature of commuting has: whereas business commuters once would travel to Paris on Monday morning and return home on Friday, these commuters are now able to travel back and forth to their jobs daily.

In Spain, high-speed rail has led to the growth of towns such as Ciudad Real, which was brought to within an hour of Madrid by the new rail line, and which has experienced both business growth and an increase in the number of people commuting from the city to Madrid. Formerly a relatively isolated town in an area of 200,000 people, Ciudad Real now serves as many high-speed rail passengers as the city of Cordoba, which is five times larger. Ciudad Real has experienced a population increase of 15 percent over the course of the past decade, with an average of 1,000 new homes built in the city each year. Commuters between Ciudad Real and Madrid make up one in four travelers between the two cities, while reverse commuters from Madrid to Ciudad Real now make up one in five passengers in that direction.

Great Britain   In England, the construction of the high-speed rail link between London and the Channel Tunnel will open up new opportunities for rapid travel between the towns of southeastern England and the capital city. Because the new high-speed rail line will accommodate both international traffic and local commuter service, the potential for development near outlying stations is great.

Local and regional governments have anticipated the arrival of high-speed rail by developing detailed plans to focus growth around new rail stations, and to do so in ways that promote environmental sustainability. For example, the principles for new development near Ebbsfleet station—which is eventually expected to create 10,000 new homes and business development with 20,000 new jobs—include an emphasis on redevelopment of previously used land, expansion of public transportation, provision of open space and community facilities, and compact, mixed-use development patterns that "offer the opportunity to live and work within close proximity, reducing travel and improving quality of life."

Creation of high-speed rail service in the United States could lead more Americans to embrace long-distance commuting, bringing new development pressures to bear on more remote, exurban areas. High-speed rail network planners should work to ensure that proper plans are in place to ensure balanced, sustainable development of cities with high-speed rail stations, rather than the creation of new, low-density residential suburbs.

Conclusion and Recommendations

The experiences of nations around the world show that the United States has much to gain from investing in high-speed rail, but also that the impact of high-speed rail depends upon the many decisions that will be made in upcoming months and years regarding the pace of high-speed rail development, the location of routes and stations, the construction of local transit networks, policies to guide development around those stations, and many other issues. . . .

Robert Poole

 **NO**

Questions Legislators Should Ask About High-Speed Rail: Testimony to the National Conference of State Legislators

My name is Robert Poole, and I'm the Director of Transportation Policy at the Reason Foundation, a nonprofit public policy think tank. After receiving two engineering degrees from MIT, I've spent nearly three decades studying both air and ground transportation and have advised a number of state DOTs as well as the Federal Highway Administration, the Federal Transit Administration, and the Federal Aviation Administration. Although Reason's policy work focuses on the United States, we draw on transportation research and experience from all developed countries, and I have participated in a number of international conferences on these subjects.

To summarize my perspective on U.S. high speed rail proposals, it's not clear to me what problem or problems high-speed rail is intended to solve. Before a state embarks on what is likely to be a very costly project, I believe it is incumbent on state legislators and other officials to first figure out what the high-speed rail project is supposed to accomplish. After that, the critically important next step is to assess whether there are ways of accomplishing those objectives that involve lower cost and risk to the state's taxpayers.

What Is High-Speed Rail Supposed to Accomplish?

As I read the various reports from public agencies and speeches by high-speed rail advocates, four rationales seem to predominate. They are as follows:

- To reduce greenhouse gases (GHGs) due to inter-city passenger travel;
- To reduce the oil dependency of the U.S. economy;
- To catch up with Europe and Japan;
- To give Americans more travel choices.

Let's look briefly at each of these.

Greenhouse Gas Reduction

Some of the most detailed work on the greenhouse gas (GHG) impacts of various air and surface transportation modes has been carried out recently by Mikhail Chester and Arpad Horvath at UC Berkeley. Their 2009 paper demonstrated that accurate assessment of the GHG impact of transportation modes must include life-cycle GHG emissions, not just those from vehicle operations. For air transportation, a life-cycle analysis adds 31% to the carbon footprint, while for road-based modes, the addition is 63%. But for rail modes, the addition is 155%. That dramatically affects the carbon footprint comparisons among modes, to the detriment of high-speed rail (HSR).

In a 2010 paper, Chester and Horvath apply their assessment methodology to the proposed California HSR project, comparing it with conventional rail, automobile, and airline travel north-south in California. Their assessment makes it clear that load factor (the percentage of seats occupied) makes a major difference to the carbon footprint. We have pretty good data on non-commuter auto occupancy and airline load factors, but HSR load factor is a major unknown. For the scenario with the average inter-city auto trip having 2.25 occupants, airlines having today's 85% load factor, and HSR achieving 50% load factor, it would take 71 years for HSR to achieve GHG "break-even"-i.e., for its GHG savings to offset the GHGs released by its construction. . . .

Reducing Oil Dependence

In most of the world, HSR denotes trains operating at speeds in excess of 150 mph. Such speeds require considerably more energy than conventional passenger rail, to overcome frictional air drag. They also require broader curves and shallower grades and, for safety reasons, complete physical separation from intersecting roadways. Thus, true HSR requires dedicated rights of way and complete grade separation. True HSR is everywhere powered by electricity, almost always via an overhead catenary system. To the extent that such HSR projects shift travelers from petroleum-based modes (auto, bus, conventional rail, airline), they will reduce petroleum use to some extent. Yet even major investments in true HSR are unlikely to produce large mode shifts in the United States. In Europe, where conditions are generally more favorable for HSR than in the United States, the average citizen uses HSR for only a very small fraction of trips.

More important for the question of oil dependence, the large majority of U.S. projects proposed under the rubric of "HSR" are more accurately termed "higher-speed rail." Of the 10 projects selected for federal funding in January 2010, eight are for diesel-powered service on existing Amtrak and freight rail corridors; only the California and Florida projects are for electrically powered HSR on exclusive right of way. Only a few of the diesel projects will produce speeds in excess of 79 mph. In a major report on HSR in 2009, the GAO included a table of all current U.S. "HSR" proposals. Of the 44 projects, 35 would be diesel-powered.

Intercity rail currently handles 0.1 percent of all passenger travel in the United States, compared with 5.8% in Europe. If very large-scale investment in HSR increased the U.S. share ten-fold, it would still account for only one percent of U.S. passenger travel. The current energy intensity of diesel-powered intercity rail is about 2700 BTUs per passenger mile, while current airliners average just over 3000 and the auto fleet averages about 3400. By 2035, diesel-powered trains will be about the same, but cars are projected to average 2500 BTUs per passenger mile, while airliners will likely be close to 2700.

Thus, in terms of what is actually being proposed as HSR in the United States, the potential for reducing petroleum dependence is very small. Rail is unlikely to shift a large fraction of inter-city trips from driving and flying, and most of the rail projects will be diesel-powered in any case.

Catching Up with Europe and Japan

Many HSR proponents argue that misguided public policy has kept the United States from enjoying the benefits of this mode of travel and that this country is in some sense "backward" by not having a national HSR network. Yet this sentiment ignores some important differences between the United States and countries where true HSR has captured the largest fraction of intercity travel-such as Japan, France, Spain, Italy, and Germany. As the Congressional Research Service has pointed out, "[C]ompared with the United States, countries with HSR have higher population densities, smaller land areas, lower per capita levels of car ownership, higher gas prices, lower levels of car use (measured by both number of trips per day and average distance per trip), and higher levels of public transportation availability and use."

For example, gasoline is taxed at eight to ten times US levels in most of Europe and Japan, and most of the intercity highway networks are toll roads. Hence, the cost of intercity car travel is much higher in those countries than here. Similarly, domestic air service in Japan has never been deregulated, and such deregulation is only a recent phenomenon in Europe. Hence, air fares are also relatively higher there than here. In short, the two modes from which HSR proponents expect most HSR passengers to come-driving and flying-cost considerably less in the United States than in HSR countries.

Another factor that differs is that European countries and Japan are not only higher in density and extent of urbanization than the United States. Their urban areas are also far more centralized. In 21st century America, the "central business district" is no longer the location of the majority of jobs in the metro area, even for New York City. The suburbanization of jobs has taken place over the last 60 years, leading to "edge cities" and later to "edgeless cities." The far more centralized metro areas of Europe and Japan are more viable as origins and destinations for HSR services, since a much larger fraction of desired trips originate or terminate in a downtown area. Moreover, those centralized downtowns are relatively easier to serve via mass transit. In the United States, the suburban locations of most airports may be easier for the majority of inter-city travelers to get to than a downtown HSR station.

With all the inherent advantages for HSR in Europe (compared with the United States), one might expect that HSR would be a major factor in inter-city travel there. Yet between 1980 and 2000-a time period that saw the introduction of HSR in France, Germany, and other countries-the mode share of inter-city rail in Europe declined from 8.2% to 6.3%. Belated airline deregulation thanks to the EU's "open skies" policy led the share of inter-city travel by air to increase from 2.5% in 1980 to 5.8% in 2000. More recently, air has climbed to 8.0% while rail has declined further to 5.8%.

Tomorrow's Cars on Tomorrow's Highways

In making transportation policy, the relevant comparison is not with historical conditions or even today's. Rather, when considering whether to make investments of tens or hundreds of billions of dollars in long-lived infrastructure, we need to consider conditions decades from now, when that infrastructure would be in service.

Most HSR corridors being planned today would not likely be in operation until a decade or more, and will then operate for 30 years or more with their initial motive power. By contrast, the motor vehicle fleet is turning over continually, with complete replacement approximately every 20 years. Hence, better technology in propulsion will be an important background factor during whatever planning period we consider-and certainly over the next three decades. The new federal fuel-efficiency (CAFÉ) standards recently finalized by the federal government require the average new vehicle in 2016 to achieve 35.5 mpg. The EPA projects that this will lead to a 21% reduction in GHG emissions from cars by 2030, as the vehicle fleet turns over. Assuming future improvements in fuel economy continue at that rate, by 2035-2040 personal motor vehicles are likely to have a lower carbon footprint than inter-city rail.

What about congestion? To be sure, traffic congestion is a major U.S. problem, but it is mostly a problem in urban areas, and mostly during weekday peak travel periods. HSR serves inter-city, not urban travel markets, so is not really relevant to urban traffic congestion (except to the extent that, operating at slower speeds, it can add to the existing commuter rail capacity on one or two corridors in large urban areas). . . .

Short-Haul Airline Service

In Europe and Japan, HSR has captured significant mode share from airlines on a small number of routes, including Tokyo-Osaka, London-Paris, Paris-Lyon, and Madrid-Barcelona. In these high-density corridors of 200 to 400 miles between centralized metro areas, HSR can be competitive with air travel, especially if the capital costs are not covered by the HSR fares. Amtrak's popular Acela service in the Northeast Corridor has captured significant share from airline shuttles, but Acela fares likewise have to cover only operating and maintenance costs, unlike the full cost recovery included in airline fares.

HSR advocates argue that airport and airway congestion makes it problematical to increase short-haul airline service in coming decades. Yet that claim has not been substantiated. Several factors suggest that the airline/airport/air traffic control system can adapt so as to accommodate continued growth in short-haul demand. . . .

Short-haul air service in California provides an important contrast with the proposed HSR system. Currently, north-south service is offered between every combination of four northern (San Francisco, San Jose, Oakland, and Sacramento) and six southern (Los Angeles, Burbank, Long Beach, Orange County, Ontario, and San Diego) airports. All those hundreds of daily flights are nonstop. The HSR system will also serve all of those points, and dozens in between. Only a relatively small number of HSR trips will be nonstop, however, with most of those leaving from "downtown" rail stations. Given the decentralized land-use patterns in California, for most north-south travelers a non-downtown airport location will be more convenient to their actual origin and/or destination than a downtown railroad station. . . .

The Cost and Risk to States

. . . The risks involved in HSR are formidable. A 2008 "due diligence" assessment of the proposed California HSR project raised serious questions about its projected capital costs, ridership, load factor, operating profits, and GHG impact. A 2010 assessment by the California Legislative Analyst's Office confirmed most of these findings, concluding that the revised HSR plan was "on the fast track to fiscal failure," as summarized by the California Taxpayers Association. Although the revised business plan increased the projected capital cost and reduced projected ridership, the agency still claims the system will cover its operating and maintenance cost from the farebox, thanks to doubling the projected fares compared to its 2008 figures. . . .

The initial $13 billion committed by the Administration ($8 billion in ARRA funds plus $1 billion per year for five years) would cover only a small fraction of the estimated cost of those initial projects. The feds committed only $2.3 billion to the California project, while the HSR Authority's current estimate of capital costs for the 520-mile Phase 1 (of the 800-mile project) is now $42.6 billion. Between the $9 billion available from the HSR bond issue and the federal grant, the state is "only" $31.3 billion short. Florida likewise faces a nominal shortfall of $1.35 billion ($2.6 billion official cost minus $1.25 billion federal grant), but if the cost ends up being close to GAO's $51 billion per mile average, the real cost could be $4.3 billion-meaning the state will need to find $3 billion just to build the 84-mile system. And if ridership ends up significantly lower than projected, there will need to be operating subsidies, as well.

State budgets are in poor shape to take on such new obligations. It is not just the current recession, though that is forcing unprecedented budget cuts in most states. More important is that states, like the federal government, are on an unsustainable fiscal path, due to unfunded liabilities for health-care programs and employee pensions. To take on huge new funding commitments this year, or this decade, strikes me as not being responsible fiscal management.

Given the near-certainty that 100% of the capital costs of HSR must come from general taxpayers, and the risk that many of these projects, if built, will require ongoing operating subsidies, state legislators and other officials must think through where the funds to support those expenditures could come from. And in doing so, they must weigh the projected benefits of HSR against those costs.

Economists make use of a concept called "opportunity cost." In simple terms, it means that the real cost of doing something is what you have to give up to do that something. In the severely constrained fiscal environment in which state governments will find themselves over the next several decades, the opportunity cost of shifting billions of dollars in general tax monies to HSR means those same billions will not be available for other public purposes-such as properly funding public pension systems, schools, highways, etc.

Given the very modest benefits of HSR, in terms of GHG reduction, energy savings, and added choices for a small fraction of travelers, it seems like a poor use of many billions of dollars in state tax money.

EXPLORING THE ISSUE

Should the United States Invest in High-Speed Intercity Rail?

Critical Thinking and Reflection

1. What do you think are the key differences between a good high-speed rail system and a wasteful high-speed system?
2. How do you expect that an HSR system in the United States would differ from the HSR systems found in France and other European nations?
3. Is it better to locate high-speed stations in the center of major cities or in peripheral communities on the edge of a metropolis?
4. Will HSR bring sufficient economic and environmental gains that justify the systems' huge costs?
5. Do you think that the governors of Wisconsin, Ohio, and Florida acted correctly when they turned down federal funds that would have supported the construction of an HSR system in their states?

Is There Common Ground?

Construction of a high-speed rail system is extremely expensive. Critics claim that the benefits do not justify the costs. But even the advocates of HSR should recognize that the United States cannot afford to build an entire national high-speed system all at once. That recognition should offer a possible basis for compromise, with construction proceeding only on those routes where state and local leaders see the value of an HSR system and where states are willing to make the necessary financial commitments that such a state-of-the-art rail system requires. The advocates of HSR may also come to see the wisdom of taking steps to mitigate the opposition to HSR, for instance, by using existing rail lines and rights of way in more populous areas. Such steps will serve to minimize costs and displacement, muting objections to construction. Such compromises may mean that HSR trains cannot always run at peak speeds; but without these compromises, few HSR trains may ever run at all.

The State of California has already sought to heed some of these cautions, seeking to mute opposition by running its first HSR line through the state's less populous Central Valley. In the flat terrain of the Central Valley trains will be able to reach and maintain a speed of 220 mph. Suburban Palmdale and Antelope Valley appear to offer a politically supportive constituency for the system's southern terminal, these are communities that see advantages in enhanced connectivity and that want the new development and job creation that HSR can be expected to bring. Critics, of course, have not been fully modified by such compromises. Opponents object to the huge state expense of building a "train to nowhere." They further argue that a line serving Fresno and Bakersfield will not generate a large number of riders and will require continuing operating subsidies. Still, completion of the Central Valley leg can demonstrate the potential of high-speed trains and allow voters to judge if they are willing to fund the extension of the system, north to the Bay Area and south to Los Angeles.

It may also be politically prudent to have the first generation of high-speed rail lines end at suburban stations rather than continuing on into the center of a region's primary city. Where necessary, system advocates should also consider the advantages of building along existing rights. Such politically sensitive strategies seek to minimize displacement and the costs of land acquisition and construction, costs that would soar if HSR lines were extended through more densely built-up areas.

Additional Resources
Internet References

American Public Transportation Association, Center for High-Speed Rail

American Public Transportation Association (APTA), an international organization of industry leaders and professionals in the transit field, expresses its commitment to improving the quality, accessibility, and safety of public transportation. APTA seeks to provide guidance as the national government and the states pursue high-speed rail.

www.highspeedrailonline.com

Californians for High-Speed Rail

A grassroots organization that seeks to make high-speed rail "a reality" in the Golden State. It supports the construction of HSR stations in city centers as well as the development of feeder transportation systems.

www.ca4hsr.org

Legislative Analyst's Office (LAO), State of California: 2011 report *High-Speed Rail Is at a Critical Juncture*

This report, issued by a state legislative bureau known for its professionalism, advised major changes in the construction of HSR in California, changing the overall vision of HSR, reducing the commitment of the state to building such an extensive HSR system in a time of fiscal troubles.

www.lao.ca.gov/reports/2011/trns/high_speed_rail/high_speed_rail_051011 .pdf

Midwest High-Speed Rail Association

The Midwest High-Speed Rail Association believes that high-speed rail can transform the ailing economy of America's Midwest.

www.midwesthsr.org

The Railist: High-Speed Rail News, a Project of Planetizen

A site where planners and other urban experts provide commentary on decisions and studies related to high-speed rail.

www.therailist.com

Reason Foundation

An organization critical of big-government projects and unnecessary public spending, the Reason Foundation points to the overly optimistic assumptions embedded in many of the advocacy studies that favor HSR. In particular, see the writings of Wendell Cox, Robert Poole, Samuel Staley, and Joseph Vranich.

www.reason.org

U.S. Conference of Mayors. 2010 Report on *The Economic Impacts of High-Speed Rail on Cities and Their Metropolitan Areas*

Written for an organization that represents big and medium-sized cities, this report claims that HSR can be the key to integrated regional economies, generating billions of dollars each year in new economic activity and creating more than 100,000 new jobs. HSR will help cities to grow as the hubs of national economic growth.

www.usmayors.org/highspeedrail

U.S. High-Speed Rail Association

An industry-based advocate of state-of-the-art high-speed rail, the USHSRA envisions a 17,000-mile dedicated-tracksystem with trains running at speeds up to 220 mph.

www.ushsra.com

UNIT 4

Debating Policies for Suburban and Regional Growth and Sustainability

*T*hroughout the nation's history, urban development in the United States has taken place under a under a sets of prevailing attitudes that historian Sam Bass Warner in The Private City labeled "privatism." Americans are an antigovernment people who resist strong urban planning requirements and land-use regulation as violations of their individual freedom and property rights. In the privatist United States, business investors and the market mechanism of supply-and-demand are dominant factors that determine the shape of urban growth. As we shall explore further in Issue 15, cities in the United States, unlike Europe, do not adopt strong policies to guide urban development and to promote mass transit, bicycling, and sustainable growth.

But are Americans well served by the resulting patterns produced by market-led growth? Certainly, freedom has enabled entrepreneurship and economic growth. But, in the United States, private-led development has also led to extensive urban sprawl, where housing and commercial development spills over a wide region. Over the last half century, Americans have gained a better understanding of the seriousness of environmental problems and the need for government action to put a halt to environmental degradation. Environmentalists bitterly attack urban sprawl for its encroachment on wetlands and agricultural acreage, its intensive energy consumption, and the air and water pollution that sprawled development generates. To visitors from abroad, the United States often seems like a wasteful throw-away society, where older communities with their existing infrastructure are cast aside in favor of new development built on the rim of the metropolis.

This unit looks at the debate over urban sprawl and the smart growth and compact city alternatives. Yet, although many Americans see great merit in governmental policies that seek to protect the environment by curbing the continued outward progression of urban areas, critics charge such action violates property rights and intrude on the individual liberty of Americans to seek homes and communities to their liking. Critics on the Left as well as the Right worry about the possible negative impacts that growth management can have on housing affordability. Housing advocates also worry that well-to-do suburbanites have been able to use the rhetoric of environmentalism as a cover story to *justify actions that are intended to maintain the exclusive character of their communities, reducing entry by less privileged newcomers.*

In the United States, a new school of thought, New Urbanism, has revolutionized how planners and architects view development. The New Urbanists seek to build more eco-friendly and livable communities, communities that encourage walking and encourage the interaction of neighbors. Critics, however, question whether New Urbanism, much like Smart Growth, will actually build the sorts of communities that the vast majority of Americans prefer.

- Is Urban Sprawl a Sufficiently Important Problem to Merit Government Corrective Action?
- Do Portland-Style Smart Growth Policies Raise Housing Prices and Hurt Urban Livability?
- Are Environmentalists Too Often the Unwitting Allies of Suburban Exclusionists?
- Does New Urbanism Represent a Viable Strategy that Can Transform Suburban Communities?

ISSUE 14

Is Urban Sprawl a Sufficiently Important Problem to Merit Government Corrective Action?

YES: **James M. McElfish, Jr.,** from *Ten Things Wrong With Sprawl* (Environmental Law Institute, 2007)

NO: **Robert Bruegmann**, from *Sprawl: A Compact History* (Chicago: University of Chicago Press, 2005, pp. 1–3 and 5–13)

Learning Outcomes

After reading this issue, you should be able to:

- Define "sprawl."
- Identify the various problems often attributed to urban sprawl.
- Identify policies that can be enacted to control or limit sprawl.
- Explain the arguments that can be made in defense of urban sprawl.

ISSUE SUMMARY

YES: James M. McElfish, Jr., senior attorney and director of the Sustainable Use of Land Program at the Environmental Law Institute, reviews the numerous environmental, health, social, and economic problems that result from sprawled development.

NO: Robert Bruegmann is professor of art history at the University of Illinois at Chicago where he also holds appointments in the School of Architecture and the Program in Urban Planning and Policy. In this excerpt from his controversial book *Sprawl: A Compact History,* Bruegmann argues that critics often exaggerate the problems that result from sprawl. He views sprawl as progress and the inevitable result of the free choice of citizens who see considerable advantages in residing in lower density settlements located at some distance from congested urban centers.

Urban sprawl entails the spread of population and economic activities over a metropolitan area. Urban sprawl denotes low-density development. The opposite of sprawl is the *compact city,* with much greater densities of population and economic activities. Sprawl is *not* just another word for suburbanization or the growth of population and economic activities outside the boundaries of a central city. Rather, sprawl entails a form of suburbanization that covers a fairly wide expanse of land, with large-lot single-family homes, shopping malls and business centers with large paved parking lots, and new multilane highways and access ramps exhausting land that previously provided valuable farm acreage, wildlife habitats, and recreational space.

When development is sprawled, relatively few people live on each acre of land. Residential sprawl in the United States is typified by large suburban homes with sizable back yards and side yards. Compact residential development, by contrast, emphasizes apartment buildings, condominiums, townhouses, and homes built on small property lots—all of which require less acreage to house a population, leaving more land for green space.

Urban sprawl in the United States is *not* uniformly low rise. Contemporary patterns of sprawl include pockets of relatively dense development that serve to support the further geographic spread of residences and economic activity in a region. Sprawl has its *edge cities,* concentrations of office towers, research parks, shopping gallerias, cinema multiplexes, and college campuses built near the intersection of major highways. Valley Forge and King of Prussia (outside of Philadelphia), Monroeville (Pittsburgh), Towson (Baltimore), Bloomington (around the Mall of America south of Minneapolis), La Jolla (San Diego), Bellevue (Seattle), Tempe/Scottsdale (Phoenix), North Atlanta, North Dallas, and the Houston Galleria—are only a few of the more prominent edge cities in the United States, giving modern sprawl a degree of diversity and dynamism that was largely absent from the string of bedroom communities that dominate the less sprawling development of suburbia of the 1950s and 1960s.

Yet, too great a focus on the rise of edge cities only serves to blind the urban observer to the sprawling decentralization that continues to take place. The office space of edge cities is surpassed by that of *edgeless development* of unglamorous strip malls and clusters of offices along secondary roads and off the exits near highway interchanges. As seen in central New Jersey, edgeless office-strip development can spill over hundreds of square miles, eating up valuable green space, wetlands, and agricultural acreage.

New residential development also continues to occur in far-off *exurban areas,* where farmers sell prime agricultural land to residential developers who build new upscale residential *gated communities* (where visitors must pass through a gatehouse before entering a development). In Wisconsin, new subdivisions on the edge of the greater Milwaukee area have driven up land prices, leading farmers to sell prime agricultural acreage to developers who build new residential complexes and shopping malls. In northern Virginia, cropland is similarly lost as farmers sell acreage to developers who build large-lot, low-density housing. Across the United States, communities of *McMansions* (super-large houses that are only a bit smaller than a typical mansion) have sprouted up on land that was once devoted to agriculture.

Sprawl compounds problems of air and water pollution. Extensive automobile travel increases tailpipe emissions, degrading air quality and increasing the generation of greenhouse gases that contribute to global warming. The runoff of oils, chemicals, and salt from the impervious roadways and parking surfaces of suburbia adds to the contamination of groundwater and nearby lakes and streams.

Sprawled residential development is also energy inefficient. High-density apartment buildings and town houses have dwelling units that share walls, lessening the need for summer air conditioning and winter heating. In contrast, the single-family homes of sprawled America are energy intensive; exposed to the environment on all sides, they radiate away heat in winter and require more extensive cooling in summer.

Urban sprawl is also associated with numerous public health problems. Tailpipe emissions can compound heart disease and chronic pulmonary and respiratory conditions such as emphysema, bronchitis, and asthma. Even more important, as we discussed in Issue 12, automobile emissions appear to be a factor in up to 3000 deaths annually in the United States.

Critics charge that sprawled residential patterns also contribute to obesity, with Americans living a sedentary lifestyle and traveling by car rather than by foot or by bicycle. Minneapolis is one of the rare U.S. exceptions, a metropolitan area where strong planning has limited outward growth and allowed the development of an elaborate network of bicycle and exercise trails.

Sprawl is also economically wasteful as it entails the expense of building duplicative facilities—roads, sewers, and physical plant—when such facilities already exist elsewhere in a region. The taxpayers in a region wind up footing the bill for the construction of unnecessary and duplicative facilities. Salt Lake City, Utah, provides just one illustration of the huge monetary waste incurred as a result of sprawl. Envision Utah argues that the Salt Lake City region can save $4.5 billion in just 20 years by taking the necessary steps to promote compact development, averting the huge expenditures for highways, water, sewers, and utilities that sprawled growth would require.

A number of social problems are also magnified by sprawl. As we discussed in Issue 9 in the debate of concentrated poverty, sprawled development helps to produce a *spatial mismatch* where new jobs in remote suburban locations are inaccessible to the inner-city poor. Sprawl also exacerbates problems of class and racial segregation, where outlying communities are able to use their land-use and zoning powers to limit new apartment and townhouse development, locking the poor and the working class in the central city in the region's older declining suburbs. Sprawled development has weakened many of the nation's *first suburbs,* the inner-ring communities just over the border from the central city. With new development moving to the outer edges of the metropolis, older suburbs are beginning to experience weakened housing markets, factory closures, boarded-up stores in neighborhood shopping districts, and a decline in the tax base necessary to support quality schools and other public services. The result of sprawled development is the continued separation of resources from need, where older cities and suburbs wind up with populations in need of assistance but cannot tap the resources that can be found in the burgeoning communities on the metropolitan rim. Sprawled development also poses an obstacle to school segregation, with whites able to flee schools undergoing integration simply by moving to new homes on the metropolitan rim.

Robert McElfish, Jr., of the Environmental Law Institute, explores the many problems that are often attributed to sprawl (in the YES selection). McElfish, like other critics of sprawl, have called for government to change its policies in order to adopt Smart Growth and other policies capable of curbing new sprawled development (which we review further in the debate in Issue 15).

Yet, a number of political conservatives have challenged the consensus position that views sprawl as a serious problem that requires more extensive governmental intervention and regulation. These defenders of property rights and individual freedom argue that critics overstate the infrastructure costs and the ecological and health consequences of sprawl. The impact of sprawl on individual health, for instance, is not easily established, and the evidence is not as overwhelmingly clear as sprawl's critics assert. Why, they argue, blame sprawl for obesity, when so many other factors contribute to that health problem?

Sam Staley (1999) observes that more compact patterns of development will not lead to the improvements in air quality that the antisprawl crowd envisions: the great majority of commuters will continue to travel by car as mass transit systems have only a sharply limited capacity to absorb new ridership. Sprawled development also does not threaten the nation's food supply or even pose much of a threat to green lands and forests, which are largely located outside of urban areas. Staley and others question whether Smart Growth planning strategies are really required, especially as sharp declines in nitrous oxide and smog levels have been achieved in recent years without enacting new government policies intended to reshape the growth patterns of metropolitan areas.

Robert Bruegmann further disputes the sprawl-is-a-problem consensus. Bruegmann argues that most assessments of sprawl are highly one-sided; they are essentially advocacy briefs that overplay the ills of sprawl without pointing to the important benefits that come with sprawl. In Sprawl: *A Compact History* (a portion of which is reprinted in the NO selection), Bruegmann argues that sprawl enables working- and middle-class families to escape from crowded cities and to realize a standard of living—with single-family homes and private backyards—that they greatly enjoy. Bruegmann sees sprawl as concomitant with increased prosperity and progress. He rejects the campaign against sprawl as culturally elitist and misconceived. In sharp contrast to McElfish, Bruegmann disapproves of Smart Growth policies that will diminish individual choice and create living arrangements that most Americans just do not like. For Bruegmann, sprawled development—with the comforts and privacy of big homes and the convenience of the automobile—is the democratic choice of people in a free society.

McElfish, in turn, responds that sprawl "enthusiasts" such as Bruegmann severely "downplay" the real and quite severe costs of sprawl. "Free choice" may give individual owners the homes they prefer. But such choice also leads to externalities and serious social problems, including the loss of prime farm acreage and diminished air and water quality.

YES    James M. McElfish, Jr.

Ten Things Wrong With Sprawl

In just the next thirty-four years, the Census Bureau tells us, we 300 million Americans will be joined by another 92 million. Where will all these people—mostly us and our direct descendants—live, work, play, worship, buy, sell, and serve? Where will 40 million additional households be located? What sort of built environment will we produce, and what will be the results for the nation's and the environment's well-being?

The prevailing form of land development is popularly known as sprawl or exurban sprawl. Sprawl is characterized by low density development that rigorously separates residential uses from other land uses, and that relies entirely or almost entirely on automobile transportation to connect the separate uses. There are strong reasons to prefer that the nation's future development does not reproduce this pattern—reasons that have nothing to do with the price or availability of gasoline.

Urban planning professor Jonathan Barnett, in his book *The Fractured Metropolis,* charges sprawl with overconsumption of resources, risks to the natural environment, and loss of community resulting from the time demands imposed by the physical separation of commercial, business, residential, and social land uses. Economic critics of sprawl emphasize the high costs of duplicated infrastructure, the cost of time devoted to delays in commuting, and the distortions resulting from the mismatch between initial economic benefits of construction in sprawl areas and the costs of meeting subsequent demands for services (schools, roads, fire and police) by these same areas. On environmental grounds, opponents of sprawl decry the rising amount of land conversion per each unit of new development (more acres per person), the paving over of some of the nation's highest quality farmland, and losses of biological diversity and open space.

Sprawl enthusiasts counter that people are getting what they want in low density housing and ubiquitous shopping, that a rising population will need more housing on cheap land, and that commute times, while rising, are not that bad for most people. They emphasize the number of construction jobs created and the higher assessed land value of developed lands over agricultural and forest lands. Sprawl enthusiasts downplay the agricultural land issue by suggesting that America still has large areas of land suitable or at least potentially suitable for agriculture (there is no "food

From *Ten Things Wrong With Sprawl* by James M. McElfish (Environmental Law Institute, 2007). Copyright © 2007 by Environmental Law Institute. Reprinted by permission.

shortage"), while further noting that the direct contribution of agriculture to the nation's gross domestic product is modest in comparison with other economic sectors.

Many of these arguments talk past one another. For example, well-paying construction jobs need not depend upon future construction in sprawl patterns rather than in alternative forms of development. Ninety-two million more people will need somewhere to live and work and go to school, after all. Likewise, the arguments over agricultural lands are not really about whether food will run out, or even whether commercial retail buildings generate more net economic value than crop lands (a hotly disputed topic, by the way), but rather whether the location of agriculture, forests, retail and housing matters. Arguments about traffic and travel times often gloss over whether alternative development patterns and transportation options can deliver comparable flexibility with fewer side effects.

Whatever one thinks of these arguments and their critique of past practices and the current built landscape, at least when considered prospectively, sprawl has ten undeniably adverse effects that should place it on the public policy agenda.

1. Sprawl Development Contributes to a Loss of Support for Public Facilities and Public Amenities

In economic terms, sprawl encourages market failure; residents of sprawl communities have access to public facilities that they do not support with their tax dollars, and residents of older communities subsidize the existence of the these facilities.

Sprawl communities typically lack parks, museums, civic spaces, libraries, and the like. This frequently occurs either because some of these amenities are privatized and made available only to a small segment (owners of large lots have less need for public open space), or because sprawl dwellers can be "free riders" on urban facilities supported in substantial part by others. Pittsburgh city officials have noted, for example, that their city's land base includes substantial tax exempt properties—museums, universities, parks, hospitals, libraries, zoos—far in excess of those in suburban jurisdictions whose citizens can enjoy city facilities while also benefitting from lower suburban tax rates. In many communities, property taxes in the exurbs are lower than those in the cities because of this mismatch.

In most metropolitan areas, piecemeal construction of new subdivisions does not include community centers and public facilities. The nearest thing to civic spaces in sprawl communities are the stone gates flanking the entrance sign. And when there are common spaces, they are often restricted to the members of homeowners' associations. There are weak or nonexistent social and financial ties to the support of regional facilities of general public benefit, such as public hospitals and parks.

2. Sprawl Undermines Effective Maintenance of Existing Infrastructure

Existing developed areas—cities and older suburbs—have sewers, water systems, city streets, bridges, schools, transit systems and other hard infrastructure to maintain. But exurban development draws population away from areas with existing infrastructure and into new areas where new infrastructure must be constructed or where some infrastructure costs are avoided, at least temporarily, through the use of wells and septic systems, or by reliance on undersized roads that are upgraded at great public expense long after the developments have been constructed. The frequent result is a shift of population regionally, leading to a decline in the urban and older suburban tax base. This decline in turn prompts increases in urban taxes and rates (needed to support the existing infrastructure across a smaller population), and/or to deferral of maintenance activities. Both of these effects further disadvantage the existing systems and encourage further exodus. John Fregonese, the Region 2040 lead planner for Portland's Metro government makes this point, "When you have sprawl, all your resources are sucked to the edge for new roads, and schools and sewers. Then you have a lack of money for rebuilding . . . and you get these rotting cores."

3. Sprawl Increases Societal Costs for Transportation

Costs rise largely because of the need for expensive retrofits. Typical scenarios include the conversion, after sprawl has occurred, of exurban two lane roads to four lanes or six lanes, adding signals, construction of grade separations for intersections, and building county or intercounty connector highways and metropolitan belt roads. This invariably occurs at great expense and disruption—because of increased right-of-way costs, difficulties in maintaining traffic flow during the construction period, and often substantial community opposition.

This retrofit dilemma is a spin-off of the problem of traffic. People hate traffic—in fact, part of the reason for sprawl is the elusive promise that commuters and commercial offices can outrun traffic by continually expanding into lower traffic areas. And, at least initially, average commute times are generally lower *within* sprawl areas than commutes *from* sprawl areas to the center city. But traffic is, in general, extremely bad in sprawling metropolitan areas—often worse on weekends when travel is more diffuse and timing strategies intended to avoid peak travel times do not work. Catch-up transportation expenditures have to be made.

Unfortunately, often they can't be made. For example, consider the sprawl area north of Chicago. Like many suburban papers, the local newspaper in Lake County, Illinois, has a daily "roads" column. A fairly typical letter printed in the column bemoaned the daily backups at the intersection of a heavily traveled two-lane road with a four-lane highway. The Illinois DOT spokesman contacted by the paper responded that the intersection complained of had been completely upgraded and re-engineered only a few years earlier. It had already been overtaken by increased traffic flow. The spokesman commented that there was no remaining engineering or right-of-way expansion solution on this road, so the only thing that IDOT could do would be new re-construction projects on parallel routes. The retrofit problem is a perennial feature of sprawl, as any sprawl dweller can personally attest, and its costs are high.

4. Sprawl Consumes More Resources Than Other Development Patterns

Because homes, offices, utilities, and other features are farther apart (requiring more asphalt, more lengths of pipe, more conduits, more wires), because each commercial and institutional structure requires its own acres of parking, and because much of the utility infrastructure is duplicative of the "stranded" infrastructure in nearby older communities—society's overall consumption of metal, concrete, asphalt, and energy is higher.

5. Sprawl Separates Urban Poor People from Jobs

Ownership of an automobile and the resources to maintain it are essential for work in the suburbs, the site of most new jobs in the modern economy. However, the prevailing sprawl model of development drastically separates different price levels of housing from one another, as well as separating job areas from residential areas. These characteristics of sprawl mean that locating new affordable homes near jobs is quite difficult, and sprawl consequently reduces the availability of jobs for those in urban areas that lack reliable automobile transportation. Overcoming sprawl patterns could result in either increasing the number of workplaces in urban areas, or making it easier to construct and maintain the availability of affordable housing near workplaces.

6. Sprawl Imposes a Tax on Time

Sprawl development requires that we spend more time on the road. Exurbia, including most post-war suburbia, rigorously separates residential housing, food stores, other retail establishments, warehouse and transfer facilities, industry, schools, and office buildings. This has adverse effects on neighborhoods, and leads to more automobile travel. In exurban areas, commercial establishments can be accessed only when people drive to each location. Non-work automobile trips now comprise more than 80 percent of all daily trips. Residents of sprawl areas do not forego the benefits of mixed uses of land, but they pay a price in time, and they lack choice in their mode of travel. Describing Tyson's Corner outside Washington, D.C., where offices and commercial buildings are completely separate from any residential housing and all access is via main arterial roads, a Washington Post writer noted that "a six-mile commute home can stretch to 90 minutes." Sprawl also makes it take much longer for the one-third of Americans who reside in central cities and inner ring suburbs to get to greenfields areas for recreation and enjoyment. Sprawl, in effect, imposes a hidden tax on time by making certain amenities more remote and harder to reach.

7. Sprawl Degrades Water and Air Quality

Sprawl development is hard on streams, wetlands, and runoff quality. It reduces the resilience of streams and other waters by degrading headwaters and impoverishing habitat. For example, in the Chesapeake Bay region, sprawl is the largest threat to water quality. It increases the area of impervious surface, decreases retention time for rainwater and diminishes its infiltration into the soil and water table, and it leads to rapid erosion and structural degradation of streams and rivers, which therefore receive runoff in much greater volumes in a shorter period of time. It also increases the frequency and intensity of flooding, placing further demands on the public treasury for preventive structures and disaster response. In metropolitan areas, air pollution can be worse over a much larger area. Vehicle miles traveled as well as time sitting in traffic rises significantly in these mega-sprawl areas; for example, motorists in the Atlanta area log about 100 million miles per day with 2.5 million registered vehicles. Another effect related to sprawl development patterns is the loss of a constituency that can be served by transit or other means. Residents' inability to substitute other modes for the automobile, including walking and transit, is an undeniable drag on every area's ability to meet clean air goals.

8. Sprawl Results in the Permanent Alteration or Destruction of Habitats

Sprawl development converts large areas to asphalt, concrete, and structures, altering the landscape hydrology and reducing the biological productivity and habitat value of the land. While any conversion of open lands to developed uses can impair the prior environmental values and there will always be trade-offs to accommodate human needs, sprawl development does so at a high rate of land conversion per unit of development.

A related problem is the loss of productive farmland near metropolitan areas. This feature of sprawl development has been documented in persuasive detail by the American Farmland Trust through repeated studies under the rubric of *Farming on the Edge*. Farmland contributes at least incidentally to wildlife habitat and potential for future restoration. Although there is, at least in the near term, no threat to the nation's total food production given the amount of remaining farmland, as well as farmland currently fallowed under federal conservation and price stabilization programs, the loss of prime farmland is not desirable from the point of view of long term uses.

Conversion of land near urban areas also presents an environmental loss in the sense that dense urbanization places stresses on habitat and aquatic systems that can best be offset by the beneficial effects of retaining larger tracts of nearby vegetated open space in the same watershed and habitat areas. Without this open space (farms, forests), metropolitan areas and their adverse environmental effects are unbuffered.

9. Sprawl Creates Difficulty in Maintaining Community

People do have communities in their suburban neighborhoods, workplaces, and in their organized activities. Modern day exurbs are not the places of alienation described by some "new urbanist" writers, many of whom draw upon affection for the older urban neighborhoods of the early and mid-20th century. But these new sprawl communities require more driving, and more complicated arrangements to maintain social connections. This also means that children are at the mercy of scheduled activities and "play dates" rather than neighborhood interactions, and exercise becomes an isolated activity on the schedule, rather than a natural consequence of walking, biking, or using public park facilities. These demands exact a social toll. Planner William Fulton recently described the effect of sprawl in the greater Los Angeles area as "a constant caravan between the residential cocoon, where citizenship is exercised only in narrow, self-interested ways, and the spending and working cocoons, where citizenship is totally surrendered to the commercial forces that run the place."

10. Sprawl Offers the Promise of Choice While Delivering More of the Same

In America, choice is not only a cherished value, it is also something that our market economy claims as its highest achievement. But, paradoxically, we have lost choice in our system of development. Sprawl constrains our choices. If you want a new house, you can have one on a half acre in the suburbs with no retail around. If you want to locate a store or an office, the arterial strip or highway interchange is for you. If you want transportation, you can use your car. If you are poor you can live in substandard housing in the inner city or manufactured housing on the farthest fringes of the metropolitan area. This lack of choice is why every part of exurban America resembles every other part.

Portions of the building industry sometimes say that our *current* development patterns perfectly reflect the satisfaction of American social demands. Whatever we have, whatever we are creating, it must be what we want, or the market would provide something else. However, this position requires us to deny the influence of laws, institutions, zoning codes, financing rules, government subsidies and market failures. Much of the sprawl we see is the unintended result of laws and policies that were imperfectly aimed at something else, such as easing transportation delays, encouraging school modernization, providing healthy settings for housing, or stimulating home ownership.

We will only be able to address these mismatches of law and policy, and to root out perverse unintended consequences, if we recognize that something is amiss with our current patterns of development.

Some things really are wrong with sprawl. *"We need to find a better word,"* said a builder representative to a program on smart growth in which I participated a few years ago. Well, that's one approach. But a better approach is recognizing that we have real problems ahead if current development patterns continue to prevail. Only such recognition will enable us to take steps to reform the laws and policies that hold us back—and enable us to find places and provide choices for our 92 million new neighbors.

Sprawl: A Compact History

When the plane banks sharply to the left about an hour and a half into the flight from Chicago, I know that we are starting our long descent into New York's LaGuardia airport. Looking down, I can see long, wooded ridges running diagonally from the southwest to the northeast, alternating with wide stream valleys between them. This part of western New Jersey is beautiful from the air. In summer the deep green of the oaks and maples on the ridge tops forms a striking contrast with the lighter greens that make up the patchwork quilt of fields in the valleys. At first glance, this landscape of cropland; farmhouses, roads, and streams seems timeless, little changed over the centuries.

Of course, the landscape is not natural but almost entirely manmade, and it was created relatively recently, mostly within the past one hundred years. Even from 15,000 feet, moreover, it is clear, if you look carefully, that a great deal has changed very recently. There are many more houses in the valleys than the small number of people who still farm there could possibly occupy; and it is possible to make out through the dense tree cover of the hillsides many other houses that clearly have no connection with agricultural production. This is not at all the completely rural scene that it might appear to be. All the evidence suggests that most of the people living here have little to do with farming or any other traditional rural activities.

It is difficult, at least at first glance, to imagine what all the people living in these houses do, where they work, shop, and play since there are no office buildings, shopping centers, or movie theaters in sight. It is possible that some of them work from their home, relying heavily on the phone, Internet, and express delivery services to keep them connected to the urban world, and it is possible that others drive to jobs in small towns nearby. The substantial number of houses, however, suggests that the majority must commute some distance to work, perhaps to nearby corporate facilities tucked discreetly into the rolling hills or, further afield, to large business centers along highways like the Route 1 strip near Princeton. Others probably make their way daily into downtown Trenton or Center City Philadelphia, twenty and forty miles to the southwest, respectively, or into downtown New Brunswick, Newark, or even Manhattan, thirty, forty and sixty miles, respectively, to the northeast. In virtually every case, however, no matter how rural the view from the living room window, these residents are more closely tied economically and socially to the urban world than they are to the apparently rural one they can see out their windows.

Indeed, the connection to the urban world is confirmed visually from the plane window within a few minutes, as the first subdivisions come into view, first one, then dozens of them, each neatly filling the land once occupied by a single farm or small group of farms. Then a freeway edges into sight, then an office park, then more subdivisions until the urban uses are dominant and are interrupted only occasionally by a patch of green—an agricultural hold-out, a golf course, or a public park. As the urban rhythm quickens, this landscape soon fills the horizon, a vast crazy quilt of nearly continuous suburbia, with subdivisions, shopping centers, and industrial parks crisscrossed by roads and railroads and dotted with parks and open spaces.

Sprawl! By almost anyone's definition this part of central New Jersey would qualify as sprawl. Once an arcane term used primarily by city planners and academics, "sprawl" has recently emerged as a part of everyday speech. Most often described as unplanned, scattered, low-density, automobile-dependent development at the urban periphery, sprawl now shares space on the covers of national news magazines with perennial "big" issues like health care and race relations, and it has become a prominent issue on talk shows and campaign trails. From every direction, Americans are bombarded by the message of anti-sprawl reformers. They are told that sprawl threatens to destroy open space, consume agricultural land, drive up utility costs, undermine urban social life, heighten inequalities, deplete natural resources, and damage the environment. And, by the way, it is ugly.

The sprawl of central New Jersey, according to these critics, represents an expensive and unsustainable pattern of development. The widely dispersed nature of this development makes everyone dependent on the automobile, which in turn, uses excessive amounts of energy, creates pollution, and contributes to global warming. Moreover, anti-sprawl activists claim, the sprawl being built today will inevitably harm the older communities that are outflanked by it.

They hold the landscape I have just described responsible for the deterioration of many of the older neighborhoods that come into view as the plane continues eastward across New Jersey, northward across Staten Island, and then across western Brooklyn and Queens into LaGuardia. Large numbers of once flourishing shops along the commercial streets of Bayonne and Jersey City disappeared when new suburban shopping centers appeared further out, they will say. In many of the tightly packed neighborhoods of Brooklyn and Queens, house prices stagnated or fell as affluent middle-class residents left for newer and more spacious houses further out in Long Island. In some cases the result was racial turmoil, abandonment, and the concentration of poor and minority residents in the oldest, least desirable housing.

According to its critics, sprawl hurts everyone and must be stopped. Instead of the unplanned, wasteful patterns visible at the edge of the New York region, they advocate new, carefully planned "smart growth," including denser urban infill and, where green-field construction is necessary, more compact "sustainable" communities, less dependent on automobiles, and more in tune with traditional urban patterns. Many of these critics hail anti-sprawl efforts underway in states like Oregon and Maryland or in communities like Boulder, Colorado.

Most of what has been written about sprawl to date has been devoted to complaints. The usual questions asked are exactly how damaging sprawl is and what are the most appropriate ways to stop it. What I decided to do instead, in this book, was to look at this issue from a historic perspective and to examine the way the concept of sprawl was invented and how it has been used over time. After all, sprawl, like "urban blight," the "slum," or many other terms connected with urban development, is not so much an objective reality as a cultural concept, a term born at a specific time and place and used over the years by a wide range of individuals and groups for specific purposes. In the process, it has accumulated around it an entire body of ideas and assumptions. . . .

Many of the things that critics of sprawl appear to agree on, moreover, are based on out-of-date or insufficient evidence. Despite a common belief that suburban sprawl is accelerating and that the most affluent people are moving constantly outward to areas of ever-lower density, in fact the suburbs of American cities are, if anything, becoming denser. Suburban lot sizes, after peaking in the 1950s, have been declining, and the number of square feet of land used by the average house in new development at the suburban edge has fallen sharply in the past ten years even as the houses themselves have grown in size. A surprising amount of the new housing at the very edge of most American cities consists of row housing and garden apartments for working-class Americans. This phenomenon is quite visible form the plane flying over the suburban edge in New Jersey but is even more conspicuous on the ground at the edge of the fastest growing cities of the American South and West, which are the very ones that have usually been described as the most sprawling.

The notion that Phoenix and Las Vegas and Los Angeles are among the country's most sprawling places is also problematic at best. Los Angeles, for example, often taken to be the epitome of sprawl, has become so much denser over the past fifty years that it is now America's most densely populated urbanized area, as measured by the census bureau. It is considerably denser than the New York or Chicago urbanized areas, for example. Although this might seem preposterous since Los Angeles has no neighborhoods with densities anything like parts of Manhattan, Los Angeles has a relatively high density spread over an extremely large area. Los Angeles also has none of the very low-density exurban peripheral growth seen in the New York region. In fact, quite unlike Eastern cities, Los Angeles has almost no exurban sprawl at all because the high cost of supplying water makes relatively compact development almost inevitable.

Turning from suburban sprawl to exurban sprawl, the picture is quite different. Exurban sprawl is apparently in the process of accelerating, with more people occupying more land at lower densities, but we know very little about exurban sprawl. It is also difficult to know what part of exurban development should be called sprawl at all. Certainly a group of four houses in central New Jersey sitting on two-acre lots behind long driveways and carefully mowed front lawns would be sprawl by most people's definition. But what about the houses visible from the airplane window over New Jersey that clearly aren't new but, instead, old farmhouses taken over by urban residents who no longer farm the land? Would this still be sprawl? And, finally, what about the houses on very large acreage, nestled into the trees in such a way that that they are all but invisible from the air or surrounding roads? Would it make any sense to use the term for this area, which might well serve as an important wildlife sanctuary?

I used to think it ironic that my interest in sprawl started as a by-product of research on central Paris. In more recent years, I have come to realize that this is actually quite a characteristic progression whenever individuals try to make sense of anything as complicated as cities and urban systems. In my case, during the period I was working on my dissertation and flying back and forth from Paris, I was forcefully struck by the tiny size of my object of study, the historical core of Paris, compared to the vast suburban and exurban areas that surrounded it. How different was this little island of tall, tightly packed apartment blocks from the large expanses of low-density housing, industrial parks, open spaces and superhighways that made up most of the rest of the urban region. Much of the recent development at the edge of the Parisian metropolitan area, in fact, looked remarkably similar to the landscape I saw from the plane window touching down at Cincinnati or Philadelphia.

After finishing my dissertation and moving to Chicago in the late 1970s, my interest in these outer urban landscapes grew, fueled by a desire to understand the vast changes I saw happening on my frequent trips out to the suburbs. Although I had been familiar with American cities and their suburbs all my life, I realized that neither my previous experience nor the existing literature was of much help in describing, let alone explaining, the vast transformations that were taking place all around me. In the Chicago area in the mid-1980s, for example, thousands of acres of agricultural countryside as far as sixty miles from the Loop, Chicago's central business district, in a great arc from Kenosha County, Wisconsin, to Lake County, Indiana, were being converted to subdivisions and industrial parks. Glossy office buildings were creating a kind of linear Main Street along the Interstate 88 tollway corridor near Naperville and Aurora, some twenty to thirty miles west of the Loop. The enormous Woodfield business district in Schaumburg, twenty-five miles northwest of the center of Chicago, already the second most important business district in the state, was starting to obtain a high-rise skyline that visitors flying into O'Hare could easily mistake for that of Chicago's Loop.

Much of what I saw contradicted the usual stereotypes about cities and suburbs. In the supposedly homogeneous suburbs, a Buddhist temple rose in a cornfield outside Aurora and a Japanese shopping center opened in northwest suburban Arlington Heights. The closing of a regional shopping mall in Harvey signaled economic woes and racial change across large areas of the south suburbs. These changes were not confined to the suburbs, moreover. The same big-box retail establishments and row houses visible in far suburban Gurnee or Tinley Park, forty or fifty miles from Chicago were sprouting in my own neighborhood, originally a German working-class community but now in the process of rapid gentrification. As an older working-class population left the area in the wake of the departure of manufacturing firms, they were replaced by new residents driving Volvos with license plate frames advertising suburban automobile dealerships. As an increasingly affluent population moved in, densities plummeted and automobile usage soared. Increasingly, althought my neighborhood looked like a traditional city neighborhood—in fact more traditional by the year as the newcomers razed small frame houses with asphalt shingles and aluminum siding and replaced them with great stone-fronted houses that appeared older and certainly much grander—it started to function in ways that made it similar to any suburb, and it gradually obtained a comparable demographic profile. In short, little of what I saw happening around me was compatible with the usual stereotypes about city and suburb. How to make sense of the whole thing?

I went to the library to see if history books, guidebooks, sociological studies, or geographic analyses could help me understand these landscapes. I found that while there were endless publications that dealt with American city centers, there was little of any substance on the suburbs and almost nothing on the much more dispersed regions beyond that. Much of the literature seemed to be a continuation of a tradition popular in the 1960s and 1970s of urban intellectuals bashing the "burbs" and then others rushing to their defense. True, by the end of the 1980s a more substantial literature had started to appear on the early history of suburban development. A few substantial articles on exurbia had appeared as well.

However, this remained a rather thin literature, given the fact that more American and Europeans live in the suburbs and exurbs than in either the central city or the countryside. And when most scholars approached the present, they tended to fall back on old stereotypes. Starting in the early 1990s, I noticed that the focus on the suburbs was starting to switch to a focus on sprawl in the works of many authors. Despite the shift in terminology, the ideas were very similar. Most of the sprawl diagnoses were still based on assumptions codified in the late 1960s when American suburbs were booming and city centers seemed to be in grave danger of collapsing. The "inner city" was portrayed as poor and filled with minorities. The suburbs were described as being white and affluent. Whatever validity these generalizations might have had in the late 1960s—and even then they were far from adequate—they were completely inadequate to describe metropolitan areas by the 1990s. Areas like the South Bronx, emptied out during the postwar decades, had started to fill up again. Many of the city centers were roaring back. Densities were rising in subdivisions at the urban periphery, many of which were being swelled by working class and minority families. A considerable number of the most troubled areas of metropolitan America were located in the suburbs, often the far suburbs.

As far as I could see, the sprawl crusade had generated a great deal of heat but not much light and was primarily of interest to a small group of academics. Then, to my surprise, in the mid-1990s, after I had done considerable work on a book on the decentralization of the American city, the anti-sprawl crusade suddenly caught fire. Articles appeared in the airline magazines, and sprawl reached the cover of the news weeklies. Virtually overnight the anti-sprawl reformers' new catchphrase "smart growth" seemed to be every-where. It appeared as though every right-minded individual and organiza-tion in the country was convinced that sprawl was economically inefficient, environmentally detrimental, socially deplorable, and aesthetically ugly—in short, an unmitigated disaster. In fact, so many "right-minded" people were so vociferous on the subject that I began to suspect that there must be something suspicious about the argument itself. Hence, I decided to shift my focus and concentrate on the construction of the concept of sprawl and the assumptions that have motivated the campaigns to combat it.

In this book, I have looked at sprawl and public policy devoted to it primarily through the lens of history. I do this in part because I was trained as a historian. I also do it because I believe that all policy analyses are based, consciously or not, on assumptions drawn from history, jut as all history is based on assumptions drawn from an observation of present circumstances. I have tried to look seriously at sprawl as a cultural issue. Although objective issues—the cost of low-density settlements or the effect of sprawl on commut-ing times or global warming—are clearly important, these are not, I believe, what has really driven and continues to drive the anti-sprawl crusade. What is actually at stake are much larger questions about planning and democracy, aesthetics and meta-physics, and differing class-based assumptions about what makes good urban life. . . .

A great deal of my research has consisted of going out and looking around. During the past fifteen years, whether I was in Chicago or Singapore, Paris or São Paolo, I rented a car and drove from the center out to the periph-ery to see what was there. Or I would make sure that I had a window seat and a daytime flight so I could see and photograph the urban built environment from the air as the plane took off or landed. I will be the first to admit that my method of research by looking has been far from comprehensive, and the result will probably seem haphazard to many readers, but I hope that it at least provides a different perspective from which to look at urban history and the questions that swirl around the term "sprawl."

In part 1 of this book I offer a compact history of decentralization and sprawl. Using the most commonly accepted and objective characteristics attributed to sprawl—that it involves low-density, scattered development with little overarching regional land-use planning—I try to show that sprawl is neither a recent phenomenon nor peculiarly American, as many reform-ers argue. It is, instead, merely the latest chapter in a story as old as cities themselves and just as apparent in imperial Rome, the Paris of Louis XIV, or London between the world wars as it is in today's Atlanta or Las Vegas or, for that matter, contemporary Paris or Rome. I try to show that our understand-ing of urban development is woefully out of date because it is based on old and obsolete assumptions about cities, suburbs, and rural areas. In fact, I argue that many of the problems that are usually blamed on sprawl—traffic congestion, for example—are, if anything, the result of the slowing of sprawl and increasing density in urban areas.

I further argue that sprawl cannot be adequately explained as a simple result of specific government policies, economic systems, or technological advances. Notions that sprawl was caused by the widespread use of the automobile, or by American tax policies, or by anti-urban attitudes, or by racism are clearly inadequate. In fact, sprawl predates the automobile and has happened in a way that is basically similar in cities with large minority populations and in cities with hardly any minority residents. It has also been visible in affluent cities worldwide, even those with policies very different from those in the United States. It is perhaps not inevitable, but it does seem to have been a logical and perhaps even predictable result of increasing wealth and the democratization of society. In this process, many more citizens have obtained the ability to exercise the choices that once were the sole prerogative of the wealthy and powerful.

Part 2 examines the three major campaigns against sprawl. . . . I attempt to show that although sprawl obviously causes considerable problems of all kinds, the same could be said of any kind of settlement pattern, and the evidence that the objective problems caused by sprawl are nearly as serious as many reformers would have us believe is weak. Moreover, a close examination of the anti-sprawl literature strongly suggests that although the case against it has been framed as an objective assessment of the problems it causes—for example, the increased cost of sewers for houses at low density or the amount of pollution generated by longer commuting distances—in fact, the driving force behind the complaints at any period seems to have been set of class-based aesthetic and metaphysical assumptions, almost always present but rarely discussed.

Part 3 outlines the history of remedies proposed to stop sprawl and how they have worked out in practice. In this part of the book I show that the solutions proposed in each of the campaigns have been similar even though conditions have changed dramatically. In practice, as often as not, these remedies have been ineffective and in some cases have led to unintended consequences arguably worse than the initial problem. Whether in London immediately after World War II or in Portland, Oregon, in the past several decades, the results of anti-sprawl policies have demonstrably not stopped the outward spread of people and jobs, and they may well have aggravated the very things, for example, highway congestion, that they were supposed to alleviate. I suggest that this is not surprising. In very complex systems, any intervention in one part of the system is likely to cause changes, often unintended, throughout the entire mechanism. In addition, anti-sprawl policies have tended to be highly inequitable. Although they are often beneficial for an "incumbents' club"—families who already have many of the urban amenities they want and who benefit from the rise in land prices that have accompanied anti-sprawl regulations—these same policies can place a heavy burden on exactly that part of the population least able to protect itself. . . .

Because the vast majority of what has been written about sprawl dwells at great length on the problems of sprawl and the benefits of stopping it, I am stressing instead the other side of the coin, that is to say the benefits of sprawl and the problems caused by reform efforts. Although I have tried to be accurate in presenting the story of how cities have sprawled and how reformers have tried to stop this sprawl, one of my goals here has been to redress to some extent the balance of opinion. My hope is to reach individuals who are concerned with urban issues, worried about the massive growth that they see around them, and willing to suspend judgment long enough to look without prejudice at some of the evidence actually visible on the ground.

Above all, I hope this book can inspire some respect for the urban landscape that we urban dwellers, whether residents of the central city, the suburbs, or the exurbs, have created. . . .

Although different in the specific forms it has taken, this process of rapid dispersal has been visible in virtually every major city on the globe—from Boston to Bangkok and from Buenos Aires to Berlin—where incomes have risen and there has been an active real estate market. It has undoubtedly created problems for many citizens as fast change always does. But, on the whole, it appears to have been beneficial to most urban dwellers. It is hard for us to imagine today the existence, in the industrial cities of one hundred years ago, of millions of urban dwellers who were obliged to endure cramped and unsanitary tenements, traffic, and pollution-choked streets and deadly factories. Today, by comparison, most residents of affluent metropolitan areas live in relatively low-density suburbs, areas that are much cleaner, greener, and safer than the neighborhoods their great-grandparents inhabited. They also have a great deal more affluence, privacy, mobility, and choice. At very least, it seems to me, our highly dispersed urban regions deserve some respectful attention before we jump to the conclusion that they are terrible places that need to be totally transformed.

EXPLORING THE ISSUE

Is Urban Sprawl a Sufficiently Important Problem to Merit Government Corrective Action?

Critical Thinking and Reflection

1. Do you think that the health and environmental consequences of sprawl are serious and real? Or do the critics of sprawl exaggerate such consequences?
2. What policies would you propose to limit the threat that sprawled development poses to a region's central city and "first suburbs"?
3. As Bruegmann notes, free choice leads to sprawl. How do you weigh the tradeoff between "free choice" and "environmental protection"? Which is more important?
4. If sprawled development poses an obstacle to school integration, just what steps would you be willing to take in an effort to increase the racial integration of a region's public schools?

Is There Common Ground?

The United States is a suburban nation. A home in the suburbs remains the American dream. Plans that seek to limit suburban home building and development are likely to face considerable opposition.

Is there possible common ground between development enthusiasts and sprawl critics? At the very least, steps can be taken to protect more valuable farm land and fragile ecological areas from development, even without imposing more general restrictions on the outward growth of urban areas. States can give favorable tax provisions to farmers who voluntarily participate in farmland protection programs and who continue to actively work the land. Alternatively, land-use measures may prohibit new residential construction on land zoned exclusively for agriculture. A policy of refusing to extend sewer and water lines to farm lands can similarly act to slow the loss of agricultural acreage. States and private associations can also purchase the development rights of land when landowners are willing to sell, thereby helping to ensure that important tracts of land are kept free of new development. Some states also allow taxpayers to voluntarily check off a box on their tax returns, contributing to a state fund that can be used for land acquisition and the preservation of farmland and green space.

As Myron Orfield (1997, 1998) has argued, a coalition of constituencies who are victimized by sprawl can seek actions to ensure that "favored quarter" communities in a region will no longer find it in their interest to push new rim development. Central cities, suburbs, farmers, environmentalists, and even the residents of overburdened working-class suburbs will benefit from policies that stress infill development as an alternative to having the state and counties continue to pay the infrastructure costs for sprawled growth.

Voluntariness may provide a key to political acceptability. Programs that embrace incentives for wise land stewardship should prove less controversial than regulatory approaches that seek to bar new suburban and exurban home building and development. Maryland's Smart Growth program seeks to incentivize home construction in already-developed areas as an alternative to continued sprawl, an approach that reduces the public's cost of building new infrastructure. The program respects local autonomy, as grassroots actors (not state officials) make the final decision of whether or not to allow a new growth program. Yet, as we shall see in the debate over Issue 15, environmentalists and central-city defenders argue that such an incentive-based approach is not always strong enough to offset the powerful political and economic forces that continue to promote sprawl.

The New Urbanism (the subject of the debate in Issue 17) can also be seen as a voluntary alternative to sprawl. The New Urbanism seeks to build communities that offer more dense, walkable, transit-oriented, community-oriented living environments than is typically found on the edges of the sprawling metropolis. New Urbanism offers an improved and more dynamic suburban aesthetic, at least for those who want it. But, as we shall also see, most residents are quite happy with their lives in more conventional suburban communities and will not seek to move to a New Urban alternative.

Finally, and maybe most significantly, new attention is being given to eliminating (or at least modifying) the single most import government policy that serves to promote sprawled development: the federal *Mortgage Interest Deduction* (MID) given to homeowners. Liberals have decried the unfairness of the MID as a "reverse Robin Hood" policy that gives the largest subsidies to the wealthy owners of the largest homes—with much smaller deductions given to working-class homeowners and nothing to renters and the poor. Urbanists scorn the MID for promoting sprawl, as the deduction essentially gives back to a homeowner a large portion of his or her monthly mortgage payments. Both liberals and conservatives have castigated the MID for leading home seekers to buy bigger homes that they could not easily afford, one of the factors that led to the foreclosure crisis that hurt the national economy in the early 2000s. Amid the nation's continuing fiscal problems, budget hawks have proposed to terminate the MID as a means of reducing the federal budget deficit by more than a hundred billion dollars each year! Economists doubt that the incentive really does much to promote new ownerships, as the great bulk of the tax expenditure is awarded to families that would have bought homes even without the deduction. A slash in the MID would not only save money and help balance the budget, it would also remove one of the great incentives for new residential construction on the metropolitan rim.

What is the major obstacle to MID reform? Politicians, of course, are reluctant to tamper with the ever-popular MID, fearful of facing the wrath of aggrieved home owners.

Additional Resources

Benfield, F. Kaid, Matthew D. Raimi, & Donald D.T. Chen. (1999). *Once There Were Greenfields: How Urban Sprawl Is Undermining America's Environment, Economy and Social Fabric*. New York: National Resources Defense Council.

Benfield, F. Kaid, Jutka Terris, & Nancy Vorsanger. (2002). *Solving Sprawl: Models of Smart Growth in Communities across America*. Washington, DC: Island Press.

Burchell, Robert, Anthony Downs, Barbara McCann, & Sahan Mukherj. (2005). *Sprawl Costs: Economic Impacts of Unchecked Development*. Washington, DC: Island Press.

Couch, Chris, Lila Leontidou, & Gerhard Petschel-Held, eds. (2007). *Urban Sprawl in Europe: Landscapes, Land-Use Change, and Policy*. Oxford, England: Blackwell.

Duany, Andres, Elizabeth Plater-Zyberk, & Jeff Speck. (2000). *Suburban Nation: The Rise of Sprawl and the Decline of the American Dream*. New York: North Point Press.

Frumkin, Howard, Lawrence Frank, & Richard Jackson. (2004). *Urban Sprawl and Public Health: Designing, Planning, and Building for Healthy Communities. Washington*, DC: Island Press.

Gillham, Oliver. (2002). *The Limitless City: A Primer on the Urban Sprawl Debate*. Washington, DC: Island Press.

Lang, Robert E. (2003). *Edgeless Cities: Exploring the Elusive Metropolis*. Washington, DC: Brookings Institution Press.

Orfield, Myron. (1997, 1998). *Metropolitics: A Regional Agenda for Community and Stability*. Washington, DC: Brookings Institution Press.

Soule, David C., ed. (2006). *Urban Sprawl: A Comprehensive Reference Guide*. Westport, CT: Greenwood Press.

Staley, Samuel R. (1999). "The Sprawling of America: In Defense of the Dynamic City," The Reason Foundation, Policy Study No. 251. Available at: http://reason.org/news/show/127576.html.

Squires, Gregory D., ed. (2002). *Urban Sprawl: Causes, Consequences and Policy Responses*. Washington, DC: Urban Institute Press.

Internet References

Brookings Institution, First Suburbs

This Washington-based think tank has issued numerous reports on the impacts of urban sprawl, especially how continued outward development has adversely affected the nation's aging inner-ring suburban communities.

www.brookings.edu/topics/first-suburbs.aspx

Envision Utah

A self-proclaimed "neutral facilitator" that seeks to bring Utah citizens and businesses together behind a vision of "quality growth" that will enable the state to meet the needs of its growing population by building healthy and "close-knit" communities while saving taxpayers tens of billions of dollars in public investment that new sprawled development would have otherwise necessitated.

www.envisionutah.org

Planner's Web: Sprawl & Growth

Planner's Web is a very useful online site where professionals in the planning field exchange news clips and their views regarding sprawl and Smart Growth alternatives.

www.plannersweb.com/articles/sprawl-articles.html

Reason Foundation

This conservative policy "think tank" argues that many of the arguments made against sprawl are overstated, that sprawl does not threaten the quality of life of most Americans, and that "Smart Growth" solutions to sprawl are ill-advised.

http://reason.org

Sierra Club: Stopping Sprawl

One of the nation's oldest organizations committed to conservation and environmental protection, the Sierra Club seeks to stop "runaway" urban growth and to find Smart Growth alternatives.

www.sierraclub.org/sprawl

Smart Growth America

Among their other reports, see their 2003 study *Measuring the Health Effects of Sprawl: A National Analysis of Physical Activity, Obesity, and Chronic Disease.*

http://smartgrowthamerica.org

Sprawl Watch Clearinghouse

An online resource center that provides a large variety of articles and reports on sprawl and Smart Growth alternatives.

www.sprawlwatch.org

Sustainable Cities

A communications hub or "portal" devoted to the future development of cities that are ecologically and culturally sustainable.

http://sustainablecities.net

ISSUE 15

Do Portland-Style Smart Growth Policies Raise Housing Prices and Hurt Urban Livability?

YES: Randal O'Toole, from "The Folly of 'Smart Growth'," *Regulation* (Fall 2001)

NO: Michael Lewyn, from "Debunking Cato: Why Portland Works Better Than the Analysis of Its Chief Neo-Liberal Critic," online publication of the Congress for a New Urbanism (2007)

Learning Outcomes

After reading this issue, you should be able to:

- Define "Smart Growth," "infill development," "priority funding areas," and "urban growth boundary" (UGB).
- Differentiate between the Smart Growth approaches of Maryland and Oregon.
- Evaluate the competing claims regarding the impact that an urban growth boundary has on housing prices.

ISSUE SUMMARY

YES: Randal O'Toole, a Cato Institute senior fellow, argues that environmentalists overstate the achievements of Smart Growth policies. O'Toole points to a number of problems that he sees resulting from Smart Growth efforts in Portland, especially increased traffic congestion and the escalation of housing prices.

NO: Michael Lewyn teaches a seminar on sprawl and the law at the Florida Coastal School of Law in Jacksonville. Lewyn contends that Portland's growth management system has succeeded in protecting recreational spaces and agricultural acreage and in reducing automobile reliance. Lewyn also counters the assertion that the UGB is responsible for home price inflation.

About 20 states have adopted *Smart Growth* policies to promote compact and transit-oriented development. Smart Growth seeks to avert sprawl and protect green areas and farm land, by steering development to sites already served by public infrastructure. Smart Growth promotes development on infill sites in older cities and existing suburbs. Smart Growth also promises to save taxpayer money by reducing the need to construct new highways and water and sewer systems; instead, growth management steers development to communities that already have the infrastructure in place to accommodate new growth.

Just how has Smart Growth fared? Has growth management lived up to expectations? Or has the effort to contain growth wound up causing new problems? We will look at Smart Growth programs in key states, observing both the successes and limitations of growth management policies.

Maryland

In the 1990s, the State of Maryland adopted a Smart Growth program in an effort to use the award of state funds to strengthen existing communities and to minimize the natural acreage lost to new development.

The Act requires state agencies in Maryland to emphasize to funding infrastructure and housing improvements in designated priority funding areas (PFAs), that is, communities that already possess the sewers, roads, and other infrastructure to accommodate new growth. Large-lot subdivisions and other developments planned for greenfields and other non-PFA areas, by contrast, do not qualify for priority funding.

The success of Maryland's Smart Growth policy has been most uneven. The Maryland Smart Growth model is essentially an advisory approach that seeks to use the leverage of state funding in an attempt to influence the location of new growth projects. The final say-so on any proposed development, however, largely remains in the hands of the local community. The Smart Growth Act does not contain strong regulations that actually prohibit development outside of the designated priority areas. As a consequence, local communities continue to approve growth projects in nondesignated areas, convinced that a project will add to the local jobs and tax base. In Maryland, developers have won local approval for thousands of new housing units constructed outside of the designated growth areas.

State agencies in Maryland, pursuing their individual missions, have also helped to fund projects in nonpriority communities. The continued consumption of land on the rural fringes of the Baltimore and Washington D.C. areas points to the Act's weaknesses.

Baltimore County, however, has adopted more stringent growth control regulations that go way beyond the state's Smart Growth effort. Predating the state's initiatives, Baltimore County in 1967 enacted an urban growth boundary (UGB), an Urban-Rural Demarcation Line (URDL). Urban development in the County often proceeds up to the demarcation line and then stops, with the land on the other side of the boundary retaining its largely rural character.

Oregon: Portland

In contrast to the Maryland Smart Growth model essentially relies on incentives, the promise of state aid, the State of Oregon has adopted a more direct strong-government approach: the state regulates land uses and requires the establishment of urban growth boundaries around each city. The Portland region's growth boundary has clearly served to minimize sprawl, keeping residential subdivisions from encroaching on farmland and recreational areas in the Willamette Valley. Portland's UGB has also promoted infill development, strengthening the city, its neighborhoods, and more established suburbs in the region.

But the Portland policies, especially its growth boundary, also have negative impacts. The boundary constricts the supply of land in a region that can serve as sites for new construction, a factor that has helped to increase property values in Portland and other communities situated inside the growth boundary. Development interests and free-market conservatives charge that, by restricting supply, the boundary winds up increasing the price of a home in the region by thousands of dollars. Such restrictive growth management practices, according to critics, produce a "new segregation" where the working class, the poor, and racial minorities find it increasingly difficult to access quality housing at a reasonable price (Pozdena, 2002).

UGB supporters, however, reply that the evidence does not support the critics' claims. Environmental activists argue that other factors, especially the growth of high-wage jobs in the Portland region's information-technology firms, bear a much greater responsibility for the region's high housing prices. They note that the rise in housing prices in Portland is not that much different from the rise in housing prices in Denver and Salt Lake City, cities that have experienced similar rates of growth but have no growth boundary (Nelson et al., 2002). Smart Growth advocates also contend that the boundary has not really curtailed housing availability in the region, as a sufficient supply of buildable land exists inside the boundary; the growth boundary only serves to alter the location where new construction occurs. Over the years, the Portland Metro Council has also expanded the boundary to help ensure a continuing supply of land for residential development.

Oregon's leaders have also adopted policies to help ensure that availability of dwelling units within the financial reach of middle- and working-class Americans. State legislation not only prohibits localities from placing a cap on the construction of new homes. State law also mandates increased housing densities and a mix of housing types in local communities. Localities in the Portland region have had to rezone land so that apartments and multifamily homes will constitute half or more of all new housing (Pendall et al., 2004). These policies help to offset the negative impact of any inflationary pressure on home prices resulting from the UGB.

The critics of the UGB are certainly correct in their claim that home buyers in Portland receive "less home" for their money. Builders construct town houses and "skinny houses" that are squeezed onto small infill plots of land with relatively tiny backyards and often with no side yards. Many

Americans dislike the loss of space and privacy that accompanies such dense development.

Beginning in the early 2000s, Oregon's Smart Growth system was subjected to a vigorous attack by property rights advocates who used the voter initiative process in an attempt to weaken state land-use planning. Measure 37 requires the state to pay compensation to owners who can show that land-use controls reduce the value of their property (Walker & Hurley, 2011). Measure 37, though, appears to have had only a modest immediate impact on planning in Oregon, especially as Oregonians later cast their ballots to narrow the scope of the development rights that were protected by Measure 37. Still, Smart Growth advocates fear that future property-rights legislation may further impede the state's ability to venture forth in the field of growth management.

The YES and NO articles continue the debate over the desirability of Smart Growth policies a seen in the Portland region. The authors clash in their assessment of the quality of life in Portland and the impact that the urban growth boundary has had on housing prices.

The author of the YES article, Randal O'Toole of the liberty- and free-market-oriented Cato Institute, is a former resident of Portland as well as an urban observer. He argues that Americans prefer to reside in low-density communities, not in the transit-oriented, compact living arrangements of Smart Growth communities with their relatively small housing units and heightened traffic congestion that too often accompanies increases in residential density. O'Toole views Portland's urban growth boundary as an unwise governmental imposition that distorts housing markets, constricting supply and raising prices.

In the NO article, Michael Lewyn attempts to rebut a number of O'Toole's claims. He reports how strong land-use planning and a willingness to invest in public transit have led to increased patronage of Portland's light rail system. Lewyn further notes that home prices in Portland are not exceptional, that economically prospering cities without growth boundaries have faced a similar escalation in housing prices. Lewyn also points to polling data that reveal that Portlanders view their community as a desirable place in which to live.

YES

Randal O'Toole

The Folly of "Smart Growth"

Throughout the United States, city and state governments are turning to "smart growth" urban planning strategies to slow suburban "sprawl." Spurred by concerns over traffic congestion, air pollution, and loss of open space, the plans are intended to improve urban livability. The strategies include purposeful efforts to increase urban population densities, boost mass transit ridership, and decrease auto driving.

In order to achieve those goals, "smart growth" governments nationwide are implementing a degree of land-use regulation that is unprecedented in the United States prior to 1990. Unfortunately, as we will see from the experiences of the Portland, Ore., area, such regulation can produce an even worse quality of life for residents. The policies' real effects appear to be increases in traffic congestion, air pollution, consumer costs, taxes, and just about every other impediment to urban livability.

Trouble in the Suburbs

In the late nineteenth century, transportation was slow and expensive. As a result, many people chose to live in dense cities so they could be near workplaces and retail shops. But that situation began to change in the 1890s with the introduction of the streetcar and automobile. Suddenly, large numbers of Americans were able to move to lower density areas outside the cities. Today, about half of all Americans live in low-density suburbs, and half of the remainder live in very-low-density rural areas. Only about a quarter live in relatively dense central cities.

Low densities provide many benefits that people value, including lower land costs, private yards with gardens and play areas, less congested roads, proximity to recreation areas, and access to a wide variety of low-cost consumer goods and services. What is more, as people moved to the suburbs, employers followed them; commute times have remained relatively constant despite the growth of suburban areas.

Despite the benefits of suburban living, some political leaders and social activists in the early 1970s began to vilify low-density suburbs as "sprawl." The anti-sprawl movement came into prominence in 1973 when George Dantzig and Thomas Saaty published their book *Compact City: A Plan for a Livable*

Urban Environment. The book unleashed a large movement of planners and architects who endorsed government efforts to mandate much higher population densities, more multi-family dwellings, and severe limits on auto driving.

However, the movement has met considerable opposition from the public. Few Americans are willing to give up their automobiles, single-family homes, and large backyards. As smart growth advocate Douglas Porter of the Urban Land Institute has lamented, there is a "gap between the daily mode of living desired by most Americans and the mode that most city planners believe is most appropriate. Americans generally want a house on a large lot and three cars in every garage. . . . Yet that dream translates into low-density sprawl and dependence on roads and highways."

Regional Governments

To the disappointment of smart growth proponents, many locally elected officials are unwilling to enact smart growth policies for fear of the wrath of voters in subsequent elections. Porter and others have suggested a way around that problem: endowing regional governments with the "powers to require local plans to conform to regional or state goals." As Brookings Institution economist Anthony Downs notes, such a regional government "can take controversial stands without making its individual members commit themselves to those stands. Each member can claim that 'the organization' did it or blame all the other members."

The nuclei of such regional governments were first created in the 1960s when the federal departments of Transportation and Housing and Urban Development required all major urban areas to form "metropolitan planning organizations" (MPOS). The organizations' original purpose was to apply for and distribute federal funds, not dictate to local governments. But they now provide a convenient framework for establishing the regional authorities that smart growth proponents want.

Oregon: A Case Study

One of the nation's most aggressive smart growth efforts has been undertaken in Oregon. There, state and local officials, along with the Portland MPO, regulate everything from the number and location of parking spaces that retailers can provide their customers to the number of people who can attend church services on Sundays.

Central to Oregon's planning system are the urban-growth boundaries that were drawn around every city and town in the state in the late 1970s. On most of the land outside of the urban-growth boundaries, the state allows people to build new homes only if they own at least 160 acres that they actually farm, and the land generated $40,000 to $80,000 per year in agriculture revenues in two of the last three years. (Ironically, less than one-fifth of existing farms meet that income test). The Oregon regulations have successfully slowed development in non-urban areas; only about 100 landowners per year have been allowed to build homes on their farms.

The urban-growth boundaries were originally supposed to be flexible planning tools. Much of the land inside the boundaries was vacant at the time the lines were drawn, and planners promised to expand the boundaries as the vacant land was used. However, soon after the boundaries were created, they became sacred lines. People who lived just inside wanted to preserve their scenic views and open space, so they fought any expansion of the boundaries.

In the late 1980s, the Portland area was growing rapidly and realtors and homebuilders began to worry that the region was running out of land. A self-styled land-use planning watchdog group called "1000 Friends of Oregon" proposed an alternative to boundary expansion: increased population densities within the boundary. In a major study begun in 1989 known as the "land use, transportation, and air quality" study (LUTRAQ), the group reasoned that higher densities would make transit service a feasible alternative to driving. Mixed-use developments that combined housing with offices and retail shops would allow people to walk to the store and work instead of driving. Thus, 1000 Friends promised, increased densities and land-use controls would allow the region to grow while maintaining its livability and minimizing congestion.

In 1991, Richard Benner, an attorney with 1000 Friends, became director of the state Department of Land Conservation and Development, the agency that oversees land-use planning. That same year, the Land Conservation and Development Commission (lcdc)—which oversees the department—issued rules requiring all major cities in the state to reduce the amount of Per capita spending by 20 percent (later modified to 10 percent). To achieve that reduction, the rules directed the cities to increase densities, promote mixeduse developments, reduce parking and discourage auto-oriented shopping areas, and emphasize transit instead of highways.

Portland's MPO, known as "Metro," projected that the population of the Portland area would grow by 80 percent over the next fifty years. To comply with the new LCDC rules, Metro wrote a plan that called for expanding the urban-growth boundary by no more than six percent over the fifty-year period. That meant that the population density inside the boundary would increase by 70 percent.

Density Targets

To achieve that increase, Metro gave population targets to each of the 24 cities and three counties inside the boundary. To meet the targets, municipalities were required to rezone existing neighborhoods or vacant lands to higher densities. The new minimum density zoning codes specified, for example, that the owner of a vacant quarter-acre lot in an area zoned for 24-unit-per-acre apartments could not build a single home—or even a duplex—on the lot. Instead, the owner would be required to build at least a six-unit complex, or else nothing could be built on the land at all.

The region's cities and counties encountered major opposition when they tried to rezone existing neighborhoods to higher densities. One Portland suburb recalled its mayor and two members of its city council from office after they endorsed higher densities over local opposition. To meet their targets, planners turned to rezoning farms and other open spaces as high-density areas. One suburban county rezoned a golf course for 1,100 new housing units and 200,000 square feet of office space. Ten thousand acres of prime farmland inside the urban-growth boundary were also targeted for development.

Light Rail

Planners were especially aggressive about rezoning neighborhoods near Portland's light-rail line, which opened in 1986. They believed that higher densities along the light rail would promote light-rail ridership. However, time has shown that few people want to live in such high-density communities and few developers want to construct them, even if there is convenient access to mass transit. As city planner Mike Saba told the Portland city council in 1996, "We have not seen any of the kind of development—of a mid-rise, higher-density, mixed-use, mixed-income type—that we would've liked to have seen" along the light-rail line. In the same meeting, city council member Charles Hales noted, "We are in the hottest real estate market in the country," yet "most of those sites [along the light-rail line] are still vacant." Hales then convinced his fellow council members to offer developers 10 years of property tax waivers for any high-density housing built near light-rail stations.

THE FRUITS OF SMART GROWTH

Metro's plans appear to have been written to favor the five- to six percent of all travel that is done on foot or bicycle and the three- to five percent that is done on public transit, at the expense of the 88- to 92 percent of all travel done by auto. What is more, smart growth policies will prove costly for everyone on virtually every indicator of urban livability. Consider the following future outcomes:

- Gridlock and air pollution will increase greatly as traffic congestion continues to mount, imposing costs on travelers and on consumers dependent on distribution of goods by truck.
- The emphasis on expensive rail transit actually will reduce the quality of the current mass transit system as fare prices are raised and bus routes are curtailed to pay for rail lines.
- The cost of housing—at least the kind of housing people want—will continue to increase dramatically.
- Taxes will have to be increased (or urban services reduced) to pay for rail transit projects and subsidies to high-density housing.
- Consumer costs will increase because of rising transportation costs from congestion and from the restrictions on new shopping areas.
- Open space in valuable locations such as people's backyards, urban parks, and golf courses will be transferred to less valuable locations such as private rural farms that are unavailable for recreation.

At the other end of the light-rail line, the city of Gresham gave developers tax breaks, waived development fees, and even provided direct grants to support higher-density development. Gresham officials claimed that the subsidies were only needed to prove to developers that high-density developments were marketable. Yet no such proof has materialized, even though Metro and local governments have used a variety of subsidies to support high-density development, including the following:

- The city of Portland sold city parklands to developers at less than fair-market value, on the condition that the buyers build high-density developments.
- Metro uses federal grants to buy land and then resells it to developers at a loss to support high-density developments.
- One county directed its county library system to use library construction funds to build four- to five-story mixed-use developments, with the library on the ground floor and apartments above.
- The nearby city of Beaverton provided $9 million in tax breaks and infrastructure subsidies to a mixed-use development that was being built near a light-rail station. The development later went bankrupt because the developer could not convince bankers to finance a project with inadequate parking.

House Shortage

Metro's land-use policies have distorted the region's housing market greatly. The urban-growth boundary and restrictions on new single-family housing have turned Portland from one the nation's most affordable markets for single-family housing in 1989 to one of the least affordable since 1996. Since 1990, the cost of an acre of land available for housing has risen from $20,000 to $200,000. According to the National Association of Homebuilders, in 1989 more than two-thirds of Portland households could afford to buy a median-priced home. Today it is around 30 percent. Meanwhile, regions such as Las Vegas that have grown much faster than Portland but without urban-growth boundaries have maintained their housing affordability.

The Portland area's response to the lack of affordable housing has been the implementation of more regulation. Both Metro and the Portland city council have endorsed or passed rules requiring developers to provide affordable housing in every development. Yet despite the shortage of single-family housing, Portland residents have failed to embrace Metro's high-density developments. In 1999, apartment vacancy rates were at seven percent, the highest in the decade, and reached 11 percent for apartments built in the 1990s. In a market where single-family home prices have nearly doubled, apartment rents have failed to keep up with inflation.

Planned Gridlock

Metro planners have also placed a stranglehold on the Portland-area road system. In order to increase the use of public transportation, the agency has publicly announced its goal of increasing roadway congestion to the point of stop-and-go traffic flow on roads parallel to existing or planned transit lines. According to Metro's Regional Transportation Plan, when rail transit is available, "transportation solutions aimed solely at relieving congestion are inappropriate."

Metro is employing three strategies to achieve its desired levels of congestion. First, it diverts most of the region's transportation funds to mass transit projects instead of road improvement. Public transit carries less than three percent of Portland-area passenger travel, yet for nearly two decades the region has invested some two-thirds of its transportation dollars into light rail and other transit rather than roads.

Second, Metro asserts that it will not add road capacity to most freeways and highways. One of Portland's worst transportation bottlenecks is located on Interstate 5 just south of the Columbia River. Most of I-5 has three lanes in each direction but, for a two-mile stretch, the southbound lanes shrink to two. As a result, thousands of commuters who moved to Vancouver, Wash., to escape Portland taxes and land-use regulation now face huge delays in commuting to Portland each morning.

To resolve the congestion, Metro wants to construct a light rail line between Portland and Vancouver. Metro requested that Vancouver pay $480 million toward the project, but city voters soundly rejected that request. Their decision is supported by a careful analysis of the economics of such projects: A typical light-rail line costs as much to build as a four-lane freeway, yet no light-rail line in the nation carries half as many people as a single lane of a typical urban freeway. Widening I-5 to three lanes for the two miles that are now bottlenecked would cost only about $10 to $20 million and would increase flow capacities by far more than would be carried on the light rail. But Metro will not allow the highway expansion until the light-rail line is fully financed.

Metro's third congestion-building strategy is "traffic calming"—the reduction of road capacities on major arterials throughout the Portland area. Auxiliary right-turn lanes are to be removed, left-turn lanes are to be filled with concrete barriers, and other lanes of traffic are to be designated as bike lanes. Metro has targeted several of the area's most heavily trafficked roads for such treatment.

Other Efforts

As another way of encouraging people to walk or use public transit instead of driving, Metro's plans require that new retail stores be built fronting on streets, instead of being separated from the streets by parking areas. Metro has also limited the construction of any new stores or shopping malls larger than 80,000 square feet—about the size of a Wal-Mart.

On top of that, the city of Portland recently passed a new design code aimed at discouraging auto-oriented homes. A central part of the new code is the prohibition on construction of what smart growth proponents derisively call "snout houses"—homes with a prominent garage in front. Supposedly, people will drive less if the garage is recessed behind the front façade of the house. Other rules require that streets be so narrow that residents can park only on one side.

Success?

Although the smart growth policies—high-density developments, light-rail transit, limited freeway expansions, traffic calming, and parking limits—are supposed to reduce per capita driving by 10 percent, Metro's own planners say that they will fail to meet that goal. In 1990, 92 percent of all Portland-area travel was done by auto, and the region's residents drove an average of 13.5 miles per day. Using one of the nation's most sophisticated transportation planning models, Metro predicts that its plans will reduce the auto's share of travel by only four percent and cut per capita driving by only 0.7 miles per day. What is more, the projections likely are optimistic; a Federal Highway Administration report indicates that, by 1998, the region's per-capita driving was already 20 percent greater than in 1990.

The state Department of Land Conservation and Development has responded to Metro's predictions by proposing additional rules. One rule requires that, if cities cannot prove that land-use and transportation policies will meet state targets, they must impose even stricter land-use and transportation policies.

Even with a five- or 10-percent reduction in per capita driving, the projected 80-percent increase in population density assures that Metro's plan will greatly increase Portland-area congestion. Metro predicts that the amount of time Portland-area residents waste sitting in traffic will quintuple by 2020. Cars pollute more in stop-and-go traffic, so increased congestion increases air pollution. Metro predicts its plan will increase area smog by 10 percent.

Empty Arguments

Supporters of smart growth argue that people would really prefer to live in high-density cities. Low-density suburbs, they claim, are the artificial result of such factors as government subsidies, zoning codes, white flight from cities, and inner-city crime or poor-quality schools. But those claims are false. Over the past fifty years, the vast majority of federal subsidies have gone to central cities, not to suburbs. Suburbs in areas without zoning codes look practically identical to suburbs that are zoned. And suburbs have grown just as fast in parts of the country that are not afflicted heavily by racial strife, crime, or poor-quality schools.

Another argument that smart growth advocates often use is that cities cannot afford to subsidize the sewers, water, and other infrastructure needed to support low-density suburbs. In fact, as noted by Harvard researchers Alan Altshuler and José Gómez-Ibáñez, it costs far less to provide infrastructure to new developments than it does to augment the infrastructure of existing areas to support the higher densities demanded by smart growth. Older studies that purported to demonstrate the "costs of sprawl"—which were based entirely on hypothetical data—seem to have gotten it backwards: An analysis of actual urban service costs by Duke University researcher Helen Ladd found that the costs are higher in higher densities. Worries that existing residents have to subsidize newcomers are also generally unfounded. When the costs of schools are assigned to residential areas, it turns out that all residential areas—both new and existing ones—are cross-subsidized by the taxes paid by commercial areas.

Using the Market

Opponents of smart growth do not necessarily endorse the status quo. Urban areas have their problems, including congestion, air pollution, inadequate transportation alternatives for people who cannot drive, and conflicts over land use and open space. But smart growth policies make those problems worse. On the other hand, many—if not all—of the problems have free-market or market-like solutions.

Transportation

For instance, since the 1960s, British transportation economist Gabriel Roth has argued that busy roadways should institute a toll system that charges higher fees for driving during rush hour than other hours of the day. That proposal has become practical thanks to the development of electronic toll collection, which has removed the need for traffic-delaying tollbooths. Such "value pricing," as supporters call Roth's scheme, is currently in use on highways in California, Texas, New Jersey, and elsewhere.

Market forces can also be used to provide incentives for auto owners to drive cleaner cars. Governments could institute annual fees for drivers that are based on the amount of pollution that each car emits. The fees would encourage drivers to install clean air technologies in their cars, purchase newer, more efficient vehicles, and do less driving.

People who are disabled, too old, too young, too poor, or otherwise unable to drive have long been the major users of public transit. Planners' attempts to attract middle-class commuters out of their autos by building expensive rail projects have often hurt transit-dependent people as fares increase and service is cut back in order to pay for rail construction. But instead of building high-cost, high-capacity rail lines and then attempting to redesign cities to provide ridership, planners should focus on designing transit systems to serve low-density urban areas. That means using low-capacity jitneys, shuttle vans, and demand-responsive transit systems. It also means demonopolizing public transit, opening the door for private providers of transportation services.

Zoning

Land-use conflicts and open space questions are best settled at the local level, not by city or metropolitan governments. In Houston and other cities that lack zoning, developers have enhanced home values by establishing protective covenants and creating homeowners associations to enforce and change the covenants in response to changing tastes and demand. University of Maryland professor Robert Nelson has proposed that cities with zoning should instead "privatize their neighborhoods" by allowing people to form their own neighborhood associations and take over zoning questions. Such neighborhoods could also protect open space and create neighborhood parks.

Such market-oriented policies allow people to choose how they want to live and insure that they pay the full cost of their choices. In contrast, smart growth advocates seem to believe that they know best how people should live. That belief seems destined to one day join the beliefs in urban renewal and public housing projects as government-directed efforts that caused enormous damage to urban livability.

Michael Lewyn

Debunking Cato: Why Portland Works Better Than the Analysis of Its Chief Neo-Liberal Critic

In a "Policy Analysis" written for the libertarian Cato Institute, Randall O'Toole calls Portland, Oregon "The City That Doesn't Work," condemning its attempts to reduce sprawl and automobile dependence through urban growth boundaries, light rail expansion and transit-oriented development. In this report, I seek to show that O'Toole's attacks on Portland often miss the mark by distorting and misrepresenting data. . . .

O'Toole suggests that:

1. Improvements to Portland's transit system have failed to increase transit ridership;
2. Portland's attempts at transit-oriented development have consistently failed;
3. Portland's attempt to limit sprawl by revitalizing its central city has failed;
4. Portland's planning system has failed to attract popular support;
5. Portland's urban growth boundary has made Portland one of America's most expensive cities;
6. Portland's transportation policies have made Portland one of America's most congested cities; and
7. Portland's plans have created a business-unfriendly environment.

. . . [I]t's worthwhile to consider carefully O'Toole's assertions about the failings of these strategies to determine how much validity there is to them. Not much, it turns out.

Let's take them in order.

I. Transit Ridership

Undeniably, Portland's transit ridership has increased since light rail was instituted in 1986. Between 1987 and 2006, the number of bus riders increased from 30.6 million to 47.7 million (an increase of more than 50%), while the number of rail riders increased from 4.7 million to 27.2 million (an increase of about 500%). Overall transit ridership has more than doubled, from 35.4 million to 74.9 million. By contrast, the population of Portland's urbanized area has grown by only about 50–60%.

During most of this period, Portland had only one light rail line. Since Portland's second light rail line opened up in 1998, ridership grew more rapidly than during the early years of Portland rail. Between 1997 and 2006, Portland's light rail ridership grew from 7.8 million to 27.2 million (an increase of over 200%), and total transit ridership grew from 51.4 million to 74.9 million (an increase of roughly 45% in just nine years).

O'Toole seeks to minimize the significance of Portland's success by pointing out that Portland's transit ridership grew more slowly than driving back in the 1980s, "when the region's first light-rail line was under construction." But for the first half of that decade, Portland's light-rail line had not yet been built. Obviously, an unbuilt rail line is not likely to contribute to transit ridership. . . .

O'Toole tries to tie light rail growth to service cutbacks, asserting that Portland cannibalized its bus system to build light rail. But the overall growth of Portland's transit ridership (discussed above) suggests otherwise. In any event, the proper balance between bus and rail is a technical and difficult issue.

What is more important is Portland's overall achievement: a transit system that has experienced increased ridership to a much greater extent than most. As noted above, transit ridership has doubled in Portland over the past twenty years. By contrast, transit ridership has increased nationally during this period—but by only about 15%. So by national standards, Portland's transit system is a success—a flawed success, to be sure, but a success. . . .

II. Transit-Oriented Development

Several transit-oriented developments have cropped up next to light-rail stations. O'Toole brands these developments as failures, because "there is little evidence that they have significantly changed people's travel habits." For example, O'Toole criticizes the mixed-use Orenco Station development. Citing a study by Lewis & Clark researcher Bruce Podobnik, O'Toole relies upon Podobnik's statement that "most residents of the neighborhood report using alternative modes of transportation far less than do their counterparts in Northeast Portland."

However, a look at Podobnik's study reveals a somewhat different story. The study points out that 18% of Orenco Station residents use public transit to get to work—a figure higher than the regional average. Although this figure is lower than the figure for Northeast Portland, this fact proves little, because Northeast Portland is the city's poorest, and thus most transit-dependent area. More important is Podobnik's finding that Orenco's design increased transit usage. According to his survey of Orenco residents, 69% of Orenco residents used mass transit more frequently than in their prior neighborhoods. Thus, the Podobnik study suggests that transit-oriented development does have a positive effect upon transit ridership.

By contrast, O'Toole's criticism of Cascade Station, a transit-adjacent office-retail-hotel development, is more persuasive. This area near Portland's airport was originally slated for development as early as 2001, but in fact is just beginning to develop. Why? According to O'Toole, "no one wanted to lease a small shop or office on a site that was miles from any residential areas."

However, O'Toole's claim actually bolsters a common new urbanist view: that mixed use development can actually be as or more profitable than single-use development. If Cascade Station had included a residential component, its residents could have lived within walking distance of its stores—a factor that might well have accelerated Cascade Station's commercial development. Thus, the answer to Cascade Station's problems is better urbanism rather than sprawl. . . .

III. Portland and Sprawl

Portland's rising transit ridership is not unique; other cities have improved their transit systems and experienced increased transit ridership. What makes Portland unique is the survival and growth of its regional core: while many central cities have grown very slowly or declined in recent decades, Portland's central city has grown almost as fast as its suburbs.

O'Toole himself writes between 1990 and 2000, Portland grew by 21 percent. This rate of increase is only slightly lower than that of Portland's surrounding suburbs; during the same 1990–2000 period, the population of the Portland urbanized area grew by about a third.

But O'Toole prefers to see the glass as half-empty rather than as half-full: according to O'Toole, the fact that some suburbs are growing faster than Portland is evidence that "people escaped Portland's planning system by moving to communities outside the reach of Portland planners." This argument overlooks the possibility that a suburb with a large amount of undeveloped land will always grow faster than a suburb or central city with less undeveloped land, even under a relatively pro-urban planning system. Thus, Portland should be compared not just to its own suburbs but to other cities with less aggressive planning policies. Is the "growth gap" between Portland and its suburbs larger or smaller than the gap between other cities and their suburbs? If the gap is larger, then maybe Portland has been doing something wrong. But if the gap is smaller, Portland's planning policies, whatever their demerits, may have limited sprawl.

Table 1 below compares Portland with other western cities of similar size and regional growth rates.

In all four regions listed above, regional population grew by about 40–50%. But Portland's results radically differ from those of other cities. In Portland, the city grew as fast as the suburbs. Elsewhere, the suburbs grew three or four times as fast as the city. Thus, Portland's policies appear to have been more successful at containing sprawl than those of comparable cities. Or put another way, comparatively fewer Portlanders chose to "escape" their central city than their counterparts in other major western cities.

Table 1

Portland vs. Other Western Cities

| | 1980–2000 population growth | |
	Cities	metropolitan area
Portland	43	43
Denver	12	47
Seattle	14	46
Salt Lake City	11	46

If Portland had always been a rapidly growing city, it could be argued that Portland's policies had nothing to do with its progress. But in fact, Portland actually lost population between 1950 and 1980, unlike Denver, Seattle and Salt Lake City (all of which experienced modest population growth during this period). So if Portland had not enacted an urban growth boundary (UGB) in the early 1980s, it might have become a declining city like Baltimore or Cleveland, rather than a slowly growing city like Denver or Salt Lake City.

O'Toole argues that regardless of Portland's overall growth rate, its high housing prices have prevented the city from retaining families with children. He points out that "only 21 percent of city of Portland residents are under the age of 18, compared to 27 percent of Portland's suburban residents."

In fact, the number of children in Portland actually increased during the 1990s. Census data show that between 1990 and 2000, the number of children under 5 increased by 6% (from 30,314 to 32,300), and that the number of children under 18 increased by about 16% (from 95,762 to 111,454). Thus, it is no longer the case that Portland is losing children to its suburbs.

In sum, Portland, unlike many other American central cities, has continued to attract new residents—both adults and children.

IV. Do Portlanders Like Portland's System?

O'Toole argues that Portland's planning system is unpopular because "several recent elections and other events have seen defeats for the planners, but they continue to plan anyway." However, most of his claims relate to events nearly a decade ago, such as rezoning decisions in the late 1990s. More recent events do not support his assertion that Portlanders yearn to turn Portland into a more conventional city.

A 2005 survey of Oregon voters showed that 69 percent believed that growth management made Oregon a more desirable place to live. An equally high percentage valued "planning-based decisions for land use" over "market-based decisions for land use." Only 32% believed that current land use regulations were "too strict"; an equal number said land-use regulations were "about right", and 21% even believed that Oregon's land use regulations were "not strict enough." In other words, planners "continue to plan" because Oregonians want them to continue to plan, even as they reject those planners' occasional excesses. . . .

V. Does Portland's Planning Create Unaffordable Housing?

O'Toole asserts that Portland's planning has caused "increasingly unaffordable housing prices." According to O'Toole, growth boundaries limit the supply of land available for new construction, and thus raise housing prices.

In Portland, the median regional income is $63,800, and the median house prices is $280,000—more than a 4-to-1 ratio. Although this situation is not ideal, other regions without regionwide UGBs have much more serious housing problems. Table 2 below compares Portland to some of America's most unaffordable markets.

As Table 2 shows, many other regions have far more serious housing affordability problems than Portland, whether affordability is measured by average housing prices or by the ratio between housing prices and income.

O'Toole is not foolish enough to deny that some other American regions are far more expensive than Portland. Nevertheless, he claims, "During the 1990s, housing affordability declined by more in Portland than in any other urban area in the United States." Since his paper was written in 2007, his reliance on 1990s data is as puzzling as it is pointless. In recent years, home prices have risen far more rapidly in the areas listed above than in Portland, as Table 3 shows.

Table 2

America's Most Unaffordable Housing Markets, as of 2nd Quarter 2007 (All Numbers in Thousands)

	Median family income	Median home price	Price/income ratio
Portland	63.8	280	4.3
San Francisco, CA	86.5	802	9.2
Los Angeles, CA	61.7	530	8.6
New York, NY	59.5	510	8.5
San Diego, CA	69.4	470	6.7
Miami, FL	45.2	290	6.4
Sacramento, CA	67.2	355	5.2
Las Vegas, NV	60.1	290	4.8
Boston, MA	76.9	353	4.6
Salt Lake City, UT	60.1	266	4.4
Orlando, FL	54.9	240	4.3

All data in this table come from the National Association of Homebuilders' Housing Opportunity Index spreadsheet for the second quarter of 2007.

Table 3

Where Prices Rose Most (All Numbers Except Percentages in Thousands)

		1995 (1st quarter)		2007 (2nd quarter)		
	income	price	price/income ratio	price	price/income ratio	% ratio increase
Portland	42.7	120	2.8	280	4.3	53 (from 2.8 to 4.3)
San Francisco	58.8	273	4.6	802	9.2	100
Los Angeles	45.2	157	3.5	530	8.6	145
New York	43	154	3.6	510	8.5	136
San Diego	45.4	157	3.4	470	6.7	98
Miami	35.7	88	2.3	290	6.4	178
Sacramento	45.2	131	2.6	355	5.2	100
Las Vegas	41.1	120	2.9	290	4.8	65
Boston	53.1	139	2.6	353	4.6	77
Salt Lake City	42.2	121	2.9	266	4.4	51
Orlando	40	87	2.2	240	4.3	95

All data are from the NAHB housing affordability spreadsheet.

In nine of the ten metro areas listed above, price/income ratios rose more rapidly between 1995 and 2007 than in Portland. The lone exception (Salt Lake City) was virtually identical to Portland.

If one disregards income changes and focuses solely on price increases, Portland again seems no worse than other markets. As Table 2 shows, the median home price in Portland increased by a factor of 2.3—hardly a result conducive to affordability. But the median home price roughly tripled in San Diego, and more than tripled in Los Angeles, New York, and Miami. In every single market listed above, home prices at least doubled. In sum, the notion that Portland's price increases are unique among American cities is just wrong.

O'Toole argues that California counties have enacted growth management policies similar to those of Portland, thus explaining California's higher housing prices. But California's UGBs, unlike those of Portland, are not region-wide: they have been adopted by local governments, and thus are easily leap-frogged by developers who can move to nearby counties. These rules have not been adopted in major regional centers, but in agricultural communities: a study published in the University of Michigan's local government policy report showed that cities and counties with UGBs are, on the average, located in counties where 40% of all land is used for agriculture. In Southern California (home of two of the cities listed above, Los Angeles and San Diego), only 15%

of all municipalities have UGBs. Thus, California's UGBs are basically tooth-less, and probably have little effect on major regional cities.

The Michigan study did find that cities with UGBs had somewhat higher housing prices than cities without. However, the "price gap" was quite minor; housing prices increased by 3.5% a year (35% between 1990 and 2000) in cities with UGBs, and 2.1% a year (21% between 1990 and 2000) in the aver-age city without UGBs. Both sets of price increases were far smaller than the housing price increases in the California regions listed above: in Sacramento, San Diego, San Francisco, and Los Angeles, housing prices increased by at least 14% per year (170% over the 1995–2007 period). Thus, it seems unlikely that the UGBs of a few rural and suburban towns had a significant effort on the housing prices of big cities and their inner suburbs.

Finally, O'Toole argues that even if Portland is not the most expensive place in America to live, other cities with less restrictive policies are cheaper. This argument lacks merit for two reasons. First, some cities not targeted by O'Toole are actually more expensive than Portland (such as Boston, Las Vegas and Orlando). Second, some of O'Toole's role models are becoming almost as expensive as Portland. For example, O'Toole claims (without citing any evi-dence) that "Portland's high housing prices led many potential employers to look at Boise, Omaha or other affordable communities." But Boise is almost as expensive as Portland. The median Boise home cost $247,000—more than four times the median family income of $58,500. O'Toole also states that Portland "is far less affordable than many less-regulated housing markets, such as Atlanta, Raleigh, and Houston." However, Raleigh and Houston both have housing price/median income ratios of just over 3; according to O'Toole him-self, "markets with ratios above 3 verge on unaffordable." Atlanta's 2.7 ratio is slightly better; however, this ratio actually understates the city of Atlanta's costliness because safer, close-in neighborhoods are far more expensive than the regional average.

Finally, O'Toole's claim that allowing additional development means lower home prices contradicts his own apparent opposition to infill develop-ment. In another section of his paper, O'Toole complains that Portland-area planners sought to "densify" existing neighborhoods by allowing additional development within existing neighborhoods. But if Portland allowed builders to develop additional housing units within the city, those units would have increased the supply of housing units, and thus (according to O'Toole's own logic) reduced housing prices. In other words, O'Toole claims that develop-ment affects housing prices when it occurs outside an UGB, but seems to think that infill development is somehow immune to the law of supply and demand. How can both propositions be true? . . .

VI. Bad For Business?

O'Toole asserts that Portland's high cost of living and traffic congestion have created an environment unfriendly to business, thus causing businesses to leave Portland for cheaper places. (He also suggests that Portland has higher taxes than other regions, but provides no data in support of this claim).

As of June 2007, Portland's unemployment rate was 4.8%, slightly below the statewide average of 5.1% and roughly comparable to the national unemployment rate of 4.7%. Thus, Portland is hardly in terrible shape economically. . . .

VII. Summary

O'Toole seeks to show that Portland's transit system is useless, and that its land use and transportation policies have caused its economy to decline, its core city to lose people to its suburbs, its roads to become more congested, and its houses to become dangerously expensive. On every point, he overstates his case; Portland has repopulated its urban core and increased transit ridership, while Portland's most serious problems (such as housing affordability) are no worse than those of other cities. In fact, rising house prices in Portland are evidence that consumers are competing to live there, hardly a sign of failure. In his own peculiar way, mostly by prompting a closer look at the facts, O'Toole has helped show that Portland has many positive lessons to teach other metro areas.

EXPLORING THE ISSUE

Do Portland-Style Smart Growth Policies Raise Housing Prices and Hurt Urban Livability?

Critical Thinking and Reflection

1. Do you think that Americans are willing to live in communities shaped by Smart Growth policies?
2. How do you personally feel about life in a Smart Growth community like Portland and its suburbs? Would you be willing to live in relatively dense, transit-oriented communities?
3. How do you evaluate the evidence of the impact of UGBs on housing prices? Does a UGB lead to serious problems of housing unaffordability?
4. Which do you prefer: the Maryland incentive approach or the Oregon regulatory approach to Smart Growth? Or do you generally oppose Smart Growth measures?

Is There Common Ground?

Of course, the "purists" on both sides of the debate will continue to see their perspective as the only just or ethical one; they will continue to spurn compromise. For rigid environmentalists, an ethic of care demands strong growth regulations to preserve the natural environment; human beings are obliged to live in harmony with the land. Antigovernment individual-rights ideologues, in contrast, tend to view all governmental regulation and domestic spending, even for the purposes of protecting the natural environment or promoting mass transit, as a denial of individual freedom and a costly intrusion on the free market.

Most Americans, however, fall somewhere between the extremes. They value individual freedom, but they also recognize how individual choices produce environmental harm. "Free choice" does not always yield the public good. Developers and home buyers moved primarily by self-interest have no concern for the *externalities* of their actions, the costs that their actions impose on others and on the community at large. Government regulation is necessary to ensure that decisions made by free individuals do not harm the common good, for instance, by destroying wetlands and natural habitats and by adding to air and water pollution. Although many Americans are quite happy with suburban living, many others give a high priority to sustainability concerns, are critical of sprawl, and would prefer the opportunities to live in denser developments built close to public transit to allow more convenient access to the jobs and amenities of the big city.

Americans recognize the necessity of laws for environmental protection. Yet, the "environment" is not the only value they cherish. Americans also want continued economic growth and prosperity and the opportunity to live "the American Dream." They oppose overregulation that impairs job growth and unnecessarily constrains residential opportunities. As the Measure 37 revolt in Oregon demonstrates, Americans also want the fair treatment of property owners; the ballot measure essentially forced state officials to pay greater attention to concerns of rural owners who claimed that strong state land-use planning had deprived them of the full economic value of their property.

The debate over the impact of an urban growth boundary also allows for possible common ground, despite the extreme voices who selectively search for data to justify their initial opinions. Undoubtedly, a UGB does add to the cost of housing, but likely not nearly to the extent that the home building industry and other critics contend. Other factors, especially the demand for housing in a hot local economy, exert a greater effect on housing prices, as is evident in the escalation of home prices in prospering cities that have no UGB.

Can growth management policies represent the balance of concerns that Americans apparently have? The first step in discovering a middle ground is to recognize that Smart Growth is not "no growth." Smart Growth is not the same as environmental extremism that bars new development; rather, it is an effort to pursue patterns of growth that will also allow for the consideration of environmental protection and equity concerns. Such a policy requires flexibility, not a rigidity of application that can turn Smart Growth into a "no growth" program.

An urban growth boundary can be flexible, with decision makers extending its borders when the supply of suitable building sites inside the boundary nears exhaustion. Decision makers can also narrow a growth boundary when there is mounting demand for home building, when local economic woes demand that greater attention be given to job creation, and where demarcation lines apparently protect areas that are of no special beauty or significance.

As seen in the Portland region, public policies—especially state and local provisions for the construction of affordable housing—can also help offset the ill effects of any UGB-induced rise in housing prices. Policies aimed at ensuring housing affordability are necessary to ensure equity in Smart Growth communities, so that land-use limitations do not wind up diminishing the housing opportunities available to working-class and lower-income families, racial minorities, and newly married couples.

Additional Resources

Abbott, Carl. (2002). "Planning a Sustainable City: The Promise and Performance of Portland's Growth boundary," in Gregory D. Squires, ed., *Urban Sprawl: Causes, Consequences, and Policy Responses*. Washington, DC: Urban Institute Press, pp. 207–235.

Benfield, F. Kaid, Jutka Terris, & Nancy Vorsanger. (2001). *Solving Sprawl: Models of Smart Growth in Communities Across America*. Washington, DC: National Resources Defense Council.

DeGrove, John M. (2005). *Planning Policy and Politics: Smart Growth and the States*. Cambridge, MA: Lincoln Institute of Land Policy.

Downs, Anthony, ed. (2004). *Growth Management and Affordable Housing: Do They Conflict?* Washington, DC: Brookings Institution Press.

Nelson, Arthur C., Rolf Pendall, Casey J. Dawkins, & Gerrit J. Knapp. (2002). "The Link Between Growth Management and Housing Affordability: The Academic Evidence," a discussion paper prepared for the Brookings Institution Center on Urban and Metropolitan Policy, Washington, DC. Available at www.brookings.edu/dybdocroot/es/urban/publications/growthmanagexsum.htm

Ozawa, Connie P., ed. (2004). *The Portland Edge: Challenges and Successes in Growing Communities*. Washington, DC: Island Press.

Pendall, Rolf, Arthur C. Nelson, Casey J. Dawkins, & Gerrit J. Knapp. (2005). Connecting Smart Growth, Housing Affordability, and Racial Equity," in Xavier de Souza Briggs, ed., *The Geography of Opportunity*. Washington, DC: Brookings Institution.

Pozdena, Randall J. (2002). "Smart Growth and Its Effects on Housing Markets: The New Segregation." A QuantEcon study prepared for the Center for Environmental Justice of the National Center for Public Policy Research, Washington, DC. Available at www.nationalcenter.org/NewSegregation.pdf

Staley, Samuel R. & Leonard C. Gilroy. (2001). "Smart Growth and Housing Affordability: Evidence from Statewide Planning Laws," a policy study of the Reason Public Policy Institute. Available at http://reason.org/files/8c953681f2d45e198d94a2c7eceea370.pdf

Walker, Peter A., & Patrick T. Hurley. (2011). *Planning Paradise: Politics and Visioning of Land Use in Oregon*. Tucson, AZ: University of Arizona Press.

Internet References

Center for Clean Air Policy: Transportation and Smart Growth

The CCAP argues that Smart Growth strategies can lessen air pollution and greenhouse gas emissions, while reducing the costs of investing in an ever-expanding road network.

www.ccap.org/index.php?component=issues&id=16

Competitive Enterprise Institute

CEI, dedicated to limited government, a free market, and individual liberty, maintains a website that provides access to a large number of news clippings and commentaries critical of Smart Growth.

http://cei.org

Environmental Protection Agency: Smart Growth Illustrated

The website of this federal agency provides numerous examples and case studies of smart growth techniques as they have been applied across the nation.

www.epa.gov/smartgrowth/case.htm

Lincoln Institute of Land Policy

The Lincoln Institute of Land Policy (LILP) seeks to promote partnerships for Smart Growth. Use the site's search engine to find LILP's collection of reports analyzing the effectiveness of various Smart Growth policies.

www.lincolninst.edu

National Resources Defense Council: Smart Growth

The website of this environmentalist advocacy organization presents a number of resources devoted to the building of sustainable communities.

www.nrdc.org/smartgrowth/

New Jersey Future

This website proclaims that New Jersey's Future is "Working for Smart Growth: More Livable Places and Open Spaces."

www.njfuture.org

Planner's Web: Sprawl & Growth

Planner's Web is a very useful online site where professionals in the planning field exchange news clips and their views regarding sprawl and Smart Growth alternatives.

www.plannersweb.com/articles/sprawl-articles.html

Reason Foundation

The Reason Foundation's website contains news articles, commentary, and studies critical of Smart Growth orthodoxy.

http://reason.org

Resources for the Future

The RFR website includes an extensive number of papers evaluating the success of Smart Growth projects, including research that was presented at the "Smart Growth @ 10" conference devoted to assessing Maryland's Smart Growth program after its first 10 years.

www.rff.org

Smart Growth Network

The website is the joint work of the U.S. Environmental Protection Agency and more than 40 nonprofit and government organizations committed to sound planning principles for healthy and environmentally friendly development.

www.smartgrowth.org

Urban Land Institute

The Washington DC-based Urban Land Institute (ULI) has developed a Smart Growth "tool kit." Also be sure to look at the 2010 ULI study "Land Use and Driving: The Role Compact Development Can Play in Reducing Greenhouse Gas Emissions."

www.uli.org

ISSUE 16

Are Environmentalists Too Often the Unwitting Allies of Suburban Exclusionists?

YES: Bernard J. Frieden, from *The Environmental Protection Hustle* (MIT Press, 1979, pp. 2–11, 178–183)

NO: W. David Conn, from "Book Review: The Environmental Protection Hustle" *Urban Studies 18.1* (1981)

Learning Outcomes

After reading this issue, you should be able to:

- Explain how zoning works.
- Identify the various exclusionary practices that affluent communities use to keep out less privileged residents.
- Explain how land-use regulations can help promote environmental values.

ISSUE SUMMARY

YES: The late Bernard Frieden, the director of the MIT/Harvard Joint Center for Urban Studies at MIT, argues that unnecessarily strict land-use regulations serve to drive up the price of housing, impairing the ability of the working class, the poor, racial minorities, and young married couples to find quality, affordable housing. Freiden contends that affluent suburban communities have used the rhetoric of environmental protection as a cover for exclusionary land-use and housing policies.

NO: W. David Conn, professor of city and regional planning at California Polytechnic State University, San Luis Obispo, responds that Frieden understates the harm that growth projects can impose on fragile natural areas. Conn worries that developers will use Frieden's claims to leverage approval of environmentally unwise growth projects.

Under state law, local jurisdictions possess the land-use authority to determine just which forms of development may or may not take place within their borders. Detailed *zoning maps* designate certain areas of a city for light industry, others for heavy industry, and other spaces for retail, office, and institutional development. Each community's land-use and zoning policies also determine whether condominiums and apartment buildings will be allowed and just where they can be located.

Zoning helps to ensure orderly land development by preventing incompatible land uses. No homeowner, for instance, wants to see a noisy factory or automobile service station built next to his or her home.

Some owners claim that zoning is a violation of property rights, that an owner should have the freedom to use property however he or she wishes. But for nearly a hundred years, since its 1926 ruling in *Village of Euclid, Ohio, v. Ambler Realty Co*, the Supreme Court has upheld the constitutionality of zoning. As the Court explained, zoning represents a legitimate use of the state's "police powers" to protect the public welfare against noise, congestion, and an unwanted change in the general character of a community.

Over the years, more affluent communities have used their zoning and land-use powers to make it difficult for lesser-privileged citizens to move into a community. Local zoning codes typically limit the construction of apartment buildings and affordable multifamily housing. Working and middle-class families are effectively excluded from a community that bans apartments and requires that new homes be built on gigantic lots with unnecessarily large rooms and other expensive construction features.

Local officials deny that such ordinances are intended to keep out racial minorities and working-class families. Instead, they argue that the restrictions are necessary to guard against congestion and the "citification" of a community, thereby protecting the local quality of life and the value of homes. The motivation underlying suburban exclusion can also be fiscal; the existing residents of a community do not wish to pay higher taxes to support schooling and other costly services for low- and moderate-income newcomers who add relatively little to the local tax base.

Suburbs use a variety of means to exclude low-income, working-class, and even middle-class families. Many communities *refuse to accept subsidized housing*. Others have zoning plans that sharply restrict or even *prohibit the construction of multifamily housing*. Most commonly, *large-lot zoning* mandates that a new house be built on no less than a half acre, one acre, or even two or more acres of land, putting homes in a price range that only more affluent families can afford. *Minimum room space requirements* (beyond that required for occupants' health and safety) and regulations requiring the use of *expensive construction materials* (such as mandates for copper pipes instead of much cheaper but quite serviceable plastic pipes) further increase home prices. Construction codes also typically require on-site construction rather than the money saving alternative of assembling prefabricated components. Communities can also burden home builders with special *development fees and access charges*, costs which are passed on to home buyers. A local *moratorium on new water and sewer lines*, can also effectively stop new construction. The designation of *agricultural preserves and green-spaces* can also be used as a tactic to obstruct new housing developments.

Studies in the greater Boston area show that such regulations, especially regulations governing minimum lot sizes, can add 11–20 percent or more to the cost of a new home. In the expensive Boston area market, such regulations can even raise the price of a home by $130,000 (figures cited in Glaeser et al., 2006).

As Bernard Frieden observes, suburbanites often hide their discriminatory intentions behind the more respectable rhetoric of environmentalism. In *The Environmental Protection Hustle* (excerpted as the YES selection), Frieden argues that environmentalists have been beguiled by calls to protect wetlands and fragile natural areas and have backed exclusionists who wave the environmental banner, even in cases where the environmental merits are not clear.

Frieden is especially scornful of a *lifeboats ethics* philosophy that bars new development from the fear that new growth will overload the "carrying capacity" of a community, severely diminishing the local quality of life. Frieden argues that in more affluent communities, the suburban "lifeboats" are indeed quite plush and comfortable and have considerable room to accommodate newcomers.

Considerations of space preclude the inclusion in this volume of the case studies that Frieden uses to show how environmental values have been perverted in the support of exclusionism. A brief review of a few of his cases will suffice to make the point.

In one instance, environmentalists opposed the construction a compact development of 2200 affordable town home and condominium apartment units in the foothills outside Oakland, California. The project's opponents blocked the development but accepted in its place the construction of 300 very expensive estate homes sprawled all over the hill side. The new plan also lacked the 480 acres of open space that was to be dedicated to public use as part of the original building plan. The new plan had less environmental merit than did the original vision of compact development vision of the original plan. But local activists accepted the compromise as it led to the construction of fewer houses, even though the homes would only be available to upper-income families.

In Marin County, residents blocked new home building, declaring the need to protect access to the beautiful Pacific coastline. Having stopped new residential development, local activists then took steps that made it all but impossible for outsiders to visit the preserve. The natural scenic beauty of the area was conserved, but seemingly for the exclusive enjoyment of persons who already lived in the area.

In affluent Palo Alto, the city blocked new homebuilding in the foothills above the city, a project which, according to a consultant's report commissioned by the city, threatened to "radically alter the ecology and the visual aspect of the foothills" (Frieden, p. 110). The city thwarted the construction of a proposed 1776-unit complex of affordable apartments, town houses, and smaller homes in the lower foothills, homes that would be within the price reach of lower- and moderate-income families. The city initially sought to thwart the project by requiring that each home in the area be built on a lot of 10 acres or larger, a requirement that the development company successfully fought in court. Although the lower foothills land was not especially unique, the city ultimately decided to buy the proposed development site and the surrounding area which would be preserved for possible park expansion. The city also blocked home development in the upper foothills area, acquiring the site near the grand vistas of Skyline Drive, which it converted into a natural park and hiking trails, with only the residents of upscale Palo Alto permitted access.

Although Frieden's case studies are rooted in the land politics of the 1970s, the alliance between suburban exclusionists and environmentalists can still be found today. Local antigrowth forces are even able to use the call of environmentalism to rally the opposition against projects that seemingly embody sustainable development principles. In 2010 and 2011, local residents continued to battle a proposed mixed-use development of 730 housing units plus offices and retail space in upscale Foster City, just south of San Francisco's airport. The project had environmental merit: An adaptive reuse of a former industrial/office site, it did not represent the loss of green space; located close to the city and near a train station, the project represented an alternative to sprawled, automobile-reliant development. Still, neighbors in surrounding communities opposed the project, citing its density, the traffic that the new development would generate, its impact on the local schools, and its potential for adding to the pollution of nearby San Francisco Bay.

Many environmentalists sharply dispute Frieden's analysis and interpretations. W. David Conn (in the NO selection) and other critics argue that Frieden seriously understates the environmental problems entailed by new development. They argue that Frieden has failed to give sufficient weight to the urgency of preserving Marin County's spectacular coastline and protecting the Bay Area's foothills against unceasing development pressures. They note the environmental degradation that can accompany a large number of new homes, even when the homes are clustered in planned unit developments. Environmentalists further fear that Frieden's analysis will serve to magnify the power of land developers who already have considerable clout with public officials, having made generous donations to the campaigns of office holders.

YES

Bernard J. Frieden

The Environmental Protection Hustle

. . . Stopping Suburban Homebuilding

While one large group of people was beating the bushes trying to find afford-able housing in the suburbs, another group, smaller but influential, was doing its best to stop suburban homebuilding wherever possible—or at least to make sure that whatever was built was expensive. This coalition against homebuild-ing consisted of suburbanites who feared it would bring higher taxes and dam-aging social consequences, environmentalists concerned about the impact of growth on the natural landscape, and local government officials sympathetic to these views. . . .

Resistance to growth began [in California] as a very reasonable political shift, concentrating on saving such priceless assets as San Francisco Bay and Napa Valley wine country. But as it gathered power, and as people discovered they could stop growth at little cost to themselves, the movement became a good deal less reasonable. Soon it turned into general hostility toward home-building for the average family, using the rhetoric of environmental protection in order to look after the narrow interests of people who got to the suburbs first. In short, the pendulum swung from one extreme on growth to the other, pausing for only a split second in the middle.

The politics of no-growth required the invention of new tactics to discour-age homebuilding. Local government staff and consultants rose to the occa-sion. Their tactics included putting land into agricultural preserves, declaring moratoria on new water and sewer connections, setting explicit growth quotas, establishing service boundaries beyond which there would be no extensions of utility lines, charging thousands of dollars in "hook-up" fees for each new house as a price for local public services, and creating a climate of hostility that encouraged all opposition groups to bring pressure against proposed new developments. Residents opposed to growth tested and polished their own techniques, which included making strategic use of public hearings, putting development issues on the ballot for popular vote, and bringing lawsuits that could tie up housing proposals for years.

Wherever possible suburban governments used methods that cost their own taxpayers nothing and that shifted the financial burden of their poli-cies to new homebuyers, to the state's taxpayers at large, or to the federal government. In Marin County, north of San Francisco, persuading the federal government to buy land for a national seashore was a key part of the plan for restricting new urban development. Once the federal government had bought the land, however, local residents decided that the environment was much too fragile to withstand recreational activity. As a result they blocked the construction of new roads to the federal lands, and they opposed recreational facilities within the national seashore that might have attracted visitors. This scheme amounts to charging the rest of the country for a plan to freeze local land from development, and then not letting outsiders come to visit the land they have bought.

One-Sided Governmental Reviews

. . . A close look at the controversies around San Francisco also helps explain what makes the new no-growth policies so effective. Opponents of growth for whatever reason—tax worries, snobbery, concern for the environment—have been able to exploit weaknesses in an elaborate process of local development reviews. The process had built-in biases against homebuilding to begin with. Numerous governmental bodies have to pass on new development proposals, and most of them act only after conducting studies and holding public hearings. The long sequence of reviews gives the opposition plenty of time to organize their campaign and then hands them repeated chances to block new developments. All the cases described in the following chapters illustrate both the complexity and the duration of these reviews. The longest review took one development proposal through nine years of regulatory proceedings before county officials finally killed it.

The review process is highly political, and the people with the greatest stake in its outcome—housing consumers—play no part in it. People who want to buy new homes come from all over the metropolitan area. They are unorganized, and probably unorganizable, since there is no way of knowing who they are until they turn up to look at new houses. Local governments conduct the reviews, and they are responsive to their own constituents who already live in the community. . . .

Redeeming Environmental Virtues?

The actual issues that lead people to oppose homebuilding are hard to discover. By far the most frequent objections that growth opponents raise have to do with environmental impacts. These range from harm to wildlife to destruction of natural resources to increases in air pollution. Yet to label all protest as environmentalism would be a mistake. Many growth opponents use environmental arguments to mask other motives, such as fears of property tax increases or anxieties about keeping their community exclusive. Environmental rhetoric has become a valued currency for public debate, with much greater voter appeal than arguments that appear more narrowly self-interested. As a result people who are not environmentalists in any sense often borrow it for their own purposes.

A large number of growth opponents are environmentalists, however. Local environmental organizations often give testimony against housing proposals at public hearings and often bring lawsuits to stop developments. Some groups seem to oppose almost any growth, others are committed to protecting only certain natural areas that interest them, while still others oppose only certain kinds of developments. Still, the prominence of these organizations in development controversies does not mean that all or even most environmentalists have joined the attack on new housing. Many environmentalists save their political activity for such issues as nuclear power or natural resources and take no part in local growth debates. And within the organizations that do take positions on community growth, there are diverse views: the national leadership is usually more willing to strike compromises between housing and environmental priorities than are local chapters. So the performance of environmental activists in California does not add up to an indictment of the environmental movement at large.

But neither is it true that the only growth opponents who use environmental arguments are impostors or members of fringe groups. Growth opponents often include respected local environmental organizations as well, who might be expected to offer cogent environmental reasons for their opposition. Yet the reason they actually cite are a tangle of contradictions that must raise suspicions about their motives.

Sierra Club chapters, for example, have opposed some suburban housing on the grounds that it would generate unnecessary long-distance commuting; have opposed other housing near suburban job centers on the grounds that it should be located closer to the central cities; and have opposed new housing near the central cities on the grounds that it would use up scarce open space there. Another California environmental group, People for Open Space, has objected to housing in the valleys near San Francisco because the valley soil is better suited to farming, and it has opposed new construction on the hillsides because it claims hill developments will increase the chances of landslides, floods, and fires.

Environmental opponents also waver between judging new developments in terms of their region-wide impacts and judging them in terms of very local impacts. As a result they argue against some housing developments on the grounds that they are poorly located from a regional point of view, while they argue against others that are in better regional locations on the grounds that their local environmental impacts will be undesirable. Growth management studies usually take a regional perspective and argue for efficient use of land through compact development. Yet environmental activists try to limit growth by pressing homebuilders to cut the amount of housing in individual projects, and, therefore, to build at lower densities that make less efficient use of land. In one case environmentalists helped defeat a proposal that was favorable to both regional and local environmental considerations, apparently on the principle that the best development is no development at all.

Environmental opposition to homebuilding has almost no connection to mainstream conservation issues, such as reducing pollution and eliminating environmental health hazards. Housing proposals seldom conflict with these goals. (In the rare cases when they do, it is usually possible to solve specific environmental problems without blocking entire developments.) Stopping homebuilding usually accomplishes nothing for the public environment. It protects certain tightly regulated communities against change, but shifts development to other places where there is less resistance. The net environmental gain for the metropolitan area is zero, and sometimes less than zero. Environmental groups have helped to stop a series of housing developments located within short commuting distances of the main job centers around San Francisco. The result has been to push homebuilding farther out to scattered sites at the fringes of the urban area, where the new residents will use more gas and pollute more air while they drive longer distances to work. . . .

Other Fallout

Growth policies have had far-reaching consequences, including some that boomeranged against the communities responsible for them. Marin County, for example, deliberately avoided tapping new sources of drinking water in the early 1970s because growth opponents were afraid that more water would encourage more development. Beginning in 1975, northern California had three abnormally dry years. Marin County with its very limited water supply was hit first and hardest. Water rationing began there early in 1976, and the rations were cut to a bare minimum by 1977. Although the national press attributed Marin County's shortage to unusual weather, the drought in Marin County was largely man-made, a result of its own growth-control policies.

Conspicuous among the victims of the water shortage were the county's dairy farmers. Earlier the county had placed their land in a special agricultural zone that permitted housing developments only if each house was on a lot of at least 60 acres, as part of a plan for restricting growth. Dairy farmers had objected to the zoning but were outvoted. Now, unable to sell their land for urban development, they had to pay exorbitant costs to bring water for their cows in rented tank trucks.

Marin County's policies, which included a water hook-up moratorium in most places where new housing was feasible, had exceptional success in deflecting growth. Not surprisingly, the county also had exceptional increases in the cost of single-family homes, both new and old. As the value of older homes escalated in a tight market, county assessors increased property valuations by as much as 40 percent. Property owners facing big tax increases were quick to protest the new assessments, but few seemed to realize that their problem was related to the county's growth policies. . . .

Regulatory policies are reducing the choices available to consumers and raising the cost of housing. They run counter to long-established national objectives of encouraging homeownership for families of average income and stimulating a large enough volume of homebuilding to take care of the growing number of families. Yet they are failing to produce environmental benefits for the public at large. Public regulation is achieving mainly private purposes. . . .

No Room in the Lifeboat

The movement to stop suburban growth has done more than disrupt home-building. In attempting to justify its position on growth, it has begun to spread a new ideology of elitism through the country's political life. This ideology has served many different uses, but with one underlying theme: it supplies a ready rationale for the defense of privilege. . . .

Using environmental arguments to defend privilege and restrict competition is a familiar enough story from the growth controversies of California. The concepts and methods perfected there are also flexible enough to help people resist change for reasons totally unrelated to community growth. In time even groups opposed to environmental protection will no doubt learn how to make use of what the environmentalists have created. And a close look at the latest anti-growth ideologies ought to persuade responsible environmentalists that their movement's rhetoric is bound to do more serious damage to the public in the future.

Environmental thinkers have begun to put together a new "lifeboat ethic" that outdoes even their own earlier efforts to justify protecting the privileged at everyone else's expense. Garrett Hardin, Professor of Human Ecology at the University of California at Santa Barbara, has developed the lifeboat ethic as a reason to keep newcomers away from our scarce resources. His essay, "Living on a Lifeboat," presents a parable in which a lifeboat full of rich people represents each advanced nation of the world. The poor people of other countries live in more crowded lifeboats, and some of them keep falling into the water and swimming around, hoping to get into one of the rich lifeboats so that they can benefit from the good things on board.

In deciding whether to let them in, the rich passengers confront the central problem of the ethics of a lifeboat. They will be tempted to make their decision on the basis of the Christian ideal of brotherhood, or the Marxist ideal of "from each according to his abilities, to each according to his needs." But every lifeboat, even theirs, has a limited carrying capacity. If they admit all the needy to their boat, it will be swamped and everyone will be drowned. Complete justice will produce complete catastrophe, according to Hardin's scenario. The sensible solution, unjust though it may seem, is to admit no more people to the lifeboat, so that those already inside may survive. Sharing would be suicidal.

Does the image of the lifeboat fit the situation in the United States, one of the least crowded of industrial countries? Hardin believes that it does: "The land of every nation has a limited carrying capacity. The exact limit is a matter for argument, but the energy crunch is convincing more people every day that we have already exceeded the carrying capacity of the land."

The question of fairness remains troublesome, however. Hardin acknowledges that critics will ask how his prescription differs from the simple selfishness of slamming the door once you are safe inside. Since almost all Americans are descended from immigrants, how can they justify keeping their own place in the rich lifeboat while refusing to admit others? . . .

An overriding concern for survival and for future generations justifies the lifeboat ethic. . . . Making this argument about foreign immigration fit the local growth policies of American suburbs goes well beyond doubt, however, and into the theater of the absurd.

Yet environmentalists and other growth opponents have applied the lifeboat ethic in just that way. By declaring their land and environmental resources to be threatened by growth, and by appointing themselves guardians of finite resources, they conclude that it is time to draw the line against further urban development. . . .

If the suburbs are lifeboats, they are exceptionally spacious and comfortable lifeboats, like Marin County with more than 90 percent of its land still open. Additional suburban growth poses no threat to anyone's survival. The only threat is to the pleasures of affluent living, including the enjoyment of not having unwanted neighbors. And indeed, the talk of survival, limited resources, and austerity does not crimp the life-style of suburban environmentalists, but only of the people they keep outside.

One Bay Area environmentalist recently showed how to honor the principles of ecological preservation while living in luxury within the lifeboat. A retired computer executive whose environmental awareness had been raised to a high level commissioned his architect to build a house that would use recycled materials as much as possible. The architect used river-washed rock from a dry stream bed on the client's 200-acre estate as the basic structural material. These large stones made attractive colonnades, terraces, and columns for the main house and a separate guest cottage and wine-storage room. They also made an unusual swimming pool. Rather than order newly cut lumber, the architect found an abandoned pier in northern California made of Douglas-fir timbers, which he disassembled and shipped to the building site. The weathered wood made handsome ceiling beams. Similarly, he used antique machine parts to make novel hardware for the doors. Further in the spirit of ecological preservation, the owner decided to recycle furniture from his last home, supplemented only with a few finds from countryside shops nearby.

This house owes as much to the tradition of Hearst Castle, where William Randolph Hearst recycled whole rooms brought over from Europe, as it does to ecological awareness. It is characteristic of the environmental outlook in another way: these gestures of resource conservation involve no real sacrifice. They are flourishes that enhance an affluent way of life and make it even more prestigious. They are only another form of conspicuous consumption, masquerading as conspicuous nonconsumption. But environmentalists who admire this extravagant use of resources on a 200-acre spread in the Napa Valley will turn up their noses at the modest homes and small gardens of average families.

People who are well-off can use the lifeboat analogy to protect what they have at no cost to themselves: the call for sacrifice and austerity is directed only to outsiders. Meanwhile the same uncritical thinking that allows prosperous suburbanites to imagine themselves huddled in a lifeboat is also warping other political debates. Lifeboat thinkers argue against many types of aid for the have-nots, on the ground that finite tax dollars must go to the productive members of society if we are to survive. "No room in the lifeboat" slogans, based on superficial analysis plus a strong measure of self-interest, are undermining a basic sense of fairness and decency in public policy.

The takeover of local growth controls for exclusionary purposes, and the selling of a lifeboat rhetoric to justify it, are both outstanding successes for the new elitism in our national politics. Recognition of this elitism will not trouble environmental purists, though. Fairness is not an important consideration for them.

But the movement's more responsible leadership will have to contend with an increasingly skeptical climate of opinion, as the public continues to question increasing regulation and as the flaws of environmental politics draw critical attention. For political effectiveness, if for no other reason, environmentalists are likely to move toward a more equitable strategy and a more considered ideology. If they want to keep a base of popular support, they will have to offer the average person something better than a rear view of a fleet of fat lifeboats sailing into the sunset while he flounders behind in the water.

W. David Conn

Book Review: The Environmental Protection Hustle

Is it true that people who use the provisions of environmental legislation to eliminate, delay, or force changes in proposed housing projects are members of a 'powerful, ideologically driven crusade to keep the average citizen from home-ownership and the good life in the suburbs'? According to Bernard Frieden, writing after a year spent in residence at the University of California, Berkeley, many of those who have made it to the suburbs, acting under the guise of protecting the environment for everyone, are really trying to keep all others out in order to preserve desired amenities just for themselves.

This claim is based on Frieden's interpretation of what has happened in a number of communities in the San Francisco Bay Area, where a variety of different tactics have been used to slow the growth of land development in general and to obstruct certain housing projects in particular. These tactics have included the establishment of agricultural preserves (with favourable tax treatment) under California's Williamson Act, land-use controls exercised under State coastal zone legislation, local ordinances restricting the issuance of building permits, moratoria on (or high fees for) utility hook-ups, public acquisition of land for open space, restrictive zoning, and environmental reporting requirements. Although California is dubbed the 'front-runner' in devising ways of halting suburban residential development, Frieden argues that the growth control movement has spread far beyond the boundaries of the State and already poses a serious threat to would-be home-owners nationwide.

Frieden contends that the maze of regulatory hurdles now facing development proposals has given opponents repeated (and, in his view, unreasonable) opportunities to challenge, delay, and generally exert pressure on developers to modify their plans or even abandon them altogether. He illustrates the problem by examining in some detail the fate of several specific housing projects, notably Mountain Village (Oakland), Harbor Bay Island (Alameda), San Bruno Mountain (San Mateo), and Blackhawk Ranch (Contra Costa). In each case, the developer initially proposed to construct a relatively large number of 'moderately' priced homes—enough, according to Frieden, to make a significant contribution to meeting the Bay Area's pressing housing needs. Frieden's account makes it appear that each of the projects was essentially environmentally sound; yet each encountered sustained opposition from members of the local

From *Urban Studies*, vol. 18, no. 1, 1981. Copyright © 1981 by Sage Publications. Reprinted by permission via Rightslink.

community, often supported from further afield by environmental organisations such as the Sierra Club. After several years of delay and uncertainty, the opposition forced either a total withdrawal by the developer or a shift toward the construction of far fewer homes, re-designed for the higher-priced end of the market.

Frieden is a very skilful writer, and the book makes compelling reading. To the casual reader, and especially to one who is unsympathetic to the environmentalist cause, his arguments will seem very convincing. However, his account suffers from several flaws: it is patently one-sided; there is a tendency to label *all* opponents of housing projects as 'environmentalists'; any suggestion that there might be legitimate environmental objections to new housing is given short shrift; at least one of the case studies is presented in a somewhat misleading way, which raises suspicions about the others; and the reader is not given enough information to be able to judge the validity of generalising from the evidence presented.

The book loses much of its impact due to the obvious anti-environmentalist bias that the author displays throughout. It is disturbing, for example, to find that the developers are always portrayed (implicitly, if not explicitly) as the 'good guys,' constantly struggling against the odds to do what is 'right' for society, while the opponents are almost invariably painted in the worst light possible. Furthermore, Frieden's tendency to describe all opponents as 'environmentalists' is misleading; in an early chapter he does distinguish between 'suburbanites,' who oppose new housing because of their concern about higher taxes and social disruption, and 'environmentalists,' who are concerned about the impact of growth on the natural environment, but even this distinction tends to get lost as the book progresses. While it is true that the *means* used to obstruct new development often stem from legislation intended to protect the environment, this is not to say that the *ends* sought are necessarily environmental. It is probably not unreasonable to suppose that, in the absence of environmental protection legislation, determined opponents would find some other means of obstruction.

Chapter 3 contains an example of the kind of problem that results from lumping all opponents together. Frieden implied that the same environmentalists who favoured the use of water policy to control growth in Marin County were also responsible for blocking the conversion of a former Dominican brothers' priory to low- and moderate-income housing for the elderly. However, it is my understanding (from two people actually involved in this controversy) that many of the environmentalists actually fought hard *against* this blatantly exclusionary action by the priory's neighbours.

By asserting that 'environmental opposition to homebuilding has almost no connection to mainstream conservation issues, such as reducing pollution and eliminating health hazards,' Frieden discounts the possibility that at least some of the hurdles presented by environmental legislation may have been erected for good purpose. However, directly or indirectly, new residential development can indeed make significant demands on the natural environment; problems may arise affecting the air, water, or soil, not all of which can necessarily be 'solved' as readily as Frieden suggests. For example, technological controls on potentially polluting residuals (such as smoke and fumes, liquid effluents, and solid wastes) typically cause them to be shifted from one place to another, or from one medium to another, but cannot make them disappear; ultimately they must be discharged in one form or another to the natural environment, whose capacity for assimilation does have a limit. Frieden fails to acknowledge the real contribution made by open space to environmental quality, especially in an area that is otherwise heavily urbanised; open space not only provides aesthetic and recreational opportunities (which are by no means unimportant in themselves) but also plays a major role in extending the assimilative capacity just mentioned, as well as providing for groundwater recharge and generally helping to maintain ecosystem stability (e.g. through species diversity).

Not being intimately familiar with the Bay Area, I have no way of judging the accuracy of all the descriptive details presented in the case studies. Although I have no reason to doubt explicit statements of fact, I am a little suspicious that information may occasionally have been used selectively or in such a way as to be misleading. A red flag was raised for me, for example, when I realised that Frieden spends seven pages on his account of the San Bruno Mountain controversy before he even slips in a mention that much of the area is 'too steep for most recreation,' or that the terrain largely consists of 'steep slopes and ravines.' Anyone who has actually seen the mountain (which I have) might be forgiven for wondering why anyone would even consider placing 12,500 housing units in a hardly accessible location part-way up! It is difficult to believe that such a proposal really warrants Frieden's description 'environmentally sound.' I am not suggesting that the opposition to the project was necessarily entirely warranted; however, I am led to wonder how objectively the cases are presented in the book.

I also wonder whether the cases themselves are truly representative, or whether they were selected very carefully to support Frieden's case. Is it fair to generalise from these cases to the entire Bay Area and beyond? Unfortunately, Frieden provides insufficient detailed information about housing needs, land availability, and alternative project proposals in the Bay Area for the uninformed reader to be able to judge. Perhaps there are more suitable locations for new housing. What about the areas of land currently targeted in local plans for development, and zoned accordingly? According to the current President of *People for Open Space,* who happens to be a former San Francisco Planning Director, there are plenty of sites available to accommodate needed growth. Of course, developers might not rush to build on them (just as they have not rushed to build in those parts of Petaluma viewed by the city as the most suitable), although in a market as tight as Frieden suggests that it is, it seems most unlikely that the dwellings would go unsold. Yet, according to Frieden, it is the developers who are the best judges of where to locate housing, and the possibility that maximising private returns might not yield the social optimum is not even considered.

Although there is much to criticise in the way Frieden presents his case, he nevertheless raises some very important issues. It is undeniable, for example, that environmental regulations do provide opponents of residential development with a great deal of power to obstruct, for whatever reason, and often at relatively low (although usually not negligible) cost to themselves. Viewed from the perspective of the person who sincerely believes that a project is environmentally undesirable, this may be considered a good thing; and Frieden's supposed 'horror story' of the lone Eagle Scout who was able to delay a major housing project near Lake Merced might be viewed in a different light altogether if a sound environmental basis for opposition were identified (in fact, Frieden is silent on the Scout's reasons). However, the same hurdles also face the developer of a 'good' project, and the possibility that the scales may have been tipped too far against development must be taken very seriously.

Also tending to tip the scales has been the sheer length of the review process and the uncertainties involved, which have inevitably acted as a discouragement to all projects (both good and bad) and have added to the costs of those that have proceeded. (It may be noted, incidentally, that California has recently adopted legislation which specifically seeks to shorten the time involved in review.)

Another important point, which Frieden aptly makes, is that those with perhaps the biggest stake in continued development, the would-be home-owners, are effectively excluded from the review process. Frieden comments that in the past, it was typical for developers and local officials to 'find a way' to get new housing started, which often led to complaints that developers had too much influence, allowing them to do essentially what they wanted regardless of the environmental or social consequences. With greater recognition given to the problems of unconstrained growth, developers have now lost some of their influence, while opponents have become better organised and more likely to gain the sympathy of local officials. Since there is generally no way of even identifying those who would occupy new housing, much less of organising them to gain an effective voice, this constituency can be (and often is) disregarded with impunity.

Returning finally to the question posed at the beginning of these comments, it is evident from not only Frieden's work but also the work of others that the problem of balancing housing and environmental priorities is not adequately resolved in the present system of local development review, and that the provisions of environmental legislation have indeed been used, at times for possibly the 'wrong' reasons, to slow residential growth. Whether it can fairly be said that a 'crusade' exists against would-be suburban home-owners by those who live there already is another question. Frieden's book is not the place to seek an unbiased answer, although it makes interesting and enjoyable reading for the person who is prepared to resist accepting uncritically all that the author has to say.

EXPLORING THE ISSUE

Are Environmentalists Too Often the Unwitting Allies of Suburban Exclusionists?

Critical Thinking and Reflection

1. Should each state require its suburbs to modify local zoning plans to accommodate a diversity of housing, including rental apartments and condominiums, not just single-family homes?
2. Do you feel that it is appropriate for wealthier communities to use land-use and zoning ordinances in an attempt to keep out affordable housing and lower- and working-class people?
3. Is environmentalism a coherent, well-ordered philosophy? Or, as Frieden charges, are there inconsistencies and contradictions in environmental thought that enable local activists to oppose seemingly sustainable growth projects?
4. Which should take precedence in a locality's land-use plan: environmental protection or the provision of affordable housing? How can you balance housing and environmental concerns?

Is There Common Ground?

This is a debate that should allow the exploration of common ground. Not all land-use and zoning regulations that are enacted in the name of environmental protection are really necessary to preserve important aspects of a region's natural ecology. But clearly, strong land-use and zoning restrictions *are* needed to protect fragile environmental areas and to protect green spaces from the excesses of an unregulated, "let-'er-rip," pro-growth development mentality.

Local land-use statutes and plans should give heavy weight to the protection of natural areas, especially areas of unique beauty. But even environmentalists should cast a skeptical eye when affluent communities adopt no-growth or slow-growth measures that seek to ban all except the most upscale development. Urbanists should be very skeptical of just "who loses" when regulation enacted for the stated goals of environmental protection somehow helps to protect a lifestyle of privilege. "Sustainable development" requires a concern for equity as well as for environmental protection. Inclusionary ordinances can require developers to build more affordable units as part of any housing development. "Open space zoning" and "planned unit developments" (PUDs) can concentrate new development on only a portion of a developable area.

Zoning and development decisions have the greatest potential for bias when only one party is represented at the table. When growth decisions are made in an arena dominated by developers, the resulting decisions are likely to favor growth and to slight local community needs and environmental concerns. When an upscale community sets its zoning and land-use policies, its decisions will reflect the interests and concerns of existing members of the community, especially as home seekers who would benefit from the new construction live outside the community and are not represented when land-use plans are set. In contrast, a process that brings a variety of interests to the table—developers, environmentalists, established community residents, and poor and working class people with housing needs—can be expected to produce more balanced decisions that respect both environmental and housing concerns.

Additional Resources

Calavita, Nico, & Allan Mallach, eds. (2010). *Inclusionary Housing in International Perspective*. Cambridge, MA: Lincoln Institute of Land Policy.

Dowall, David E. (1984). *The Suburban Squeeze: Land Conversion and Regulation in the San Francisco Bay Area*. Berkeley: University of California Press.

Glaeser, Edward L., Jenny Schuetz, & Bryce Ward. (2006). "Regulation and the Rise of Housing Prices in Greater Boston: A Study Based on New Data from 187 Communities in Eastern Massachusetts." A joint research paper of the Pioneer Institute for Public Policy Research and Harvard University Rapport Institute for Greater Boston. Available at: www.hks.harvard.edu/var/ezp_site/storage/fckeditor/file/pdfs/centers-programs/centers/rappaport/applied/regulation_housingprices.pdf

Levine, Jonathan C. (2006). *Zoned Out: Regulation, Markets, and Choices in Transportation and Metropolitan Land-Use*. Washington, DC: Resources for the Future.

Wolfe, Michael Allan (2008). *The Zoning of America: Euclid v. Ambler*. Lawrence, KS: University Press of Kansas.

Internet References

Cato Institute

A conservative organization committed to liberty and free markets, the Cato Institute website has a fair number of reports and articles critical of zoning.

www.cato.org

Urban Land Institute

The ULI seeks to promote balanced development around the globe, development that allows for job and housing growth consistent with environmental values.

www.uli.org

Planner's Web: Sprawl & Growth

Planner's Web maintains a variety of informed articles on such topics as planning, zoning, and housing.

www.plannersweb.com/articles/sprawl-articles.html

ISSUE 17

Does New Urbanism Represent a Viable Strategy That Can Transform Suburban Communities?

YES: Robert Steuteville and Philip Langdon, from "The New Urbanism: A Better Way to Plan and Build 21st Century Communities," *New Urban Network* (June 10, 2009)

NO: Myron A. Levine, from "The New Urbanism: A Limited Revolution," in *Redefining Suburban Studies: Searching for a New Paradigm*, ed. Daniel Rubey (Hempstead, NY: National Center for Suburban Studies, 2009)

Learning Outcomes

After reading this issue, you should be able to:

- Identify how the following concepts are a part of the New Urbanism: neotraditionalism, community, front porches, traffic calming, and connectivity.
- Identify the three or four most important guiding principles and goals of the New Urbanism movement.
- Explain how New Urbanism seeks to rediscover the lost sense of "community" in America's cities and suburbs.
- List two or three charges that critics level against the New Urbanism.

ISSUE SUMMARY

YES: Robert Steuteville and Philip Langdon, the coauthors of *New Urbanism: Best Practices Guide,* argue that New Urbanism is a reaction-sprawled development. The New Urbanism builds compact mixed-use developments that, in a number of ways, resemble the small towns that dominated the U.S. landscape before the rise of the automobile. Steuteville and Langdon show how New Urban design emphasizes environmental sustainability while also seeking to reinvigorate the sense of "community" critical to neighborhood life.

NO: Myron A. Levine, professor of Urban Affairs at Wright State University and the author of the present volume, argues that the New Urbanism, despite its laudable goals and many achievements, does not really pose a challenge that is capable of reshaping the American landscape. Most Americans are quite content to live in large detached homes in automobile-reliant suburbs. As a result, developers will continue to build, and the vast majority of Americans will continue to buy, homes in conventional suburbs rather than in New Urban communities.

*T*he *New Urbanism* (NU) "is arguably the most influential movement in city design in the last half-century" (Marshall, 2000). Architects and city planners from around the globe have visited the United States to learn how the guiding principles and techniques of New Urbanism can improve living environments in their home countries.

Put most simply, the New Urbanism seeks to build better communities, in particular, communities that are ecologically sustainable and that can offer residents a better quality of life than found in conventional suburbs. New Urban construction stresses energy conservation and the preservation of wetlands and the natural terrain. The NU also emphasizes design elements that foster the interaction of residents in a neighborhood. New Urban enthusiasts offer the vision of an engaged community that stands in sharp contrast to the perceived loneliness and isolation of life in conventional suburbs where a homeowner may not even know the people who live next door. In New Urban communities, houses are typically built close to one another—not separated by garages—with front porches overlooking sidewalks, all design elements that allow residents to meet and talk with their neighbors.

New Urbanism emphasizes *walkability*. New Urbanism seeks to get Americans out of their cars and back on the street and in touch with their neighbors. Houses are built close to property lines, close to one another. Each neighborhood also has its own convenience stores, schools, parks, and other community facilities, located in such close proximity that than can be reached by foot or by bicycle. New Urbanist planners also seek to build homes that are located within a 5- to 10-minute walk of such neighborhood facilities.

In the conventional suburb, walking can be a dangerous venture, with streets designed for the fast movement of automobiles, not for pedestrians. New Urban design, by contrast, utilizes *traffic-calming measures* such as speed bumps and narrow street widths to reduce the speed of traffic, a necessity if streets are to be conducive to walking. New Urbanism encourages on-street parking, which provides pedestrians with a protective buffer against oncoming traffic. New Urban communities also have tree-lined pedestrian paths and bicycle ways, separated from automobile traffic.

New Urbanism design emphasizes front porches rather than back yards. Front porches allow residents to talk with children playing on the sidewalk and with neighbors strolling by. Front porches also help to provide the "eyes" that watch over streets, keeping streets safe.

NU breaks with the sort of zoning ordinances found in a great many suburbs that seek to enforce local exclusivity and a homogeneity of land uses in a community. NU design, by contrast, seeks a *diversity of population and a mixture of residential and commercial uses*. NU developers embrace a mixture of housing types and styles, seeking places for apartments, townhomes, and condominiums as well as single-family homes.

NU communities are intended as an alternative to sprawl development. Rather than "spread" single-family homes thinly across a large geographical area, NU planners envision *population densities* that can support neighborhood schools, thriving town centers, and *mass transit*. Rather than prohibit townhomes and garden apartments, as many more privileged suburbs do with exclusionary land-use and zoning plans, NU embraces multifamily dwellings as the key to providing the population densities necessary to support neighborhood stores, town centers, and public transit.

More dense settlement also enables NU development to preserve open space. The more compact nature or smaller "footprint" of NU communities lessens the acreage lost to home construction, roadways, highway access ramps, and the sea of impervious parking lots that surround the shopping malls and offices of suburbia. Compared to more conventional suburban developments, NU communities are more land-intensive and *environmentally sustainable*.

As discussed in Issue 9, the design principles of the New Urbanism have also been applied in the inner city, as part of the *HOPE VI* effort to transform public housing and deconcentrate poverty. New Urban consultants worked with the Department of Housing and Urban Development to design replacement housing built to human scale, with brick texture and "rich architectural detail" (Calthorpe p. 52). Many of the new units even had front stoops and porches, bringing activity to the front of the houses, helping residents to get to know one another while also providing the "eyes" for natural surveillance of the streets. Units for the former public housing residents and other subsidized rental units were "blended" into the mixed-income developments and, from the outside, were indistinguishable from the market-rate units.

In the YES selection, Steuteville and Langford emphasize how New Urbanism seeks to recapture a sense of "neighborhood" that is too often missing in contemporary urban and suburban America. Elements of New Urbanism can also be found in attractive commercial "town centers" that have been built across the nation as alternatives to the enclosed shopping mall.

Yet, despite its successes, the New Urbanism will not substantially alter the face of urban and suburban America. As I point out in an article that appeared in *Redefining Suburban Studies* (the NO selection), New Urbanism cannot undo patterns of land use that have taken root over many decades. Nor will the New Urbanism do much to alter the preferences of most Americans who will continue to conventional suburbs for homes with large backyards and the convenience of an attached two-car garage.

NU communities will also tend to be auto-reliant. Despite the addition of walking and bike paths and neighborhood convenience stores, residents will still need a car to travel to work or to go to supermarkets and major retail outlets found outside the boundaries of New Urban communities. The quite limited availability of federal fiscal assistance for public transit has also precluded the construction of transit-oriented developments part of the full-fledged New Urbanism vision.

YES

**Robert Steuteville and
Philip Langdon**

The New Urbanism: A Better Way to Plan and Build 21st Century Communities

Through the first quarter of the 20th century, the United States developed mainly in the form of compact, mixed-use neighborhoods. The pattern began to change with the emergence of modern architecture and zoning and the ascent of the automobile. After World War II, a new system of development was implemented nationwide—one that, instead of being based on neighborhoods, was based on a rigorous separation of uses. The separate-use system has become known as sprawl or conventional suburban development (CSD). The majority of US citizens now live in suburban communities built during the last 60 years.

Although CSD has been popular, it carries a significant price. Lacking a town center or pedestrian scale, CSD spreads out to consume large areas of countryside even when the population grows relatively slowly. Automobile use per capita has soared, because a motor vehicle is required for the great majority of household and commuter trips.

Those who cannot drive are significantly restricted in their mobility. The working poor living in suburbia spend a large portion of their incomes on cars. Meanwhile, the American landscape in which most people live and work is dominated by strip malls, auto-oriented civic and commercial buildings, and subdivisions without much individuality or character.

The New Urbanism is a reaction to sprawl. A growing movement of architects, planners, developers, and others, the New Urbanism is based on principles of planning and architecture that work together to create human-scale, walkable communities. New urbanists take a wide variety of approaches—some work exclusively on infill projects, others focus on transit-oriented development, still others are attempting to transform the suburbs. Many are working in all of these categories. The New Urbanism includes traditional architects and those with modernist sensibilities. All, however, believe in the power and ability of traditional neighborhoods to restore functional, sustainable communities. The trend had its roots in the work of visionary architects, planners, and developers in the 1970s and 1980s who coalesced into a unified group in the 1990s. From modest beginnings, the trend is growing to have a substantial impact. More than 500 new towns, villages, and neighborhoods are built or under construction in the US, using principles of the New Urbanism. Additionally, hundreds more smaller-scale new urban projects are restoring the urban fabric of cities and towns by reestablishing walkable streets and blocks in communities throughout the US.

On the regional scale, the New Urbanism is having a growing influence on how and where metropolitan regions choose to grow. Large-scale planning initiatives now commonly incorporate new urban planning ideas—such as walkable neighborhoods, transit-oriented development, and sociable, pedestrian-scale streets. Form-based codes and better-connected street networks are two instruments by which new urban ideas can be implemented at the scale of the region.

Principles of the New Urbanism

Let's look more closely at the core beliefs of new urbanists. Seven key principles have been identified by Richard Bernhardt, a leading new urbanist who heads the Nashville-Davidson County Planning Department in Tennessee.

1. The basic building block of a community is the neighborhood.
2. The neighborhood is limited in physical size, with a well-defined edge and a center. The size of a neighborhood is usually based on the distance that a person can walk in five minutes from the center to the edge—a quarter-mile. Neighborhoods have a fine-grained mix of land uses, providing opportunities for young and old to find places to live, work, shop, and be entertained.
3. Corridors form the boundaries between neighborhoods—both connecting and defining the neighborhoods. Corridors can incorporate natural features such as streams or canyons. They may take the form of parks, natural preserves, travel paths, railroad lines, major roads, or a combination of all these.
4. Human scale sets the standard for proportion in buildings. Buildings must be disciplined in how they relate to their lots if public space is to be successfully demarcated. Because the street is the preeminent form of public space, buildings are generally expected to honor and embellish the street.
5. Providing a range of transportation options is fundamental. For most of the second half of the 20th Century, transportation agencies focused almost exclusively on optimizing the convenience of automobile travel, and dealt with transit riders, pedestrians, and bicyclists as little more than afterthoughts. We must give equal consideration to all modes of transportation to relieve congestion and to provide people with useful, realistic choices.
6. The street pattern is conceived as a network, to create the greatest number of alternative routes from one part of the neighborhood to another. This has the effect of providing choices and relieving vehicular congestion. The streets form a hierarchy, from broad boulevards to narrow lanes and alleys.
7. Civic buildings (town halls, churches, schools, libraries, museums) belong on preferred sites such as squares or neighborhood centers, or

where the view down a street terminates. Such placement helps turn civic buildings into landmarks and reinforces their symbolic and cultural importance.

New Urbanist Prototypes

The first full-size new urbanist community was Seaside, the 80-acre resort development that Robert Davis began building on the Florida Panhandle in the early 1980s with lead designers Andres Duany and Elizabeth Plater-Zyberk.

Seaside is an amazing project, both in its style and in its pursuit of community interaction. Davis's pioneering project demonstrated that New Urbanism (or Neotraditional planning, as it was first called) is capable of reviving many of the best elements of small-town design.

New Urbanism has always been concerned with cities as well. At around the time that Seaside was being planned, architects like Daniel Solomon and Raymond Gindroz were applying similar ideas to revive neighborhoods in historic cities.

Solomon honed his architectural approach to building design in part by closely observing traditional development patterns, especially those in his own city, San Francisco. Solomon recognized that the most essential elements of the old patterns could be perpetuated if new construction followed the right principles.

While Solomon was exploring how San Francisco could redevelop in a satisfying way, similar work was under way on the East Coast. In 1979 in New York, a group of architects that included Alexander Cooper and Stanton Eckstut produced a revised master plan for Battery Park City, a 92-acre endeavor that was destined to become the most significant Manhattan development in half a century. Cooper and Eckstut had seen that when street walls are interrupted too frequently—as happened during in the 1960s and 1970s, when office towers with barren plazas proliferated—the city lost some of its interesting, walkable qualities.

Battery Park City was enormously successful as a real estate venture, and was celebrated for rediscovering critical elements of effective city planning. The complex along the Hudson provided a case study in how a large, dense urban precinct, or several of them, could respect human scale and enhance the public realm.

A catalyst to this movement arrived in 1993 when leaders in urban design came together to form the Congress for the New Urbanism (CNU), now based in Chicago. The founders were Andres Duany, Elizabeth Plater-Zyberk, Peter Calthorpe, Daniel Solomon, Stefanos Polyzoides, and Elizabeth Moule, all practicing architects and town planners. CNU has since grown to more than 2,500 members and is now the leading international organization promoting new urbanist design principles.

It did not take CNU long to have a significant impact on public policy. In the mid-1990s, the US Department of Housing and Urban Development (HUD) adopted the principles of the New Urbanism in its multibillion dollar program to rebuild public housing projects nationwide. Gindroz, of Urban Design Associates in Pittsburgh, was one of the influential new urbanists who helped to set the design guidelines for public housing redevelopments.

Redesigning Commercial Centers

Another setting in which New Urbanism has proven useful is the single-purpose retail center. During the postwar decades, Americans threw up thousands of shopping and business centers that catered to the automobile, at the expense of pedestrians and community life. One of the first attempts to transform a suburban commercial district took place in the Town of Mashpee on Cape Cod. There, in the mid-1980s, developers Buff Chace and Douglas Storrs acquired a generic shopping center and then set about altering and adding to it—a process that has continued for over 20 years now.

The result, Mashpee Commons, is a town center serving a community that previously lacked one. At the impetus of Chace and Storrs, the sixties shopping center added a post office; a cinema complex that opens onto a public square; narrow streets and wide sidewalks comfortable for pedestrians; second-floor offices; apartments and live/work units; and civic and religious structures, including a public library and a church. The center has acquired many of the traits that made 19th-century downtowns appealing.

About half the new urbanist projects now under way in the US are on land that had previously been built upon. Many of these occupy reclaimed polluted land ("brownfields") or fit into existing neighborhoods ("infill") or convert failed shopping centers ("grayfields") into sociable, mixed-use developments or renovate subpar urban buildings. Most of the early new urbanist projects were on "greenfield" sites—virgin soil.

The first large suburban greenfield project to employ New Urbanism's principles was Kentlands, a 352-acre project in Gaithersburg, Maryland. Designed for developer Joseph Alfandre by Duany Plater-Zyberk & Company in a charrette in 1988, Kentlands demonstrated that some of the development components common to the Washington, DC, region could be assembled in a more attractive and much more convivial manner.

Alleys and Accessory Units

This was made possible in part by placing most residents' parking behind the houses, along alleys. When Kentlands and other early greenfield new urbanist projects were getting under way, there was doubt that alleys would ever catch on in the suburbs; in fact, alleys have become a well-accepted part of contemporary development, helping the facades of the houses to form visually appealing streetscapes.

Another innovative feature of Kentlands is the accessory unit—small quarters above a garage or in some other portion of a single-family home. These apartments provide opportunities for homeowners to obtain some rental income, and offer relatively inexpensive housing for the renter—usually a single tenant or a couple, since the units are small. Initially (and incorrectly) viewed as an assault on the character of suburban neighborhoods, auxiliary apartments are now common in new urbanist developments, adding to diversity, density, and affordability.

Many of the best-known examples of New Urbanism are early greenfield developments like Seaside; Celebration, Florida; Harbor Town in Memphis, Tennessee; and Kentlands. New towns on greenfield sites continue to be built—more recent examples include New Town at St. Charles in Missouri, Seabrook on the Washington coast, and The Waters in Montgomery, Alabama.

New urban infill developments in older cities and towns are proliferating as well—probably to a greater degree than greenfield developments. Redevelopments of suburban sites are also increasingly common. Some of the infill communities occupy formerly industrial properties. Others are redevelopments of public housing projects, shopping malls, apartment complexes, or even military bases. Still others consist of revitalization of underpopulated parts of cities. The diversity of new urban developments is steadily growing.

The new urbanists have taken on three other projects worth mentioning in this brief report. One is the reform of zoning codes, which were established in the first half of the 20th Century largely to separate uses and restrict density. Zoning played a major role in suburban development for the last six decades.

The problem of codes has inspired some of the most innovative work by new urbanists. A reform movement toward "form-based codes," so-called because they regulate the three-dimensional shapes or forms of buildings and the public realm, has taken hold in recent years. These codes focus less on a property's uses than on factors that determine the character of places—such as building frontage and placement. A substantial number of municipalities have adopted the SmartCode—which first became available in 2003—and other form-based codes. But many more municipalities still have conventional codes.

Streets for People, Not Just Cars

The second project is the reform of thoroughfares. Conventional street design focuses primarily on the expeditious and safe movement of automobiles. The concerns of pedestrians and mass transit are secondary. That single-minded focus is fading, due in part to the New Urbanism. Since the 1980s, new urbanists have made the following arguments that were radical in the context of late 20th Century street planning.

- Mobility is not measured primarily by automobile movement. Other modes of transportation such as walking and mass transit should be given an equally high priority on all but the highest-speed thoroughfares.
- Streets must have character as well as capacity. Streets consist not just of two-dimensional pavement, but also of building frontages, landscaping, sidewalks, lighting, and street furniture. The ensemble gives the street its character.

- Streets serve a vital social function. They are the heart of the public realm—the glue that holds communities together—and should be designed as pleasurable places to interact, to see and be seen, and just to be.
- Streets should be highly interconnected. Conventional planning employs a dendritic (tree-like) pattern, with local streets branching off of arterials and collectors. The blocks tend to be large, overall connectivity is low, and traffic is concentrated on major streets. New urbanists argue for well-connected street layouts that disperse traffic and allow for narrower, more human-scaled thoroughfares.

Finally, new urbanist designer Peter Calthorpe and others have been strong advocates for transit-oriented development (TOD). In the last five years, mixed-use, higher-density TODs have been built all across America with great success.

In terms of urban planning, we have come a long way in the last two decades. In the 1991 book *Edge City,* author Joel Garreau was able to say that Americans have not built "a single old-style downtown from raw dirt in 75 years." Today we can see new mixed-use centers and downtowns in many places in the US, Canada, and abroad. There are strong indications that this return to urbanism will carry on well into the future. In the deep housing recession that began in 2006, urban housing has generally outperformed that of the distant suburbs. Demographic trends, such as the aging of the Baby Boomers and the emergence of the Millennial generation, promise to make urban places even more popular in the decade to some.

The looming climate and energy crises, likely to be dominant forces in the next half century, also favor the prospects of walkable, urban, mixed-use places. It appears that the 21st Century will be a new urban one.

NO

The New Urbanism: A Limited Revolution

The New Urbanism "is arguably the most influential movement in city design in the last half-century."[1] New Urbanist developers and planners have reacted against the environmental degradation and the perceived lost sense of communal life in suburbia. The New Urbanism seeks to build better suburbs—sustainable communities that offer alternatives to reliance on the automobile. The New Urbanism embraces the more efficient use of land, reducing the vast acreage that is lost to wide roadways, access ramps and a sea of parking lots that surround suburban shopping malls and office galleries. Just as significantly, New Urbanist design seeks to re-inject a sense of community into suburbia reestablishing the small-town connections among citizens that, as critics charge, have been lost to privatization of lives in backyards and big houses separated by side yards and driveways.

The New Urbanism promises a better alternative to the traditional suburb. But just how realistic and viable is this new and better vision of suburbia? Before this question can be answered, we must first review the core principles and promises of the New Urbanist movement.

The Guiding Principles of the New Urbanism[2]

In its attempt to offer an alternative to both the sprawl and anomie of suburbia, the New Urbanism emphasizes such principles as compact development, walkable communities, identifiable town centers, and the integration of suburban communities in regional mass-transit systems. New Urbanists seek to get Americans out of their cars and back on the streets and in touch with their neighbors. Conventional suburbs, designed for the convenience of the automobile, place virtually insurmountable barriers in the way of walking. Homes are located far from commercial destinations. High schools and office centers are situated on virtual islands surrounded by acres of parking that are not easily traversable on foot. Multi-lane highways and access ramps are nearly impossible for pedestrians to cross; they pose virtual moats that separate one office building and retail development from another. The workers in a suburban office tower simply cannot walk to a café or convenience store; they have no alternative but to get into their cars and drive across one parking lot into another. The highway- and parking-dominated landscape of suburbia further

From *Redefining Suburban Studies: Searching for New Paradigms* by Daniel Rubey, ed. (National Center for Suburban Studies, 2009), pp. 25–30. Copyright © 2009 by Hofstra University. Reprinted by permission.

lacks visual attractions and walkable destinations; it is "an incredibly boring place to walk."[3]

New Urbanist design encourages people to return to the streets. Homes can be built close to sidewalks and located within a five-minute walk to schools, convenience stores, and other key facilities that serve as neighborhood focal points. Town homes and apartments are included in suburban developments, as their existence helps to provide the population densities needed to support walkable neighborhood facilities and town centers. With more people walking and with more homes being built with front porches (town homes can even share porches) located close to the street, residents are encouraged to interact and learn and care about their neighbors.

Front porches also help to restore the "eyes" that watch over streets, making streets safe and free of crime. In commercial areas, "live-works," where owners reside above their stores, help to restore 24-hour-a-day surveillance and a sense of life necessary for the vitality of shopping areas. Just as walkability can be promoted (and the sense of suburban isolation reduced) by having homes located close to one another with parking moved to the rear, stores are similarly located, one abutting another in order to promote walking.

Narrow and tree-lined streets, lower speed limits, and the preservation of on-street parallel parking to protect pedestrians in shopping districts from the flow of automobile traffic and various other traffic calming measures, all serve to make communities more walkable. A conventional street grid, as opposed to dead-end suburban *cul-de-sacs,* further allows residents to choose from a variety of paths, adding to the interest of walking from one destination to another. Walkways and bike paths provide pleasant alternatives to the automobile.

The New Urbanism also emphasizes the construction of attractive, old-style town centers with cafés and interesting shops that serve to promote a leisurely, community lifestyle. Where central facilities require automobile access, parking is pushed to rear garages so that pedestrian-friendly shopping and an environment conducive to civic activity can be maintained in the town center.

New Urbanists emphasize diversity as an alternative to the insularity of life in more conventional (especially exclusive) suburbs, where homogeneity is rigidly enforced through zoning. At its visionary best, the New Urbanism seeks to blend well-designed and visually-attractive apartments into communities with single-family homes. New Urbanists even accept subsidized housing, again stressing the "blending in" concept so that the subsidized units are made part of the community as their appearance is not easily distinguishable from marketrate apartments. These New Urbanist principles have also been applied to the creation of better public housing environments in Chicago, Atlanta, Baltimore, Pittsburg, Charlotte, and other cities across the nation.[4]

New Urbanist communities are not meant to be isolated developments. Rather the New Urbanism seeks an environmentally sustainable vision of communities embedded in a larger metropolis As a result, New Urbanists propose greater residential densities around a rail station, with the goal of establishing a transit-oriented village that provides shopping and other conveniences as well as a mass-transit connection to work.[5] In Portland, Oregon, transit stations have served as the nodes for new development and pedestrian-friendly activity. The sustainability of New Urbanist communities enmeshed in their larger surroundings depends, to a great extent, on the existence of a well-funded and functioning regional mass transit system.

Preliminary evidence from Orenco Station, an affluent New Urban sub-division in Portland, shows that residents exhibit a higher sense of commu-nity or "within-neighborhood cohesion" than do the residents of more typical Portland communities. Orenco Station citizens, however, do not exhibit any great sense of responsibility to citizens who live outside, beyond the borders of the local community.[6] The question remains as to what extent New Urbanist design can truly increase a community's stock of social capital.

Limitations and Criticisms of the New Urbanism

Does the New Urbanism provide a viable alternative to conventional suburban development? Can the New Urbanism, as celebrated as it is, reshape suburbia?

One obvious limitation is that the New Urbanism cannot greatly alter patterns of land use that have taken root over time. New Urbanist developers and planners have been most successful where they have had the freedom to design new housing developments according to their community-oriented principles; but, overall, they have not been able to greatly reduce automobile commutes, as residents choose to travel to jobs, shopping centers, and strip malls located outside the borders of the ideal New Urban community.

The New Urbanism creates highly desirable communities for those who choose, and those with the buying power, to live in them. But the New Urbanism lacks the ability to change the suburban preference of the vast majority of Americans. Homeowners in conventional suburbs express a great deal of satisfaction with their lives. As a result, the vast majority of Ameri-cans can be expected to continue to use their buying power to purchase big homes with spacious backyards and a sense a privacy; they are satisfied with the escape and exclusiveness that affluence and the automobile have placed within their grasps.

Not only does the New Urbanism lack the power to reverse the suburban housing choices that most Americans have made, but also this architectural and design movement does little to alter the provision of road-building subsi-dies and homeowner tax breaks that continue to promote sprawl development. As a result, New Urban developments often fail to attract the population densi-ties necessary to support neighborhood facilities and thriving town centers.

Compared to most New Urban developments, Celebration, Florida, is noteworthy for its attractive town center with a town hall, bank, post office, upscale grocery store, theater, trendy cafés, and a lakeshore path; yet, the resi-dents of Celebration routinely drive to supermarkets, shopping malls, power stores, and restaurants in the suburban shopping strips beyond its borders. Celebration, like other New Urban communities, lacks the population density to support major stores of its own. For a long while, Celebration was able to maintain its town center only as a result of the subsidized store leases offered by the Disney Corporation.[7]

In Kentlands, Maryland (located within Gaithersburg, a suburb of Washington, D.C.), there was no deep-pockets Disney Corporation to subsidize store leases. In Kentlands and similar communities, developers had to respond to market forces, compromising New Urbanist ideals where the market required. Indeed, Kentlands Square is like any other strip mall, only a bit more aesthetically pleasing. The stores facing the parking area have proved economically viable; but vacancies quickly appeared in areas of the center that were not visible to, or easily accessible from, the parking lot.[8]

Constrained by market forces and reliant on private developers, the New Urbanism has not produced communities with great social balance. Seaside, Florida, in the state's panhandle, is a New Urban community much celebrated for its small-town appearance—white picket fences, front porches, gabled roofs, narrow streets, walkways to the beach, homes of architectural distinction, public spaces, and striking beach pavilions. The setting for Jim Carrey's film, *The Truman Show,* Seaside is pleasant and attractive. But Seaside fails to represent an authentic revival of small-town life. Seaside is little more than a fashionable beachfront community, with housing that sells at high prices attesting to the community's aesthetically-pleasing qualities. Seaside's homes mainly cater to short-term vacationers, not permanent town residents.

The decline in federal subsidies for the new construction of subsidized housing has seriously impaired the ability of New Urbanist developers to achieve their ideal vision of social balance. In the absence of government subsidies to build extensive affordable housing, New Urbanist developers have found that their efforts to design ideal communities are still highly constrained by a market in which many homebuyers value exclusivity and distance from lower classes. Even where New Urban communities have offered affordable housing, the lower-income units tend to be relatively few and are usually separated from the more high-status and attractive residential developments. As a result of these constraints, New Urbanists "are producing only slightly less exclusive suburbs than the ones they dislike."[9]

Celebration, Florida, developed by the Disney Corporation, is not strictly a New Urban community yet is noteworthy for a number of its New Urban design features. As already noted, the development, just south of Disney World, contains an attractive, upscale town center with cafés, a theater, and a community store, but no full-scale supermarket. The development also contains different neighborhoods with different housing styles. Yet, Celebration has only the most limited class diversity. Disney did not support the construction of affordable housing within the community; instead, the developer chose to meet its obligations under state law by contributing to a fund to assist people with rents and housing down payments outside of Celebration's borders. Celebration's housing is priced beyond the reach of the area's Hispanic service workers: "It's true that Celebration does have some mix of housing, but it's a mixing of the upper class."[10] Despite its aesthetically pleasing appearance, in important ways, Celebration is not all that different from other exclusive suburbs.

"You Say You Want a Revolution, Well, You Know, We All Want to Change the World."

—The Beatles

Regardless of the shortcomings and incompleteness of the New Urbanism, the residents of New Urban communities often express great satisfaction with their lives—with biking and hiking trails, with the sense of freedom that comes with the ability of children to walk safely to schools and recreation, and with the sense of community that they report they have found. Homeowners in Celebration, for instance, report that they value community and neighborliness: "You *can* be isolated in Celebration, but unlike in traditional suburbs, you have to work at it."[11]

Overall, the New Urbanism offers a relative few citizens, who desire it, a more aesthetically-pleasing alternative to the conventional suburb. The movement, however, falls short of achieving its goal of offering residents a revival of small-town community life with a respect for true social diversity. The goal of having a community in which residents "live, work, shop, and play in close proximity" is "more theory than reality," especially as New Urbanists have been unable to build at high densities and have failed to counter Americans' automobile-oriented lifestyles.[12] The New Urban communities that have been built fall far short of the ideal vision of compact, socially-balanced, mixed-use, transit-oriented communities. Instead, New Urbanists have succeeded in building only "a slightly reconfigured suburb," an "automobile-oriented subdivision dressed up to look like a small pre-car-centered town."[13]

The practitioners of the New Urbanism have created a number of highly desirable communities. Residents often express great satisfaction with life there. Still, the movement, despite the overstated claims of its enthusiasts, promises no great reshaping of suburbia. While the New Urbanism does offer a more sustainable alternative to the conventional suburb, it is a choice that the great majority of Americans will resist. Rather than revolutionize suburbia, the New Urbanism poses only the smallest of counterweights to continued sprawl.

Notes

1. Alex Marshall, *How Cities Work: Suburbs, Sprawl, and the Roads Not Taken* (Austin, TX; University of Texas Press, 2000), p. xix.

2. For a good review of the guiding principles of The New Urbanism, see Andres Duany, Elizabeth Plater-Zyberk, and Jeff Speck, *Suburban Nation: The Rise of Sprawl and the Decline of the American Dream* (New York: North Point Press, 2000); Peter Katz, *The New Urbanism: Toward an Architecture*

of Community (New York: McGraw-Hill, 1994); Congress for The New Urbanism, *Charter of The New Urbanism* (New York: McGraw-Hill, 2000); Calthorpe and Fulton, *The Regional City.*

3. Duany et al, *Suburban Nation*, p. 30.

4. Calthorpe and Fulton, *The Regional City,* pp. 253–265; Janet L. Smith, "HOPE VI and The New Urbanism, Eliminating Low-Income Housing to Make Mixed-income Communities," *Planner's Network* 151 (Spring 2002): 22–25; Sabrina Deitrick and Cliff Ellis, "New Urbanism in the Inner City: A Case Study of Pittsburgh," *Journal of the American Planning Association* 70, 4 (Autumn 2004); 426–442.

5. Michael Bernick and Robert Cervero, *Transit Villages in the 21st Century* (New York: McGraw-Hill, 1997); Peter Newman and Jeffrey Kenworthy, *Sustainability and Cities: Overcoming Automobile Dependence* (Washington, DC: Island Press, 1999).

6. Bruce Podobnik, "The New Urbanism and the Generation of Social Capital: Evidence from Orenco Station," *National Civic Review* 91, 3 (Fall 2002): 245–55. F. Kaid Benfield, Jutka Terris and Nancy Vorsanger, *Solving Sprawl: Models of Smart Growth in Communities across America* (Washington, DC: Island Press, 2001) present Orenco Station as a model "smart growth" community. Also see Thomas H. Sander, "Social Capital and The New Urbanism: Leading a Civic Horse to Water?" *National Civic Review* 91, 3 (Fall 2002): 213–34.

7. Marshall, *How Cities Work*, pp. 8–14.

8. Alexander Garvin, *The American City: What Works, What Doesn't,* 2nd ed. (New York: McGraw-Hill, 2002), pp. 415–416.

9. Susan F. Fainstein, "New Directions in Planning Theory," *Urban Affairs Review* 35(4), (March 2000), p. 464.

10. Marshall, p. 27. For a more detailed and nuanced discussion of life in Celebration, see Douglas Frantz and Catherine Collins, *Celebration, U.S.A.: Living in Disney's Brave New Town* (New York: Owl Books/Henry Holt, 2000), pp. 74–77 and 219–225.

11. Frantz and Collins, *Celebration, U.S.A.,* p. 313; also see pp. 255–56.

12. Garvin, *The American City: What Works, What Doesn't,* pp. 336–337.

13. Marshall, *How Cities Work*, pp. xx and 6. Also see Alex Krieger, "Arguing the Against' Position: The New Urbanism as a Means of Building and Rebuilding Our Cities," in *The Seaside Debates: A Critique of The New Urbanism,* ed. Todd W. Bressi (Rizzoli, 2002), pp. 51–58. For a defense of The New Urbanism that attempts to rebut many of the critiques, see Cliff Ellis, "The New Urbanism: Critiques and Rebuttals," *Journal of Urban Design* 7, 3 (2002): 261–291. For a most useful overview of The New Urbanism movements, the international reach of The New Urbanism, and the potential and limitations inherent in The New Urbanism, see Jill Grant, *Planning the Good Community: The New Urbanisms in Theory and Practice* (London: Routledge, 2006).

EXPLORING THE ISSUE

Does New Urbanism Represent a Viable Strategy That Can Transform Suburban Communities?

Critical Thinking and Reflection

1. How do you view life in the suburbs? Is life in the suburbs satisfactory or stultifying?
2. Are New Urbanists accurate or culturally elitist in their view of life in conventional suburbs?
3. Should "sustainability" be a guiding goal in urban development?
4. New Urban communities have seldom developed as transit-oriented communities. NU communities also have often fallen short when it comes to serving a diversity of population. What public policies would you suggest to help New Urban communities reach their goals?

Is There Common Ground?

New Urbanism has built only a relatively small number of new free-standing communities. Nonetheless, NU has had a wide influence on urban and suburban planning and architecture. Numerous housing developers seem to have rediscovered the virtues of front porches. The developers of new "town centers" and HOPE VI housing likewise have borrowed heavily from the New Urbanism. The NU has even affected the design of the single-store suburban power center, with a superstore emphasizing brick and other traditional building materials in its construction and, in some cases, even hiding behind false-front paintings that make the store appear, at least from the outside, to be a collection of quaint old-fashioned stores.

Further development of New Urban developments will require the relaxation of local zoning codes and regulations that bar apartments and condominiums from certain parts of town. Conventional zoning ordinances serve to segregate activities, not to mix land uses. A zoning map designates just which sort of activities are—and are not—allowed in each portion of a community. As New Urban founders Andrés Duany and Elizabeth Plater-Zyberk have advocated, such segregative zoning plans can be replaced by a "Smart Code" that allows more flexible and mixed-use patterns of development to take place throughout a community. Modifications are also required in cases where local land-use regulations require stores to provide parking on site. Such regulations are responsive to the demand of neighbors who fear that shoppers may park in their neighborhoods. But such regulations have the unfortunate effect of creating strip malls, with parking spaces built in front of stores. Such strip malls effectively break up the connectivity of the cityscape, building places that can be accessed comfortably only by automobile and not by foot.

Similarly, local ordinances that require wide streets to accommodate the large turning radius of the biggest fire trucks also serve to increase vehicular speeds, impeding walkability. "Skinny streets" can promote pedestrian use without jeopardizing citizen safety—at least in cases where the local fire department has smaller vehicles that can capably do the job, where parking is banned on street corners to facilitate turns by emergency vehicles, and where there exists sufficient alternative routes for fire trucks to speed to their destination.

New Urban developments can also be brought closer to the ideal vision of transit-oriented diverse communities. Local regulations, for instance, can require that new town centers be transportation-oriented, with public transit stations centrally located. Public funds can be used to help support such facilities. Similarly, public funds can help provide for affordable units in New Urbanism developments, a target of opportunity given how few other developments seek the inclusion of subsidized housing.

Additional Resources

Bressi, Todd W., ed. (2002). *The Seaside Debates: A Critique of the New Urbanism*. New York: Rizzoli, 2002.

Calthorpe, Peter. (2009). "HOPE VI and New Urbanism," in Henry G. Cisneros & Lara Engdahl, ed., *From Despair to Hope: HOPE VI and the New Promise of Public Housing in America's Cities*. Washington, DC: Brookings Institution, pp. 48–63.

Calthorpe, Peter, & William Fulton. (2001). *The Regional City*. Washington, DC: Island Press.

Congress for the New Urbanism. (2000). *Charter of the New Urbanism*. New York: McGraw-Hill.

Duany, Andres, Elizabeth Plater-Zyberk, & Jeff Speck. (2000). *Suburban Nation: The Rise of Sprawl and the Decline of the American Dream*. New York: North Point Press.

Dunham-Jones, Ellen, & June Williamson. (2009). *Retrofitting Suburbia: Urban Design Solutions for Redesigning Suburbs*. Hoboken, NJ: Wiley.

Marshall, Alex. (2000). *How Cities Work: Suburbs, Sprawl, and the Roads Not Taken*. Austin, TX: University of Texas Press.

Sobel, Lee S., Ellen Greenberg, & Steven Bodzin, eds. (2002). *Greyfields Into Goldfields: Dead Malls Become Living Neighborhoods*. San Francisco, CA: Congress for a New Urbanism.

Internet References

Congress for a New Urbanism

The principle organization in the New Urbanism movement, the CNU's website presents a copy of The Charter of the New Urbanism as well as numerous helpful articles describing the inspiration, goals, principles, and tools of NU.

www.cnu.org

Newurbanism.org

This site contains a variety of material on sprawl, Smart Growth, walkability, and transit-oriented solutions.

www.newurbanism.org

New Urban Network

The site, to which members of the Congress for a New Urbanism may subscribe, provides a variety of articles and commentary on New Urbanism and compact-city growth projects.

http://newurbannetwork.com

Planetizen

Planetizen is an online site where urban planners and interested citizens exchange posts, articles, and perspectives on various topics related to urban planning and design, including the New Urbanism, alternatives to sprawl, and the continuing debate over Smart Growth.

www.planetizen.com

Planner's Web: Sprawl & Growth

Planner's Web is a very useful online site where professionals in the planning field exchange news clips and their views regarding sprawl and Smart Growth alternatives.

www.plannersweb.com/articles/sprawl-articles.html

Smart Growth America

Among their other reports, see their 2003 study *Measuring the Health Effects of Sprawl: A National Analysis of Physical Activity, Obesity, and Chronic Disease.*

http://smartgrowthamerica.org

Debating the Future Direction of Urban Policy

*W*_{hat} *will the future city look like? Of course, no one really knows for sure. Still, we can expect that the future will alter patterns of urban settlement in important ways.*

Advances in technology and communication may serve to cut even further the ties of suburbanites to the central city. The rise of telecommuting and e-commerce may help open relatively distant exurban and rural areas to new development. Advances in transportation and technology can even lead to a regional shift in population and development, to small towns and rural areas not yet plagued by high land prices, crime, and other urban problems.

Technological innovation may even reduce some of the problems associated with continued suburban development and sprawl. More fuel-efficient engines and breakthroughs in automotive design can lessen pollution and the emission of greenhouse gases. Green construction practices and the introduction of new building materials, including higher grade insulation, can also reduce suburban energy consumption.

But the changes may not all be for the better. Many urban observers believe that future trends will for the most part exacerbate urban ills, producing an urban dystopia—not a utopia—unless government intervenes with effective corrective action. Most troubling will likely be the virtual disappearance of good-paying jobs for workers of low education and little skills. The manufacturing jobs of the old industrial city have already largely disappeared, lost to automation and lost to outsourced locations overseas. At its worst, cities may more and more come to resemble the picture of urban life portrayed in the classic scientific film Blade Runner, *where the future city suffers from a magnified urban dualism, the deep chasm that separates the "haves" and the "have nots." In* Blade Runner, *technologically competent knowledge workers are well paid but have little choice but to seek the safety of gated communities and secure entry-controlled high rises and office buildings. These* urban citadels and fortresses *keep out the threat posed by the growing numbers of the urban poor, a superfluous population who lack the skills to do work of great value in the new global economy.*

Other countries around the world have taken stronger actions than has the United States in their efforts to guide urban growth and to promote more equitable and sustainable patterns of urban development. Countries in Europe have strong social welfare and planning programs that seek to reduce the social stratification and polarizations typical of living patterns in the United States. European nations and cities also initiate stronger actions to ensure that growth is compatible with environmental protection.

But not every policy tried overseas represents a good "fit" for the United States. Just what exactly can the United States learn from countries around the world? Just what urban approaches in Europe and elsewhere can be appropriately transferred to the United States?

- Should Urban Policy in the United States Be Guided by the Model of the European City?

ISSUE 18

Should Urban Policy in the United States Be Guided by the Model of the European City?

YES: Elisabeth Rosenthal, from "Across Europe, Irking Drivers Is Urban Policy," *New York Times* (June 26, 2011)

NO: Joel Kotkin, from "The War Against Suburbia," *The American: The Journal of the American Enterprise Institute* (January 2010)

Learning Outcomes

After reading this issue, you should be able to:

- Differentiate between market-led urban development in the United States and plan-led development in Europe.
- Identify the various tools that European policymakers use to shape urban growth, tools that are much less frequently used in the United States.
- Identify the policies that European policymakers use to decrease automobile reliance.
- Identify the various "costs" of European urban policies and why European-style actions may not be an appropriate fit in the U.S. setting.

ISSUE SUMMARY

YES: Elisabeth Rosenthal, reporter for *The New York Times*, reviews the various means by which European countries discourage automobile use and encourage walking, bicycling, and public transit.

NO: Joel Kotkin, presidential fellow in Urban Futures at Chapman University and author of *The City: A Global History*, argues that Americans prefer automobile-orientated lives and the freedoms and privacy of large single-family homes as contrasted the smaller housing units and greater population densities of Europe.

$\mathbf{A}$s a visitor to Europe quickly sees, cities in Europe differ markedly from their American counterparts. The downtowns of European cities are less dominated by high-rise office development and instead feature outdoor plazas, sidewalk cafés, automobile-free pedestrian zones, and low-rise historic buildings adapted for modern use. Residents in Europe have less need for a car, as trains and trams run frequently and serve the entire region.

The differences are not accidental. European cities and suburbs are shaped by strong government planning. Urban development patterns in the United States are more the product of free-market choices and private investment decisions.

European cities make more extensive use of *land banking*, where governmental authorities acquire and save land parcels in order to control just what development will ultimately take place. Many European nations use *greenbelts* to delimit urban growth and protect green space and agricultural acreage from the threat of sprawl. Compared to the United States, European cities place more extensive regulation on building facades and heights, whereas National governments in Europe also assume greater responsibility for the provision of health care, welfare, education, mass transit, and social housing and provide a greater share of local budgets, relieving much of the fiscal burden that American cities bear (Savitch & Kantor 2002).

The major differences between the U.S. and the European cities are summarized in Table 1. A brief look at the development of Paris and Stockholm will serve to underscore the greater role that governments in Europe play in shaping the growth of cities and suburbs.

In the decades following World War II, Paris was in need of modernization. The central state, not private businesses, directed the change. The national government gave its delegate for the Paris region, Paul Delouvrier, the authority to undertake the capital region's massive transformation. Delouvrier implemented a master plan to provide the housing, transportation, and other infrastructure to modernize the city and provide for the region's future vitality. The government's plans assured that new facilities would be built without destroying what was unique and wonderful in the "old city" of Paris (Savitch, 1988). To avoid overcrowding the historic city center, Delouvrier built suburban "new towns" that were connected to Paris by a new commuter rail system.

Delouvrier's planners sought to build a Paris that could accommodate global business headquarters without sacrificing the beauty of the city's historic core. Private developers were not allowed to change the face of Old Paris by constructing new glass office towers and high-rise apartments in the city's historic neighborhoods. Strict regulation of building heights and façades served to preserve the texture of the old city. Instead of allowing high-rise development in the city center, the planners designated an entirely new area for office construction, just over the city boundary line at La Défense. Formerly a small town, La Défense became France's equivalent of New York's Wall Street New office development, was concentrated on the outskirts of the city, thereby preserving the architectural integrity and ambience of the city's world-renowned center.

Table 1

Comparison Between U.S. and European Cities

United States	Europe
Low-density cities and urban sprawl	Development at higher densities and protection of green space
Local autonomy and metropolitan fragmentation that impedes effective land-use planning in a region	Regional governments are given considerable control over development and land uses
City power limited by both federalism and the constitutional doctrine of Dillon's Rule that gives each state the ability to define and limit municipal powers	Cities historically possess real authority
High automobile usage and widespread automobile ownership, promoted by extensive government investment in road construction	High taxes on gasoline, high automobile registration fees, and extensive government investment in rail, tram, and bus systems and in bicycle trails
Market-led land use; private business owners and the housing market help to determine patterns of land use	Government owns and controls large tracts of land; government engages in "land banking;" strong government regulation of building heights and facades
Farm land on city's rim is sold for residential and commercial development	Large agricultural subsidies and strict regulations serve to preserve farm land
Low taxes; relatively high levels of individual entrepreneurialism	Higher taxes; welfare state social supports, and an emphasis on "social cohesion"
Tax code promotes home ownership; subsidized housing programs reinforce the spatial segregation of the poor	Mixed-income rental housing is provided for a fairly large portion of the population, not just the very poor
Heavy municipal reliance on property taxes and own-source revenues; inequalities in public school finance	Greater fiscal burden sharing by the central government with central spending emphasizing leading to greater service equalization
Growth of suburban shopping malls and "big-box" superstores	Preservation of vibrant central-city "high streets" as a result of regulations that help to protect small shops from some of the competition offered by malls and suburban megastores

In Sweden, strong governmental planning similarly helped Stockholm to emerge as a lively urban center, with downtown pedestrian zones and shopping areas accessible by mass transit. To create an automobile-free center, planners developed a regional rail system and moved parking off site. Regional planners also built a number of new suburban residential towns along the "fingers" or spokes" of the rail lines radiating from the city center. High-density housing was sited close to the rail stations to provide the population base necessary for mass transit; densities were less in neighborhoods located at greater distances from the station. Feeder bus routes and walking and bicycling trails fanned out from the station area, offering an alternative to the automobile. Transit-oriented, compact, and surrounded by a growth boundary to protect abutting green areas, the new towns acted to avert sprawled development.

A system of congestion pricing (see Issue 12), where drivers are charged a fee to enter central Stockholm, also served to promote the use of mass transit.

As the case studies presented above reveal, urban regions in Europe developed under the guidance of strong state planning. European governments provide "social housing" (subsidized housing) and social welfare assistance to a greater degree than is common in the United States. European planning also pays attention to matters of ecological sustainability, including the provision of mass transit and the preservation of open space.

Yet, the differences that distinguish the European city from the American city, while still very real, are not as great as they once were. As we saw in our discussion of Smart Growth (Issue15), U.S. cities are also beginning to show a new concern for ecological sustainability, including the adoption of "green" building codes and, in some cases, even European-style urban growth boundaries.

European states, in turn, have begun to retreat from—or at least greatly modify—their strong government planning approach. Even in countries that can still be considered welfare states, urban policies are increasingly marked by decentralization, local initiative, and the priority accorded local economic development (Le Galès 2002, 175). "New mayors" (Clark & Hoffman-Martinot, 1998) in Europe are more business- and partnership-oriented than were their predecessors.

In Europe, rising affluence has increased automobile ownership and the demand for suburban homes (Couch, Leontidou & Petschel-Held, 2007). Across Europe, stores on neighborhood "high streets" (to use the British term) have lost market share to big-box superstores and suburban retailers such as Wal-Mart, Carrefour, Tesco, and IKEA.

Still, despite trend toward increased convergence, the fundamental difference between the European city from the American city remains. Even with the increased acceptance of privatization, public–private partnerships, and decentralization, strong government policies and planning continue to shape the European city to a degree that is unimaginable in the United States.

A good example of the difference is provided by transportation policy where, as Elisabeth Rosenthal describes (in the YES selection), U.S. planners largely seek to improve traffic flows and to ensure that new developments provide an adequate number of parking spaces. European planners, by contrast, have been "openly hostile" to driving and have removed parking places, pedestrianized streets, increased the frequency of red lights, and lowered permitted traffic speeds. High vehicle registration fees and gas prices, too, serve to discourage automobile use. The creation of segregated bicycle lanes has helped to make cycling an important part of the transportation system of Europe's cities.

Joel Kotkin, in "The War Against Suburbia," argues that it would be undemocratic to impose similar policies on an unwilling American population. Kotkin further objects to what he sees as the efforts of liberal policy elites to copy European practices and "force densification" on an American public that prefers the comforts and privacy of the automobile and of large single-family homes. Kotkin rejects the strong top-down planning approach of Europe. He argues for the adoption of alternative environmental policies that are more consistent with the suburban lifestyle preferences of most Americans.

YES

Elisabeth Rosenthal

Across Europe, Irking Drivers Is Urban Policy

ZURICH—while American cities are synchronizing green lights to improve traffic flow and offering apps to help drivers find parking, many European cities are doing the opposite: creating environments openly hostile to cars. The methods vary, but the mission is clear—to make car use expensive and just plain miserable enough to tilt drivers toward more environmentally friendly modes of transportation.

Cities including Vienna to Munich and Copenhagen have closed vast swaths of streets to car traffic. Barcelona and Paris have had car lanes eroded by popular bike-sharing programs. Drivers in London and Stockholm pay hefty congestion charges just for entering the heart of the city. And over the past two years, dozens of German cities have joined a national network of "environmental zones" where only cars with low carbon dioxide emissions may enter.

Likeminded cities welcome new shopping malls and apartment buildings but severely restrict the allowable number of parking spaces. On-street parking is vanishing. In recent years, even former car capitals like Munich have evolved into "walkers' paradises," said Lee Schipper, a senior research engineer at Stanford University who specializes in sustainable transportation.

"In the United States, there has been much more of a tendency to adapt cities to accommodate driving," said Peder Jensen, head of the Energy and Transport Group at the European Environment Agency. "Here there has been more movement to make cities more livable for people, to get cities relatively free of cars."

To that end, the municipal Traffic Planning Department here in Zurich has been working overtime in recent years to torment drivers. Closely spaced red lights have been added on roads into town, causing delays and angst for commuters. Pedestrian underpasses that once allowed traffic to flow freely across major intersections have been removed. Operators in the city's ever expanding tram system can turn traffic lights in their favor as they approach, forcing cars to halt.

Around Löwenplatz, one of Zurich's busiest squares, cars are now banned on many blocks. Where permitted, their speed is limited to a snail's pace so that crosswalks and crossing signs can be removed entirely, giving people on foot the right to cross anywhere they like at any time.

As he stood watching a few cars inch through a mass of bicycles and pedestrians, the city's chief traffic planner, Andy Fellmann, smiled. "Driving is a stop-and-go experience," he said. "That's what we like! Our goal is to reconquer public space for pedestrians, not to make it easy for drivers."

While some American cities—notably San Francisco, which has "pedestrianized" parts of Market Street—have made similar efforts, they are still the exception in the United States, where it has been difficult to get people to imagine a life where cars are not entrenched, Dr. Schipper said.

Europe's cities generally have stronger incentives to act. Built for the most part before the advent of cars, their narrow roads are poor at handling heavy traffic. Public transportation is generally better in Europe than in the United States, and gas often costs over $8 a gallon, contributing to driving costs that are two to three times greater per mile than in the United States, Dr. Schipper said.

What is more, European Union countries probably cannot meet a commitment under the Kyoto Protocol to reduce their carbon dioxide emissions unless they curb driving. The United States never ratified that pact.

Globally, emissions from transportation continue a relentless rise, with half of them coming from personal cars. Yet an important impulse behind Europe's traffic reforms will be familiar to mayors in Los Angeles and Vienna alike: to make cities more inviting, with cleaner air and less traffic.

Michael Kodransky, global research manager at the Institute for Transportation and Development Policy in New York, which works with cities to reduce transport emissions, said that Europe was previously "on the same trajectory as the United States, with more people wanting to own more cars." But in the past decade, there had been "a conscious shift in thinking, and firm policy," he said. And it is having an effect.

After two decades of car ownership, Hans Von Matt, 52, who works in the insurance industry, sold his vehicle and now gets around Zurich by tram or bicycle, using a car-sharing service for trips out of the city. Carless households have increased from 40 to 45 percent in the last decade, and car owners use their vehicles less, city statistics show.

"There were big fights over whether to close this road or not—but now it is closed, and people got used to it," he said, alighting from his bicycle on Limmatquai, a riverside pedestrian zone lined with cafes that used to be two lanes of gridlock. Each major road closing has to be approved in a referendum.

Today 91 percent of the delegates to the Swiss Parliament take the tram to work.

Still, there is grumbling. "There are all these zones where you can only drive 20 or 30 kilometers per hour [about 12 to 18 miles an hour], which is rather stressful," Thomas Rickli, a consultant, said as he parked his Jaguar in a lot at the edge of town. "It's useless."

Urban planners generally agree that a rise in car commuting is not desirable for cities anywhere.

Mr. Fellmann calculated that a person using a car took up 115 cubic meters (roughly 4,000 cubic feet) of urban space in Zurich while a pedestrian took three. "So it's not really fair to everyone else if you take the car," he said.

European cities also realized they could not meet increasingly strict World Health Organization guidelines for fine-particulate air pollution if cars continued to reign. Many American cities are likewise in "nonattainment" of their Clean Air Act requirements, but that fact "is just accepted here," said Mr. Kodransky of the New York-based transportation institute.

It often takes extreme measures to get people out of their cars, and providing good public transportation is a crucial first step. One novel strategy in Europe is intentionally making it harder and more costly to park. "Parking is everywhere in the United States, but it's disappearing from the urban space in Europe," said Mr. Kodransky, whose recent report "Europe's Parking U-Turn" surveys the shift.

Sihl City, a new Zurich mall, is three times the size of Brooklyn's Atlantic Mall but has only 225 more parking spaces than Atlantic's 625, and as a result, 70 percent of visitors get there by public transport, Mr. Kodransky said.

In Copenhagen, Mr. Jensen, at the European Environment Agency, said that his office building had more than 150 spaces for bicycles and only one for a car, to accommodate a disabled person.

While many building codes in Europe cap the number of parking spaces in new buildings to discourage car ownership, American codes conversely tend to stipulate a minimum number. New apartment complexes built along the light rail line in Denver devote their bottom eight floors to parking, making it "too easy" to get in the car rather than take advantage of rail transit, Mr. Kodransky said.

While Mayor Michael R. Bloomberg has generated controversy in New York by "pedestrianizing" a few areas like Times Square, many European cities have already closed vast areas to car traffic. Store owners in Zurich had worried that the closings would mean a drop in business, but that fear has proved unfounded, Mr. Fellmann said, because pedestrian traffic increased 30 to 40 percent where cars were banned.

With politicians and most citizens still largely behind them, Zurich's planners continue their traffic-taming quest, shortening the green-light periods and lengthening the red with the goal that pedestrians wait no more than 20 seconds to cross.

"We would never synchronize green lights for cars with our philosophy," said Pio Marzolini, a city official. "When I'm in other cities, I feel like I'm always waiting to cross a street. I can't get used to the idea that I am worth less than a car."

Joel Kotkin  **NO**

The War Against Suburbia

A year into the Obama administration, America's dominant geography, suburbia, is now in open revolt against an urban-centric regime that many perceive threatens their way of life, values, and economic future. . . .

The lesson here is that political movements ignore suburbanites at their peril. For the better part of a century, Americans have been voting with their feet, moving inexorably away from the central cities and towards the suburban periphery. Today a solid majority of Americans live in suburbs and exurbs, more than countryside residents and urbanites combined.

. . . For the first time in memory, the suburbs are under a conscious and sustained attack from Washington. Little that the adminstration has pushed—from the Wall Street bailouts to the proposed "cap and trade" policies—offers much to predominately middle-income-oriented suburbanites and instead appears to have worked to alienate them.

And then there are the policies that seem targeted against suburbs. In everything from land use and transportation to "green" energy policy, the Obama administration has been pushing an agenda that seeks to move Americans out of their preferred suburban locales and into the dense, transit-dependent locales they have eschewed for generations. . . .

Many Obama appointees—such as at the Departments of Transportation and of Housing and Urban Development (HUD) and at the Environmental Protection Agency (EPA)—favor a policy agenda that would drive more Americans to live in central cities. And the president himself seems to embrace this approach, declaring in February that "the days of building sprawl" were, in his words, "over."

Not surprisingly, belief in "smart growth," a policy that seeks to force densification of communities and returning people to core cities, animates many top administration officials. This includes both HUD Secretary Shaun Donovan and Undersecretary Ron Sims, Transportation undersecretary for policy Roy Kienitz, and the EPA's John Frece.

Transportation Secretary Ray LaHood revealed the new ideology when he famously declared the administration's intention to "coerce" Americans out of their cars and into transit. In Congress, the president's allies, including Minnesota Congressman James Oberstar, have advocated shifting a larger chunk of gas tax funds collected from drivers to rail and other transit.

From *The American*, January 2010. Copyright © 2010 by American Enterprise Institute. Reprinted by permission. www.american.com

In addition, the president's stimulus—with its $8 billion allocation for high-speed rail and proposed giant increases in mass transit—offers little to anyone who lives outside a handful of large metropolitan cores. Economics writer Robert Samuelson, among others, has denounced the high-speed rail idea as "a boondoggle" not well-suited to a huge, multi-centered country like the United States. Green job schemes also seem more suited to boost employment for university researchers and inner-city residents than middle-income suburbanites.

. . . Administration officials have also started handing out $300 million stimulus-funded grants to cities that follow "smart growth principles." Grants for cities to adopt "sustainability" oriented development will reward those communities with the proper planning orientation. There is precious little that will benefit suburbanites, such as improved roads or investment in other basic infrastructure.

But ultimately it will be sticks and not carrots that planners hope to use to drive de-suburbanization. Perhaps the most significant will be new draconian controls over land use. Administration officials, particularly from the EPA, participated in the drafting of the recent "Moving Cooler" report, which suggested such policies as charging tolls on the Interstate Highway System, charging people to park in front of their homes, and steering some 90 percent of all future development into the most dense portions of already existing urban development.

Of course, such policies have little or no chance of being passed by Congress. Too many representatives come from suburban or rural districts to back policies that would penalize a population that uses automobiles for upwards of 98 percent of their transportation and account for 95 percent of all work trips.

But the president's cadres may find other ways to impose their agenda. New controls, for example, may be enacted through the courts and regulatory action. . . .

Such threats will become more commonplace as regulating greenhouse gases fall under administrative scrutiny. As can already be seen in California, regulators can use the threat of climate change as a rationale to stop funding—and permitting—for even well-conceived residential, commercial, or industrial projects construed as likely to generate excess greenhouse gases.

These efforts will be supported by an elaborate coalition of new urbanist and environmental groups. At the same time, a powerful urban land interest, including many close to the Democratic Party, would also support steps that thwart suburban growth and give them a near monopoly on future development over the coming decades.

Glimpse the Future

One can glimpse this future by observing what takes place in most European countries, including the United Kingdom, where land use is controlled from the center. For decades, options for new development have been sharply circumscribed, with mandates for ever-smaller lots and smaller homes more the norm for single-family residences.

In Britain the dominant planning model is widely known as "cramming," meaning forced densification into smaller geographic areas. Over the past generation, this has spurred a rapid shrinking of house sizes for a generation. Today the average new British "hobbit" house, although quite expensive, covers barely 800 square feet, roughly one-third that of the average American residence. Even in quite distant suburbia many of the features widely enjoyed here—sizable backyards, spare bedrooms, home office space— are disappearing.

But these suburban hobbits will be living large compared to the sardines who would be forced to move into inner cities. In London, already a densely packed city, planners are calling for denser apartment blocks and congested neighborhoods.

This top-driven scenario may be playing soon in America. Following the proposed edicts of "Moving Cooler," the urban option increasingly would become almost the only choice other than the countryside. Unlike their baby boomer parents, the next generation would have few affordable choices in comfortable, low- and medium-density suburbs and single-family homes.

Ownership of a single-family home would become increasingly the province only of the highly affluent or those living on the fringes of second-tier American cities. Due to the very high costs of construction for multi-family apartments in inner cities, most prospective homeowners would also be forced to remain renters. Although widely hailed as "progressive," these policies would herald a return to the kind of crowded renter-dominated metropolis that existed prior to the Second World War.

Are Suburbs Doomed?

The anti-suburban impulse is nothing new. Suburbs have rarely been popular among academics, planners, and the punditry. The suburbanite displeased "the professional planner and the intellectual defender of cosmopolitan culture," noted sociologist Herbert Gans. The 1960s counterculture expanded this critique, viewing suburbia as one of many "tasteless travesties of mass society," along with fast and processed food, plastics, and large cars. Suburban life represented the opposite of the cosmopolitan urban scene; one critic termed it "vulgaria."

Liberals also castigated suburbs as the racist spawn of "white flight." But more recently, environmental causes—particularly greenhouse gas emissions as well as dire warning about the prospects for "peak oil"—now drive much of the argument against suburbanization.

The housing crash that began in 2007 added grist to the contention that the age of suburban growth has come to an end. . . .

Yet fundamentally the attack on suburbia has less to do with market trends or the environment than with a deep-seated desire to change the way Americans live. For years urban boosters have proposed that more Americans should reside in what they deemed "more livable," denser, transit-oriented communities for their own good. One recent example, David Owens' *Green*

Metropolis, supports the notion that Americans should be encouraged to embrace "extreme compactness"—using Manhattan as the model. . . .

What Do the Suburbanites Want?

In their assessments, few density advocates bother to consider whether most suburbanites would like to give up their leafy backyards for dense apartment blocks. Many urban boosters simply could not believe that, once given an urban option, anyone would *choose* to live in suburbia.

Jane Jacobs, for example, believed that "suburbs must be a difficult place to raise children." Yet had Jacobs paid as much attention to suburbs as she did to her beloved Greenwich Village, she would have discovered that they possess their own considerable appeal, most particularly for people with children. "If suburban life is undesirable," noted Gans in 1969, "the suburbanites themselves seem blissfully unaware of it."

Contrary to much of the current media hype, most Americans continue to prefer suburban living. Indeed for four decades, according to numerous surveys, the portion of the population that prefers to live in a big city has consistently been in the 10 to 20 percent range, while roughly 50 percent or more opt for suburbs or exurbs. The reasons? The simple desire for privacy, quiet, safety, good schools, and closer-knit communities. The single-family house, detested by many urbanists, also exercises a considerable pull. Surveys by the National Association of Realtors and the National Association of Home Builders find that some 83 percent of potential buyers prefer this kind of dwelling over a townhouse or apartment.

In other words, suburbs have expanded because people like them. A 2008 Pew study revealed that suburbanites displayed the highest degree of satisfaction with where they lived compared to those who lived in cities, small towns, and the countryside. This contradicts another of the great urban legends of the 20th century—espoused by urbanists, planning professors, and pundits and portrayed in Hollywood movies—that suburbanites are alienated, autonomous individuals, while city dwellers have a deep sense of belonging and connection to their neighborhoods.

Indeed on virtually every measurement—from jobs and environment to families—suburban residents express a stronger sense of identity and civic involvement with their communities than those living in cities. One recent University of California at Irvine study found that density does not, as is often assumed, increase social contact between neighbors or raise overall social involvement. For every 10 percent reduction in density, the chances of people talking to their neighbors increases by 10 percent, and their likelihood of belonging to a local club by 15 percent.

These preferences have helped make suburbanization the predominant trend in virtually every region of the country. Even in Portland, Oregon, a city renowned for its urban-oriented policy, barely 10 percent of all population growth this decade has occurred within the city limits, while more than 90 percent has taken place in the suburbs over the past decade. Ironically, one contributing factor has been the demands of urbanites themselves, who want to preserve historic structures and maintain relatively modest densities in their neighborhoods.

Multicultural Flight

Perhaps nothing reflects the universal appeal of suburban lifestyles more than its growing ethnic diversity. In 1970, nearly 95 percent of suburbanites were white. Today many of these same communities have emerged as the new melting pots of American society. Along with immigrants, African-Americans have moved to the suburbs in huge numbers: between 1970 and 2009, the proportion of African-Americans living in the periphery grew from less than one-sixth to 40 percent.

Today minorities constitute over 27 percent of the nation's suburbanites. In fast-growing Gwinett County outside Atlanta, minorities made up less than 10 percent of the population in 1980; by 2006 the county was on the verge of becoming "majority minority." In greater Washington, D.C., the Northeast's most dynamic region in economic and demographic terms, 87 percent of foreign migrants live in the suburbs, while less than 13 percent live in the district, according to a 2001 Brookings Institution study. . . .

Perhaps most intriguingly, this diversity is itself diverse, including not only African-Americans but also Latinos and Asians. Suburban areas such as Fort Bend county, Texas, and the city of Walnut, in the San Gabriel Valley east of Los Angeles, already have among the most diverse populations in the nation. And this is not merely a California phenomenon: Aurora (outside Denver), Bellevue (the Seattle suburb), and Blaine (outside Minneapolis) are becoming ever-more diverse even as the nearby city centers become less so. By 2000 well over half of mixed-race households were in the suburbs, a percentage that continues to grow.

Today the most likely locale for America's new ethnic shopping centers, Hindu temples, and new mosques are not in the teeming cities but in the outer suburbs of Los Angeles, New York, and Houston. "If a multiethnic society is working out in America," suggests California demographer James Allen, "it will be worked out in [these] places. . . . The future of America is in the suburbs."

A War Not Worth Fighting

If most Americans clearly prefer suburbs, then why would our elected representatives choose to pick a fight with them? Perhaps the most widely used explanation lies with densification as a means of reducing greenhouse gases. But this rationale itself seems flawed, and could reflect more long-standing prejudice than proven science.

For example, a recent study by the National Academy of Sciences found that a nationally imposed densification policy would at best cut greenhouse gas emissions between less than 1 and 11 percent by 2050. Other research suggests that, by some measurements, low-density development can use less energy than denser urban forms.

Although automobile commuting now consumes more energy resources than well-traveled traditional urban rail systems, the future generation of low-mileage cars may prove more efficient than often underutilized rail systems that are now seen as critical elements of fighting climate change. A public system running at low capacity—commonplace in many regions—may actually produce more emissions than the coming generation of personal vehicles.

Moreover, tall buildings may not be as green as some advocates suggest. Recent studies out of Australia show that townhouses, small condos, and even single-family homes generate far less heat per capita than the supposedly environmentally superior residential towers, particularly when one takes into account the cost of heating common areas and the highly consumptive lifestyle of affluent urbanites (with their country homes, vacations, and frequent flying). In terms of energy conservation, the easiest and least expensive option may be to retrofit single-family houses and wood-shaded townhouses.

Two- or three-story homes or townhouses often require only double-paned windows and natural shading to reduce their energy consumption; one Los Angeles study found that white roofs and shade trees can reduce suburban air conditioning by 18 percent. Such structures are particularly ideal for using the heat- and water-saving elements of landscaping: after all, a nice maple can cool a two-story house more efficiently than it can a ten-story apartment.

Of course, density advocates can and do produce their own studies to justify their agenda. But there seems enough reasonable doubt to focus on more efficient, and less intrusive, ways to create greener communities by improving energy efficiency of automobiles and changing the way suburbs fit into metropolitan systems.

Turning Deadwood into Greenurbia

The "green" assault on suburbia also largely ignores changes already taking place across the suburban landscape. In a historical context, the latest suburban "sprawl" may be compared to Deadwood. That rough-and-ready mining town on the Dakota frontier was developed quickly for the narrow purpose of being close to a vein of gold. But over time these towns developed respectable shopping streets, theaters, and other community institutions.

One change already evident can be seen in commuting patterns. Density advocates and the media often characterize suburbanites as people who generally take long commutes to work compared to the shorter rides enjoyed by city-dwellers. But with the continuing dispersion of work to the suburbs over the past two decades, suburban work locations actually enjoyed shorter commutes than their inner city counterparts in virtually all the largest metropolitan areas.

This is true even in New York. Although Manhattanites enjoy short commutes and can even walk to work, most people who live in New York City and work in Manhattan suffer among the longest commutes in the nation. In fact, residents of Queens and Staten Island spend the most time getting to work of all metropolitan counties. Residents in suburbs and particularly exurbs actually endure generally shorter commutes, in large part because of less congestion and closer proximity to employment.

Such pairing of jobs and housing will shape the suburban future and represents among the easiest ways to cut transportation-related emissions. Even more promising has been the continuing rise in home-based employment. According to Forrester Research, roughly 34 million Americans now commute at least part time from home; by 2016 these numbers are predicted to swell upwards to 63 million.

Oddly, despite these tremendous potential environmental benefits, the shift toward cyberspace has elicited little support from smart-growth advocates. Indeed most reports on density and greenhouse gases virtually ignore the consideration of telecommuting and dispersed work.

One reason may be that telecommuting breaks with the prevailing planning and green narratives by making dispersion more feasible. The ability to work full time or part time from home, notes one planning expert, expands metropolitan "commuter sheds" to areas well outside their traditional limits. In exchange for a rural or exurban lifestyle, this new commuter—who may go in to "work" only one or two days a week—will endure the periodic extra long trip to the office.

Yet although it may offend planning sensibilities, the potential energy savings—particularly in vehicle miles traveled—could be enormous. Telecommuters drive less, naturally; on telecommuting days, average vehicle miles are between 53 percent and 77 percent lower. Overall a 10 percent increase in telecommuting over the next decade will reduce 45 million tons of greenhouse gases, while also dramatically cutting office construction and energy use. Only an almost impossibly large shift to mass transit could produce comparable savings.

Ultimately, technology will undermine much of the green case against suburbia. If we really want to bring about a greener era, focusing attention on low-density enclaves would bring change that conforms to the preferences of the vast majority of people.

Think Twice Before You Act

Ultimately, the war against suburbia reflects a radical new vision of American life which, in the name of community and green values, would reverse the democratizing of the landscape that has characterized much of the past 50 years. It would replace a political economy based on individual aspiration and association in small communities, with a more highly organized, bureaucratic, and hierarchical form of social organization.

In some ways we could say forced densification could augur in a kind of new feudalism, where questions of land ownership and decision making would be shifted away from citizens, neighbors, or markets, and left in the hands of self-appointed "betters." This seems strange for an administration—and a party—whose raison d'être ostensibly has been to widen opportunities rather than constrict them. . . .

Given these realities, it seems more practical not to work against such aspirations but instead to evolve intelligent policies that would reconcile them with our long-term environmental needs. Suburbanites like their suburbs but would also like to find a way to make them greener as well as more economically and socially viable. Right now neither party has developed such an agenda, and so the suburbs, now clearly leaning right, remain up for grabs. To win suburbanites over, politicians first have to respect the basic preferences while offering a realistic program for improvement. This remains a key to building a sustainable electoral majority, not just for the next election, but for the decades to come.

EXPLORING THE ISSUE

Should Urban Policy in the United States Be Guided by the Model of the European City?

Critical Thinking and Reflection

1. What is your attitude toward planning? Is strong planning necessary to promote an appropriate balance of land uses and good community development? Or is strong governmental planning intrusive?
2. Which type of city do you prefer, the low-rise, mixed-development, center-focused European city or the more dynamic glass-tower-downtown and sprawling large-lot-home American city?
3. Should governments make costly investments to extend and modernize subways and commuter rail systems?
4. Should governments seek to promote compact development?

Is There Common Ground?

As we discussed earlier in the debate of Issue 15, the defenders of America's suburbs and the advocates of Smart Growth and compact development will continue to clash over just what constitutes good development. But there may be common ground in certain areas, if, as Joel Kotkin suggests, the defenders of suburbia are willing to entertain policies that will help make suburban living more "green."

Environmentalists, must, begin to recognize the practical importance of "greening" practices in existing suburbs, as opposed to simply designing more perfect eco-friendly new communities. Compact development can only be obtained when a mass transit system is introduced first, with housing later built around it. American metropolitan areas, however, have not been built in such a manner. Instead, developers built and sold homes, often after buying up large tracts of land, without waiting for the development of public transit. As a result, the housing in the American suburb is already spread out; mass transit systems do not provide a good "fit" for the low-density development and sprawl of the American suburb.

Even the imposition of extraordinarily high taxes on automobile ownership and gasoline, a feature of the European city model, cannot realistically be expected to alter substantially the physical structure of a metropolis that has already been built. High fuel costs will not lead many Americans to reject suburban living. Faced with high energy costs, suburbanites may simply dial down their heating and air-conditioning a bit or cut back on a few shopping and leisure trips. Politicians attempt to win the votes of suburbanites with the promise of governmental assistance to help them cope with soaring energy bills.

What realistically can be done? There are communities where environmental sentiment is strong. In those communities, policy makers can follow the compact-city, transit-oriented model.

But in most regions, where single-family homes have already been built, policy makers can seek environmental gains by introducing sustainability principles into already-developed communities:

Step 1: Construction codes can emphasize green development. Project approval should require such factors as: adequate insulation to reduce energy costs, passive use of solar energy and natural lighting, reuse of recycled materials in construction, and landscape design and the use of ground pavers to promote on-site water runoff and the natural filtration of contaminants from groundwater.

Step 2: Continue to develop alternatives to the automobile, including bicycle routes as well as public transit, for those people who are willing to take alternate transit. In communities as diverse as Minneapolis, Sacramento, Portland, Seattle, and Atlanta, there is greater local public support for the provision of a public transit, including a network of bicycle trails, than opponents recognize.

Step 3: Develop more fuel-efficient and less polluting vehicles. Incentivizing or mandating greater automobile fuel efficiency, however difficult politically, still represents an easier task than trying to reshape American housing preferences and to restructure patterns of settlement.

Step 4: As the practitioners of New Urbanism advocate, build interesting places that promote walkability. New Urbanism-style lifestyle and entertainment centers have already shown that people are willing to get out of their cars and walk, if there is something fun or interesting to do.

Step 5: Institute policies that present Americans with a choice of living environments. Although most Americans greatly enjoy their single-family home and suburban lives, other citizens express their boredom with suburban living, prefer a style of living that is more compatible with environmental values, and would prefer a residence that allows them to be part of a community rather than merely the occupant of a large isolated McMansion. Many Americans will choose to live in more compact, transit-oriented, European style centers, if appropriate living options are made available to them.

Step 6: Increase investment in public education and in law enforcement in the nation's cities and inner-ring suburbs. Americans will undoubtedly continue the migration to the suburbs, especially if suburbs offer the only good public schools and safe living environments. Even Americans who prefer a more active city life will often opt to leave for the suburbs in cases where a city's schools are of poor quality and where neighborhoods are unsafe. Making the commitment to strengthen city schools and promote public safety is absolutely essential if Americans are to be more like Europeans in viewing cities as the centers of civilized living.

Additional Resources

Bagnasco, Arnaldo, & Patrick Le Galès, eds. (2000). *Cities in Contemporary Europe.* Cambridge, UK, and New York: Cambridge University Press.

Beatley, Timothy. (2000). *Green Cities: Learning from European Cities.* Washington, DC: Island Press.

Bontje, Marco. (2003). "A 'Planner's Paradise' Lost? Past, Present and Future of Dutch National Urbanization Policy." *European Urban and Regional Studies* 10(2): 135–151.

Cervero, Robert. (1998). *The Transit Metropolis: A Global Inquiry.* Washington DC: Island Press.

Clark, Terry. N., & Vincent Hoffman-Martinot, eds. (1998). *The New Political Culture.* Boulder, Colorado: Westview Press.

Couch, Chris, Lila Leontidou, & Gerhard Petschel-Held, eds. (2007). *Urban Sprawl in Europe: Landscapes, Land-Use Change & Policy.* Oxford, UK, and Malden, MA: Blackwell.

de Roo, Gert. (2003). *Environmental Planning in the Netherlands: Too Good to be True.* London, England: Ashgate.

Dutt, Ashkok K., and Frank .J. Costa, eds. (1985). *Public Planning in the Netherlands.* Oxford, UK: Oxford Univversity Press.

Gordon, David, ed. (2006). *Planning Twentieth Century Capital Cities.* London and New York: Routledge.

Kazepov, Yuri, ed. (2003). *Cities of Europe: Changing Contexts, Local Arrangements, and the Challenge to Urban Cohesion.* Malden, MA: Blackwell.

Le Galès, Patrick. (2002). *European Cities: Social Conflict and Governance.* Oxford, UK: Oxford University Press.

Levine, Myron A. (1994). "The Transformation of Urban Politics in France: The Roots of Growth Politics and Urban Regimes." *Urban Affairs Quarterly,* 29(3): 383–410.

Levine, Myron A. (2004). "Government Policy, the Local State, and Gentrification: The Case of Prenzlauer Berg (Berlin), Germany. *Journal of Urban Affairs,* 26(1): 89–108.

Marshall, Tim, ed. (2004). *Transforming Barcelona.* London, England: Routledge.

Newman, Peter, & Andy Thornley. (1996). *Urban Planning in Europe: International Competition, National Systems and Planning Projects.* London, England: Routledge.

Newman, Peter, & Andy Thornley. (2011). *Planning World Cities: Globalization and Urban Politics,* 2nd ed. New York: Palgrave Macmillan.

Savitch, H.V. (1988). *Post-industrial Cities: Politics and Planning in New York, Paris, and London.* Princeton, NJ: Princeton University Press.

Savitch, H.V., & Paul Kantor. (2002). *Cities in the International Marketplace: The Political Economy of Urban Development in North America and Western Europe.* Princeton, NJ: Princeton University Press.

Internet References

Carbusters

A website devoted to the development of car-free communities, including pedestrian plazas and auto-free public places, as seen in cities around the world.

http://carbusters.org

Carfree Cities

The companion website to two books by J.M. Crawford, *Carfree Cities and Carfree Design Manual*, including a "virtual tour" of Venice, "Europe's largest carfree city."

http://carfree.com

International Making Cities Livable

Dedicated to replacing sprawl with compact development on a human scale, the IMCL website provides numerous examples of sustainable growth from Europe and around the globe.

www.livablecities.org/articles

New Geography

A collection of essays and news articles by Joel Kotkin and other urbanists who question much of the prevailing orthodoxy in urban circles, including the desirability of strong planning models.

www.newgeography.com/

Planum

A European-based online journal that offers extensive reports on urban planning projects and models across Europe and around the globe.

www.planum.net

The Transport Politic

A Web collection maintained by Yonah Freemark that looks at a large variety of innovative transit ideas across the United States and around the world including light rail, high-speed rail, and car sharing.

www.thetransportpolitic.com

World Carfree Network

A clearinghouse of information from around the world.

www.worldcarfree.net

Contributors to This Volume

EDITOR

MYRON A. LEVINE is professor of urban affairs at Wright State University in Dayton, Ohio. He is the author of *Urban Politics: Cities and Suburbs in a Global Age* and is editor of *Annual Editions: Urban Society*, a McGraw-Hill Higher Education publication. His writings on urban policy in the United States and Europe have appeared in the *Journal of Urban Affairs*, the *Journal of the American Planning Association*, and the *Urban Affairs Review*. He has been a Fulbright Foundation Fellow in Germany, Latvia, the Netherlands, and the Slovak Republic, as well as a NEH Fellow in France. He has interests in city-suburban cooperation and is coauthor of reports examining the possibilities of regional governance reform in Ohio. A political scientist by training, he has also written books on presidential elections and American government.

AUTHORS

PHILIP ASHTON teaches in urban planning and policy at the University of Illinois-Chicago. His writings on the subprime mortgage crisis have appeared in *the Journal of Urban Affairs, Urban Affairs Review, Urban Geography, and Environment & Planning A.*

WILLIAM J. BRATTON gained national renown as Commissioner of Police in New York City. Appointed to the post by Mayor Rudolph Giuliani in 1994, Bratton introduced broken-windows style policing and other innovations such as CompStat, a "real time" system of management that uses computer-generated statistics and maps to help police target their resources and improve their performance. In 2001 he became Chief of Police in Los Angeles.

ROBERT BRUEGMANN, author of *Sprawl: A Compact History*, is an historian of architecture, landscape, and the built environment. He is professor of art history at the University of Illinois at Chicago where he also holds appointments in the School of Architecture and the Program in Urban Planning and Policy.

DICK M. CARPENTER II is associate professor of educational leadership at the University of Colorado, Colorado Springs. He is also the director of strategic research for the Institute for Justice, a conservative "think tank" committed to the preservation of liberty.

DENNIS COATES is professor of economics at the University of Maryland, Baltimore County. He has written extensively on the economics of sports.

THE CONGRESSIONAL BUDGET OFFICE (CBO), in existence for more than 35 years, is charged with providing nonpartisan expert advice to help Congress in preparing the national budget. CBO prepares economic forecasts, estimates future tax revenues, and program costs and analyzes major programs and policy choices that have substantial budgetary implications.

W. DAVID CONN is Academic Vice-Provost and professor of city and regional planning at California Polytechnic State University, San Luis Obispo.

SHEILA CROWLEY, PhD, MSW, is the president and CEO of the National Low Income Housing Coalition. She is a former Congressional Fellow and received the "Making a Difference" PhD alumni award from the Virginia Commonwealth University.

ROBERT ENLOW is president and CEO of the Foundation for Educational Choice, the legacy foundation of Milton and Rose Friedman. He is the co-editor of *Liberty and Learning, Milton Friedman's Voucher Idea at Fifty.*

LANCE FREEMAN, author of *There Goes the 'Hood*, is associate professor of urban planning at Columbia University. His research focuses on gentrification and affordable housing issues. He has worked for the New York City Housing Authority and the New York City Department of Environmental Protection.

BERNARD J. FRIEDEN (deceased) was a nationally renowned professor of urban planning and housing and director of the MIT/Harvard Joint Center for Urban Studies at MIT. He served on various White House task forces and as a consultant to state and federal agencies. Among his noteworthy books are *The Environmental Protection Hustle* and *Downtown, Inc.: How America Rebuilds Cities*.

JAY P. GREENE is department head and 21st Century Chair in Education Reform at the University of Arkansas. He has written extensively on the subject of school choice, including his book *Education Myths*.

BERNARD HARCOURT is Julius Kreeger Professor of Law, the Chair of Political Science at the University of Chicago. Among his books are *Language of the Gun: Youth Crime and Public Policy* and *Illusion of Order: The False Promise of Broken-Windows Policing.* He received both his law degree and a PhD in political science from Harvard University.

LORI HEALEY is principal at The John Buck Company, a Chicago-based real estate firm. She has served as City of Chicago Commissioner for Planning and Development, Chief of Staff to Mayor Richard J. Daley, and as president of the Chicago 2016 effort.

BRAD R. HUMPHREYS is professor of economics at the University of Alberta in Canada where he holds the Chair in the Economics of Gaming. He received his PhD in economics from the Johns Hopkins University.

GEORGE L. KELLING is professor of criminal justice at Rutgers University and a Fellow in the Kennedy School of Government at Harvard University. He is coauthor (with Catherine Coles) of *Fixing Broken Windows: Restoring Order and Reducing Crime in Our Communities*.

JOEL KOTKIN, Presidential Fellow in Urban Futures at Chapman University in Orange, California, is a noted commentator on global trends and their impact on city and suburban development. He is the author of *The Next Hundred Million: America in 2050* and *The City: A Global History*.

PHILIP LANGDON is senior editor of *New Urban News*. He is author of *A Better Place to Live: Reshaping the American Suburb* and coeditor of *New Urbanism: Best Practices Guide*.

STÉPHANE LAVERTU is a faculty member at the John Glenn School of Public Affairs at The Ohio State University. He previously taught at the University of Colorado at Boulder. His work reviewing charter school performance in eight states was published by the RAND Foundation.

MICHAEL LEWYN teaches at the Florida Coastal School of Law in Jacksonville, FL. He is a member of the Congress for the New Urbanism and teaches a seminar on sprawl and the law.

JOHN F. MCCORMICK served as Tax Increment Financing (TIF) Financial Manager in the Chicago Department of Finance.

JAMES M. MCELFISH, JR., is senior attorney and director of the Sustainable Use of Land Program at the Environmental Law Institute. His writings on the law and environmental protection have appeared in various law journals.

DANIEL MCGRAW is a freelance writer who resides in Fort Worth, Texas.

GARY MIRON is professor in the College of Education at Western Michigan University. He is the author of numerous reports and publications that assess the impact of charter schools. He received his PhD from Stockholm University.

KATHE NEWMAN is associate professor urban planning and policy development at the Edward J. Bloustein School of Planning and Public Policy. Her work on housing and community development has appeared in *Urban Studies, Urban Affairs Review,* and *Housing Studies.*

RANDAL O'TOOLE is a Cato Institute Senior Fellow who writes on urban growth, public land, and transportation issues. Director of the American Dream Coalition, he is also the author of *Gridlock: Why We're Stuck in Traffic and What to Do About It.*

BART PETERSON, senior vice president of corporate affairs and communications at Eli Lilly and Company, served two terms as Mayor of Indianapolis (1999–2007). He also served as president of the National League of Cities. A former resident fellow at Harvard University, he teaches classes at Ball State University.

ROBERT POOLE is director of transportation and former president and CEO of the Reason Foundation. Beginning with his classic book *Cutting Back City Hall (1980),* he has written extensively on privatization and the use of market mechanisms to bring greater efficiency to public service provision. He has advocated the use of privately financed toll lanes to relieve congestion.

SUSAN J. POPKIN, senior fellow at the Urban Institute and director of the Institute's Program on Neighborhoods and Youth Development, is a nationally recognized expert on assisted housing programs and the poor. She led the *HOPE VI Panel Study,* the first systematic look at families involuntarily relocated from public housing. She has also examined public housing transformation in Chicago, the *Gautreaux* housing desegregation program, and the national government's Move to Opportunity (MTO) program, all efforts aimed at deconcentrating urban poverty.

ELISABETH ROSENTHAL is an MD who left a career in internal medicine to become a full-time journalist. She covers health, environmental issues, and social trends for the *New York Times,* having also served as a correspondent in the newspaper's Beijing bureau.

MARK S. ROSENTRAUB, Bickner Endowed Chair and professor at the University of Michigan's Center for Sports Management has written widely on the subject of sports and local economic development. His writings include *Major League Losers: The Real Costs of Sports and Who's Paying for It* and *Major League Winners: Using Sports and Cultural Centers as Tools for Economic Development.*

JOHN K. ROSS, research associate at the Colorado-based Institute for Justice, has written widely on the subject of *eminent domain.*

SOL STERN is a Manhattan Institute senior fellow and contributing editor to the Institute's *City Journal.* He is author of *Breaking Free: Public School Lessons and the Imperative of School Choice* and frequent contributor to the *New York Post* and other newspapers and magazines.

ROBERT STEUTEVILLE is editor and publisher of *New Urban News*, a newsletter covering the New Urbanism design and planning movement. He and Philip Langdon are the primary authors and editors of *New Urbanism: Best Practices Guide*.

CHRISTOPHER SWOPE edits the website *Stateline*, a Pew Foundation-funded resource for policymakers and journalists that covers policy developments in state capitals. He previously was a staff writer, author of the Urban Notebook column, and managing editor for *Governing* magazine, the Congressional Quarterly publication that focused on the innovative practices of statehouses and city halls.

MARGERY AUSTIN TURNER is vice president for research at the Urban Institute. She has written extensively on housing policy, including Section 8 housing vouchers and the HOPE VI program. She is author of *Public Housing and the Legacy of Segregation*.

JULIA VITULLO-MARTIN, senior fellow at the Manhattan Institute and director of the Center for Rethinking Development, is the author of *Breaking Away: The Future of Cities*. She has a PhD in political science from the University of Chicago.

PETER J. WALLISON holds the Arthur F. Burns Chair in Financial Market Studies and is codirector of American Enterprise Institute's (AEI) program on financial market deregulation. Prior to joining AEI, he practiced banking, corporate, and financial law. He also served as White House counsel to President Ronald Reagan and general counsel of the United States Treasury Department, where he helped to develop the Reagan administration's proposals for the deregulation of the financial services industry. He is author of *Ronald Reagan: The Power of Conviction and the Success of His Presidency*.

JAMES Q. WILSON, Ronald Reagan Professor of Public Policy at Pepperdine University, has written 14 books on urban problems, crime, bureaucracy, and police behavior. A past president of the American Political Science Association, he has also taught at Harvard University and UCLA. He also chaired the White House Task Force on Crime, the National Advisory Commission on Drug Abuse Prevention, and the Attorney General's Task Force on Violent Crime. Wilson and George Kelling are often credited with conceiving the idea of broken-windows policing.

JOHN WITTE is professor of political science and public affairs at the University of Wisconsin, Madison, having served previously as the director of the university's Robert M. La Follette School for Public Affairs. He served as Wisconsin state evaluator of the Milwaukee Parental Choice and has authored *The Market Approach to Education: An Analysis of America's First Voucher Program* and numerous other books and reports on the subjects of charter schools and school vouchers.

ELVIN K. WYLY, professor of Geography and Chair of the Urban Studies Program at the University of British Columbia in Canada, has written extensively on gentrification, housing issues, and urban change.